Jacopo de Barbari, perspective map of Venice (1500); detail of the ghetto.

The Ghetto of Venice

RICCARDO CALIMANI

The Ghetto of Venice

Translated by Katherine Silberblatt Wolfthal

M. EVANS AND COMPANY, INC.

Library of Congress Cataloging-in-Publication Data

Calimani, Riccardo, 1946–
  The ghetto of Venice.

  Translation of: Storia del ghetto di Venezia.
  Bibliography: p.
  Includes index.
  1. Jews—Italy—Venice—History.   2. Venice (Italy)—
Ethnic relations.   I. Title.
DS135.I85V422613   1987   945'.31   87-9036

ISBN 0-87131-484-3

M. Evans and Company, Inc.
216 East 49 Street
New York, New York 10017

Design by Lauren Dong

Manufactured in the United States of America

9 8 7 6 5 4 3 2 1

Acknowledgments

This book would not have been the same without the help of many people. I would like to thank Marino Zorzi of the Biblioteca Marciana in Venice, Marika Michieli and Pietro Falchetta of the Biblioteca R. Maestro, who provided valuable help in tracing original book titles, Paolo Sereni, Vittorio Levis, Sandro Romanelli, Roberto Bassi, Anna Campos Calimani, Dario Calimani, Emanuela Trevisan Semi, Claudio Disegni, Nello Pavoncello, Mario Infelise, Cinzia Nicoletto, Shlomo Simonsohn, Benjamin Ravid, Giulio Lepschy, Susanna Biadene, Luciano Sinigaglia, Raneri da Mosto, Marina Reinisch and Giovannina Sullam Reinisch, Franca Bonfante, Nino Vascon, Carla Boccato, and Rabbi Raffaele Grassini, who prepared the glossary and was very generous with advice and suggestions.

Special thanks are due to Elena Sereni Angelini, who edited the final Italian version.

Thanks to my wife, Anna-Vera, without whose assistance this book could not have been written.

For Anna-Vera and Davide

Table of Contents

From Elie Wiesel   xv

Chapter One
ORIGINS   1
*The census of 1152—The tax of 1290—The origin of the name Giudecca—
The fourteenth century: the two charters and first loans*

Chapter Two
JEWS, CHRISTIANS, AND MONEYLENDING   14
*The position of the rabbinate and the papacy on moneylending—The
pawnshops and their operation—The monti di pietà and the Minorite
preachers—Bernardino da Feltre—Accusations of ritual murder*

Chapter Three
THE BIRTH OF THE GHETTO:
THE "GERMAN NATION," 1516   28
*The war with the League of Cambrai—Asher Meshullam and Zaccaria
Dolfin—The founding of the ghetto—The dispute over the monti di pietà
and the Jewish pawnshops—Jews, foreigners, and prostitutes*

Chapter Four
THE "LEVANTINE NATION": 1541,
THE "OLD GHETTO"   41
*Isaac Abrabanel—Arrival of the merchants in the Old Ghetto—Burning
of the Talmud in St. Mark's Square—The expulsion of the Marranos—The
papal bull of Paul IV, Cum nimis absurdum*

Chapter Five
THE MARRANOS   52
The difficulty of defining Marrano—Relations between Jews and Marranos, and between Christians and Marranos—Venice and the papacy—The Inquisition in Venice

Chapter Six
JEWS, MARRANOS, AND JUDAIZERS BEFORE THE INQUISITION: STORIES OF EVERYDAY PEOPLE   62
Giuseppe Francoso, 1548—Francisco Oliviero, 1549—Elena de Freschi Olivi, 1555—Gomez and Enriquez, 1555—Licentiato Costa, 1555—Aaron and Asser, 1563—Marco Antonio degli Eletti, 1569

Chapter Seven
PRINTING AND PUBLISHING IN SIXTEENTH-CENTURY VENICE   80
The first printers: Daniel Bomberg—The Bragadin-Giustiniani affair—The burning of the Talmud—Censorship—De Medico hebreo—Discourse on the Birth of a Monstrosity

Chapter Eight
JOAO MICAS, GIOVANNI MICHES, JOSEPH NASI, DUKE OF NAXOS: A MAN OF FOUR NAMES AND MANY IDENTITIES   90
The feuds and adventures of the Mendes family—The abduction of young Beatrice—Gracia Nasi in Constantinople—The Jewish colonies at Tiberias

Chapter Nine
LEPANTO   97
The question of Cyprus—The Holy League—The battle of Lepanto—The expulsion of the Jews—Salomon Askenazi

Chapter Ten
DANIEL RODRIGA AND THE "WESTERN NATION"   106
The Port of Spalato: the plan—Vacillation of the Senate and the Five Sages of Commerce—The Charter of 1589—The Port of Spalato: its realization

Chapter Eleven
THE UNIVERSITY OF THE JEWS IN THE SIXTEENTH AND SEVENTEENTH CENTURIES   116
Discord between Venice and the papacy—The new activities of the German Nation—The Cattaveri, the Five Sages, and the Sopraconsoli, and their attitudes toward "the Ghettos"—Doge Leonardo Donà and the Marranos—The Jewish merchants in the sixteenth and seventeenth centuries—The Interdict—Paolo Sarpi and the baptism of Jewish children —The charter of 1624

Chapter Twelve
THE GHETTO OF VENICE A CENTURY LATER: SOCIETY, RELIGION, AND CULTURE 129
The etymology of the word ghetto—*The environment—The synagogues— How the ghetto was organized—The rules of the Italian School—The cultural debate—Jewish doctors in Padua—The* Great Book—*The notaries' documents—Population figures*

Chapter Thirteen
LEONE DA MODENA, OR ON CONTRADICTION 152
*Early works, dreams, and marriage—Gambling obsession and preaching career—The study of alchemy—*Diffesa da quello che scrive Fra Sisto Sanese—*The University leaders' edict against gambling—The* Historia de' Riti Hebraici—*The* Kol Sakhal

Chapter Fourteen
SARA COPPIO SULLAM, POETESS 173
Correspondence with Ansaldo Cebà—Controversy with Baldassare Bonifacio on the immortality of the soul—The Codice *of Giulia Soliga*

Chapter Fifteen
SIMONE LUZZATTO, OR ON CONSISTENCY 179
Luzzatto and the legend of Venice—The Discorso circa il stato de gl'Hebrei et in particolar dimoranti nell'inclita città di Venetia—*The success of the* Discorso

Chapter Sixteen
GIULIO MOROSINI ALIAS SAMUEL NAHMIAS: HIS UNCERTAIN IDENTITY AND ANTI-JEWISH POLEMIC 189
Via della Fede: *a spiritual journey suspended between rejection and nostalgia—Leone da Modena: former teacher and imaginary interlocutor— Circumcision, the feast of Simchat Torah, Purim, kosher wine, and the Sabbath*

Chapter Seventeen
VENICE AND THE GHETTO IN THE SEVENTEENTH CENTURY: FROM OPULENCE TO DECADENCE 201
The German, Levantine, and Western Nations and their relations with the Sopraconsoli, the Five Sages of Commerce, and the Cattaveri

Chapter Eighteen
HELL, THE MESSIANIC HOPE, AND A NEWBORN BABY 210
Mosè Zacuto, the Jewish Dante—The Jews of Venice await the Messiah— An infant abandoned in the ghetto

Chapter Nineteen
THE BANKRUPT UNIVERSITY: FROM 1700 TO 1750   222
The debts of the ghetto—The Cattaveri and public morals—The tax problem—A new magistracy: the Inquisitors over the University of the Jews—Plans for rehabilitating the ghetto finances—The new charter of 1738

Chapter Twenty
MOSÈ CHAIM LUZZATTO AND SIMONE CALIMANI: TWO RABBIS COMPARED   231
Mystical visions and rabbinical invective—The life of a Venetian rabbi in the eighteenth century

Chapter Twenty-One
THE END OF THE GHETTO: FROM 1750 TO 1797   238
The economic crisis of the University—The conflict between physiocrats and mercantilists—The charter of 1777

Chapter Twenty-Two
FREEDOM IN CONTRADA DELL'UNIONE   248
The demolition of the ghetto gates—The report of Pier Gian Maria Ferrari, battalion leader—The article in the Gazzetta Veneta Urbana—Speeches by Citizen Vivante and Citizen Grego—The 1797 census

Chapter Twenty-Three
BETWEEN AUSTRIA AND ITALY: VENICE AND THE JEWS IN THE NINETEENTH CENTURY   257
The Jews and the Republic under Manin—The Castillero-Ravenna case—Jewish integration into Venetian life—The unification of Venice and Italy

Chapter Twenty-Four
CAN A JEW BE A MINISTER OF THE REALM?   268
The telegram to the king—A violent press campaign—Senator Musio's letters—Rabbi Mortara—Isacco Pesaro Maurogonato declines the ministry

Chapter Twenty-Five
THE TWENTIETH CENTURY: A HISTORY YET TO BE WRITTEN   275
The ghetto at the turn of the century—The Nazi-Fascist persecution

Conclusion   281

Glossary of Hebrew Terms, by Raffaele Grassini   283

General Bibliography of Reference Works   287

Index   305

The
Ghetto
of
Venice

From Elie Wiesel

The average tourist goes to Venice to visit the Rialto or the Lido, but Jews go there to see the ghetto. This is because, of all the medieval ghettos, the one in Venice is the most famous.

Likewise, of all the books written about that ghetto, Riccardo Calimani's is the best. The author writes with the erudition of a historian, the terseness of a journalist, and the captivating style of a memorialist. In a long series of events and portraits, he gives us a document that reads like an adventure story.

His book tells it all, from the questions concerning the first Jews to appear in Venice (perhaps in the tenth century) to the deportation of the Jews by the Germans and their collaborators in 1944. One thousand years of history—exciting, upsetting, sometimes agonizing, at other times ennobling. Bankers and rabbis, talmudists and free-thinkers, mystics and followers of a false Messiah, poets and scientists: all these abound.

1516: for the first time the Jews are ordered to confine themselves to the old walled ghetto, whose two gates are closed at midnight. The ghetto is guarded by four Christians, and it is the Jews who have to pay them. Yes, that's the way it was then: the prisoner had to pay his jailer. And four centuries later, the Germans would make the Jews pay for their railroad tickets to Auschwitz.

It's strange. The recent past seems, in other respects as well, to reflect the distant past. What is the yellow Star of David if not *la rouelle** brought back into fashion? The anti-Semitic decrees of the thirties and forties are reminiscent of the anti-Jewish laws of the sixteenth century: a ban on sexual relations between Jews and Christians, Jews prohibited from practicing certain professions and holding public office, Christians prohibited from working for Jews.

On April 24, 1516, the Venetian authorities published the following decree: "The Jewish doctors must also live in the ghetto." As I read that sentence, I recall that in the spring of 1944, in Sighet, in the Carpathians, all of the Jews were herded into the ghetto except for the doctors, since the Christian inhabitants needed them. On the eve of our deportation, we learned that the doctors were compelled to leave their apartments and come join us in the ghetto. . . .

Our ghetto did not last long, but the one in Venice did: almost three centuries from the date of that decree until the arrival of Napoleon's armies.

Read this book and you will discover characters who astound you with their wisdom, their piety, and their imagination as well. In it you will find my great hero, Don Isaac Abrabanel, who renounced fame and fortune at the court of Ferdinand and Isabella and chose exile rather than conversion. It was to Venice that he came to write his mystical works and his biblical commentaries. Did you know that in them he compared the Constitution of Venice to the Mosaic Law?

In *The Ghetto of Venice*, so rich and enriching, you will also meet Don Joseph Nasi, the Duke of Naxos, who had the audacity to declare economic war against the Venetian Council of Ten, and who had even greater courage to hope he would emerge the victor. This whole war began with an abduction inspired by romantic ideas. . . .

A mirror of the Jewish world, of Jewish history, in which everything is reflected: the life of the Marranos, the machinations of the Inquisition, the dreams of Sabbatai Zevi's followers. . . . Did you know that Nathan of Gaza, Sabbatai Zevi's spokesman, had visited the ghetto of Venice? And that he caused disturbances there because some Jews had been unable to resist the facile and dangerous promises of the false Messiah?

And do you know the name of Leone da Modena? That scholar who, by his own account, practiced twenty-four professions and who stirred up many controversies with his attacks against mysticism. Did you know that he was afflicted with a disease I'm ashamed to mention? An inveterate gambler, he lost his money and stopped gambling only when the Venetian community declared that whoever gambled would

---

*a star-shaped patch of yellow or green cloth that Jews were forced to wear in medieval times (called the "yellow badge" in the text of *The Ghetto of Venice*)

be excommunicated. He is a fascinating personage in a gallery that the visitor refuses to leave, so captivating are the portraits he finds there.

Take, for instance, Rabbi Moshe-Chaim Luzzatto, the famous Ramchal, who decided that the ghetto of Venice was the chosen place where a few friends would study the Zòhar without interruption. They fasted every ten days. In their daily exchanges, no profane word was uttered. Their goal? To repair the fractures and fissures in the world and in the heart of humankind. Ramchal was attacked by some rabbis and defended by others. He left for the Holy Land, where he died at the age of thirty-nine.

Of course not all the Jews of the ghetto were saints or sages. Among them were also weak persons, cowards, and heretics. Consider the son of the great Asher Meshullam. A very rich man and head of the community, he converted and took the name of Marco Paradiso. Pope Clement VII himself came to the grandiose ceremony to offer his blessing. . . . As is always and everywhere the case, the converts were especially fanatical within the framework of their new religion. After all, the ghetto of Venice was not all that different from other places where Jews studied, worked, suffered, hoped, and waited for redemption. But what distinguishes the ghetto of Venice is that it is the oldest. That, and the fact that it lasted much longer than the others.

Finally, there is this: the ghetto of Venice is also special because it has, in Riccardo Calimani, a magnificent biographer who knows how to talk about it with melancholy and love.

So read this book, and you will understand why I, too, talk about it with a melancholy love which, with all my heart, I invoke.

Translated by Guy Daniels

CHAPTER ONE

Origins

The census of 1152—The tax of 1290—The origin of the name
"Giudecca"—The fourteenth century: the two charters and first
loans

"The Jews must all live together in the Corte de Case, which are in the Ghetto near San Girolamo; and in order to prevent their roaming about at night: Let there be built two Gates, on the side of the Old Ghetto where there is a little Bridge, and likewise on the other side of the Bridge, that is one for each of said two places, which Gates shall be opened in the morning at the sound of the Marangona,* and shall be closed at midnight by four Christian guards appointed and paid by the Jews at the rate deemed suitable by Our Cabinet."

The scene is La Serenissima, the Most Serene Republic of Venice; the date, March 29, 1516. The words of this edict would toll like a knell in the history of the Jewish Diaspora, and the ghetto walls, a concrete, physically insuperable barrier, were to become the ghetto's most powerful and pervasive symbol.

It is difficult to say with exactitude when the first ties were formed between Venice and her Jews. Time has erased many clues, and the fragments that remain have taken on ambiguous meanings. In the end, reality merges with conjecture. For while many documents bear witness to the presence of Jews in the city before 1516, historians in their attempts to reconstruct reality from partial evidence have often themselves created new legends.

---

*the main bell of St. Mark's Cathedral

1

Many students of Venetian history have freely (and sometimes un-critically) drawn on G.B. Galicciolli's *Storie e memorie venete profane ed ecclesiastiche,** printed in Venice in 1795. On the basis of copious evidence Galicciolli confirms the active role of the Jews in Venetian trade during the twelfth and thirteenth centuries, and writes, "That the Jews were therefore of great antiquity in Venice emerges from incontrovertible documents."

He cites a manuscript by Pietro Vanzi describing a census taken on May 12, 1152, which indicates the presence of 1,300 Jews. "But I truly fear," observes Galicciolli, "that there is an error in the date, possibly made by the person who copied the chronicle, and that the figures refer to a later century . . . since we know . . . that such a large number of Jews was improbable at that time." Subsequent research has in fact set the date of the census at 1552.

A tax decree enacted in 1290 is judged by some to be evidence of the stable presence of Jews in the city as early as the thirteenth century. Galicciolli writes, "And truly it must be recognized that . . . the Jews in our state, and chiefly in Venice, sojourned and did business, for there is a decree dating from 1290, which obliged the Jews to pay 5% on the purchase and sale of their goods."

B. Ravid disagrees with Galicciolli, however, and refutes this alleged proof: the tax decree enacted in 1290 by the Maggior Consiglio** of Venice, he points out, ordained that all the Jews of Negroponte (the modern island of Euboea in the Aegean sea) and "all those who travel on the sea" were to pay 5 percent for every import or export transaction. So that tax would not in the least have affected the Jews of Venice.

When, then, did the first Jews actually settle in Venice?

A third provocative theory suggests that the answer lies in the origin of the name *Giudecca,* given to the island of Spinalunga in Venice. The etymology of the name has not yet been conclusively determined. There were *giudecche,* or Jewish quarters, in many Mediterranean cit-ies, but when did Spinalunga acquire the name?

In the eighteenth century, Ludovico Muratori wrote a *Dissertazione* in which he says that the name *Giudecca* appeared as early as 1090. But whether this name was associated with the presence of a Jewish settlement on the island, a theory that had already been considered by fifteenth- and sixteenth-century writers, is debatable. Francesco San-sovino, the seventeenth-century author of *Venetia città nobilissima e singolare,*† appears to accept this thesis in his first edition, expresses some doubts in the second, and in the third creates an ambiguous synthesis of the first two editions. In the eighteenth century, Tommaso Temanza's *Antica pianta dell'inclita città di Venezia** (1781) tells us that the Giudecca had been mentioned in several earlier documents of the Piovego (a judicial organ of the Venetian government). Temanza also found a fourteenth-century map, drawn by a Franciscan friar, on which the island of Spinalunga was already called Judaica.

Others, including Gallicciolli, felt that the original term was probably *del giudicato,*** based on the fact that conspirators had been banished to the island of Spinalunga. In Venetian dialect the term became *Zudegà*, and later *Judecha, Zuecca,* and *Giudaica*. Gallicciolli, with characteristic moderation and insight, reports both theories, while reminding his reader that they are only opinions. In his *Memorie venete* he writes: "But since this is so uncertain, and mere supposition, I can propose no other conjecture than the following. At the end of the ninth century, the conspirators of the Flabanici and Caloprini families, whose property had been confiscated, were assigned some land on Spinalunga as compensation after their reconciliation, a fact attested to by the historians who mention these events. It would have been said, at the time, that the land was awarded by the judges, that is by the Magistrate and the Council . . . At that time, the term Zudega came into use on its own. So it often became necessary to 'act as Zudegà,' or 'Zudega judicatum facere.' This manner of speaking soon degenerated into Zudega, then Judecha, Zuecca and finally Giudaica, because the notaries, preferring to write in Latin but unfamiliar with the origin of the word, thought it was correct to say Judaica or Judea. I myself, however, would not venture to guarantee the accuracy of this opinion."

Such uncertainties naturally gave rise to legends. There was a report of a stone with Hebrew inscriptions found on the Giudecca and subsequently lost. It was also said that there were two synagogues on the island, but this has never been confirmed and in any case would not, by itself, have proven the existence of a Jewish quarter there.

Curiously enough, a Jewish source was also drawn into the debate. An anonymous seventeenth-century author of a Jewish history (a strange documentary work of somewhat masochistic tone) entitled *Storia delle disgrazie che hanno colpito gli Ebrei d'Italia†* relates: "In the great city of Venice, capital of the Dominant Republic, many terrible events have afflicted the people of God. In particular the Venetians did not at all like to have the Jews living in the center of town, so in ancient times they drove them to a bowshot's distance from the city. The name of the place was originally Giudaica, from the name of the Jews that lived there . . . Certain Venetians, envious of the Jews, decided to take

---

**Ancient Map of the Noble City of Venice*
**(island) of the judges
†*History of the Misfortunes that have Afflicted the Jews of Italy*

away their possessions and to attack the Jews. They occupied their property and killed them all, except for a little boy from a German family called Lippmann. The Venetian rulers were angry and went to the Giudaica island, where they found the child alive and decided to convert him to Christianity and marry him to a Venetian noblewoman. Thence, from the name Lippmann, the origin of the noble Venetian family Lippomano."

One manuscript describing the origins of noble Venetian families says that the Lippomano family was of Jewish descent, and while many historians have judged this to be apocryphal, such legends are typical of the mingling of fact and fantasy that colored the history of the Venetian Jews when their lives began to intermesh with that of the Most Serene Republic.

All seeming evidence of a stable Jewish settlement in Venice during the twelfth and thirteenth centuries has thus been refuted: the 1152 census actually took place in 1552; the 5 percent import-export tax of 1290 referred not to Venice but to the Jews of Negroponte and the overseas territories; the origin of the name "Giudecca" is still being debated. A considerable degree of uncertainty about the earliest presence of Jews in Venice thus seems inevitable, and we would be well-advised to emulate Gallicciolli's cautious methods.

E. Ashtor, an important modern scholar of Mediterranean history, has found additional evidence in the curious case of the Damascus *Keter* and in an episode concerning Isaia da Trani. The *Keter* is a beautiful Old Testament thought to come from Babylon or Palestine and probably dating from the ninth century. The binding of the *Keter* has Latin writing which, according to specialists at the British Museum, mentions Venice. It seems legitimate to suppose that the book was bound in Venice, and if this is so, one might be led to speculate that Jews were already living in Venice at the time of the Crusades. But it seems a shaky clue.

Further, Sedecia ben Abramo ha Rofe wrote that in 1244 a renowned rabbi, Isaia da Trani, crossed the Venetian canals on a Saturday. V. Colorni thinks Isaia was the first rabbi of the Jewish community on the Giudecca and that the island at the time housed the two synagogues whose existence is corroborated by Cristoforo Tentori and Gallicciolli. The fact that the rabbi traveled by gondola on Saturday, a day on which Jews are not allowed to do any form of work, provoked a dispute, thus providing us with documentation of Isaia's presence. Rabbi Simone Luzzatto, in supporting the arguments of Rabbi Isaia da Trani, maintained that it was permissible to travel by gondola on Saturday, but the Jewish community council of the time denied the legitimacy of any such behavior.

Modern historians feel that documents dating back to the Crusades or earlier are too scanty to support any definite conclusions about the origin of the Jews in Venice. For example, a prohibition enacted in 960 against transporting Jewish merchants on Venetian ships, while authentic, is more indicative of a transient than of a settled population. Neither the *Codice Diplomatico Veneziano,** published by the Republic's two major assemblies, the Maggior Consiglio and the Senate, nor the various notarized deeds and judicial acts recording events of daily life, make any explicit mention of the Jews, which leads us to think that there were no Jews residing in Venice until the thirteenth century.

Another matter variously interpreted by historians is the residence in Venice, in 1281, of a Jew named Jacob, who, on commission from a medical student of Padua, translated from the Hebrew the medical treatise *Teicrin* by the Arabian author Ibn Zohr. Some identify Jacob the Jew as Jacob ben Elia "da Venezia," the author of a polemic letter against the apostate Paolo Cristiani, while other historians feel the name should be read Jacob "da Valenza" and not "da Venezia."

Further evidence dating from the late thirteenth century remains fragmentary. But in 1314 we find a petition from a Cretan Jew, a certain Ulimidus, submitted to Doge Soranzo on behalf of the local Jewish community. Not much later, a Jewish doctor is allowed to practice in Venice, and from then on we find increasingly frequent signs of Jews coming and going from Negroponte and Zurich. In the future, waves of Jewish immigrants would come to the region of Venetia from the north, seeking to escape the persecution that followed the Black Death, and from central and southern Italy, looking for less oppressive homes than the Papal States.

The mid-fourteenth century was a particularly delicate time in Venetian history. Wars with Verona and Genoa and the outbreak of the plague had created severe financial problems: trade was laboring under heavy taxation and cash flow was diminishing, while the poor grew in number. Interest rates spiraled as high as 40 percent.

In December 1356 the Maggior Consiglio, forced to deal with the financial question, discussed a plan that would have brought to Venice the pawnbrokers who for some time had been doing business in nearby Mestre and Treviso. The plan was voted down, but from that time onward the issue of moneylending, with all its religious and moral implications, would remain a matter of perpetual political debate in the Senate and Collegio.**

---

*The Venetian Code of Diplomacy
**The Cabinet, the administrative branch of the constitution, above the Senate and the Council of Ten. All matters of state passed through its hands and were sent for deliberation to the Senate or the Council of Ten.

The Council of Ten, a powerful Venetian magistracy, was instituted in 1310 as a temporary inquisitional body. It soon became permanent, acting as a political tribunal and absorbing many important functions of the state.

There was a strongly felt need to bring moneylenders to Venice, both to satisfy the demands of the city's poor and to provide merchants with credit. At that time the Jews were not the only ones offering this service, but they soon would be. With the authorization of the Maggior Consiglio, the Venetian *podestà** in Mestre finally negotiated with the moneylenders of Mestre, who were eager to set up shop in Venice. Reinhold Mueller notes that, while this first step has been interpreted by many historians as specific permission for the Jews to reside in the city, it applied generically to all moneylenders, known as *feneratori* (from the Latin *fenus*, meaning loan), many of whom were Christians.

Banking and moneylending in any form were considered usury and had been strictly forbidden in the city for religious reasons. From 1300 on a special office, the Piovego, in addition to its concerns with the public domain and drainage of the canals, exercised judicial authority over heretics and usurers. One function of this magistracy was to prevent illegal moneylending in the city. Yet it appears certain that it was difficult if not impossible to stem the flow of people between Venice and Mestre, seeking the services of the moneylenders.

The wars with Genoa and subsequent conflicts with Chioggia (1378–1381) had drained the coffers of the Republic. Forcible levies were at their highest, government securities had plunged in value, and many financiers were forced to sell their securities at a loss in order to pay the high property taxes. In this climate of widespread economic malaise, the instruments of credit previously used proved inadequate. Fresh capital was needed, ideally originating from outside the city. In March 1381, Marco Corner, one of the leaders of the Quarantia,** proposed that moneylenders be allowed to lend at interest rates not to exceed 15 percent for secured loans, or 18 percent for loans against written guarantee. Although the Senate rejected the proposal, it continued to find support among the Venetian ruling class, drawing new strength from the discontent caused by further taxation. In February 1382, the Maggior Consiglio voted on a bill submitted by Giovanni Corner and Giovanni da Canal, the leaders of the Quarantia, similar to the one proposed a year earlier. This time the moneylenders were approved. The new law made no distinction between Jews and Christians, but in practice, as Mueller observes, it was the beginning of the first Jewish charter, even though "the invitation was conceived in broad, open terms."

The arrival of the Jewish moneylenders gave rise to a new financial system. They brought in fresh capital and lent it at fixed rates of interest, subject to control by the government (which not only taxed the

---

*the chief magistrate in the republics of medieval Italy
**A high court consisting of forty magistrates, instituted in the thirteenth century. In the fifteenth century two distinct Quarantie were formed, "al Civil," for civil cases, and "al Criminal" for criminal offenses.

moneylenders but also obliged them to grant loans to defray its own expenses). One important effect of this new availability of credit was the alleviation of poverty, resulting in a general lessening of internal political tension. As a further consequence, popular hostility would henceforth be directed not at the State, but at the moneylenders. The Jews in particular—and not only in Venice—became a shield to deflect resentment away from the political authorities. In consideration of all these benefits, the Venetian oligarchy soon abandoned all its previous reservations.

The magistrates of the Piovego continued to hold authority over the moneylenders and their activities. Fixed interest rates could not exceed 10 percent for secured loans and 12 percent for loans against written guarantee (in the other cities of Venetia, rates ranged as high as 20 or 30 percent). Transgressors would be penalized. The Piovego sold forfeited pledges at auction in the Rialto district and was responsible for keeping a list of the moneylenders in the city, who were allowed to stay for a maximum of five years. Any Venetian who dared even request the revocation of this measure was liable to a fine of one thousand ducats. So after much resistance, moneylending at fixed rates of interest, *pro evitandis maximis usuris*,* was established in Venice. According to the notaries' deeds, nearly all the moneylenders were Jewish.

In 1385, when the first charter expired, it was decided to renew the agreement. The negotiations between Venice and the Jews, with each side anxious to obtain the best terms, were the first in a long series, which went on for centuries. The Jews were offered permission to reside in Venice, but they were obliged to restrict their activities, lower their rates, and, in substance, serve the interests of the Venetian oligarchy's power politics. Now the Senate no longer referred to generic *feneratores*, but specifically to *Judei*. The new agreement would be valid for ten years, and established a tax of 4,000 ducats to be paid by the Jewish community, whose leaders would be independently elected and who would in turn set the quotas to be paid by individuals within the community. The Jews were subject to no other taxes, except for the usual import-export duties. They thus became a codified legal exception to the authority of the Piovego, subject instead to that of the Sopraconsoli.** They were also promised an area of the town in which to live—and this, too, was a great privilege.

Although the traditionally precarious situation of the Jews was stabilized, for a decade at least, the hand of authority weighed no less heavily on them than before. The attempt to raise taxes, on the one hand, and to lower interest rates, on the other, would become a constant in the conflictual relationship between the two sides. Sometimes the

---

*"in order to avoid the greatest of usuries"
**a municipal magistracy that tried bankruptcy cases and supervised the pawnshops

Jews refused to lend small sums, and other times the Republic pressured them by delaying assignment of the promised residential district, thereby arousing unrest and protest. The Senate appointed commissions of experts and from time to time made marginal corrections in the basic provisions of the charter. One particular amendment, in 1389, provided that special pawnshops, some to be run by German Jews from Nuremberg, or Jews of French origin, should be opened for the purpose of making small loans.

Although the Jews almost certainly preferred large commercial loans and important transactions, they were thus obliged to lend small sums as well, by a Republic desirous of achieving social peace and controlling the urban poor.

On one occasion, the government obliged the Jews to make a risky loan to Antonio Della Scala, the ruler of Verona, who offered his family's jewels as collateral. The jewels were brought to Venice, but remained in the hands of the authorities, who had them appraised. They then persuaded certain wealthy Venetians to guarantee repayment of the loan by pledging an amount equivalent to the value of the jewels and promising to purchase them if need be. A consortium of Jewish pawnbrokers then lent the money to Della Scala, whose military fortunes, however, continued to decline until his death in exile at Faenza in 1388. Two years later, the pawnbrokers had still not been completely reimbursed, and this caused them a severe shortage of cash.

After 1389 Venetian finances improved, thanks to the renewed expansion of maritime trade. At the same time, clashes between Jewish moneylenders and the Senate increased sharply. A fine was proposed, to be paid by those who did not comply with the regulations on small loans, and religious objects were decreed unpawnable. The promise to give the Jews a district of their own as their permanent residence remained unfulfilled, and the Senate even decided not to renew the charter. The Jews were accused of oppressing rather than aiding the urban poor. It was said that they had become too influential, that all the wealth of Venice was accumulating in their hands, and that they refused to lend money to anyone who did not pawn gold and jewels.

In August 1394, the Senate accused the moneylenders, who were demanding reimbursement of loans made to the city government, of not lending to the poor as agreed. The Senate therefore decided that when the charter expired in February 1397 the Jews were to be expelled. Gallicciolli states that this expulsion decree is the earliest known to him.

There were a few exceptions to the expulsion, however. By 1395 a number of Jews had distinguished themselves as physicians in Venice, and on April 3, in confirming the expulsion decree which was to take effect in 1397, the Maggior Consiglio explicitly exonerated the physician Salomone from compliance. Gallicciolli also tells of a doctor named Abramo who came to Venice after studying in Arabia and Cairo and in 1401 was awarded a diploma of merit for his activities by Pope Boniface IX.

When the charter expired in 1397 the Jews withdrew to Mestre, but they continued coming to Venice to sell their unclaimed pledges. Side-stepping the laws "with fraudulent design," they spent increasingly less time in Mestre and more in Venice, thus thwarting "the pious spirit of the Decree." Yet amid much polemic, moneylending continued to be tolerated even after 1397, and representatives of the Jewish pawnshops in Mestre were allowed in Venice on days when forfeited pledges were to be sold.

The Jewish moneylenders were permitted to return to the city for a maximum of fifteen days at a time, and at all such times they had to wear a circular yellow badge. Transgressors would be heavily fined, without appeal. The Venetians knew that the Jews had been obliged to dress differently from Christians in 1221, by order of Frederick II of Sicily, and in 1311 under the *Codice Ravennate*.*

The Venetian authorities resolved to prohibit Jews from acquiring or possessing real estate in the Venetian domains, except within the Jewish quarters in the overseas territories; nor could real estate belonging to Christians be pawned as collateral for loans. The Jews were thus obliged to keep all their assets in cash. This favored their moneylending activities and gave them a great deal of mobility since it allowed them to move quickly from one place to another. At the same time, however, it also made it difficult for them to establish permanent settlements.

Galicciolli writes, "The Jews, having thus settled in Venice, and deluding themselves, perhaps, that the Sentence of expulsion served only for the sake of political appearances, and that they could already consider their domicile perpetual, decided to purchase a piece of land that they could use to bury their Dead." On September 25, 1386, the doge granted the Jews a piece of land to be used as a cemetery, and the transaction was handled by the Piovego. Although the land was uncultivated farmland, the religious community of San Nicolò did not give it up without a fight, and sued the Venetian magistracy. In February 1389 an agreement was finally reached, and the area was walled in. The oldest Jewish tombstone, that of Samuele the son of Sanson, dates from that year.

On September 7, 1402, noting that the Jews were still coming and going and that they tended to congregate in certain areas of the city (Sant'Apollinare and San Silvestro), the authorities decreed that once a Jew had been in Venice for fifteen days, he could not return again for four months. They also revoked the privilege exempting doctors from

---

The Code of Ravenna

the yellow badge, for many Jews persisted in passing themselves off as doctors or Christians in order to avoid wearing it.

After the expulsion decree the Jews spread through all Venetia, but in fact they never entirely left Venice. In 1423 a new decree was enacted obliging them, within two years, to sell any real estate purchased in violation of the law. It was not uncommon, however, for the Republic to issue repressive laws which were then mitigated by diluting their enforcement over time.

The political pragmatism of the Venetians is clearly reflected, too, in their different attitudes regarding the city proper and the overseas territories, where the presence of Jews was not only tolerated but often encouraged. In contrast to the Jewish population in Venice, still very small, there were flourishing settlements of Jewish tradesmen in the territories of Crete and Candia, and on Negroponte, as early as the beginning of the thirteenth century.

If official relations between Venice and the Jews were subject to changes in mood and tone, there is plentiful evidence that normal business negotiations, and even closer relations, were developing between individual Jews and Christians. Documents dating from 1402, 1409, 1424, and 1443 contain references to sexual acts between Jewish men and Christian women. A decree enacted on July 19, 1424, formally prohibited such affairs, with penalties including a heavy fine and six to twelve months' imprisonment, depending on whether or not the woman was a public prostitute. Barely two days later, an infraction was recorded.

The Senate itself intervened on April 11, 1443, in the case of an academy where Jews taught singing and dancing to young Christian girls of patrician families. The Jews were forbidden to run schools of any kind, under penalty of a fine of fifty ducats and six months' imprisonment.

The Venetian economy seemed propelled by an inner force of its own. By the end of the twelfth century, the Jews had developed their moneylending trade in all the principal cities of Venetia, from Mestre to Treviso, from Conegliano to Cividale, from Padua to Este. The Republic had become the guarantor of numerous charters, establishing their terms and arbitrating the conflicts between the local authorities and the Jewish moneylenders. The renewal of the charters was always a crucial issue, involving complicated negotiations between the Republic and the Jews. Although it taxed the Jews heavily, the Venetian government demonstrated a certain benevolence, ordering the local authorities to protect the Jews and allow them to practice their religion. Indeed, it was this religious tolerance that attracted increasing numbers of German, Spanish, and Levantine Jews to Venice from all directions, over a period of centuries.

The relationship between the common people of Venice and this initially foreign community was an ambivalent one. The differences between them were many: the Jews' language, religious observances, customs, dress, and food were a mystery. Foreigners they were, and foreigners they remained—indeed, they were doubly foreign, for in addition to being Jews they were Germans, Levantines, and, later, Spaniards.

As for the Venetians, the man in the street was sometimes friendly, but he could also be hostile if incited by the preachers and religious, who could not look with favor on these involuntary challengers of the Christian faith. By contrast, the ruling classes used the Jews as suited their needs, with flexible political and economic pragmatism, often as a lightning rod to deflect social tension. The greatest uneasiness was caused by the Jews' financial operations; their aggressiveness, resulting from the need to meet the heavy tax burdens imposed by the Republic, made them objects of distrust and provoked hostility.

But by obliging the Jews to lend money at interest in exchange for permission to live in the city, the Republic was beginning to implement a policy of tolerance that served its own interests and cared very little about showing the Jews in a bad light. The expulsion decree of 1395 reads, *"Antiqui nostri numquam eos voluerunt videre in Venetiis."**

Measures against the Jews were often justified by references to divine law. With regard to the yellow badge, in fact, the decree contains some very revealing words: *"Secundum Deum et bene vivere . . . optime factum."*** The Jews tenaciously resisted the repressive measures. Obliged to wear the yellow badge, they contrived every possible trick to render it virtually invisible. In the course of the fifteenth century, the Venetian authorities re-examined the issue at least eight times, and there are reports of Jews being convicted for failure to comply. Unable to enforce the law, the Senate in 1496 ruled to replace the yellow badge with a more easily visible head covering of the same color. As before, exemptions were granted for certain individuals, especially physicians.

The yellow hat was a hazard to Jews who had to travel, exposing them to constant perils. They therefore obtained permission to wear the same head covering as Christians while traveling, in order to avoid recognition. In 1517 the Council of Ten, in a new ruling, revoked all dispensations and restored the obligation of the yellow hat even for illustrious doctors. There may have been exceptions in the colonies; Alvise Corner, in his early-seventeenth-century *Historia de Candia*, recounts that the descendants of David Mavrogonato of Candia were all dispensed from wearing the yellow hat and nicknamed "Mavroberti" or "black hats."

---

*"Our ancestors never wished to see them in Venice."
**"According to the will of God and upright living . . . it was excellently done."

Could a Jew be a Venetian citizen? The question is controversial. Many noted historians, including Samuele Romanin and Pompeo Molmenti, feel that he probably could. The French historian David Jacoby, on the contrary, holds that the privileged legal status conferred on certain deserving Jews did not constitute full citizenship, but was comparable to the status of a non-Venetian resident of a Venetian colony. Ashtor, too, has studied this issue and examined the documents, preserved in the Venetian State Archives, of the Venetian notary Nicolò Venier, active in Egypt and Syria chiefly from 1417 to 1422. Among the most interesting is a document drawn up for Elia Capsali, a member of a family that had been influential in the Jewish communities of Candia and the eastern Mediterranean for at least three centuries, in which Capsali authorizes one Isaia ben Chayim to apply for Venetian citizenship on his behalf and that of his heirs, emphasizing the fact that he already enjoyed privileges conferred by the Republic.

But, Ashtor observes, "The Republic granted different degrees of citizenship. Sometimes the privilege was personal and not hereditary. Citizenship was often granted for a set period, for example, twenty-five years. Other times it was granted to the applicant and his son, or extended to all his heirs. There were cases of foreigners obtaining the privileges of 'nobles.' Many were granted citizenship on condition that they not engage in maritime trade (*de intus* citizenship) or do business with the Germans." Different degrees of citizenship were granted to those who had served the Republic of Venice or had married Venetian women (according to a decision of the Maggior Consiglio dated July 5, 1407), or to merchants who had lived in Venice for many years. All these opportunities were closed to Jews. We do not know whether Capsali's request was granted or whether he achieved the legal status he sought. It is unquestionable that Venetian citizenship was a coveted prize not only because of the financial advantages it conferred, but also, and perhaps especially, for the political protection it ensured.

Many historians have emphasized the two faces of Venetian policy regarding the Jewish communities: one, repressive, in the city proper and the other, more permissive, in the colonies. After the conquest of Padua, for example, the obligation of the yellow badge was extended to that city, "*quod sit bene apparens*,"* while in the colonies the law was less zealously enforced. In Venice the Jews were closely supervised, while on Corfu and Negroponte they enjoyed considerable liberty, interrupted by occasional outbursts of religious zeal, tempered, however, by the pressing need to enable the poor to borrow small sums of money at reasonable rates of interest.

In 1408, the Senate revoked the four-month interval between visits and allowed the Jewish merchants to come and go as they pleased. But

---

*let it be clearly visible

the struggle between hawks and doves within the Maggior Consiglio was by no means over and led to a different outcome a bare seven months later. The expulsion decree was restored and, as before, the Jews were allowed to return to the city only at four-month intervals. Six months later, there was a new about-face and a new rule: the four-month interval was abolished and permission was granted to Jews who did not practice usury to return to Venice. The only restriction: the yellow badge.

In 1430 the Maggior Consiglio ruled that any Jew from Corfu (normally exempt from wearing the badge) who embarked on a Venetian ship had to wear the yellow badge. This apparently repressive measure actually held a hidden benefit, for it formally abrogated the prohibition dating from the tenth century against carrying Jewish merchants and their goods.

Around the mid-fifteenth century, echoes reached Venice of the theological disputes on moneylending between the Franciscan and Dominican orders. Although the pope had approved the establishment of *monti di pietà*,* he did not intervene to settle the controversy. In 1463 Cardinal Bessarione, the emissary of Pope Pius II, came to Venice in view of a possible crusade against the Turks, and the Republic took advantage of his presence to consult him on the delicate and thorny question of Jewish moneylending. The cardinal's letter to Doge Cristoforo Moro, dated December 18, 1463, is an important document. After reminding the doge of the advantageous past relations between the Venetian government and the Jews, Bessarione, without ever actually mentioning usury, rhetorically asked whether it was legitimate to let the Christian and Jewish communities live as neighbors. Could it be beneficial to keep Christians in contact with Jews? The cardinal answered his own question in the affirmative, expressing the hope that such proximity would lead to the conversion of the Jews. With the weight of his pastoral authority, he maintained that all agreements stipulated with the Jews should be strictly respected. The Venetian authorities could therefore do business with them without fear of reprisals from the Church.

In 1478, after a lengthy debate within the oligarchy, a new decision confirmed the current laws in all their forms (a victory for the liberals of the time) and revoked the expulsion of 1426, with the one usual exception: the yellow badge.

---

*Originally, charitable pawnbroking institutions run by the Church that made interest-free loans to the poor. The Italian term has been used throughout, to distinguish the Christian from the Jewish pawnshops.

CHAPTER TWO

Jews, Christians, and Moneylending

The position of the rabbinate and the papacy on moneylending—
The pawnshops and their operation—The monti di pietà *and the*
Minorite preachers—Bernardino da Feltre—Accusations of ritual
murder

The issue of moneylending is one of the aspects of Jewish history most charged with ideological tension, not only in Venice, but throughout the rest of Italy and indeed all of Europe. Although moneylending flourished chiefly in the Middle Ages, its roots stretch much further back in time. The Bible contains injunctions and prohibitions that made it permissible for the Jews to trade in money, creating yet another deep chasm between Jews and Christians. In the Old Testament it is written, "Unto a foreigner thou mayest lend upon interest; but unto thy brother thou shalt not lend upon interest." In the Talmud, the implications of this sentence were hotly debated. The Babylonian Talmud cites the opinion of Reb Hunna: "The profit deriving from usury, even if gained by an idolater, is vowed to perdition." Many other rabbis studied the problem, and what emerged, in keeping with the best Jewish tradition, was a wide range of interpretations and nuances. The rabbis were especially concerned with assuring the survival of the Jewish community, and to do so they were willing to justify moneylending by tortuous economic and theological rationalizations.

In medieval, Christian Europe the social environment itself, hostile to the Jews, ultimately led to a more pragmatic outlook. Trading in money was a matter of life and death, as is clear from the responsum of the great rabbi and Talmudic commentator Rashi de Troyes: "When this prohibition [against trade] was pronounced, the Jews all lived together and could trade with one another; but now that we are a minority, we cannot survive unless we trade with non-Jews, because we live among them and also because we fear them."

Moneylending at interest and the specialization in lending against pawned objects had become confirmed practices among the Jews in Italy as early as the thirteenth century, even though they were not an integral part of Jewish custom. In the fourteenth century Jacob Landau of Pavia wrote, with a twinge of bitterness, "I have no power to forbid the practice, but he who proves strict on this matter shall be blessed."

Rabbenu Tam, a twelfth-century Talmudist, emphasized that moneylending was a choice dictated by necessity: "Today people are in the habit of lending at interest to non-Jews . . . because we have to pay taxes to the king and the nobility, and all these things are necessary for our sustenance. We live among non-Jews, and we cannot earn a living unless we trade with them. It is therefore no longer forbidden to lend at interest."

Although their discomfort was repressed and rationalized, Jews never entirely stopped feeling uneasy about moneylending. Leon Poliakov asks a provocative question that encompasses the entire psychological world of the Jew: "What value judgment could the Jews themselves have made of a profession that the educative efforts of the Church clothed in growing discredit?" One answer is supplied by the thirteenth-century Provencal rabbi Jacob ben Elia in his reply to apostate Paolo Cristiani's queries on moneylending: "Among the Eastern Jews, each man lives by the labor of his own hands . . . in our lands things are different . . . because our kings and our princes have no other thought than to strip us of all our money. And now look at this court of Rome, to which all Christians are subject . . . everyone chasing after profit . . . What is our life, then, to us? Our strength and our power? We should thank God for having multiplied our wealth, since this allows us to defend our lives and those of our children, and to frustrate the designs of our persecutors."

Poliakov also tells of an erudite though little-known book published in the early seventeenth century, Scherzi di Purim. Il libro di chi presta e di chi chiede in prestito,* in which the subject of moneylending is treated with irony. The anonymous author threatens with dire curses those who do not lend at interest or who lend without making sure they receive an adequate pledge. The borrower is to be flogged even if he pays back his loan, "not because the law so prescribes, but because the times so demand."

Leone da Modena, an illustrious rabbi of the Venetian ghetto, expressed his discomfort in Historia de' Riti Hebraici**: "It is true that

---

*Purim Pranks: The Book of the Lender and the Borrower
**History of Jewish Ritual

THE GHETTO OF VENICE

in the deplorable state to which their [the Jews'] dispersion has reduced them, since they are forbidden to own land almost everywhere, and since they cannot trade and accumulate wealth, their spirit may have become corrupt and have degenerated from the ancient Israelite candor."

Leone's realism is also reflected in a responsum: "If we open new banks the people will be angry and will have the Jews expelled, because everyone knows how the people detest usury, and more than the approval of the rulers, the Jew needs the good will of the people. For when the people are hostile to the Jews they petition their rulers to have them expelled, which does not please God, and the ruler listens to them, as has occurred for our sins in various places, but above all because of usury."

These words show much greater perception than those of another responsum by Rabbi Joseph Colon, written in the late fifteenth century. Colon, concerned with the advisability of opening new banks in an Italian city, observes that, while prior to the sermons of the Minorite preachers the opening of a new bank would automatically have lightened the tax burden of the entire Jewish community, today the banks "have multiplied, because of the sins of the Jews, and become 'scourges of oppression.' " Rabbi Colon further observes: "This is what happens to him who adds his own burden to a camel already heavily laden. The beast collapses, and he is responsible because, but for him, the camel would have supported the load." He adds: "As I wrote that day, because of our sins the hand of the preachers will strike heavily down upon us, and we live each year in fear of that day. It is certain that no man can come to a city and lend money at interest without the permission of the people of that city."

While Leone da Modena's arguments reflect greater political maturity and a different ideology, both rabbis show their awareness of the difficulties encountered by the Jewish moneylenders in their dealings with the Christian populace.

Canon law regarding the freedom to charge interest on loans, as applied to both Jews and non-Jews, dates from before the twelfth century. An Aristotelian maxim influenced the financial thought of all later periods: *Pecunia pecuniam parere non potest* (Money does not gain in value; it is sterile and perpetual). These two characteristics are incompatible with the concept of interest. Another maxim that appears in the Gospel of Luke, "Lend, hoping for nothing again," is not only a prohibition against lending at interest but also an implicit order not to disturb a person who owes money by asking to be repaid. These two concepts had long inspired Christian doctrine and were now applied to medieval economics.

In 443, Pope Leo I condemned moneylending by the laity. The councils of Rheims (1049) and Rome (1059), and the Lateran Council (1139), confirmed this policy and added new rulings to the *Corpus Juris Can-*

*onici.** Little by little, the Church assumed authority over all questions relating to moneylending, denying moneylenders the sacraments, communion, and burial (Alexander III, 1179) and annulling their testaments (Gregory X, 1274).

Church sources are unclear as to whether the prohibition against moneylending also applied to the Jews, who were obviously outside the Church. They do not deal with the question, possibly to avoid granting infidels privileges denied to believers. Thomas Aquinas writes in his *Summa Theologica*: "The Jews were forbidden to lend to their brothers at interest, that is, to fellow Jews. From this prohibition, we understand that lending at interest to any individual is always a blameworthy action, because we must treat all men as our neighbors and brothers, especially out of respect for the Gospel, to which all are enjoined. They were, however, allowed to lend to foreigners at interest, not as though this were right, but to avoid a greater evil; that is, given the avarice to which they were prone, according to Isaiah, to prevent their lending at interest to other Jews, their brothers in God's faith."

Francesco Sforza, a theologian as well as a military leader, wrote, "The Church and the Christians commit no sin when they allow the Jews to observe their rituals, since they do not approve them but only tolerate and permit them, for it is impossible to totally eradicate the bad will of men." Since the Jews were considered lost souls, they might as well be moneylenders.

During the fifteenth century, the issue of whether to permit or prohibit Jewish moneylending was the subject of heated debate. Between the two extreme positions there grew up an ambiguous acceptance of the situation as it stood. Around the middle of the century, in the Venetian territories, Paolo di Castro and Alessandro de Nevo took opposite sides on the issue. Di Castro felt it was important to leave moneylending to the Jews and "necessarius et salutifer"** to deal with them. De Nevo, in his *Consilia contro Judaeos fenerantes*,† published in Padua in 1450, proposed that the Jews be forbidden to practice moneylending so they could be saved. De Nevo's writings merit a reading because many of the friar preachers used them as points of reference in their anti-Jewish attacks. The first *Consilium* is couched in question-and-answer form. Was it a sin for Jews to lend at interest? Should the Church combat this Jewish sin? The answer is yes, "for he who borrows money becomes the servant of the usurer." Should the Church tolerate this sin in the interest of avoiding greater evils and in the name of a greater good? As St. Augustine said, the Jewish rituals must be tolerated because they bore witness to the truth of the Christian faith.

---

*Body of Canon Law
**necessary and salubrious
†Counsels Against Jewish Usurers

Could the rulers, city councils, or communes grant licenses to the Jews? Could the pope grant dispensations to the rulers or cities, allowing them to do business with Jewish moneylenders? The answer was no.

The Dominican Sisto Medici later wrote in his *De foenerare Judaeorum*, "If the worst crime of the Jews is their infidelity and perfidy, which offend God, since our mother Church tolerates these why not tolerate their usuries when the latter are not contrary to the public good?"

The Church did not hold a unanimous position on Jewish moneylending. On the contrary, the issue often gave rise to heated debate. Religious and purely theological considerations were frequently overridden by the need to alleviate the hardships of a great mass of poor people, and the Church had no intention of renouncing practical control over pawnbroking activities; indeed, it was impossible to open any pawnshop in the towns without the permission of the local religious authorities. Disobedience was punished by fine or even excommunication.

Despite all the obstacles and restraints posed by friars and rabbis, for opposite reasons, a solid Jewish monopoly on moneylending was established during the fourteenth and fifteenth centuries. The rapid expansion of the economy made it increasingly difficult for Christian thinkers to reconcile conflicting concepts—religious purity, on the one hand, and economic development, on the other—by dialectical tricks and theological cavils. It could not be denied that the Jewish moneylender provided an essential credit service. Marin Sanudo, writing about the 1519 renewal of the Jewish charter in Venice, said in his *Diarii* that Jews were as important as bakers. Banned from the arts and trades, from public office and military service, from the professions and from landowning, only one means of livelihood was left open to the Jews: the banking and loan activities that the Middle Ages called usury. The Jews, desired and detested, settled in the major Italian cities, and in establishing their pawnshops they often managed to obtain financial benefits and other privileges as well. In 1312, in the aftermath of a siege laid by Orvieto, the city of Montefiascone applied to the Jews of Rome for a loan. The Jews agreed to grant it on condition that they be granted citizenship and full membership in the local guild of arts and trades. Often the Jews entered into such agreements just for the purpose of obtaining a "charter" that would allow them to settle in the town and grant them "civil rights."

What exactly was a "charter"? In substance it was an agreement, a set of clauses and regulations, often the fruit of tense negotiations between the Jews and the municipal authorities. It became a mutual code of behavior that governed relations between the state and the bankers, and gave the Jews a license to trade. The form of the charter was almost always the same: it established types of loans and their terms, the number of pawnshops, their hours, and the district where they were located or some appropriate alternative point of reference. The identities of the lenders, their families, and their assistants were specified. If the pawnshop was a partnership, the charter specified the respective shares of the partners in terms of capital contributions and management responsibilities.

The Venetian pawnshops were indicated by colors: red, green, or black. Closing times were subject to regulation. The Jews were allowed to close on their own holidays, but there was a conflict when it came to the Christian holidays. The priests wanted the pawnshops closed as a sign of respect, while the Jews wanted to take advantage of the holiday crowds to do business. Often a compromise was reached: the pawnshops would be open in the morning and on minor holidays, and closed all day on Easter and on the feast of the city's patron saint. Special closing days were decreed in situations of social tension. The book *Scherzi di Purim* contains some interesting details: "The principal director of the bank, whether he be the sole owner of the capital or have a partner, or whether the capital belong to another, must be a humble, modest man." Further on, "The room in which the pledges are kept should be built of stone so light cannot penetrate or dust filter in, and so that thieves, having climbed thereupon, cannot look inside." Additional recommendations were a standard blue awning at the entrance, disinfection against rodents, and rules about the places where pawnshops should be established. The book suggested concealing the contents of the pawnshops from the sight of the poor so they would not be tempted to burglary, and advised locating the entrance of the bank in a street that was not too central or busy, so that noblemen might feel more comfortable about entering.

Interest rates varied considerably from one charter, region, and period to another. The terms and conditions that emerged from the lengthy negotiations were generally respected, although exceptions and violations did occur. Favorable interest rates were established for large loans to governments or rulers. University students also received special rates. Jewish moneylenders typically accepted written guarantees as well as actual pledges. Loans secured by solid collateral had lower interest rates, and appraisal of the pledges was left to the discretion of the interested parties, although both the Church and the rabbinate forbade the pawning of Christian religious objects, weapons, or books. Moneylenders could not refuse to lend a pre-established minimum sum to anyone who requested it, as long as the pledge was adequate. There was also a special clause protecting the lender in case anyone pawned a stolen object. He was not obliged to return such objects until both principal and interest had been repaid. Loans were granted for periods ranging from one month to a year and a half. Interest was computed monthly and could not be compounded. Each pledge was entered in a register. The Jews either wrote in Hebrew or used Italian words transliterated in the Hebrew alphabet, a system which resulted in frequent infractions, despite strict supervision by the city officials. In case of accident (fire or flood), the lender was not held responsible. Pledges not redeemed by a given date were sold at auction, always by city officials. The rules for the auctions were set down in minute detail and favored the borrower. If the auctioned pledge was sold for more than the amount of money borrowed, the difference, minus petty costs, was returned to the borrower.

Loans secured in writing were granted for longer terms and larger sums, but the interest rate was higher. The degree of actual security in such cases was much less, and loans of this kind were granted much less readily. In fact, certain charters gave moneylenders the right to refuse loans without pledges.

The term of the charter varied from five to ten years. If the community grew, differentiated rulings were sometimes established, with one set of rules for bankers and another for the rest of the group.

Is it possible, today, to draw an accurate financial picture of a pawnshop? Interest rates, the crux of the moneylending business, fluctuated according to time, place, and economic conditions. Even when the established rates were not strictly complied with, they did constitute a clear basis for reference. The overhead of a pawnshop could be broken down into rental of the premises, salaries, legal costs for trials, contributions to the Jewish community and for religious services, the cost of inactive capital, and interest paid on funds deposited by the partners in the pawnshop enterprise. Add to this losses of various kinds and taxes, both normal and extraordinary, called licensing fees. The bankers often lent money without security to the local political authorities. One rabbi said, "Getting something back from the prince is like getting something back from the lion."

Was moneylending profitable under such conditions? Were profits actually greater than the interest income reported? We have an excerpt from an accounting book of a Jewish pawnbroker who lent money in Padua around 1450 and who took advantage of conflicts between the town authorities and other Jewish moneylenders to extend his activities to a broader territory than had been allotted him, including Este, Piove di Sacco, and Padua itself. The Paduan authorities tried him for his illegal operations and his books ended up in court, providing historians with a valuable and unprecedented opportunity to conduct a financial analysis of a pawnshop. One indication we find is that the real rate of interest seems to be inversely proportional to the duration of the loan. We also have the impression that profits could be increased by juggling the various calculations. Rounding fractions of months to whole months, approximating sums above the half-lira, profiting on rates of exchange between different currencies, and charging fixed commissions were all ways of pushing profits above the official rates.

There were hidden tricks of other kinds as well: The sum lent could be entered as greater than it actually was. Or the lender might charge compound interest—usury upon usury—which was formally prohibited. Almost all the lender's entries were written in Hebrew, and he sometimes gave the borrower a receipt in that unknown and totally inaccessible language.

Amid so many restrictions and obligations, the Jews made moneylending their lifeline in a highly precarious situation. In studying the reasons for their characteristic role, some historians have departed from religious considerations entirely and give greater weight to the intrinsic dynamics of the laws of economics, according to which highly civilized merchant populations tend to withdraw with their capital into the world of finance when they are displaced from the commodity trade by younger rivals. The Jews, no longer allowed to be merchants, became the first bankers, to a certain extent foreshadowing the credit mechanisms of modern finance.

Many conflicting factors came into play in consolidating the role of the Jews as moneylenders. The Church, for example, harshly repressed moneylending at first, and this generally favored the financial activities of the Jews, to whom their sanctions did not apply. Later, in order to remedy that undesirable effect, it attempted to repress the Jews with even greater severity, in an effort to exert some degree of control over the situation. The religious authorities, under pressure from rulers who wanted the Jews at their courts and unable to put a stop to moneylending, were obliged to levy taxes. This interweaving of religious and economic factors constantly created new situations to which the Church, the Jews, and the rulers all tried to adapt, often belatedly, constantly re-adjusting their positions in the game. Poliakov emphasized the close relationship between tolerance of the Jews and tolerance of "Jewish usury" in Christian society.

Toward the mid–fifteenth century, the situation deteriorated. The Franciscan Friars Minor were preaching against usury, considered a grievous blot on the purity of the faith. The champion of that battle was Fra Bernardino da Siena, who disseminated his ideas from Umbria throughout central Italy. According to Bernardino, lending money for profit, even the smallest profit, was usury. Those who practiced it (the Jews) were enemies of the people. Those who allowed or authorized it (the rulers or communal authorities) deserved excommunication. This marked the beginning of a great crusade against the moral laxity of the times. The Minorites fostered a potentially subversive climate of fierce social and religious protest, and were uncompromising in their practice of the principles they espoused. One way of actuating these principles was through charity toward the poor. The first *monti di pietà* were established in an attempt to combat the Jewish pawnshops.

By the mid–fifteenth century the conditions of the Jews had improved, thanks to their moneylending activities. The charters had given them the longed-for right of residence, a certain religious freedom, and relative financial comfort compared to the vast majority of the population, most of whom were poor. Most Jews did not wear marks distinguishing them from Christians, and they attempted to extend their activities beyond the oppressive confines of moneylending to commercial and financial activities of broader scope. The violent campaign against Jewish moneylending kindled by the Minorites put an abrupt stop to that process of assimilation. Vast masses were inflamed by the words of the friars. For one thing, the need for greater social justice was already deeply felt by many poor people. The renewed social fervor did not affect the ruling classes but was instead diverted toward the Jewish communities, which suffered new persecutions.

The *monte di pietà* was the Minorite answer to the growing social demands, in the name of the purest religious spirit. In every city, capital to serve the Christian lending institutions was accumulated through donations and contributions paid for indulgences. That capital was parceled out into many tiny loans, granted interest-free to the poor of the towns, "hoping for nothing in return." Pledges were required, and it was forbidden to use the borrowed money for commercial transactions. A pledge was kept for six months, at the end of which time it was sold at auction. The *monti di pietà* were usually located in towns, and their services were available only to the townspeople.

Around the turn of the century this new financial institution gained a solid foothold throughout Italy, but the very fact that it was based on charitable, humanitarian ideals meant that it was not always economically viable. The original capital often seeped away and had to be reconstituted several times in the same town by continual contributions from the faithful. The *monti* therefore functioned only in part as credit organizations; they tended, rather, to take on the character of charitable institutions, which indeed had been the original pious intention of their advocates.

There was no direct conflict between the Jewish pawnshops and the *monti di pietà* on a purely financial level, because their original nature was so different. The credit activities of the pawnshops were broader and afforded protection to both lender and borrower. The pawnshops were better organized (on the strength of past experience), more professional and aggressive, and also more widespread, for they were present in the country as well as in the towns. The *monti di pietà*, governed not by financial opportunism or interest but by religious ideals, were better attuned to the needs of a static culture than to those of a society in the process of commercial expansion. In later years their management was taken over by a class of hired employees who became increasingly parasitic, having no direct interest in their efficient operation.

The conflict between *monti di pietà* and Jewish pawnshops was initially a religious and political issue. Not until later, when the *monti* finally began to charge interest, albeit at minimal rates, in order to recoup part of their operating costs, did the financial competition become fiercer. The most able propagandist of the charitable ideas behind the *monti* was Fra Bernardino da Feltre. In only nine years, from 1484 to 1492, he succeeded in founding twenty-two *monti di pietà*, most of them within the Venetian Republic. In his fight to defend the poor and derelict, Bernardino da Feltre was driven by religious intransigence and absolute conviction. He was intolerant of everything and everyone; he inveighed against the moral laxity of the ruling classes and against every earthly joy or amusement. He was a puritan and a bigot, to the point of banning Ovid and Petronius. During the plague epidemic in Padua, he was reportedly prodigal in his devotion to the poor and the plague-ridden, and always bore in mind the words of Bernardino da Siena, according to whom a man who dies as a result of his charitable deeds during an epidemic was to be considered a martyr. It seems, too, that he did not balk at the meanest tasks, such as washing the feet of the sick. Inflamed by his faith, he defied the authorities of many Italian cities from Florence to Venice, Naples to Mantua, and possibly even Rome. Throughout his campaign he discerned one natural enemy: usury, and by extension, the Jews. In the cause of his faith, he never hesitated: he condemned, persecuted, and instigated expulsions with the same implacable determination that he poured into his defense of the disenfranchised. "Oh, what a fever consumes the Jews! The chill of infidelity and the fire of greed," he said. And further, "Oh—says he—here was a good Jew who kept his word—Oh, you might as well say a scoundrel as a good Jew."

He preached in the region of Umbria, in Mantua, Ferrara, and Genoa, and, especially, throughout Venetia. His first battles in Florence were not successful. He had many supporters, but the socially subversive impact of his impassioned preaching was not looked upon with favor either by the Medici or by the Jews who tried to defend themselves against his accusations, or even by the Dominican and Augustine friars, who, in the name of purity of the faith, obstinately denied the legitimacy of his plan for *monti di pietà* that would charge a minimal interest. The battle was waged on the theological front, relying on mass psychology and rhetoric, with complicated judicial and religious overtones, and on the political front, involving complex issues tied in with the growth of the merchant bourgeoisie. Despite the discord between the political powers and the friars, both groups agreed when it came to curtailing the influence of the Jewish pawnbrokers. The new competition created by the conflict between pawnshops and *monti di pietà* was welcomed by the rulers, who stood to come out ahead. And yet, between the vehement and impassioned friars and the Jews, who paid extra taxes and were less troublesome politically, the ruling classes were likely to prefer the latter.

The friars' violent attacks often provoked persecution and false accusations against the Jews. During the Lenten sermons at Trent in 1475, Fra Bernardino da Feltre fiercely attacked Christians who were on good terms with Jews. To those who objected that the Jews were good people, albeit of a different religion, he grimly prophesied, "You do not know the evil they whom you consider good do you, but before the Lord's Easter, they will give you proof of their goodness." On the evening of Holy Thursday, 1475, a little boy called Simone disappeared. Despite the fact that the Jews had been shut in their homes (the Fourth Council of Toledo in 633 had decreed that "Jews and Moslems of both sexes . . . on the day of the Passion must not be seen in public, nor go about boldly in scorn of the Creator"), they were accused of ritual murder on the strength of the testimony of Giovanni da Feltre, a converted Jew. The accused were tortured, and many died; others confessed under torture to whatever they were charged with. Even before the trial was over, Bishop Hunderbach confiscated the Jews' property just for good measure and in anticipation of their conviction. The papal commissioner sent from Rome declared the Jews innocent, and the murderer was ultimately found. Although the accusation of ritual homicide was ultimately proved to be an obvious fiction, many men were tortured to death, and the women and children were expelled from Trent and obliged to move to Rovereto. After several attempts to beatify the little Simone, in 1562 Gregory XIII included him in the *Martirologium Romanum* and Sixtus V granted his beatification. Later, the Jews declared *chèrem* (excommunication) against the city of Trent: they would never return there as long as it observed the cult of the Blessed Simone of Trent.

The accusation of ritual murder recurs again and again in history; its symbolic significance plays on the imagination of great masses of people. The early Christians were repeatedly accused of that crime, and the Jews' turn came later. The intervention of many popes between 1250 and 1540 was of no avail to stem the dissemination of the infamous charge; the slander had enormous power. In a bull dating from roughly a century after the Trent affair, Paul III wrote, "The enemies of the Jews, blinded by hate and envy or, even more plausibly, by greed, as an excuse for usurping the possessions of these same Jews falsely accuse them of killing little children and drinking their blood and of committing other frightful crimes of all kinds against our Faith, and in this way they attempt to incite against them the simple souls of the Christians, so that they, the Jews, are often unfairly deprived not only of their property, but also of their lives." Paul III did not stop there. He ordained that the Jews were to enjoy the protection promised by his predecessors (Pope Martin V in particular), even if it had to be enforced by the secular arm of the law.

The fear of ritual murder spread throughout the territory of the Republic and moved Doge Pier Mocenigo to action. He wrote three official letters in an attempt to remedy the problem. Shortly before 1480, an episode similar to the Trent affair took place at Portobuffolé in Venetia, resulting in the annihilation of its small Jewish community. The alleged ritual murder in Marostica of a child named Lorenzino, venerated there since the end of the fifteenth century, dates from the period of Bernardino da Feltre's fiery sermons. The Marostica murderer was never found, and the affair remains undocumented, but that did not stop Barbarano, a Capuchin preacher and the author of a *Historia ecclesiastica della città, territorio e diocesi di Vicenza,* * from writing: "The perpetrators of that infanticide were never found, but Vicenza, shaken by so horrifying a tale, sent Giacomo Trento and Alvise Thiene to Venice as representatives of the city in order to calm the anxious populace; and a decree by Doge Marco Barbarigo on 12 April 1486 banished all Jews from Vicenza and its territory. In this manner Vicenza and its territory are freed of this Nation of perdition, nor did it ever again admit into its midst this race of people thirsting equally for gold and for Christian Blood. Therefore if this Blessed Innocent earned no other merit by his Martyrdom, he gained a very great one by having driven the Vicentines, through his suffering, to rid themselves forever of this detestable and pernicious Nation." The legend of Blessed Lorenzino of Marostica persisted for centuries. In 1867 he was beatified by Pope Pius IX. In 1885 the cardinal of Venice took part in the solemn celebration of the fourth centennial of his murder, and in 1945 the heavily bombed town of Bassano made a vow to build a new chapel to Lorenzino in the church of Santa Maria. As recently as the 1950s, a reprint of an 1885 publication with the Church's imprimatur, containing accusations against the Jews, was distributed in church.

Legends of ritual murder in general, and murdered children in particular, were often discounted, especially by Christian intellectuals. But they hovered in the air all the same, deeply penetrating the minds of the common people. As late as 1964 Gemma Volli, an expert on these issues, wrote an article for the journal *Il Ponte* requesting reexamination of the "Tridentine Trials" and the cult of the Blessed Simone of Trent. This was done shortly thereafter, during the Second Vatican Council.

Toward the end of the fifteenth century, Bernardino da Feltre in-

---

*Ecclesiastical History of the City, Territory and Diocese of Vicenza

tensified his anti-Jewish campaign, thereby arousing concern in Venetian government circles.

Citing the bull of Pope Martin, the Republic reaffirmed the right of the Jews to lend money "as provided in their charters." In particular it ruled that, until and unless the Republic decided otherwise, no interference of any kind would be tolerated by anyone. The Jews were to be left unmolested, and the preachers were firmly warned against making trouble of any kind. The podestà Bragadino admonished Fra Bernardino, but the latter, unfazed, turned his defeat into a victory: at the end of 1491, the commune of Ravenna sent two ambassadors to Venice, requesting the institution of a *monte di pietà*. In March 1492, a new dogal decree was issued. Although the Jews were not expelled from Ravenna, Venice did approve the request of the communal ambassadors. They prohibited the Jews from lending money and authorized the *monte di pietà*. The Jews were also forbidden to build a synagogue in the city's finest square, near the church, an initiative much feared by the communal delegates.

In the summer of 1491 Pietro Barozzi, the bishop of Padua, agreed with Bernardino to set up a *monte di pietà* in Padua. The plan was opposed, for different reasons, by both Jews and Dominicans: the former hoped to avoid expulsion and the latter, in the person of Fra Domenico da Gargnano, considered the officials of the *monte* no better than the Jews, for in charging interest, no matter how nominal, they violated canon law.

In 1492 (a year of dire significance for the Spanish Jews, expelled not only from Spain but also from Sardinia and Sicily, then under Spanish rule), Venice wrote to the governors of Brescia "to advise them that Bernardino, while preaching in Padua and in these other places, had incited the people against the Jews, and great tumults, disturbances, and scandals therefore ensued, which we do not wish to believe or hear of happening here." That same year, the tireless preacher delivered fiery sermons at Camposampiero, Castelfranco, Asolo, Feltre, Serravalle, and Bassano. The script was the same everywhere, with minor variations. The sermons were followed by riots and persecution; the Jews were temporarily expelled and the local *monte di pietà* established. Sometimes expulsion was total, but sometimes the Jews were allowed to return. In more than one town the two institutions, pawnshop and *monte di pietà*, existed side by side.

The Minorites' preaching never accomplished all it set out to do. The *monti di pietà* prevailed in the cities, but in the small towns of the Venetian mainland the Jews held their own. In Venice proper, the pawnshops enjoyed a strong position because they afforded significant advantages to whomever needed a loan: the Jews asked no questions, they did not require official declarations of poverty, they appraised pledges generously, they sometimes lent against written guarantee with no pledge, and in rural areas they accepted the future harvest as security. Moreover, the Venetian government could levy extra taxes on the Jews in times of crisis. The war of the League of Cambrai drove the Jews still closer to Venice, so that in the end they concentrated their financial activities in that city and left most of the Venetian countryside to the Minorites.

How did the papacy react to this situation, rife with conflicting demands, permeated with religious zeal and ideological fanaticism? In the face of the unrest in Italian society, with the ascent of Jewish moneylending on the one hand and the establishment of the *monti di pietà* on the other, the Church bowed to the Minorites' initiative without fully espousing their cause. Papal "tolerance" was a way of maintaining control over moneylending. The rulers, when negotiating new charters for the Jewish pawnshops, tried to involve the Church, avoiding sanctions or excommunication by unloading their theological dilemmas onto ecclesiastical shoulders.

At the end of the fifteenth century the Jews were given permission to sell *strazzaria*, or second-hand clothing. Gallicciolli writes: "And yet the Jews sometimes ingeniously succeeded in eluding that law too. For while actually selling new suits and garments of their own making, in some invisible place they made a tiny spot or other flaw and, having charged the customer for a new garment, they pocketed the money and then told him that in a certain place there was a spot, and in this way they pretended to be able to say that the garment was used if any complaint reached the Magistrates." Sometimes even a little spot hidden in a new suit was enough to ensure survival.

CHAPTER THREE

The Birth of the Ghetto: The "German Nation," 1516

The war with the League of Cambrai — Asher Meshullam and Zaccaria Dolfin — The founding of the ghetto — The dispute over the monti di pietà and the Jewish pawnshops — Jews, foreigners, and prostitutes

After their expulsion from Venice, the Jews fled to Mestre.* There, under the control of the local podestà, they carried on their moneylending business in three authorized pawnshops. They were allowed to return to Venice for no more than fifteen days at a time.

Through most of the fifteenth century, the Jews were officially banned from Venice. Nonetheless, they resorted to all manner of subterfuge for the sake of living in the narrow streets and little squares of the city on the lagoon. They went back and forth from Mestre far more often than allowed, wore Christian dress, and, as in the case of the doctors, sought exemptions and exceptions. There is much evidence of this constant, invisible Jewish presence in the city. One document, dated March 1408, states that Jews were renting houses from Christians and using them as synagogues to "pray Hebraically," and brands this practice a sign of great disrespect for the Christian faith. Additional complaints came to light in 1483, when certain violations were reported to have been committed by Jews who, instead of entering the pledges pawned by patricians in their books in Mestre, where the rate was 15 percent, entered them in more distant inland cities, where the interest

---

*a town on the mainland, directly across from Venice

rates were higher. In 1493, the Senate ordered the Avogadori* to keep a tighter control over the running of the pawnshops. According to the Senate, the Jews were earning more than they should, "to the great detriment of the poor people living in Mestre and in the district." In 1496 new rules were made: only one representative of the Jewish pawn-brokers could go to Rialto for the sale of forfeited pledges, the yellow hat was introduced, and the longest period of residence allowed was fifteen days a year.

The decisive turning point came in the sixteenth century. Pompeo Molmenti, the author of a monumental *Storia di Venezia nella vita privata,** * * writes: "The end of the fifteenth century marks the cul-mination not only of Venetian power, but also of that illusory splendor that harbors the germs of corruption and decadence; a frenzy for life, a combination of theatricality and luxury, an awesome ostentation of magnificence. Powerful on the seas with innumerable galleys, splendid in her marble palaces and churches encrusted with gold and precious stones, sumptuous in her festivals, receptions, weddings, and funerals, the true home of Giorgione, Titian, Palma, Pordenone, and Veronese, the court of elect intellects such as Bembo, Aretino, Bernardo Tasso, Sansovino, Jacopo Zane, and the Manuzio family; rich in banquets, balls, ornaments, garments, where more than six hundred women went out adorned with gold, silver, jewels, and silks, a majestic sight indeed." But this was only one side of the Venetian reality. The crisis in the economy was growing steadily worse, and had already led to the failure of the Garzoni, Pisani, and Lippomano banks in 1499.

When the time came, in 1502–1503, to discuss the renewal of the Jewish charter in Mestre, the Jews of Mestre thought circumstances were ripe for gaining new concessions. For one thing, the Venetian government was laboring under pressure from certain patricians who had been very generous during the recent war with Ferrara and now held a joint interest, along with the Jews, in the matter of a loan to Mestre. In practice the new agreement, drawn up for a ten-year term, brought the Jews of Mestre to Venice.

These provisions amounted to a true about-face in the relations between Venice and the Jews: the Jewish moneylenders could rent homes in the city for their families and the personnel employed in the pawnshops, and they could also store the pawned pledges in the city. They could come and go in and about Venice "as many times as they please . . . and also when war threatens they can come to sojourn and

---

*The Avogadori de Comun, a Venetian magistracy originally created in the twelfth century to uphold the rights of the Treasury in civil and criminal trials. They eventually became judges and examiners in charge of public finance.

* *History of Venice in Private Life*

live here without opposition." The headquarters of the Jewish community stayed in Mestre. The highest rate of interest for residents of Venice and Mestre was 15 percent against security and 20 percent on written guarantee; for everyone else it was 20 percent against security and 30 percent on written guarantee. Pledges could be accepted in Venice, but the term of a loan was considered to have begun only when the pledges were entered into the books in Mestre. The Jews were also allowed to bear arms in order to protect themselves and their possessions, and to go without the yellow hat in potentially dangerous circumstances. These new rules had priority over all previous Senate decisions. In case of danger, the Jews would be allowed to move all their assets to Venice, a guarantee that worked to the advantage of their customers as well as to their own. Finally, the articles of the charter drawn up with Venice could be compared with those negotiated by other Jewish communities in the mainland cities of Venetia, and any advantageous provisions contained in the latter could be taken into account.

In 1508, war broke out with the League of Cambrai, an alliance formed against the Republic by Pope Julius II, Emperor Maximilian, and King Ferdinand of Spain. Venice rapidly lost almost all her mainland cities and saw the enemy troops come very close. Numerous refugees, including many Jews, sought asylum in Venice. At Treviso, in particular, the arrival of the enemy resulted in rioting and violence. We know that a group of people from Treviso escorted to Venice a Jewish "gentleman," a banker named Calimano, in order to save him from the violence of the crowd. The population of Venice suddenly grew, and with it grew problems: there were many poor people to be fed and the risk of epidemics was increasing. The Jewish bankers of Mestre also fled to Venice, under the provisions of their charter, and were well received because they brought in capital at a time of great need.

That same year the Senate again discussed the situation of the mainland Jews. Pressed by impelling and urgent financial need, they decided to raise the taxes that the Jewish communities on the mainland had to pay. In exchange they offered new guarantees, laying the foundation for a new agreement which the lawgivers intended to last another five years. The Jews were authorized to go on lending money, against either security or written guarantee. They could accept pledges of any kind, except weaponry or sacred objects such as crucifixes, chalices, altar cloths, missals, "and other similar things on pain of having to return them without any payment." They were also exonerated from any responsibility in case of accident, theft, fire, or looting. The loan could run for a maximum of fifteen months. They were allowed to rent houses but not own them, and they could have a cemetery, a synagogue, and a hotel to receive "visiting Jews according to custom." From Holy

Thursday to Easter Sunday they were to stay shut in their homes, as much for the sake of their personal safety as out of respect. In return they were guaranteed protection against harassment, and the local authorities would be responsible for their safety. When traveling, they were exonerated from wearing the yellow hat.

In May 1509 the town of Agnadello fell, creating a dramatic situation on the mainland. Bands of French, Spanish, and Imperial troops threatened Venice, taking up positions on the shores of the lagoon. More refugees poured into the city, and among them were many Jews.

In his *Diarii*, Girolamo Priuli describes the moral corruption that had brought divine chastisement upon Venice and decreed the fall of Agnadello. This Venetian nobleman cites examples of broken oaths, immorality in the convents, and the sale of church benefices for profit. Many preachers considered the presence of the Jews in the city and the leniency they enjoyed as the root of all evil and hurled anathemas against the infidels and against the Jewish doctors, who fraternized dangerously with Christian invalids. At the news of grave and imminent peril, the Venetian populace reacted with strong emotion, deep religious fervor, and moral anguish, whipped to still greater intensity by the fiery sermons the preachers were delivering from the city's pulpits. This explosive situation is described by Sanudo and Priuli in their diaries. According to Sanudo's estimate, there were about five hundred Jews in Venice at that time, most of them apparently living in the parishes of San Cassiano, Sant'Agostino, and San Geremia. With the increasing hardships, hostility against them grew.

By 1513 and 1514 Venice had succeeded in overcoming her most critical political and military difficulties, but she was still beset by domestic problems that showed no signs of abating. There was plague in the city and fires had broken out, including one especially fearsome blaze at Rialto. Nobles, commoners, refugees, peasants, and Jews were all crowded together. And yet a number of witnesses, including Priuli, still talk about a merry atmosphere, the affectation of French vogues, violence, sodomy, and great confusion. Even in this highly charged atmosphere the Jews, scattered throughout the city, were still enjoying great freedom. They lent to the poor and to anyone else in financial trouble, and they had no dearth of clients. The political authorities tolerated them because they needed them: not only was credit essential to the economy, but the Jews could be used as a lightning rod to deflect mass hostilities. Already in 1512, the constant tug-of-war between the leaders of the Jewish community and the Venetian political powers had led to a heated conflict. The Senate wanted 10,000 ducats. The banker Asher Meshullam (called Anselmo del Banco in Italian) and the other Jewish leaders who had refused the loan on the terms offered were thrown in jail in an attempt to induce them to reconsider. The Jewish bankers threatened to close their pawnshops and leave town.

Not until a year later did the Council of Ten accept Meshullam's terms, with certain modifications, and permit lending against collateral in exchange for an annual tax of 6,500 ducats.

Two years later the Senate, again in need of funds, authorized the opening of nine second-hand shops in the Rialto district in exchange for a fee of 5,000 ducats. The presence of the Jews in the city was thus explicitly accepted, and new business enterprises started to grow up alongside the traditional moneylending establishments. At that precise moment there was a counter-reaction that seems almost surprising: some of the nobles gave their support to the preachers, one of the most virulent of whom was Fra Zulian Maria di Arezzo. Sanudo observes that by this time the Jews were scattered all through the parishes of San Cassian, San Polo, San Stin, and Santa Maria Mater Domini, and that while they had formerly stayed home during Easter week, "now they are always about." Bitterly, he writes: "Nobody says anything to them for they are needed because of the wars, and so they do as they please. The Minorite preacher Fra Zuan Maria di Arezo preaches against them and against the Jewish doctors, most of all Master Lazaro, who has been the ruin of Christian woman, has consorted with Christian women, and nothing is done about it." A few days after Sanudo's outburst, in March 1515, the Senate received a proposal from Emo Zorzi requesting that all Jews be confined to the Giudecca. The Jewish leaders objected to that choice of location, for they considered the Giudecca dangerous, and suggested Murano instead. Argument was heated, but the Senate could not reach a decision.

The following year, on March 20, 1516, Zaccaria Dolfin launched a violent attack in the Collegio against the Jews, accusing them of numerous iniquities, including the illegal building of synagogues and corruption of the State. He requested that they be confined to the Ghetto Novo, or New Ghetto, an ancient site resembling a fortress in the parish of San Gerolamo, where there was a foundry that had fallen into disuse. The doge approved the plan, as did a number of patricians who felt the situation should be corrected and the Jews' freedom curtailed. Asher Meshullam and the other Jewish leaders tried to object, warning of the dangers of isolation and reminding the authorities that they had just recently opened their second-hand shops at Rialto and had recently been obliged to make heavy investments. In what may have been a desperate attempt to gain time, they proposed that any decision be suspended until Venice won back her mainland possessions, at which time the Jews would be happy to return to the mainland. It was all to no avail: the proposal, discussed first in the Cabinet and then in the Senate, was approved by a crushing majority of 130 to 44, with 8 uncertain.

On March 29, 1516, the Senate enacted the following decree: "The Jews must all live together in the Corte de Case, which are in the

Ghetto near San Girolamo; and in order to prevent their roaming about at night: Let there be built two Gates on the side of the Old Ghetto where there is a little Bridge, and likewise on the other side of the Bridge, that is one for each of said two places, which Gates shall be opened in the morning at the sound of the Marangona, and shall be closed at midnight by four Christian guards appointed and paid by the Jews at the rate deemed suitable by Our Cabinet." The enclosure was to be completed by two high walls; all the exits were to be locked and the doors and windows walled up. The guardians were to live there day and night, to guard it "with the other Orders that shall be established by the Cabinet." The Jews also had to pay two boats to unceasingly patrol the canals surrounding the ghetto. Progressively severe penalties were established for any Jew found outside the ghetto at night. The first and second offenses were punishable by a fine, the third by a heavier fine and two months' imprisonment. Appointed to control and enforce these measures were the Cattaveri, government officials in charge of public assets and, in particular, Jewish moneylending and "the manner in which they were to reside in Venice." The Cattaveri were authorized to make suggestions to the Cabinet, in an advisory role. To change any of the rules, a five-sixths majority was required in the Senate. The Senate decided that the houses in the ghetto should be evacuated immediately, and that their new occupants should pay a third more rent than the landlords had previously been receiving. That third was exempt from tithes.

The old idea of granting the Jews a residential quarter, which dated back to the fourteenth century, had finally been actuated. But while the Jews at that time had considered it an important, though disregarded, provision of those early charters, they now looked at it with fear and suspicion.

One question remains unanswered: why did the proposal to confine the Jews to a ghetto, defeated in 1515, carry the Senate so quickly and by such a large majority only a year later?

Some historians have seen this as reflective of the Venetian position in the overall international situation. In 1515, a certain optimism still reigned in the city: in particular, the Republic was convinced that with the aid of the French troops it would soon succeed in reconquering Verona and part of the Venetian mainland. In the spring of the following year, however, the outlook had grown bleaker. Emperor Maximilian had come down from the Alps at the head of an Austrian army and the French had barricaded themselves in Milan without giving battle. The French seemed inclined to reach a compromise with Austria, and Venice had been excluded from talks between the king of France and the pope. On the eastern front, troubling news was arriving from Friuli, and many feared a new Turkish invasion. This unfavorable train of events left its mark on the minds of populace and nobility alike. The general mood was one of gloom and pessimism. For months the Minorite preachers had been insisting that Venice, to survive, would have to regain God's grace and atone for all her sins—and one of the most grievous of those sins was letting the Jews live freely in the town. The ghetto was seen as an act of expiation, a request for indulgence.

Before the end of July, Asher Meshullam and his brother Chaim were forced to move into the ghetto. On moving to Venice, Chaim had imprudently rented the Ca' Bernardo palace in the parish of San Polo, ostentatiously flaunting his wealth and thereby arousing envy. The Meshullams were the heads of the wealthiest and most important banking family of Venetia, and according to some historians they were the sons of a certain Salomone da Camposampero who had been persecuted as a result of Bernardino da Feltre's impassioned sermons. At that time a new decree was enacted, establishing the wages of the ghetto boatmen and the Cattaveri, naturally at the expense of the Jews. Asher was forced to play a double role: on the one hand he was personally responsible for guaranteeing and advancing the taxes owed by the entire Jewish community, and on the other he had to apply to the community for reimbursement. Despite Asher Meshullam's authority as leader of the Jewish community, or possibly due to the very delicate position in which he found himself, members of his family were often involved in infighting and scandals. Jacob the jeweler, Asher's son, got into a bitter fight with his uncle Chaim over matters of money. On another occasion Jacob was accused of having purchased stolen goods. He apparently managed to avoid conviction by bribing the judges. The fortunes of this legendary family, which had guided the Jewish community of Venice through the first hard years in the city, reached their lowest ebb in 1533, when Jacob, the son of Asher (hero of innumerable battles with the Venetian authorities), converted to Christianity and took the name of Marco Paradiso in a sumptuous ceremony at the Church of the Frari, with the blessing of Pope Clement VII and the doge.

In December 1516, the Treaty of Noyon brought peace to the mainland, and in Venice the tensions associated with the ghetto relaxed (the number of guards was reduced from four to two, and the gates were kept open longer); but the question of the Jewish presence in Venice again came up for discussion. The alternative between Jewish pawnshops and *monti di pietà* was always in the air, and at the Easter season of both 1518 and 1519 the Minorite preachers, particularly Giovanni de l'Anzolina, attacked both the Jews and the alleged laxity of the authorities in dealing with them. The charter was about to expire and the usual precarious period of negotiation was beginning. In the summer of 1519, there was new talk of expulsion.

To the point, as always, is the testimony of Marin Sanudo, who remarks in his *Diarii* that it could be debated whether to let the Jews stay in Venice or Mestre, or whether to discuss the details of the charter, but that there was no point in arguing about the Jews themselves (especially on religious grounds) as long as the pope was keeping them in Rome.

Indeed, there were some very ambivalent opinions. Piero da Ca' Pesaro, for one, although favoring the restriction of the Jews to the ghetto, wrote, "It would be to drive them from the world," and recalled their expulsion from Spain and Portugal. Such disputes shed light on the Venetians' differing attitudes not only toward dealing with the Jews, but also toward governing the Republic. Antonio Grimani agreed with Marin Sanudo, saying, "The Jews are necessary to subsidize the poor people and it makes no difference whether they stay in the ghetto or go live in Mestre, but the six articles must be confirmed and there must be no more of this bigotry and the Jews must be allowed to lend at interest." When Tommaso Mocenigo, in November 1519, proposed renewing the charter, with interest rates fixed at 15 percent and a tax of six thousand ducats, Antonio Condulmer requested that the Jews be expelled in the name of Christianity, exhorting the nobles to fear the wrath of God. Francesco Bragadin, although hostile to the Jews, stressed their important role in the Venetian economy and argued that, for lack of a *monte di pietà*, they should be kept in the city. Some insisted on associating the presence of Jews with the misfortunes that had befallen the countries where they had lived, while others emphasized the advantages the Turks had derived from their presence.

Marin Sanudo gives an accurate interpretation of the dispute: nobody in the Senate was sincere. The speakers opposed one another with ambiguous arguments, but they all, at least verbally, took positions against the Jews so that no one could accuse them of weakness. Certainly, there were some who did not want the Jews in Venice proper, for the sake of "goodness and piety," but others were simply eager to take over the moneylending business for themselves, no longer at the controlled rate of 20 percent but at 50 percent or more, as was being charged at Rialto. Sanudo thus concludes his chronicle with an outburst which has become famous: "And if I, Marino Sanudo, had been one of the Senate, as I was last year, I would have taken the floor not to speak of the sons of Israel and the swindles they perpetrate lending at interest, but to speak of their charter, to have it amended, to show that the Jews are as necessary as bakers in a town, and in this town in particular, for the general good, citing the law and what our ancestors always did, who advised having Jews to lend at interest; this is whereof I would have spoken. We need no such imbecility in this State, as that of banishing the Jews without having a *monte di pietà*."

Although they were seen as interchangeable, *monti di pietà* and pawnshops did not serve exactly the same economic function. A *monte di pietà* operated as a losing venture; it created no wealth and could not be heavily taxed. The Jews, whose role in the economy was more dynamic and flexible, and less bound up with public welfare, to use a modern expression, paid high taxes to the state and could be forcibly obliged to lend. They lent to the poor at reasonable rates without the need for the heavy initial investments required by the *monti di pietà*.

Furthermore, the *monti di pietà* had often shown a tendency to deviate from their original charitable purpose and were subject to the influence of the patricians in whose hands they became centers of power. The ones on the mainland had come a long way from the idea of inexpensive loans. During the latter half of the sixteenth century they gradually became private banks and provided fertile terrain for corruption and scandal. Such bad examples ultimately discouraged spontaneous donations. Interest-bearing deposits were accepted and became a form of investment. In the final analysis, Jewish capital was more easily controlled, could not become a political force, and worked extremely well as a tool for containing poverty. Venice, sensitive to the advantages of capillary social control, had no desire to lose the use of such a tool.

The discussions and quarrels among the nobles were intensified by the precarious financial situation of the Republic and the unanimously acknowledged need to strengthen the Arsenal. Rather than imposing an extraordinary tax on all the citizens, it was decided to heap the entire burden on the shoulders of the Jewish community, offering a ten-year charter in exchange for a tax of ten thousand ducats, with the interest rate for loans set at 15 percent. Apart from the heavily increased tax burden, there was little substantial difference between that charter and the earlier ones. Asher Meshullam asked for time to consult the mainland communities, but in the end he was obliged to give in. "When will struggles with power, power wins out," he is reported to have said on that occasion. Cynical pragmatism often became the key note in Venetian politics.

The supporters of the *monti di pietà* spoke up again in 1523. This time they asked only that the *monti* be instituted without demanding that the Jews be expelled.

The following year, in an incontestable show of authority, the Council of Ten forbade the members of the Senate to concern themselves with the question, on pain of death. This prohibition lasted for over two centuries, until 1734, although the *monti di pietà* again came under discussion in 1573 in conjunction with a new plan to expel the Jews.

To a further demand for money in the spring of 1526, Asher Meshullam replied that the Jews would rather leave Venice than pay. At about the same time, Gabriele Moro, long known for his anti-Jewish position, maintained that in accordance with the past tradition of the Republic the Jews should be sent to Mestre. He asked that rules be established limiting any new attempt to gain access to the city. He also demanded strict enforcement of the obligation to wear the yellow hat. Moro was opposed by Zaccaria Trevisan and Giacomo Loredan, who pointed out that the charter still had three years to run, that much could happen in the meantime, and that the Senate could not afford to be bound by a hasty decision made so far in advance. Moreover the Jews themselves, through their leader, had announced that they would leave. Gabriele Moro's motion passed by a small majority, but the government had other problems in those times of hardship and it was never enforced. The Jews, too, sought a compromise.

The Council of Ten reached a decision in September 1528. The Venetian Jews addressed a poignant petition to the Council, stressing their long tradition of obedience and the importance of their contribution to the finances of the Republic. They made it clear that only their dire need and the fear of not being able to pay had provoked them to say they intended to leave Venice, but that to do so would cause them great sorrow. They therefore requested, with the prudence demanded by the situation, to be allowed to stay in Venice under the conditions accepted by the mainland Jews, with a five-year charter authorizing, among other things, their second-hand shops and the making and selling of veils, and of course their usual pawnbroking activities. In exchange for these much-desired concessions, they offered the government a loan of seven thousand ducats and an annual tax of five thousand, to the exclusion of any other ordinary or extraordinary payments. The agreement was to be automatically renewed for five years if neither of the two parties canceled it; if, on the other hand, the contract were broken, the Jews would be granted a year to wind up their business. The Council of Ten accepted the petition with no serious reservations: in fact, it looks almost as though the reply had been agreed on beforehand. The amount of the loan was raised to ten thousand ducats and the maximum rate of interest was maintained at 15 percent for loans against security. The agreement was to remain in force until 1533.

When the charter came up for renewal in March of 1532, there was a new tug-of-war between the Cabinet and the leaders of the Jewish community. Once again the Council of Ten renewed the charter, changing the terms and increasing the tax but, in substance, maintaining the previous agreement unaltered until October 31, 1538.

In February 1537, just a year before the charter was due to expire, the Council of Ten came up with a new, drastic ultimatum: either the Jews agreed to donate 5,000 ducats within fifteen days, increase their mandatory loan to 6,750 ducats by the end of April, and pay a yearly tax of 7,000 ducats, or they would have to leave the city and the territories of the Republic at the expiration of the charter. Before accepting those conditions, the Jews requested that they be allowed to stay in the city for ten years rather than five. The Council of Ten accepted this proposal, but demanded an increase of the donation from 5,000 to 6,000 ducats, a yearly tax of 7,000 ducats, and an additional 6,750 ducats to be deducted from the annual sum over a five-year period. The gift and loan, amounting to 12,750 ducats, were earmarked for the reinforcing of the artillery and the fleet stationed at Corfu.

A unique period in the history of the Venetian Jews was drawing to a close. Although they were confined to the ghetto, their residence in the city was legally recognized. Their situation was one of precarious stability, charged with tension, but it was a good one compared to that of Jews elsewhere in Italy and Europe, and the fame of the Venetian ghetto spread to the most remote corners of the Diaspora.

The restrictions imposed on the Jews at that time must be viewed in the overall context of the times. They were not the only group or the only foreigners subject to such restrictions. Many attempts had been made, for example, to confine prostitutes to a special district, but the very proliferation of laws to this effect bears witness to their inefficacy. Obviously the prostitutes had ways of reaching the ears of the powerful, and repressive measures against them were never strictly enforced. But like the Jews, the prostitutes were to begin their business only after the ringing of the Marangona, the great bell in the campanile of St. Mark's.

The German merchants in Venice had long been subject to restrictions similar to those imposed on the Jews, under a law passed by the Maggior Consiglio in 1314. A provision enacted in 1478 prescribed that the gates of their Fondaco* must stay closed until the sound of the Marangona. For that matter, confining foreigners was not an exclusively Venetian custom. In Alexandria, Egypt, the Venetians themselves were forbidden to go out during the Moslem prayer times or on Fridays. And at night they were locked in. The need to cultivate good business relations was probably what induced the merchants to accept these restrictions in silence.

The situation of the Turks in Venice was very particular, changing according to their alternately serene and stormy relations with their powerful enemy. Following the conflicts of the 1570s, the Turks, too, demanded a residential district like the one assigned to the Jews. But the Senate granted them only a Fondaco on the Grand Canal, known to this day as the Fondaco dei Turchi. There, too, the doors were locked at night and guarded by soldiers. The Turks were never allowed to spread out too much, for in case of war they could become a dangerous Trojan horse. In fact, they aroused much greater mistrust than the Jews.

---

*in the Middle Ages, a building that served as both a dwelling and warehouse for foreign merchants in Mediterranean seaport cities

The Greeks, on the other hand, were less dangerous politically but were greatly feared from a religious standpoint, having broken off from the Roman Catholic Church. Not until the mid–fifteenth century were they granted the right to build a church, and not until the end of the century were they allowed to establish a "school" for Greeks. Of course, there were vast differences between the Greeks and the Jews: the constitution of the Greek community, in the neighborhood of the church of San Giorgio dei Greci, was the spontaneous, or almost spontaneous, result of an act of will on the part of its members, motivated by their feeling of religious identity.

The most important group in the newly constituted ghetto was that of the German Jews, as can be deduced from the family names, even those that had been Italianized. Even at this time there were noticeable differences between Jews of German ancestry, accustomed to a hostile environment and themselves suspicious and unbending, and the Italian Jews, who were reproached with not being sufficiently well-versed in the analysis of rabbinical texts and with being too indolent and "Mediterranean." The first group of Jews in the newly founded ghetto was called the "Natione Todesca," or the German Nation, and comprised Jews who had lived in Italy and Venice for hundreds of years, as well as recent immigrants of German and, more generally, Ashkenazic origin.

We unfortunately know very little about the daily life of the ghetto during those early years, because the sources that have come down to us are primarily official documents, almost all relating to moneylending. The bankers themselves probably doubled as tradespeople. We find traces of the presence of rabbis, learned men, writers, proofreaders, and printers, but no record of those in humbler, but equally essential, walks of life.

Physicians were especially important and carried great weight in that restricted society. When Venice decreed the isolation of the ghetto, we find written on April 24, 1516, "The Jewish doctors must also move into the Ghetto." But how could they answer night calls if they were confined to the ghetto? On July 20 of that same year, it was decided to allow them to leave the ghetto at night. Their freedom was controlled, however: they had to inform the guards, in writing, of where they were going and where they had been, and they had to give the names of their patients. Violations or false statements would be punished by fines and imprisonment.

The Jewish doctors were much respected; certainly they differed from their Catholic colleagues not only in religion, but in their attitudes toward life, health, and illness, as well as in the modernity of their ideas, the fruit of stronger international influences and continual travels. The Church thought they cured the body but damned the soul, and felt that the bonds of gratitude that inevitably grew up between doctor and patient should be strenuously fought. Nevertheless, Calò Calonimos and Joseph De Dattolis received financial aid in the form of brokerage licenses. Lured by the myth of Venice, David De Pomis came from his native Umbria, and Calonimos from Naples, to live in the ghetto.

Our sources depict an ambivalent line of conduct, wavering between generosity and distrust. The Jewish doctors obtained privileges, but they aroused much suspicion; they were accepted by bishops and popes who needed their services, but were denounced from the pulpits so the people would learn to fear their "long and crafty hand." In 1517 the Council of Ten ordered doctors to wear the yellow hat, but in 1529 permission was granted to "Mastro Jacob Mantino, a Jewish physician, to wear the black cap in this our city of Venice, freely living in the Ghetto where the other Jews live." Originally granted for a month, the privilege was later extended. An interesting note is the phrase, "freely living in the Ghetto where the other Jews live." After the bitter conflict that had led to the creation of a segregated district, the words "freely living" attest to the fact that this state of affairs was now considered normal.

This marks the beginning of a relationship between the Most Serene Republic and the ghetto of Venice dense with changing moods and resentments, desires, and fears—a relationship unique in the history of the Jews of the Diaspora.

CHAPTER FOUR

The "Levantine Nation": 1541, The "Old Ghetto"

Isaac Abrabanel—Arrival of the merchants in the Old Ghetto— Burning of the Talmud in St. Mark's Square—The expulsion of the Marranos—The papal bull of Paul IV, **Cum nimis absurdum**

I n the history of the Mediterranean Jews, the sixteenth century was an age of constant migration. Precariously balanced between a cruel and uncompromising "purity" of faith and a hidden intense religiosity mixed with fear and anxiety, many changed their identities as they found new homes in Turkey, Venice, Leghorn, or Rome. At the dawn of that century, the splintering and the expulsion of the Jewish communities of Spain and Portugal was already a *fait accompli*, with many forced to convert and others dispersed throughout the Mediterranean region.

In 1474, when Ferdinand and Isabella came to the throne, Spain espoused a policy of *limpieza de sangre*—purity of the blood. The prime mover behind the persecution and expulsion of the Jews was a Dominican friar, Tommaso de Torquemada, suspected of having Jewish blood himself. He was the queen's confessor and notorious for his inflexibility. He also inspired the revival of the Inquisition, that great repressive machine created in 1212 to combat the Albigensian heresy, and later a tool for repressing new Christians and Judaizers. In the wake of the religious intolerance that swept the country, an edict enacted on March 31, 1492, obliged all unbaptized Jews to leave all lands under Spanish rule (then including Sardinia and Sicily) within four months. In December 1496 Don Manuel, king of Portugal, having asked for the hand of the Spanish king's daughter, gave the Jews ten months to leave his own territory. Any Jew failing to conform was forcibly baptized, and these "converts" were called Marranos. Many other Jews refused conversion (some sources number them in the tens of thousands) and fled the Iberian peninsula seeking new, more hospitable lands.

These events have been interpreted by almost all historians as manifestations of religious intolerance. Only Fernand Braudel has relegated such ideological factors to the background, focusing instead on physical anthropology. In his view the frequent expulsions of the Jews at the end of the fifteenth century and later were the result of overpopulation, and evidence of a true attempt to redistribute the scarce resources of Mediterranean Europe.

The years spanning the end of the fifteenth and the beginning of the sixteenth century were dramatic not only for the Iberian Jews, but for the Most Serene Republic as well. The voyage of Vasco da Gama, which opened up new commercial routes to the Orient, suddenly threatened the position of Venice on the chessboard of international trade, creating new uncertainties and conflicts in the Mediterranean. Global patterns of trade changed rapidly as new oceanic routes came into being alongside the customary Mediterranean routes, and the traditional trading centers of the Mediterranean saw themselves cut off from the new international traffic lanes. The first to adapt were the Iberian refugees, expelled in consecutive waves. In search of a homeland and a true identity, they would travel, if need be, to the most remote corners of the Mediterranean.

Among these refugees was the Abrabanel family. Their wanderings over vast reaches of land and sea, as well as their exemplary intellectual itinerary, have lent them symbolic significance. Not only do their lives embody the traits of two centuries, the fifteenth and the sixteenth, they also highlight the differences between these two periods. The foremost representative of the family was Isaac Abrabanel, born in 1437 in Lisbon. He had been a powerful man, the treasurer and finance minister of Alfonso V, but when the king died he was unjustly accused of conspiracy. Abrabanel fled to Spain, where his financial acumen won him the task of reorganizing the State budget, heavily strained by a fierce war with the Moors. Even for such an illustrious statesman, however, 1492 meant exile and long wanderings through the Mediterranean. In 1493 he was at the court of Ferdinand I, but in 1494 was forced to follow Alfonso II, the son of Ferdinand I, who was routed by the French army of Charles VIII. In 1495 he went to Corfu, and in 1496 to Monopoli, in Italy.

Don Isaac Abrabanel reached Venice in 1503. An elderly statesman, full of glory and experience, he immediately tried to act as political mediator between Venice, his new home, and Portugal, where the tide had turned and he was again in favor. He submitted a plan to the Council of Ten, pleading his case so eloquently as to provoke an exhaustive discussion. The Senate considered the plan advantageous and sent Josef Abrabanel, a relative, on a mission to Portugal. This last diplomatic endeavor of Don Isaac's (he died in 1508 at the age of seventy-one and was buried in Padua) bore no fruit, despite the Senate's approval. But Don Isaac did not neglect his intellectual activity in those last years and completed many writings, including *Docens Justitiam*, a commentary on Maimonides's *Guide for the Perplexed.*

Abrabanel is the symbol of a certain Jewish way of being at that time. Even in history's darkest tumults he devoted himself to abstract philosophical speculation, and this, though it may have prevented his focusing on the reality around him, enabled him to survive. Faced with the alternatives of conversion or exile, he unhesitatingly chose the latter, comforted in his odyssey by a deeply rooted metaphysical messianism. In his writings, a messianic conception of history mingles with hope for the future role of Israel: "It has been taught in the houses of Eliahu that the duration of the world is six thousand years: two thousand of confusion, two thousand of Torah and two thousand of Messianic times." Abrabanel had made his calculations, and was convinced—as he writes in *Fontes salutis* *—that the Messiah would come in 1503. These deductions influenced many Jewish exegetists and scholars during the first half of the sixteenth century. Abrabanel is a symbol: his thoughts embody the contradictions of the Middle Ages and the ferment of the Renaissance; his political and intellectual life is the mirror of Jewish existence.

Certain aspects of his relationship with Venice are emblematic, too. In his *Commentary on the Pentateuch*, originally written in Hebrew, Abrabanel elaborates the myth of Venice. The first of the Jewish thinkers to do so, he discusses the Venetian constitution, comparing it to the government given by Moses to the people of Israel according to the counsel of Jethro, and upholds the superiority of republican government over monarchy. Thus Abrabanel identifies the "governors of thousands," mentioned in the Bible, with the Maggior Consiglio, the "rulers of hundreds" with the Senate, and the "rulers of tens" with the Council of Ten. In order to draw this analogy, however, this Iberian philosopher was obliged to bend the biblical text, for while in the Mosaic constitution the "governors of thousands" were at the apex of the pyramid, Abrabanel had to set the "rulers of tens" at the top so they could be identified with the Council of Ten. His ideal constitution was also more markedly republican than was that of Venice. Despite Abrabanel's interpretation of the Bible in the light of contingent reality,

---

*The Sources of Salvation

this first Jewish contribution to the creation of the Venetian legend, on the threshold of the Renaissance, remains a document of considerable importance.

The events culminating in the expulsion of the Jews from Spain in 1492, and from Portugal in 1496, left deep scars. Although the effects were felt most keenly during the first half of the sixteenth century, the entire Mediterranean region underwent a radical transformation throughout the century. The changes were not only social and commercial, but cultural, religious, and psychological as well. The first massive migrations of Jews, who had settled in all the seaports from Constantinople to Salonika, Venice to Ragusa,* and Ancona to Leghorn, were followed by a slow but steady stream of small Marrano family groups or lone individuals with contorted and tormented histories. Trade was enlivened by these perennial fugitives, whom poverty had emboldened and homelessness unsettled.

Around the 1540s, Portuguese trade began to decline. One reason for this may have been Portugal's policy of cheap exports (we would call it dumping), which limited the opportunity for reinvestment and had failed to take into account the high cost of traveling over long routes.

Venice, meanwhile, had worries of her own. New and lesser-known cross-routes, from Ancona to Constantinople by way of Ragusa, had begun to encroach on the traditional longitudinal itineraries from Egypt and Constantinople to Venice. In both cases the Adriatic emerged as an independent reality whose two shores were to a large extent complementary, with grain and oil traveling toward the Slavic side and meat, wool, and leather coming to Italy. The Ancona-Ragusa axis, a short, safe sea route, was an efficient alternative to sailing the length of the Adriatic from Venice, amid the perils of corsair attacks and Uskok** ambushes. The revival of international trade drove Venice to seek new ways of reinforcing her privileged lifeline with Egypt. Once again the Republic, in an attempt to save her economy and maintain her status as the chief port of call for merchants and adventurers, the bridge linking the great Christian powers of the West with the Ottoman Empire, made use of the Jews.

The residents of this city, a true bazaar of peoples of different nations, origins, and destinies, included many wayfaring Levantine Jewish merchants of Marrano origin, people of ambiguous religious affiliation. They were all attracted by the ghetto, in which they sought a fixed point of reference and support, a place where they might be able to put down roots and find some degree of cultural and psychological identity. These merchants, Jews of Portuguese and Spanish origin, were called

---

*present-day Dubrovnik
**Serbo-Croatian pirates who infested the Adriatic in the sixteenth century

Rio di Ghetto Novo. The bridge and one of the entrances to the ghetto.

Levantines because they had lived in or passed through such eastern ports as Constantinople and Salonika before coming to Venice. Gradually they settled in the ghetto alongside the group of Jews called the German Nation, the core of the original community. The differences between Germans and Levantines were considerable: their language, history, and personal backgrounds differed, as did their religious traditions and their trades. The Germans were moneylenders, veteran city dwellers, while the Levantines were seafaring merchants.

There is no evidence of any instinctive empathy between the two Nations. Elias Levitas writes in his *Paris und Wien*, a Yiddish transcription of a popular Italian novel written in verse: "In the Venetian ghetto nobody speaks to the foreigner and it never occurs to anyone to do so. He is forced to wander the ghetto for a long time before finding company among them. If anyone be found who has done this, that man is certain to have gained something from the foreigner."

The Most Serene Republic, which had already exploited the lending aptitudes of the original Jewish nucleus, soon realized the potential usefulness of the Levantine Jews in fighting for trade supremacy with the rival cities of the Adriatic. When the Levantines complained that their life in the New Ghetto was made difficult by lack of housing and storage space, the Senate made an unusually speedy decision on June 2, 1541: "Let the Magistrates have the freedom to lodge the traveling Levantine merchant Jews in the ghetto, and if they cannot be accommodated there for lack of space, let them have authority to lodge them in the Old Ghetto . . . but always locked and guarded as are at present those in the New Ghetto . . . since said Levantine Jewish merchants cannot yet keep pawnshops, second-hand shops or any business save only simple commerce."

Thanks to a singular network of human and family relationships, the wandering merchants put their international connections to good use in the very areas of influence essential to the survival of Venice. They had especially close ties with Rumania, the Balkan peninsula, and the vast Ottoman Empire. This is explicitly mentioned in the text of the motion approving the expansion of the New Ghetto to include the area of the Old Ghetto: "And given that most of the merchandise coming from upper and lower Rumania is brought by and is in the hands of the traveling Levantine Jewish merchants, they say they have no room, as verified by the Five Sages of Commerce.*"

Once more the fate of the Jews is interwoven with that of Venice. That year, 1541, marked the beginning of a thirty-year period that many historians have called a golden age, and which set the tone for the rest of the sixteenth century. The Serenissima established the terms for

---

*The *Savi*, or Sages, were senior magistrates whose function was to advise and assist the executive organs of government.

the new situation. It was decided that: "At the entrance to the small Square of the Old Ghetto on the Cannaregio side, running down toward the canal, where the well is, let there be erected a wall of appropriate height that joins with the walls to the left and right, and let a door be made therein, and this wall shall continue up to the boundaries of said Ghetto so that there will be no other exit toward Cannaregio, except for said door. Let the Ghetto be guarded so that they cannot leave by any door, as from the New Ghetto . . . Let the guardian who watched the gate of the New Ghetto leading toward the Old be removed and set at the Cannaregio gate. Let the doors of the three Christian houses that look onto the small square with the well be walled up and their doors be made to open on the other side, nor may they make balconies except at windows enclosed in the wall that crosses the Ghetto on the Cannaregio side." The aristocrat Leonardo Minotto, who owned the property in that area, was ordered to evict his tenants. He was promised that the new tenants would pay a third more rent than the current ones (in effect, he would enjoy the same benefits as the New Ghetto landlords, except for exoneration from the tithe).

This edict sanctioned the passing of Venetian trade, albeit only in part, from the hands of the Venetian patricians to those of the new foreign merchants. Venice had come around to granting these concessions to the traveling Levantine Jewish merchants only after much hesitation and, in 1541, was the last of the Adriatic cities to do so. Ancona had already given the Jews a stable settlement in 1526, in addition to the traditional exemption from customs duties. In Ferrara, Duke Ercole II d'Este had tried to attract Levantine merchants in 1538 by offering them a safe-conduct that would enable them to live in the town and trade indefinitely.

Had the Levantine Jews lived in the New Ghetto up to that time, or had they been scattered throughout Venice? The latest research by Ravid has now supplied a clear answer to this previously controversial question: all the Jews lived in the New Ghetto. The expansion to the Old Ghetto was not a new restriction, therefore, but a tardy and reluctant acknowledgment of the importance of the Jews in the city's economy. Pragmatic as usual, Venice was keeping up with the times by finally according the Levantine Jewish merchants, most of whom were not Venetian citizens but subjects of the Ottoman Empire, a special legal status. They were authorized to live in Venice for no more than four months at a time, without their families, and could engage in no business but trade. Initially, because they were foreign subjects, the Levantines enjoyed more business privileges and fewer rights than had the first Jewish moneylenders, but in time the restrictions grew less rigid and were often disregarded entirely. One historian ironically remarked that the agreement ultimately carried a double advantage:

Venice did not lose her precious trading routes, and the Venetians did not lose their faith.

The German Nation lived in the New Ghetto and the Levantine Nation in the Old. Although they were neighbors, the two groups were now separate, and their functions in the economy were different. Yet almost immediately, despite a certain mutual distrust, a process of gradual osmosis began to integrate them through the exchange of homes, marriages, cultural and religious debate, and business. The financial supremacy of the German Jews, who were the founders of the ghetto and its pawnshops, declined, while the trading fortunes of the Levantine and, later, the Western Jewish groups rose.

Higher taxes and lower interest rates were the Venetian government's most forceful method for squeezing maximum profit from the ghetto Nations during the 1540s and 1550s. Under these hard conditions, the pawnshops struggled through a period of instability accentuated by the worsening of the underlying economic crisis.

On the Venetian mainland, several cases of persecution were verified. When Jewish families were massacred in Asolo, Venice intervened with a firm hand not only against the perpetrators, but also against the feeble local authorities. The guilty were arrested and punished with the implacable severity characteristic of the times and the laws of the Republic.

Levantine merchants, meanwhile, were building up good will in many Mediterranean ports. Both Jews and Portuguese Marranos could conduct their business freely in Ancona, and the situation did not change when that city came under papal rule in 1532. Between 1547 and 1552, in fact, both Paul III and Julius III (despite his attack on Jewish books) continued to guarantee a certain degree of tolerance: "No mark of differentiation from the Christians."

But the 1550s saw an abrupt change involving both the Levantines, suspected of being Marranos, and the Jews. In 1553, Venice and the papacy, in one of their rare moments of harmony, agreed to fight heresy and Jewish culture by the public burning of books in Rome and Venice. Volumes of the Talmud were burned in St. Mark's Square; Cardinal Varallo, an exponent of the Roman Inquisition, in a letter to the Venetian ambassador called them "Hebraic books, the most pestilential . . . against the Christian religion."

Actually, Venice had preceded Rome with her attack against resident Marranos in 1550. In June of that year the Senate, after a reminder that as early as 1497 "the Marranos, infidels with no religion and great enemies of the Lord God, had been driven from the State," observed that despite this it was easy to see that their numbers had increased and that the time was ripe to "renew such a useful and holy measure." The expulsion decree was reconfirmed; would-be transgressors were threatened with confiscation of their property and a two-year sentence to the galleys, in chains. Although authority still rested with the Avogadori de Comun, enforcement of the order was delegated to the Senate Censors' Office. The motion was passed, 146 to 25, with 24 uncertain. In August of the same year the Senate was obliged to re-examine the matter. Many citizens and merchants "of the Rialto district," of all nationalities, afraid of being tainted by alleged contact with the Marranos despite their best efforts, asked to be exonerated from the suspicion of dealing with possible infidels. The merchants explained that they bought from the Spaniards, who traded with Apulia, Rome, Naples, and Sicily, and that their business involved unknown traders and many different countries, and that they wanted to work "safely and with peace of mind," without running the risk of being chained, possibly even through trickery, to the oars of a galley "which frightens all who hear of it." The Senate made it clear that it was not opposed to trade with the "Marranos of other nations," but wanted only to prevent their coming to roost in the city.

In both Rome and Venice the Jews lived in separate quarters, were obliged to wear distinctive signs on their clothing, and were forbidden to own real estate. They were also obliged to attend sermons (during which they plugged their ears with wax), for the predecessors of Paul IV had increased the pressure on them to convert. A "Domus Conversorum" or House of Catechumens was instituted and the property of new converts protected, while Jewish culture was attacked by the destruction of Talmuds.

A few years later, in 1555, the extremist leader Giovanni Pietro Carafa was elected pope, taking the name of Paul IV. One of his first actions was to send emissaries to Ancona to investigate the orthodoxy of the Portuguese Jews. His bull *Cum nimis absurdum*, in which he emphasized the Jews' error of faith and the need to keep them subservient until they understood its gravity, was already in the air. The bull marked a change in relations between Christians and Jews; conversion would be obligatory rather than spontaneous, and any Jew who moved to Italy after having lived in Spain or Portugal would be considered an apostate even if he denied, under torture, having been baptized or having lived as a Christian. The official explanation was that, since Jews had not been officially allowed in Portugal for the past sixty years, anyone coming from there must necessarily have been baptized and lived as a Christian.

Economic repression was particularly harsh and effective from 1555 to 1558, both in Venice and in Rome. The Jewish leaders in Venice sent a memorandum to the government of the Republic emphasizing the impoverishment of the Jewish community and asking for tax relief.

The arrest of the Marranos in Ancona, in 1555, cast a still darker cloud over the Italian scene. Totally disregarding the promises made

A building in the ghetto: the ceilings are very low and the windows very close together.

by his predecessors, Paul IV ordered the Inquisition to throw the Marranos of Ancona into prison. Some fled to nearby Pesaro or Ferrara. About a hundred Marranos were captured; of these, forty were Turkish subjects. In March 1556, Suleiman the Magnificent demanded that the pope free his subjects, adding, "Thereby you will give us reason to treat with friendship your own subjects and the other Christians that trade in these parts." The sultan's firm stand contributed to the speedy liberation of the Turkish citizens. Other prisoners saved their lives by abjuring their faith and were deported to Malta. On the way there, they organized a successful escape and, on reaching Turkey, openly declared themselves Jews. Twenty-four prisoners were left in Ancona who refused to deny their faith; they paid for their steadfastness at the stake. The news of this tragic mass execution ordained by Paul IV spread like wildfire to all corners of the Mediterranean and provoked strong reactions. The Levantine Jews, especially the powerful Don Joseph Nasi, alias Giovanni Miches, organized an economic boycott against Ancona. Participation was not unanimous, but important communities, including Salonika and Constantinople, joined the protest. The government of Ancona turned to the pope, and even to the much-embarrassed local Jewish community, in an attempt to get the boycott suspended. There were violent polemics among the Jews of Ancona, many of whom had no desire to be involved in matters concerning Marranos. The boycott lasted for two years, and little by little ceased to be enforced. But the events left a deep scar and marked the beginning of a dark period for Ancona, while Venice benefited from the problems of her traditional rival.

In November 1558, the Venetian charter was again renewed. Renewal was automatic unless the charter was canceled by at least one of the parties a year in advance. That year could be used to settle debts and credits, but no moneylending would be allowed. The principles governing all the charters were reiterated yet again: the general tax, the Jews' right to live in the city and observe their religion, the prohibition on selling new merchandise, and the permission to sell second-hand clothes. Pawnshops could not charge more than 12 percent and were obliged to meet the needs of anyone who asked for a loan "from five Ducats down." These regulations were followed by new ones, but these were mere formalities, seemingly of minor importance. The banks were still accountable to the Sopraconsoli. The cashiers had to write their lists and accounts in Italian (the first moneylenders had written them in Hebrew) and provide minutely detailed and comprehensible descriptions of the sums loaned and the pledges received. The activity of the pawnshops was subject to strict control, and as far as we can gather from reading the regulations approved by the Senate, there was no margin for transgressions of any kind, large or small, even when it came to holding the pledges and selling them at auction. Increasingly, the Jews were becoming mere executors of the will of the Republic. The many other provisions in the new charter simply retraced old patterns.

When the charter came up for renewal in 1563, the tensions that had lain dormant in earlier years resurfaced. For two years there was no talk of renewal, and in September 1565, a new decree established that the Jews could live in the ghetto for only one more year, to settle their debts and credits, without lending money or buying any more stock to sell in their second-hand stores.

As the year wore on, the situation became even more entangled, and the time when the Jews would have to leave Venice was drawing dangerously near. In a new, poignant petition the Jews enumerated their problems: many of them had left, and other important Jewish taxpayers had gone bankrupt, irreparably crippled by two years of uncertainty. They were at their last gasp. This petition, which may have been agreed on in advance, led the Cabinet to stress its concern for the city's poor, and to present to the Senate a bill in which this was expressed. Unexpectedly, the Senate voted down the proposal to renew the charter for five years. This came as a shock to the Jews in the ghetto, accustomed as they were to the usual tug-of-war with the government of the Republic and to their life in the city.

They submitted yet another sorrowful petition: they and their ancestors had by now lived in Venice for generations, they could not bear the thought of being driven away. They were desperate, not only because of their looming banishment, but because there was simply not enough time left to organize such a mass exodus. Once more they appealed to the mercy of the government, convinced that it could not possibly mean to expel men, women, children, and old people just when winter was coming. It would be impossible to move everyone. They would be murdered en route. They might as well all throw themselves into the canals—at least they would all die together. At the end of this appeal, the Jews asked for only a year's extension and requested that anyone who so desired should be allowed to leave for Palestine, traveling on safe galleys. In that year of special suspension, they promised not to take any initiative or to harm anyone in any way. Once again the Cabinet passed on to the Senate a proposal granting the Jews' requests to all practical effects. But the Senate was divided, and no decision was taken. Again the Cabinet submitted a proposal for discussion: the extension was to have a strict time limit and the Avogadori de Comun were to be charged with its enforcement. Any new decision would have to be voted by a large majority.

After a long debate, the Senate approved the year's extension by a large majority, suspending the expulsion of the Jews.

In February of 1566, the Cabinet sent the Senate a new bill which represented still another sudden about-face in Venetian policy. Concern for the poor made it necessary to restore the lending operations suspended as a result of the earlier negotiations. The Jews could stay in their ghetto, but on different terms. Instead of automatic renewal, there would now be automatic expulsion unless the government decided otherwise. The terms for moneylending were also revised: Bankers were now obliged to deposit a sum as security against bankruptcy and were not allowed to refuse loans of five ducats or less. They could no longer take money from Christians. This meant the interruption of all financial cross-flow. Segregation between Jews and Christians, which daily living had tended to reduce, was again the guiding principle of Venetian government policy. And on the horizon loomed old problems, still unresolved: the antagonism between pawnshops and *monti di pietà* was flaring up again; Pope Pius V, in his bull *Hebraeorum Gens*, branded the Jews unnecessary and instituted a policy of religious and economic repression.

Meanwhile, friction between the Christian West and the Ottoman Empire was mounting. The Turkish designs on Cyprus, growing clearer day by day, were creating the inevitable conditions for war. In 1570 some Venetian citizens were arrested in Constantinople and two ships were confiscated. Venice retaliated by freezing the property of the Turks living in the city, as well as that of the Levantine Jews, who were considered Turkish subjects.

This was the first link in a chain of events that would eventually lead to open conflict, culminating in the famous battle of Lepanto.

CHAPTER FIVE

The Marranos

The difficulty of defining "Marrano"—Relations between Jews and Marranos, and between Christians and Marranos—Venice and the papacy—The Inquisition in Venice

What, exactly, is a Marrano? When the expulsion edict of 1550 aroused angry protest among the merchants of Rialto, the government of the Most Serene Republic was faced with that difficult question. If the answer was problematical even in the sixteenth century, when the elusive and ambiguous Marranos lived openly in the city, clearly visible to all, how can we, today, even free of the opportunistic considerations that may have swayed the Venetians, hope to identify them?

In its literal sense, the word *marrano* is an insult: it means "pig" in both Spanish and Portuguese. Used figuratively in Italian, it has remained a derogatory epithet.

The Marrano phenomenon evolved as a result of the expulsions, forcible conversions, autos-da-fé, and general persecution of the Jews that took place in 1492 in Spain and 1496 in Portugal. The Marrano was a forced convert to Christianity who remained a Jew in his heart, observing Judaism as well as he could in the privacy of his home.

With the passing of time, Marranism assumed so many different forms that it is impossible to define it in a single image, or even in two—as in the suggestive dichotomy between decisive religious experience and eternal heresy. As intriguing as such definitions may be, they offer but a static view of a dynamic phenomenon.

The violent repression that struck like a sledgehammer, shattering the Jewish social groups, undermining their unity, and wiping out the fertile Jewish culture of the Iberian peninsula (which had bred Ibn Gabirol and Maimonides), was not entirely successful in its object of annihilating the small family microcosms, which were impervious to outside reality. Tenacious and stubborn, they survived, like myriad droplets of oil on water. Families and individuals were forced to protect themselves in the only way they could, hiding underground like karstic rivers, which alternately surface and submerge as the terrain permits. Therein lies the great, elusive variable of Marrano existence: collective history is replaced by the innumerable histories of individual families and figures. Each Marrano becomes an original expression of the more complex Marrano phenomenon, with its burden of sorrow, ritual, and religious belief. Judaism, publicly denied, recedes to the level of an inner debate, a personal conflict that feeds on secret thoughts, until it becomes an incurable disease.

In the forty years between 1497 and 1537, before the king of Portugal brought the Inquisition to his country with the support of the pope, Marranism had ample time to develop. From then on, the experience of each generation of Marranos was unique. As these people spread through the Mediterranean, the intrinsically fragmentary nature of their culture was accentuated by contact with geographically and politically diverse areas: Salonika and its Turkish culture, Venice the eternal frontier, Rome and the papal influence. It is not surprising that the Marrano, accustomed to being chased like a stray dog, found protection in camouflage.

Certain traits are indeed recognizable as common to all Marranos, and many historians have attempted to pinpoint them: hostility toward the persecutor, Christianity; a strong attachment to a simplified form of Judaism; and a firm faith in the coming of the Messiah. The pattern is accurate in many cases, but not all. The entire Marrano phenomenon is anomalous; their history is more that of flesh and blood men with passions and vices than that of saints and martyrs. The victims of persecution may very well have been weak, stupid, or corrupt; seeking no halos, their only concern was survival. The Marrano was often totally alone, deprived of the solace of a community, bearing alone the tensions that the world heaped upon him. Even his moral and religious ethic was solitary. The Marrano read the Bible without guidance, and although his interpretations may have been more original, they were teeming with the seeds of heresy. In the seventeenth-century Marrano communities of northern Europe (Amsterdam is one example), this cultural soil produced a rich flowering of skeptics, heretics, and Averroists. The solitude of Spinoza and the torment of Uriel da Costa were but two expressions of that climate.

A minority group must either love its own condition, mark out the boundaries of its identity, and seek the means to perpetuate that identity, or hate itself and attempt to hide under protective coloration. Thus the individual Marrano either became a more ruthless persecutor of other new Christians, or tended to cleave to his group of origin, no matter how innately ambiguous the relationship. Either choice entailed an intense confrontation with memory. The transition from collective memory to that of the family and the individual was all the more tortured for being haunted by the ghosts of the Inquisition.

Inquisition. The word evokes ancient torments, prolonged for centuries. In Portugal, the Marrano problem was a constant of political and civil life. The first auto-da-fé took place on September 20, 1540, the last on October 27, 1765.

One singular characteristic of the Marrano phenomenon is that the harder the historian tries to bring its constituent elements into sharper focus, the more entangled they become. For historical inquiry, Marranism is a complex development whose several interpretations lie at various points between two opposite poles; it may be viewed as a concrete form of potential Judaism or, at the other extreme, as an illusory projection, more present in the thoughts of the authoritative investigators than in social reality.

In its continuous evolution, Marranism took on many different forms, from its origin as secret Judaism to a bare and essential Judaism, finally becoming a distant, inner memory which the very Inquisition helped perpetuate through its persecutions. As it gradually forgot its birth trauma, Marranism became less a collective event than the sum of individual choices, subjected to incessant and tormented revision by people living in a perpetual state of instability. The Marranos' changes from Jew to Christian, half Christian and half Jew in a constant state of flux, were too numerous not to engender suspicion and accusation. The family, originally a locked strongbox closely guarding the secrets of its members, was ultimately weakened by these subterranean tensions: sons, daughters, husbands, wives, for different personal reasons, through youthful impatience or marital discord, sometimes made conflicting life choices that created strife and embarrassment and resulted in the whole family's being dragged up before the Inquisition. Amid these contradictions and vacillations, the Inquisition stepped in, enforcing its own concept of order. While in Spain this concept was partly based on an ideal of purity of the blood, in Venice it was more a question of preserving a tradition of clearly defined social roles.

Given the difficulty of drawing an unequivocal portrait of the Marranos as a class, it may be best to devote our attention to the individual. The Marranos of the sixteenth century spread throughout Europe, even where official Judaism was outlawed. Charles V of Spain accepted them under his rule from 1537 to 1542, and Henry II of France offered them more privileges than his own subjects enjoyed. Some Marranos were even protected by papal privileges while still others, well thought of in the Ottoman Empire, traveled as far as Constantinople. In every city, the Marranos lived alongside the Jews and sometimes assimilated gradually with them, forming the core of the Sephardic line that would grow to represent the counterpart of the Ashkenazic current originating in the East.

The history of the Jewish communities of Marrano origin reveals the existence of pervasive heterodox tendencies: the traditional barriers with which the rabbis encircled the Torah were considered superfluous; the Oral Law, the Mishnah, and the Talmud, always sources of religious debate, were harshly criticized as the root of rabbinical power. The most strongly heretical opinions attributed the authorship of the Bible to men. In the seventeenth century, this vast assortment of subversive opinions, flaring up after nearly a hundred years of dormancy, created bitter contention within the Jewish world and a deep split between Kabbalists and anti-Kabbalists.

If the Marranos were disliked by the Christians, neither were they much loved by the Jews, who had no real understanding of their insecurities and constant transformations, but simply considered them insincere and opportunistic. Even among the Jews, however, there was more than one attitude toward the Marranos, the persistence of whose ambiguous behavior caused the rabbis' initial understanding, benevolence, and empathy to give way to more severe judgments. In 1556, at the time of the troubles in Ancona, Yehoshua Sonino, the rabbi of the Italian Jews in Constantinople, opposed the boycott because in his opinion there was no point in siding with men who had abjured their faith.

The Venetian attitude toward the Marranos was one of instinctive mistrust. In Venice, precisely defined social roles reflected rigid criteria of order and segregation. In 1497 the Marranos had been expelled from Venice and the cities in Puglia under her rule. The renewal of the expulsion in 1550, which on the one hand reflected a Venetian policy even harsher than that of the papacy itself, on the other made it clear how difficult it was to define the Marrano. Venice, a quintessential city of transit, was also the site of many metamorphoses, and it is more than likely that the Marrano refugees had a number of friends there. They came to Venice on their way to the Orient, returning with new merchandise and ready for new transactions. Some revealed their Jewish identity while others wavered between the two worlds, trying first one, then the other. The presence in their city of men of uncertain faith troubled the Venetians, who gladly welcomed foreigners but always liked to know with whom they were dealing. If the Marranos wanted to declare themselves Jews, well and good; they would move to the ghetto where they would live unmolested. Jews by birth were rarely bothered by the Inquisition in Venice. Those who came from the East after fleeing Spain and introduced themselves in Venice as

Levantine Jews and Turkish subjects were protected by the Ottoman Empire, whatever their personal background.

In practice, the city was open to many wealthy, useful, and influential Marranos alongside whom lived a mass of poor ragpickers. The figures recorded by the papal nuncios, having been used for propaganda, may not be very reliable; indeed, ten thousand seems too large a number. It may simply have been one way of putting pressure on Venice, for though officially hostile to the Marranos, the city was secretly unwilling to break with them entirely.

Toward the late 1560s, trade patterns in the Mediterranean began to change. These changes immediately affected the Marranos, who were loved or hated only in function of the commercial strategies of their adopted countries. Venice was left with a reduced naval force that chiefly plied the Adriatic, seldom venturing further abroad. Ancona and Ragusa were dangerous competitors that lay on an imaginary axis between France and the Ottoman Empire, cutting out Venice entirely. The situation worsened in the seventies with the loss of Cyprus, and loss of her influence in the salt trade limited Venice's function as mediator. Ragusa, which had maintained a neutral position and was now enjoying a healthy economy, offered merchants many advantages.

In this changing scene the Marrano merchants, the connecting threads in a worn fabric, were in danger of being split up and their mediating role stifled. But the Christian nations, allied against the Turks, were divided and competing with one another. One of the most noteworthy initiatives, in the seventies, was the decision by Duke Emmanuel Philibert of Savoy to develop the port of Nice Villefranche and his attempt to channel various economic and trade forces into that project. The duke offered a generous safe-conduct to the victims of the Inquisition, arousing the jealousy and hostility of Spain, Venice, and the papacy, each for different reasons. International pressure finally put a stop to the plan, and within six months, in a partial reversal of policy, Savoy expelled all Marranos who had returned to Judaism.

This turn of events was not entirely disadvantageous for the vast and fragmented Marrano population. Once again the Marranos, on the brink of annihilation, were spared the destiny that would have been inevitable had the Christian world stood united. Events were coming to a head. Six months after the apostate Marrano Jews were expelled from Nice, Venice offered them a safe-conduct. While in substance it accorded the same benefits offered by the duke, its form was different in that those who entered Venice as Jews were obliged to live in the ghetto, wear the yellow hat, and obey all the other restrictions applying to Jews. Its granting was symptomatic of an about-face that would take deeper root in Venice during the 1580s.

Here, too, as we learn from the many records of Inquisition trials, an attempt was made to clearly define the identity of the Marranos.

Were they the new Christians hailing from foreign shores, now living as Jews in Venice, or those who had been Jews elsewhere but behaved like Christians in Venice? Or were they the Levantine Jews, Turkish subjects of dubious origin? Even the most astute Inquisitor might well have been confused. For one thing, the histories of these individuals were fragmentary and vague, with intricate family complications. The Marrano identity was hazy even within individual families, often taking different forms in husband and wife, parent and child, even among siblings. The Venetian Inquisition came up against many such cases, and the judges made every effort to clarify the issues.

It must be recognized, too, that the Inquisition in Venice was quite different from similar tribunals in other countries at that time. It was concerned primarily with those whose way of life or imprudent speech gave rise to scandal and caused them to be suspected of straying from their assigned social roles. Such people disturbed the guardians of the rigid Venetian social order, with its stratified system of rights and obligations. The Jews themselves, though considered inferior to the Venetian patricians, citizens, and merchants, could still live with dignity as long as they respected the social role assigned to them. The University of the Jews,* a single body representing all the Nations in the ghetto, distinguished according to their different ancestries and countries of origin, was treated as an equal by the government of the Republic which, except in rare cases, scrupulously respected the pacts signed after long and exhausting negotiations. The Jews of the German Nation, the group around which the ghetto had been established, were very well aware of this; in fact, they were hardly ever the target of the Inquisition. Among the most recent immigrants, however, were many who had lived as adventurers, whose identity was not so clear, and who had arrived in Venice erroneously believing that here they would be accountable to no one for their behavior.

We have had frequent occasion to note the complex interaction of religion with politics in the Most Serene Republic. It was common belief in all social strata that the city had been founded with the help of God and could only survive by the grace of His continual support. Military defeats, too, were interpreted in a religious light, as signs of God's rejection. On such occasions the Senate and the Council of Ten, with amazing speed, would approve laws and decrees aiming to guard public morals against corruption, blasphemy, prostitution, or the deviation of the clergy, in the attempt to win back the lost grace. The 1537 ordinance instituting a special magistracy expressly for that purpose, the Executors against Blasphemy, spoke explicitly of the "fear of

---

*The Latin *Universitas Judeorum* and its literal Italian translation *Università degli Ebrei* are derived from the Hebrew *Talmud Torah*, the school where Torah was studied. This term was used, by extension, to indicate the Jewish community as a whole.

God," on whom "the public and private weal" of the Republic depended. The duties and powers of this new magistracy soon extended to the control of gambling and the press, spheres not originally included in their mandate.

But religious piety in Venice never became political subservience to the pope. Venice and Rome were often in opposition, driven by divergent interests. On several occasions members of the Venetian nobility who had relatives in the Curia argued the need for a special tie with Rome, but such was the Venetian aristocracy's desire for independence that the Senate and the Council of Ten questioned whether those with such close ties to Rome should be allowed access to the more delicate public offices. The considerable economic benefits accompanying the privileges conferred by the Church on the noble families that served it only compounded the complexity of the political conflicts engendered by such issues.

The coming of the Counter-Reformation to Venice cannot, therefore, be interpreted simply as the handing down of decisions made in Rome. In July 1542, Pope Paul III issued a bull, *Licet ab Initio*, instituting the Roman Inquisition. From that time on the papal nuncios in Venice repeatedly pressed the government of the Republic to combat Protestant heresy. But the existence of conflicting attitudes in Venice resulted in a stalemate, with neither victors nor vanquished. Domestic policy changed only as a reflection of the changing international scene, and only after repeated Protestant defeats did Venice belatedly take sides. By a decree enacted on April 22, 1547, Doge Francesco Donà brought the Inquisition to the lagoon. It was not an absolute novelty, but an old institution into which new life and energy had been breathed. The papal legate, the Patriarch of Venice, and the Franciscan Inquisitor were flanked by three Venetian nobles. The doge appointed three magistrates, patricians of untarnished Catholic piety: Nicola Tiepolo, Francesco Contarini, and Antonio Venier. They were called the *Tre Savi sopra l'Eresia*—the Three Sages on Heresy—and they represented the authority of the Council of Ten to the Holy Office. They attended trials and expressed opinions. They also acted as a buffer between Venice and Rome when the pope pressured the Venetian government with injunctions or protests. But only the ecclesiastical judges had a vote when it came to passing sentence.

Until 1560, the Venetian Inquisitor was a member of the Franciscan order. Although his appointment came from Rome, he swore an oath of obedience to the laws of the Republic. After 1560 the Dominicans took over from the Franciscans and ran the Inquisition until its abolition in the eighteenth century. The Three Sages on Heresy, selected with special care from among the most influential members of the aristocracy, had the delicate task of mediating between Venice and

Rome. Their role is most clearly portrayed in the reports of the papal nuncios resident in Venice, and appears to have been designed primarily to moderate the demands of the clerics. While often agreeing with the clerics in substance, the Sages did their best to make sure that the proceedings, including punishment of the guilty, or those so judged, were carried out quietly. Discreet drownings at sea were preferred to public executions.

From analysis of the large volume of trial records, many historians have concluded that the Holy Office in Venice, probably due in part to the moderating influence of the Three Sages, was fair in its sentences (considering the times), attentive in its inquiries, and scrupulous in its evaluation of the evidence. The Inquisition tried 1,560 cases in Venice during the sixteenth century, with 14 sentences of death by drowning and 4 more executions in Rome, where the accused were extradited. Throughout Italy the Inquisition was far more moderate than were the regular city courts. The Council of Ten, for example, sentenced to death 168 thieves, murderers, traitors, and homosexuals in the course of the sixteenth century. Venice at that time was much more lenient in its day-to-day justice than many other Italian cities, including Ferrara and Mantua.

Furthermore, the Holy Office in Venice offered reduced sentences in exchange for confession or repentance, and sometimes even imposed light sentences. Almost all the trials were for heresy (Lutheran or Anabaptist), for reading or trading in forbidden books, or against Judaizing Marranos. Some historians have calculated that the approximately seventy trials against Judaizers accounted for about 5 percent of the total. Almost all the accusations involved offenses against religion. Very few ghetto Jews were accused of such crimes: charges against them usually involved threats or bribery. Rather than on the Jews as individuals, attention focused on Jewish culture, considered close to the Anabaptist heresy, which was viewed as deceitful and subversive. There were repeated attacks on the Talmud, thought to be a dangerous book that encouraged false testimony and contained, it was said, numerous insults to the Christian religion. These accusations were repeated not only in 1553 and 1568, when Jewish books were publicly burned in St. Mark's Square, but in the early 1570s and 1580s, two particularly critical moments in the history of Venice. Only in the eighties were Jews accused of apostasy and heresy, even though they were generally seen as merely treacherous, rather than as true heretics. The Old Testament origin shared by Jews and Christians made it all more complicated. According to St. Thomas Aquinas, the Jews were midway between pagans and heretics, whereas a heretic was a person who, through continual vacillations, ended up with one foot on each side of the fence. Boniface VIII had a narrower conception: any baptized person of Jewish origin who wished to revert to Judaism would be considered a heretic, unless baptism had been inflicted upon him by *absoluta coatio*—not merely by threats, that is, but by actual physical force.

The Venetian Inquisition was unusual in that it reflected the different interests of Rome and Venice. It did not indulge in gratuitous persecution and avoided becoming embroiled in family diatribes or unrelated vendettas. Nor was it desirous of trying baptized Jews who wished to revert to Judaism, since that might appear as a defeat for Christianity. The records that have come down to us, which of course illuminate only the overt doings of the court and not what went on behind the scenes, do, however, provide glimpses into the mentality of both the judges and the judged.

If the relationship between the Inquisition and the heretics and Marranos was by its very nature vague and problematical, that between the Holy Office and Jews who had become Christians and wished to revert to Judaism was much clearer. Christianity placed Judaism at the bottom of its scale of values; any motion from there had to be irreversibly upward. Repeated conversion was considered an abuse of the sacrament, a mockery that diminished its indelibility. While Rome had always used every means to encourage conversion, the same cannot be said of Venice. The ghetto had been established to protect the Christians, but Jews were not overtly courted. True, the son of Asher Meshullam was received with great pomp and full honors upon his baptism in the church of the Frari, but his was a special case: he was the son of the ghetto founder and leader. Conversion was certainly welcome in Venice, but there was no blatant proselytizing or mandatory attendance at sermons, as in Rome. The House of Catechumens in Venice, founded in 1557, did not win official recognition until 1571, the year of the tormented renewal of the controversial charter. This new institution was intended to provide security for the new converts and eliminate deception; it became an element of order, an obligatory corridor between Judaism and Christianity. Passage was not immediate, however. It generally required at least forty days, which could be reduced if a student demonstrated particular zeal and knowledge. Conversions were infrequent, and the flow of new arrivals to the Jewish community from other European countries and the Mediterranean region compensated for the loss of those converted. The latter, who frequently adopted their godfathers' family names, such as Pisani, Morosini, and the like, or the name of that day's saint, were helped by the catechumens to take their place in the new life. The bond between the Inquisition and such catechism schools grew closer in the 1580s, when both became tools of a single strategy.

Pullan has observed that the Inquisition in Venice lived by compromise. Both Church and State were inspired by ideals of social order, but their interpretations often differed. Their treatment of cases concerning Jews exemplifies both the coincidences and the divergences. Freedom in Venice meant leaving one's past outside the city gates and conforming quietly to the social order. The Inquisition had little interest in the Jews, partly because other magistracies had jurisdiction over religious offenses, and partly because it preferred to avoid institutional conflicts with the Venetian government. Too-frequent attacks on the ghetto would have been embarrassing for the government, which would have inevitably retaliated.

The Inquisition trials supply colorful testimony about anonymous individuals picked out of the crowd. Though mere fragments of a larger picture, the records offer unforgettable impressions of secondary figures, men and women who have been remembered by history due to some single nonconformist act, possibly no more than a simple offense against the current ideal of modesty or some instance of irregular or ambiguous behavior.

CHAPTER SIX

Jews, Marranos, and Judaizers Before the Inquisition: Stories of Everyday People

Giuseppe Francoso, 1548—Francisco Oliviero, 1549—Elena de Freschi Olivi, 1555—Gomez and Enriquez, 1555—Licentiato Costa, 1555—Aaron and Asser, 1563—Marco Antonio degli Eletti, 1569

Giuseppe Francoso, 1548

Giuseppe Francoso, a young man of twenty, of middle height, with a blond beard, was accused of having been baptized several times. He immediately confessed, confirming that, indeed, he had been baptized four times. "The first, as I said, in San Hereima . . . as a Jew my name was Aaron . . . and they christened me Jacomo . . . the second was in Modena, where I took the name Paulo, the third in Ravenna, where I took the name Battista, and the fourth at the abbey of Monsignor Loridan, where I was christened Francisco." At his baptism in Venice, he said, "My godfathers were Jacopo de Paternostri and the fruit-seller who lives near the Cannaregio bridge," a bare few yards outside the ghetto gates. Ingenuously, according to the trial records, the young man related the encounters and experiences in Modena, Padua, and Ravenna that had led him to repeat the ritual, almost as if he thought repeated baptism would strengthen his new faith.

The Inquisitors wanted to know whether he had received gifts or money. "In Venice," replied the young man, "the only alms I received were 14 soldi . . . in Modena I refused to take anything . . . when I left Ravenna [Monsignor Spirito Santo] gave me two gold scudi . . . at the Abbey on Palm Sunday I was baptized by the Vicar there, but he gave me only clothing and six ducats for charity, after which I came here."

He seemed resigned. "I was baptized because my clothes were in rags and in order to have someplace to go." His words reveal very little Christian inspiration but, rather, a fatalistic attitude toward life: "I knew it was wrong and that it went against the principles of the Christian religion, and that it was a sin, but I did it because I had no livelihood." He went on to say that he had tried to unburden himself of the sin on his conscience by making confession. But one priest had brusquely rebuffed him and another had refused him absolution, after his first baptisms. Having nothing else to fall back on, he had converted over and over again despite their admonitions, as though impelled by some irresistible urge. In concluding his deposition he begged forgiveness, "and he was questioned no further."

So that no one would go unpunished for "errors and failings against the baptismal sacrament and the Christian faith," the Inquisition sentenced Jacomo alias Aaron to "forced labor in the galleys" for twenty years, and to perpetual exile thereafter. If he tried to escape and were captured, "let him be hanged by the neck at the usual place of judgment." As a final note the court added that he could be recognized by one distinctive feature: "Note that said Jacomo has a mark on his right ear, a sort of wart or mole."

Francisco Oliviero, 1549

The story began when Oliviero was wounded at the home of a courtesan, Laura Romana, who lived in Calle del Pestrin in the parish of Santo Stefano and "whom he visited wearing the black cap and sword and dagger of a Christian."

It would have been a banal affair except for the unusual incident that occurred after two days spent at the home of Zuan* Paolo. The latter "sent him from his own house and took him to the Jewish inn in the ghetto to be cared for." This cast doubt on the man's identity: was he a Jew or a Christian? The Inquisition investigated and called witnesses. One was Antonio de Bernardi, subdeacon in the church of Sant'Angelo, whose story ran: "One night at around four in the morning I was called to confess a man who had been wounded and I rushed to the Corte del Pestrin, over the wooden bridge to the group of new houses near the bridge, I don't remember if it was the first or second door and I don't know who lives there, but I confessed a man who had been wounded." He added that the man looked like a foreigner, possibly Spanish; he confessed and absolved him "according to the order of our Holy Mother."

Another witness was Victorio da Pesaro, who lived in the house of the lawyer Zuan Battista Contarini. Was Francisco Oliviero a Jew or

*"Zuan" is Venetian dialect for "Giovanni."

a Christian? His answer: "I don't know, but I know he's one of those Portuguese Marranos." The witness told of his visit to the wounded man and said he knew that the next day Oliviero had been taken to the home of Paolo Paruta at Santa Marcuola (near the ghetto) and had been moved to the ghetto the day after that.

Zuan Francesco Brandi, whom the Inquisition asked for reliable details about Oliviero's alleged identity, replied that he had met the man at the home of the Spanish ambassador and had heard rumors from certain friends of his who were in some doubt about the defendant's true religion. It was said that he had a Jewish brother in the ghetto and had been seen wearing a yellow cap.

Yet another witness, the innkeeper Bondi di Vitali, was asked "whether this witness knows Francesco called Oliviero, a tall, dark young man with a thin beard . . . and whether he is a Jew or a Christian, whether he has Jewish relatives and whether Francesco Oliviero generally dressed as a Jew." The witness answered that he had been told of the arrival of a wounded man by the name of Joseph and that, as they could see from his register of Jewish foreigners, he had given him a room, registered him as "Joseph the Jew," and considered him Jewish, feeding him "according to Jewish law and in the Jewish style." He added that this Joseph had a brother by the name of Davide who "comes and goes every week" between Ferrara, Venice, and Ancona, "a respectable Jewish man who dresses as a Jew, and this Joseph sometimes dresses as a Jew and sometimes as a Christian, that is with the yellow hat." Bondi di Vitali ended by saying: "I consider him a Jew and I registered him as a Jew, as you can see from my book . . . and to tell you the truth I took him into my house so he wouldn't be buried among Christians if he died."

"At present detained in the prisons of the Magnificent Lords of the Night," the tall, thin, dark young man with a sparse beard, Francisco Oliviero de Ulsbona, was summoned before the Inquisition. He asserted that he had no idea why he was being held, "unless it were because I was wounded." His deposition took on dramatic tones. At the courtesan's house he had narrowly escaped a conspiracy: an old woman "put out the candle and left me in the dark where a man came up, wounded me with seven mortal blows and left me for dead." At death's door, his first thought was to call a priest, who came and heard his confession.

The Inquisition finally asked Oliviero whether he was a Jew or a Christian. The young man answered, "I am a Christian. It's true that I am circumcised, and that it was my father who circumcised me." But he said he had no recollection either of when he was circumcised or when he was baptized. "I have always lived as a good Christian."

The Inquisitors were quick to object. Why, if he was a good Christian, did he live like a Jew in the ghetto and wear a yellow cap? "I had no money and nothing to live on, and I was taken into the ghetto where I have many Jewish relatives, and have been in the Jewish hostelry until now, where my family paid for me." But now the whereabouts of those relations were unknown. Oliviero solemnly declared that if they could prove he wore a yellow cap or ate and drank according to Jewish law, he would submit to any punishment (what choice did he have?). Immediately thereafter, however, he added, "It's true that I ate with the Jews, my relatives, but I did not observe their rituals."

A porter named Leonardo was called. He confirmed having seen Francisco Oliviero wearing a yellow cap, "and he was under the little portico of the old ghetto, in Cannaregio." Yes, but did the people in the ghetto consider him a Jew or a Christian? The porter was uncertain. "I think he behaved more like a Jew than a Christian," he said, but without much confidence "because those Jews don't let any Christians know about their affairs, and don't talk to them about their business."

The same questions were asked of another witness, Messer Antonio, a grain and turpentine merchant who confirmed that he had known the defendant "before he was wounded at the strumpet's." Certain friends of his, said Antonio, although they thought him a worthy fellow, were "in doubt as to whether he was a Jew or a Christian." Yes, he had seen him with a yellow cap and remembered the exclamations of surprise!

Another porter, Jacobo Veronese, told the court about an exchange of banter with the defendant: "I saw this Francesco on the ghetto bridge with a yellow cap on his head, and he said, 'Well, what what do you think?' To which I said, 'I think it's well you've recovered!' "

Francisco Oliviero testified again. What were his relations with the mistress of the house where he was wounded? "She was a friend and courtesan, and my relations with her were casual, the usual sort of thing for young men." Jew or Christian? The defendant firmly protested, "I am a Christian and I wish to die a Christian, nor have I worn Jewish clothing and if there are witnesses to say that I have dressed otherwise why ask me?" He added that he had associated with Jews only after being wounded. Why did he receive money from Jews in prison? "I don't know; they happen to be Jews and they come from my country, which is why they help me."

Had he ever changed his name? "No."

The sentence: Francisco Oliviero, "a circumcised Jew," had confessed to having had "commerce with a Christian woman"; furthermore, after being wounded he had confessed to a priest "as a Christian" in "derision" of the Catholic faith; he had been taken to the ghetto where he called himself Joseph and ate and drank "according to Jewish custom," and when he was well again he wore the yellow cap "to the great scandal of the faithful." He was sentenced to four years as a galley slave and lifelong banishment from Venice and her domains.

Elena de Freschi Olivi, 1555

The story of old Elena de Freschi Olivi began on a Sunday.

One witness said: "Last Sunday . . . the priest told me he had it from the Magnificent Lady Paula Marcelo . . . who was with the wife of the Magnificent Messer Andrea Diedo of the S. Fosca parish and the wife of Messer Bernardin Grappina . . . that the mother of Messer Zuan Battista, that Jewish doctor turned Christian, while the priest was reciting the Credo: 'Et Incarnatus est de Spiritu Sancto ex Maria Virgine et homo factus est' said these very words: 'You're lying in your teeth, he's a bastard son of a whore.' "

Further testimony confirmed that Elena de Freschi Olivi, the mother of Zuan Battista, a converted Jew known for his uncompromising stand against Jewish books, had given vent to insults and foul language in church, during mass. "She was kneeling right behind me," declared one witness. "She said: look at what these brutes, these bastards, are saying," confirmed Donna Lucretia, another witness, adding that Elena Olivi often went into the ghetto and Donna Paola Marcello had heard her say that "this faith wasn't the true one and she didn't want to stick with it."

Donna Paola Marcello, summoned to testify, confirmed that Olivi had been in high dudgeon with the priest "and she was making faces and talking a lot, and among the other words I heard her say 'You're lying in your teeth. . .' and I saw her make the gesture of a fig toward the altar." Donna Paola had spoken with "Salomone, a German Jew who teaches music." When she asked him why he didn't become a Christian he had replied, "Milady, a man who is not a good Jew is not a good Christian, and those who have turned Christian would like to become Jewish." "He mentioned the mother of Messer Zuan Battista," added Donna Paola, "saying that 'she comes into the pawnshops, crying that she wishes she could get out of that damned religion and come back to her own.' "

Donna Margherita, who had lived in Zuan Battista's house with her husband for three years, and taken care of his daughters, also related her experience with the de Freschi Olivi family, recent converts to Christianity and suspect, therefore, despite Zuan Battista's anti-Jewish pronouncements. During the sermon at the church of the Santi Apostoli, when the priest said that the Virgin was a virgin before, during, and after the birth of Christ, "that Donna Helena shuffled her beads in her hands and said, 'You're lying in your teeth, you bastard, you mule,' and made a sign with her hand, that looked like a fig. When I asked her what she was saying," went on Donna Margherita, "she answered, 'I didn't say a thing, Madame,' and laughed." The witness added: "There were other people that I didn't know, and the wife of their family boatman, Cadorin . . . and . . . [donna Elena] said: 'Christ, he would deserve to have his nose and ears cut off . . . It's a lie that she's a virgin.' " She recalled that the woman muttered these things not only in church, but often from her balcony, too, "in Hebrew, and mentioned the government, and the Doge, and I don't know what she said . . . I don't think she's out of her mind . . . she knows exactly what she's doing." Donna Margherita testified to having been the confidante of Grazia and Orseta, Elena's two granddaughters. That was how she knew old Elena ate meat on Friday and Saturday; in fact, "when Messer Zuan Battista bought meat on Saturday for Sunday, she made cutlets on Saturday afternoon." The witness lost no opportunity to show the defendant in a bad light, and concluded by saying, "And even the girls told me that when the old woman killed chickens in the house, she slit their throats the way the Jews do."

Salomone the Jew stood up to testify, swearing on the point of the clerk's pen according to Jewish custom; but he did not confirm Paola Marcello's report. He denied having seen Elena Olivi in the ghetto after her conversion, and if he had seen her he would certainly say so, because he wished more evil than good on Messer Zuan Battista "who had a part in getting our books burned."

"It's quite possible," he added, "that I may have said a man who is not a good Jew cannot be a good Christian. But I can tell you no more."

Donna Agnese, a new witness, considered the defendant a good Christian, at the worst slightly crazy or possessed: "She talks a lot of nonsense and says things like, 'Go to the whore-house, get out of here, you sluggard!' "

Donna Julia: "It's true that at times she seemed possessed by a thousand sprites, at home or in the street, or even in church, and would say, 'Go be hanged, go be quartered!' "

Giovanni Battista de Freschi Olivi, the son of the defendant, was a Jewish physician converted to Christianity. When he came before the Inquisitors, his words echoed the medical theories of his time. "Reverend and most Illustrious Judges over Heresy, I . . . tell you truly that the poor woman, affected for long years by a severe illness caused by melancholy humors, has been left mentally infirm and suffers from a weak mind and speech impediments, and is obfuscated by various false and corrupt fancies represented in her mind by many evil vapors from the several superfluous humors that rise up . . . as the doctors determine, or by some evil spirit as the theologians would have it, on which images the poor woman fantasizes, talking to herself disconnectedly, now loud, now soft, in front of everyone, with no shame . . . and not knowing whether she's in church or in St. Mark's Square or on the terrace over the public thoroughfare." Involved in a heresy trial despite his best intentions, Zuan Battista eloquently defended himself and his mother, telling the Inquisitors that the poor woman, when her mind was cloudy, was in the habit of yelling, heaping insults on everyone, and talking disconnectedly. If she were no longer allowed to live with her family and see her granddaughters, which would go against Christian charity, her demented condition might deteriorate even further. Nor did he stop at the details of his mother's infirmities—he went on to attack the witnesses. Donna Agnese, for instance, whom he had taken as a governess for his daughters and specifically ordered not to bring men into the house, had disobeyed him. Four or five of her "nephews" frequented his house, to the great dismay of Zuan Battista, who wanted his home to be like a convent "especially since I have a grown daughter" whom he wanted to become a nun, and "with the help of the blessed Jesus Christ, for the sake of my poor mother, a good and true Christian when she's in her right mind." How could they possibly—asked Messer Battista—take the word of infidels over that of a good Christian? It defied the holy laws. "And all the more so," continued de Freschi Olivi, "because all the Jews in the world are my enemies since I was present along with the reverend father Friar Thomaso d'Urbino of the Dominican Order of Castello, while he burned the Talmud in honor of the blessed Jesus Christ," in obedience to the decisions of the "reverend Cardinals General, Inquisitors over Heresy 'which Talmud teaches them that it is permissible to swear a false oath with the lips and break it with the heart, and all the more so against Christians, they swear a hundred thousand.' " Continuing his testimony, he said that Donna Cadorina had tried to "lead my elder daughter astray and convince her not to become a nun," and that as soon as he found out about it he had thrown her out of his house and fired her husband "who rowed in the poop and was a good boatman."

Old Elena, his mother, was baptized of her own accord and was a good Christian when lucid, even though "being a woman and of weak mind she is not capable of discussing religion, for she might talk foolishness." Further, "My poor mother is a lunatic and an energumen, a Greek word used by the holy canonists in the Decree and defined by them as one suffering alienation and weakness of mind more or less according to the waxing and waning of the moon and tormented by evil spirits." Citing St. Thomas Aquinas, Zuan Battista observed that lunatics are those who suffer a certain mental alienation at the waning of the moon, when they are "possessed by demons, and the devil torments and afflicts them . . . at the waning of the moon the humors decline and dryness abounds and the melancholy humor with its evil vapors," weakening the brain and its powers, especially in those already susceptible to illness. And the devil inflicts suffering on the weak parts of the body, causing these persons to curse and despise God, so that the poor creatures know not what they're saying, it's the demon speaking within them, and if you ask them, when the crisis is over, what they said, they deny having said anything at all. All the holy doctors, theologians, and canonists agree that those who suffer mental weakness and alienation in conjunction with the lunar phases are often suffering because of the demons in their heads. "And if it were simple madness without the torment of spirits, she would not have uttered those horrendous curses in church."

Finally Elena de Freschi Olivi, herself, appeared before the court. "I have told no lies, I have not murdered, I have not stolen. Send me to my son's house . . . I was talking in the church of S. Marziale before the priest began mass and I mumbled: 'Virgin Mary help me and deliver me from these torments because I will die and be slandered by that bastard of a servant of mine . . . let him stop pestering me to marry him, because I wish to remain a widow and he called me a whore.' " The defendant firmly denied having ever blasphemed, but confessed to having entered the ghetto once with her daughter-in-law to visit some relatives and having gone to the pawnshops, once to pawn some things and a second time to redeem them. She denied ever having repented her conversion and heatedly replied: "Why should I repent? Why should I want to be a Jew? I never left God, on the contrary when I say, 'In nomine Patris et Filii et Spiriti Sancti,' I've found God. I'm a good Christian and I became a Christian inspired by the Holy Spirit." She denied ever having said she wanted to leave that "damned religion." She denied having uttered the words numerous witnesses had sworn they heard her say. "Don't ask me whether I believe Mary was a virgin before, during and after the birth," said Elena, "just because you want to hear me say it . . . it's enough for me that Christ was born of the Holy Spirit without worrying about whether she was a virgin or not." She denied having eaten meat on Friday or Saturday, but as for the hens slaughtered according to Jewish law, she answered, "Women don't kill them that way because very few women know how. It is true that we did sometimes behead a hen."

"We're afraid to wring their necks," she added, "and we also do it to let the blood run out, but it's not a Jewish thing, that's all just gossip."

More witnesses were summoned, including Donna Magdalena who lived near the Aceto bridge, just outside the ghetto. She described Messer Zuan Battista's troubles and assured them that, even as a young woman, his mother had behaved strangely. Her husband had kept her tied with a rope to the chairs and bed even when they lived in Ferrara, before moving to Venice.

Donna Agnese was summoned, and she described Elena de Freschi Olivi's anguish when her sons Zuane and Jacomo were baptized along with her granddaughters, and her uncertainty as to what she should do. According to Donna Agnese, the woman agreed to follow her sons, but remained a Jew in her heart. "She Jewishly slaughtered and slit the throats of all the hens, capons, chickens and pigeons that they ate in their house, and after having cut their throats she chopped off the heads and threw them away."

The witness Jacobo de Gastaldi de Pinerolo testified that he had considered her a weak-minded woman even before her conversion. The priest of the church of San Basso recalled that she had come to the baptismal font happy and content. Donna Menega of the parish of Santa Fosca did not remember her as a zealous Christian. Michiel, the barber from Calle dei Cinque at Rialto, who also considered her more crazy than sane, swore he had heard her earnestly reciting her Pater Noster. Donna Antonia "of the Vendramin soap-works" at Santa Fosca, a witness for the defense, described her as wise and pious. Agostino Maripietro, who had known the defendant and her family when they were all still Jews, recalled that he had often heard her talking to herself. Marco Trevisan, a ferryman who plied to and from Santa Sofia and stated that he had known her since 1550, said that she had always talked from her balcony "saying this one be damned and that one be damned." He concluded, "I have heard it said in the street, but I don't remember by whom, that while they were still Jews a daughter was taken from her and that trouble was what drove her out of her mind." Donna Mora, who lived at San Marziale near the priest's house, said, "A sane woman would never do what she did." Donna Veneranda considered her a good Christian, but "she often comes out on her balcony and says . . . you pig, you lout, you go around saying you've taken my Venetianity!"

In reaching its decision, the Inquisition acknowledged that Elena de Freschi Olivi was sometimes "out of her mind, even though she does have lucid intervals"; but just to make sure no similar scandals would occur in the future, they sentenced her to life imprisonment, to be served at the "chief hospital of this city." To guarantee the enforcement of the sentence and overcome any resistance from the hospital authorities, the court took it upon itself to vouch financially and morally for this woman, now seventy years of age.

Odoardo Gomez and Augustino Enriquez, 1555

The story of Gomez and Enriquez ties in with that of the Mendes family* and the Marranos in Venice.

The Inquisition summoned Donna Julia, demanding information about Odoardo Gomez and Augustino Enriquez, two Spanish merchants living in a large house over the engraver's shop at Santa Maria Formosa near the Angelo bridge. "Many people frequent that house,"

---

*See Chapter Eight

the witness told them, "Jews and women, and I used to live on the floor below but they sent me away."

The witness Mastro Simone was concise in his appraisal of the defendants' identities: "As for their religion, I think they're Jews, even though they say they're Christians." Their many dealings with Jews and Marranos automatically made them suspect, "and they are stewards of Beatrice de Luna, a Jewess who lives in Constantinople, and with her one of Odoardo's brothers."

Another witness, Gottardo Arcari, stated that he had known both men for four years and done business with them, that he had seen them in the company of the Spanish ambassador and at mass in St. Mark's, that he had often taken meals with them and seen them eat all kinds of food. All the same, he was not convinced. In fact, the more he thought about it, the less confident he felt, and said, "As far as outward appearance is concerned, I don't think they're as good Christians as they ought to be, for we have often compared the Christian, Turkish and Jewish ceremonies, saying that the Christian ceremonies are much more beautiful than the others, and they never answer."

The Inquisition summoned Odoardo Gomez, one of the two defendants. "My age is forty-five years, one month and a day," he said. His father, he added, had not been a Christian, nor did he remember when he had converted, but it might have been at the time of the great conversions in Portugal in 1492. He said he had three brothers, Thomaso, Guglielmo, and Vincenzo, all Christians, but now living as Jews in Constantinople and going by the names of Abramo, Joseffo, and Jona. Although he was a merchant, said Gomez, he had studied the arts, humanities, philosophy, and medicine in Medina. His wife, Clara, as well as his four sons and four daughters, were all Catholics who made confession and took communion several times a year, sometimes even at St. Mark's in Venice. He went on, "We do business with Jews from the Levant and Ancona, and trade with them but with no others." He did not deny having discussed Turkish, Jewish, and Christian rituals with the Spanish ambassador and others, but said, "The conclusion of our talk was that the Jewish religion is all vanity and the Christian religion is good and holy." The judges, very interested in the controversial affairs of the Mendes or de Luna sisters, asked Gomez whether he knew any of them. Yes, said Gomez, he had known Beatrice de Luna, who was a Christian at the time. Now, he had heard, she had become a Jewess.

The Inquisitors called the physician Zuan Battista de Freschi Olivi to examine and report on the circumcision of Gomez and his son Consalvo. Once again Zuan Battista, once a Jew but now a zealous Christian, the son of Elena de Freschi Olivi who had recently been in the spotlight of the Inquisition herself, stood before the court. His testimony was disappointing. "And to further clarify my deposition as regards this Odoardo, I can say that, compared with his son's member, he appears to me to be circumcised; as compared with my own I am in doubt, having never seen a circumcised adult."

The defendant repeatedly insisted that he was a firm believer, but the court seemed skeptical. He had said that his whole family confessed and took communion, but if so, why did he send his sons to Ferrara just before Easter? "I sent them to spend the holiday with their mother and sisters, since they had nothing to do here at that season."

Other witnesses confirmed the substance of his statements. According to one merchant, "I have seen images of Christ and the Virgin in every room of his house." Another told of having seen him at mass and attending sermons at St. Mark's, the Frari, and San Polo—and not only him, but his friend and co-defendant Agostino, both accompanied by their children and servants. Another witness confirmed that the family did normal business on Saturday and ate whatever they were served, even pork and other foods forbidden to the Jews. In fact, if they received letters written in Hebrew they asked other Jews to read them, which would lead one to think they did not know Hebrew themselves. Testimony in their favor was plentiful: "A good Christian who leads a Christian life," and, "I have seen him in church many, many times," or, "I've heard that the brothers and relatives of Messer Odoardo are angry with him because he refused to become a Jew, and I've heard it said very often."

Augustino Enriquez, who was ill at Ferrara, sent a letter to say he would soon be arriving in Venice. Although no clear record of the verdict has been found, both defendants were probably absolved.

Licentiato Costa, 1555

The case of Licentiato Costa, summoned before the Inquisition in 1555, is a very typical Marrano story. Thomas Zornoza, an administrator for Brianda de Luna,* said of him: "For my part, I consider him a heretic, for I saw him when he came from Spain and he was a Christian, then he went to Salonika and became a Jew. I heard that he was circumcised in Ferrara. Odoardo Gomez and Augustin Enrichez have told me he's a Christian."

A man dressed in foreign costume with a long, grey beard, looking about sixty years old, came before the court. He identified himself as Tristano da Costa de Vienna from Portugal, the son of Isaac Odoardo Costa. His mother's name? Unknown. She remained a Jewess when her husband was forced to convert by the king of Portugal along with all the other Portuguese Jews. He was too young to remember exactly

---

*See Chapter Eight

what had happened; anything he knew he heard from his father and brothers, who had been thrown in prison and baptized by force. The Inquisitors demanded more information, but Licentiato Costa repeated, "My father and brothers have told me I was snatched from my mother's bed and baptized." Had he then lived as a Christian? The answer was vague. "At the time they told me, I was living outwardly as they told me to, and I sometimes went to mass with other Christians for fear of being thrown in jail, and I sometimes made confession to a friar, but I never took communion . . . Inwardly I lived as a Jew, and then I left for Lisbon. I stayed eight months, and never gave any sign of being a Christian because at home I did as I liked. From Lisbon I went to Flanders and Antwerp, and then I came here." Those, he said, were not his only wanderings. Before Lisbon he had passed through Salamanca and then gone to Viana where he had married "one of our own nation." Five children were born to them, and he had had them all baptized, but only for fear of the Inquisition.

In short, was Licentiato Costa a Jew or a Christian? The defendant said he had been sent for by Donna Brianda de Luna, who was feuding with her sister and had been issued a safe-conduct for Venice by the Council of Ten, not only for herself but for some thirty people in her retinue, servants and stewards, all new Christians. He would never have come to Venice if he had known or even thought he would be tried by the Inquisition. For as he admitted and confirmed, "Inwardly I live as a Jew but outwardly I go as a Christian by the name of Tristano da Costa."

The Inquisition refused to give up. Was Tristano a Jewish or a Christian name? Here, it seems, was an attempt to trace at least a glimmer of the defendant's identity. But judging from the trial chronicles, Costa was reluctant to give them any satisfaction whatsoever: "When my father gave me that name, he said it was just as well that he had so named me."

Jew or Christian then? Had he ever recited "Jewish prayers" in Venice? The defendant replied that he had never behaved as a Christian or prayed as a Jew. Was he circumcised? "I have no recollection of it, unless it was when I was a baby."

"Do you use a Christian name in Venice?" "I have never said it was either Christian or Jewish, and I was never asked." But why would an observant Jew dress as a Christian, especially in Venice where everyone knew Jews dressed differently? The defendant said he thought it was tolerated, given the privilege of the safe-conduct.

Once more attention focused on the famous Mendes sister, alias de Luna. Did Brianda de Luna live as a Christian or a Jew? Costa confirmed that she lived as a Christian. Then how could he, a Jew, eat in the home of a Christian? Without batting an eyelash, Costa replied that he did not eat the same things as Brianda, but lived on goose or fish or fruit. If he did want meat, he went to the ghetto to buy it. Brianda ate meat only on Saturday, with the written permission of her priest.

The Inquisitor asked Licentiato Costa if he knew why he had been arrested. Certain Marranos, answered Costa, namely Odoardo Gomez and Augustino Enriquez, were enemies of Brianda de Luna and in the service of her sister, Beatrice, and wanted Brianda to follow Beatrice to Constantinople. They had denounced him in order to make trouble for his mistress.

In concluding his deposition, Licentiato Costa once again proved to be the archetypical Marrano, meticulously calling the attention of the court to his double life, his outward-inward life as he called it, living as a Jew but wearing a black hat in all innocence, under the protection of the safe-conduct. Anything he had done as a Christian was only out of fear of the Inquisition.

The outcome of the hearing was realistic: Licentiato Costa was indeed protected by the safe-conduct of the Council of Ten and was immediately released.

Aaron and Asser, 1563

Aaron and Asser were two young Jews who had been attending the House of Catechumens with the intention of converting. Aaron came from the ghetto, but Asser was Polish.

One day, while standing together under the loggia looking out on the square, they were seen by the porter Salomon (alias Mona), who spent much of his time in the ghetto. He spoke to them, and from that time on the two young men cooled off and lost their desire to convert. Asser had blasphemed, saying that "the Virgin Mary had slept two nights with a flesh and blood man" and had gotten "pregnant with Christ by him," and he had even thrown a ball at her image. Moreover, they did not pray with the other catechumens, and they even poked fun at the saints. One Saturday morning Asser had put on his "clean Sunday silk shirt." When his companions asked why he didn't wait for the Christian sabbath, he had answered, "I'm not a Christian, I'm a good Jew, because all Christians go to hell." Another catechumen, Samuele, a Jew from Cairo, the son of Isaac de Sidat, then said to him: "Hush, you should be ashamed. Take off that shirt," to which "he began saying that the Lord God was a bastard son of a whore, and saying in Hebrew that the Lord God was conceived while the Virgin had her period, and calling him a *mamzer barhanid,* which means what I said before." Asser kept repeating: "When I've become a Christian and they give me a fine suit of clothes, I'll run away."

Giovanni Gabriel, another Jewish catechumen, told the Inquisitors, "We were parading about the house singing the Virgin's litanies," and Asser came in with a ball and threw it "at the face of the painting, laughing and making fun . . . I said to him: 'If you don't behave like a good Christian they'll throw you in jail.' He answered, 'Quiet, you ass, I want to be a good Jew, not a Christian.' "

Chaim of Salonika, the son of Salomone, now a catechumen, was called to testify and said that he had seen the porter, the tempter who had lured Aaron away from Christianity, telling him, "Come to the ghetto, what are you doing here; you won't lack money." But Asser "wore his clean shirt on Saturday out of spite, saying: I want to be a Jew, and uttered blasphemies too odious ever to be said, talking about the Lord God and the Madonna and all the Saints."

The German Paolo also said that on the day Asser and Aaron, "Jews who had come here to the House of Catechumens to become Christians," were arrested, he had heard them say they no longer wanted to be Christians. "This Asser wanted to be free and obey no man, nor even the Virgin Mary."

Donna Angela testified: "I saw a porter who looked very young, I thought he had no beard, in porter's dress, neither very tall nor very short, saying to that Jew . . . 'Come on, let's go; come on, get moving.' " And according to Donna Filippa, "I heard Donna Anzola . . . shouting at someone, 'Hey, you scoundrel, you deserve a beating for leading people astray who want to do the right thing!' "

One of the defendants was finally called to testify before the court. "My name is Aaron the German from Bohemia and Prague, I have no trade, I was a Jew in the ghetto and lived in poverty, with no livelihood." He was asked, "If you have no trade, what did you live on?" "It's the custom among Jews that if a man has nothing he asks those who are comfortable, and they give him money."

Aaron told the court he had always wanted to be baptized, but at another time and place, and denied ever having spoken ill of Jesus, the Virgin, or the saints. He denied having seen Asser throw a ball at the face of the Virgin. He denied having heard Asser say the Virgin Mary had slept two nights with a man. If he had, he would have spit in his face. He confirmed having met the porter Mona, who had insisted that he come back with him to the ghetto, and that this man Mona ate meat on Friday or Saturday, he wasn't sure, even if it was true that many people in the service of the Levantines "eat as they do and are neither Jews nor Christians, nor Turks, and follow I don't know what law."

"What are your intentions?" the Inquisitor asked Aaron. Aaron confirmed his desire to be a good Christian, insisting that they both did intend to be baptized, not necessarily right away, but at the first place where they felt inspired by God.

Asser was also called before the court and questioned through an interpreter. He said he was born in the little Polish village of Chelm, east of Lublin. Yes, it was true that a man by the name of Salomon had convinced him to postpone his baptism, but he, Asser, wanted to convince Aaron to do the same. Yes, it was true, he had argued with the prior who had refused to give him dinner because he had left the house without permission. He had suddenly felt uncomfortable at the House of Catechumens, and thought he would rather leave and be baptized elsewhere, possibly after having earned a little money with the help of Messer Salomon the porter. What did Asser do before coming to the ghetto? He delivered water and firewood, and carried a child in his arms for a Jewish widow in the city, the sister of a brother-in-law of Cervo del Banco. Why did Asser change his shirt, that famous Saturday? Because the shirt was dirty and he had put on a clean one. Why all the run-ins with the prior? The prior wouldn't feed him and all Germans get peevish when they don't have enough to eat and drink. Was it true that the defendant had called the Virgin Mary a "bad woman"? The defendant: "What did I do wrong? I asked a lot of questions when I was a newcomer among the Catechumens, just to find out the truth."

Through the interpreter, the court warned the defendant to tell the truth. To which he replied: "The Virgin was a Saint. The Angel said she would bear Christ, and he would be the true Messiah." What about the ball in the Virgin's face? And his blasphemy against the saints? The defendant denied it all; he was only joking. He said he had only behaved as the Jews behave when they pray: some pray, others joke—and not having been baptized yet, he still behaved as a Jew and didn't think it was all that important.

Once more through the interpreter, the court gave him to understand that they considered him an opportunist and not to be taken seriously. His only reason for becoming a Christian, they suspected, was to avoid the hard work in store for him in the ghetto.

Marco Antonio degli Eletti, 1569

Had Isaaco, the son of Mandolin Pugliese, baptized in 1569, already been baptized once before at Alessandria della Paglia? The case came up before the Inquisition, and inquiries were made. Certain sources said that one Isaac, the son of Mandolino Pugliese, had in fact been baptized fifteen years earlier in the church of San Girolamo of the Calzetta friars. So the suspect was summoned before the court.

"My name is Marc'Antonio degli Eletti,* formerly a Jew called Isaac son of Menachem Thodesco. My mother's name is Mir and I was born at Vigevano, near Milan, and I am currently a simple broker here in this city of Venice, but I used to make certain round mirror balls, together with a certain Nicolò dell'Aquila, a glass-blower of Murano,

---

*meaning "the Chosen"

with whom I fell out over a year ago on account of those balls . . . I have brothers, the eldest called Simion and the second Moisè, I am the third and was named Isaac Paltiel. Later there were born two others whom I never knew by name, but hearing I was in Venice they came to see me."

Who was Mandolin Pugliese the Jew? "Our family name is Pugliese, and my father's name is Menachem Mandel in Hebrew and Michiel in Italian. I don't know whether he was called Mandolin, but Mandel and Mandolin are the same name, for adults are called Mandel and children Mandolin."

The defendant recounted his travels and wanderings, first to Salonika, then Belgrade, where he had married and lived for two years. He had left his wife and children there and now lived in Venice, where he had married again.

To the crucial question of whether he had ever been baptized prior to his baptism in the church of Santa Maria Mocenigo, he replied: "I'll tell you the truth, gentlemen: when I was a boy of twelve or thirteen, I had a very pretty face and there was an outlaw in Alessandria, who taught me the guitar and lived at a church, the name of which I don't remember, where there was also another outlaw living in a room in their monastery, and he kept me there at his command, saying 'I want you to become a Christian and be baptized.' " The defendant could not remember the details, but he knew he had been baptized hastily. To avoid being reproached by his family, he had decided to move in with those Christians. After a while he set out on his travels, first to Venice, then to the East. "I was baptized," recalled the defendant, "without ceremony; there was laughter and joking, and water was poured on my head."

"Having continued to live as a Jew," queried the court, "having married a Jewish woman and had children with her, what induced you to be baptized again?"

"I'll tell you: it was through having to do with Christians in the trade I practiced on Murano, and having received permission from the Cattaveri to stay outside the ghetto at night in order to work by night at that trade, making glass balls by permission of the illustrious Authorities, and Magnificent Messer Antonio Boldù having obtained for me the permission of the Cattaveri, and having discussed and debated religious issues many a time for three or four months." Finally he had gone to hear a sermon at the church of San Giovanni e Paolo, by a preacher from Ferrara learned in the Hebrew language. Little by little, the defendant confessed, he had begun to understand the importance of the Messiah's coming. He had been in a state of dire mental torment: "So talking and discussing and constantly thinking for more than a year, by different methods, prayer and fasting, I prayed God to send me light and grace to understand these difficult questions of Scripture, and God's teaching inspired me and led me to the holy Catholic faith through Holy Baptism."

Why were you, an educated and responsible man, baptized twice? The accused answered that he had not realized it was wrong to be baptized twice, and that he had never considered the first baptism to be a true one. Marco Antonio insisted that he had been baptized "not to deceive myself or anyone else, or out of any desire for profit or gain, but simply because I realized that the faith of Jesus Christ is the true one, and that of the Jews is shadow and appearance, but I never thought I would be made to suffer in this cruel prison for this accusation, to my total ruin and the desolation of my wife who is now pregnant, and of my family."

A few days later the court received a letter from Francesco Dario, a lawyer, confirming the state of physical and emotional prostration of his client, incarcerated in the prison of San Zuane alla Bragora. If the man were not released very shortly, he would not have long to live. He therefore requested that his client be placed under house arrest, possibly at the home of his father-in-law, who would vouch for him and make sure he appeared in court when summoned. Meanwhile, information on Marco Antonio degli Eletti alias Isaac the son of Menachem Pugliese arrived from Alessandria, delayed on account of the witnesses' absence. The copious, though vague, testimony confirmed the defendant's own account.

A few questions were left unanswered, and certain contradictions emerged. Did the youth make confession after his first baptism? Did he take communion? Did he receive money? The defendant firmly denied having done so. Early in May of 1570 he wrote a letter to the Inquisition saying, among other things, "I confess that in Alessandria della Paglia, that act was performed upon me over twenty years ago, which I myself never took for baptism; but I say further that anyone considering the reasons preceding that act, and the things that followed, my tender years, my inexperience with worldly affairs, my ignorance of the Scriptures, my having been born and brought up a Jew among Jews and taken by them to distant lands, and in short, all the other incidents that should be mercifully considered in my case, will say that I deserve pity and clemency, rather than punishment." In a second document abjuring Judaism, he again reaffirmed his innocence.

The sentence: Marco Antonio degli Eletti, having made an act of abjuration on his knees, was absolved from excommunication for having been baptized twice, but in order that his error not go unpunished, "the aforesaid Marco Antonio must personally move to the monastery of S. Secondo of the reverend Dominican fathers on the island outside Venice . . . *loco carceris* . . . and living therein, at no cost shall he ever leave it without express written permission from this holy tribunal for as long as we shall see fit. Every Wednesday and Friday as long as he shall stay in that monastery, he shall dine on bread and water, reciting the seven penitential Psalms before the altar of the Holy Sacrament, with litanies and prayers of penitence for the remission of his sins."

Some time later the Inquisition received a letter beginning: "Most reverend and illustrious gentlemen, eight months have now passed since I, poor Marco Antonio degli Eletti, was detained by order of this holy tribunal and sent to this prison where I have greatly suffered in my person and property, for I am at death's door and have consumed what little I had earned through my industry, which was to have been the sustenance of myself and my poor Family." The long letter begged for mercy. The court agreed to let him go home, albeit still under house arrest. Eventually he was allowed to leave his house and again go about his business throughout the city of Venice and on Murano, with no fear of being troubled by anyone in the name of the Holy Office.

CHAPTER SEVEN

Printing and Publishing
in Sixteenth-Century Venice

The first printers: Daniel Bomberg— The Bragadin-Giustiniani
affair— The burning of the Talmud— Censorship— De Medico
Hebreo— Discourse on the Birth of a Monstrosity

The quadrangle formed by St. Mark's Square, Campo Sant'Angelo,
Rialto, and Campo Santa Maria Formosa was the booksellers'
district. There they lived and worked, their shops concentrated mainly
in Campo San Bartolomeo and on the street called Mercerie.

The relationship between Venice and the printed page was fertile
and far-reaching in the sixteenth century. Cautious estimates calculate
that fifteen thousand different books were published, with average
printings of at least a thousand copies. Once more the city was an
important pole of attraction for European and extra-European culture,
favorable to the development of a refined intellectual environment
centering on the book industry. Singularly enough, the rapport between
Venice and her Jews was enriched by the birth, amid many difficulties,
of a Hebrew publishing center important for the quantity, and especially for the high quality, of its output. Attracted by this hospitable
climate, Jewish intellectuals looking for work in the publishing field
and scholars seeking to have their books published converged from all
of Europe. Cultural debate within the ghetto contributed to the dissemination of Hebrew books in all the Mediterranean countries by
producing a rich crop of philosophical, grammatical, and religious works,
which made it possible to codify the most important rabbinical thought,
past and present, in beautifully printed and richly illuminated volumes.

Venice was already one of the world's prime publishing centers. It was advantageously located, and its ghetto was a meeting ground that attracted Jews from the world over, both because of the presence of the outstanding personalities who laid solid foundations for the success of their businesses, and the favorable economic, cultural, and religious conditions. There may also have been an abundance of good manuscripts ready to be printed. With capital, good technical skills, and quality paper, Hebrew printing in Venice won international renown within a very short time.

The birth of the ghetto and the printing of the first books in Hebrew characters were contemporaneous events, although some authors think Hebrew books may have been printed even earlier than 1516 and destroyed during the Inquisition. This, however, seems unlikely. In any event, Jews could not go into business for themselves either as printers or as publishers, except in very rare circumstances, and therefore almost always worked for the most important publishers only as indispensable employees. They came and went through the city, but were obliged to return to the ghetto at night.

Daniel Bomberg, a Christian with a Jewish-sounding last name, with the invaluable assistance of a friar, Felice da Prato, was the first to print works written in Hebrew characters, aided by numerous Jewish editors and proofreaders. Bomberg began with the Pentateuch, a selection from the Prophets, and three consecutive editions of the great rabbinical Bible (one in 1516–17, one in 1524–25, and one in 1548). The Bible contained not only the Hebrew text but the Aramaic translation and comments by noted medieval Jewish commentators. Fra Felice supervised the preparation of these first editions; he was in charge of the writers as well as of the text itself, and in 1515 he applied to the Cabinet to obtain the assistance of "four very learned Jewish men," preferably of foreign origin and therefore privileged to wear the black hat. The first edition of the Bible was dedicated to Pope Leo X, which leads us to believe that Jews were not the only readers of Hebrew books, but that interest in Hebrew culture was widespread among humanists and clergy. So the Hebrew books were welcomed at first, although they were looked upon with a certain fear and suspicion by the general populace, possibly because of the mysterious characters in which they were printed. The prestige of Bomberg's establishment contributed to the wide circulation of commentaries which, while in manuscript form, had necessarily been restricted to a very limited readership. Within a few years this daring publisher, with the permission of the Venetian Senate, undertook a grandiose project: the printing of the Babylonian Talmud, in twelve volumes (1510–1523), and the Palestinian Talmud (1522–23), in addition to the prayer books commissioned by many Jewish communities of the Diaspora in Rome, Spain, Germany, Greece, and even Aleppo, in Syria.

Although internationally known for the quality of its work, Bomberg's printing shop was inactive from 1533 to 1537, for reasons unknown. The publication of a major Jewish classic, Elias Levitas's *Massoreth ha-Massoreth*,* dates from 1538. Just a year later, surprisingly enough, Bomberg published a book of anti-Jewish polemic, *Itinera deserti de judaicis disciplini*** by Gérard Veltuyck. Johannes Treves and Meir Parenzo worked for the printer in later years, when his star was on the wane, although he continued producing books of high quality to the last, including *Hovot ha-Levavot*† by Ibn Pakuda and works by the Jewish-Spanish poet Ibn Gabirol.

Bomberg's declining fortunes crossed paths with the rising star of Marco Antonio Giustiniani. Shortly after setting up in business in 1545, Giustiniani printed eighteen Hebrew books in close succession, including Moses Nahmanides's *Commentaries on the Pentateuch*. In 1548–49 Bomberg retired, after publishing a new edition of the Talmud and a Hebrew edition of the Proverbs, the Song of Songs, and Ecclesiastes. His chief assistant, Cornelius Adelkind (Israel ben Baruch before his conversion), and his son Daniel carried on his work, although they never equaled his quality. They no longer possessed Bomberg's famous Hebrew type, which had been bought by a number of printers who prized its elegance.

Marco Antonio Giustiniani opened his printing shop on the Calle dei Cinque in the Rialto district. Between 1546 and 1551 he printed the Babylonian Talmud and enjoyed a monopoly as the only large-scale Hebrew publisher in Venice. The De Farri brothers published only twelve Hebrew books and Brucello's only Hebrew publication was a glossary of philosophical terms.

As international relations changed, the climate of tolerance toward Hebrew books changed, too. In 1550 (the year of the Marrano expulsion from Venice) Cardinal Varallo lodged a protest with the Venetian and Roman ambassadors against the edition of the Talmud that Giustiniani would complete in 1551. And in 1551, partly in response to papal concern, the Cabinet ordered the Executors against Blasphemy to examine the Talmud and report on any incriminating passages.

The tension was heightened by another seemingly banal episode. That same year, a new printing shop had opened in Venice. It was called La Bragadina, after its owner, Alvise Bragadin, and its first publication was Maimonides's great *Mishneh Torah*, with a commentary by Meir Katzenellenbogen of Padua. Almost contemporaneously, Giustiniani published the same work without Rabbi Meir's notes. A furious quarrel broke out between Bragadin and Giustiniani, with the former accusing the latter of attempting to provoke a boycott of his estab-

---

Tradition of Tradition
**The Wanderings in the Desert Away From the Jewish Disciples*
†*Duties of the Heart*

lishment, especially with regard to the Talmud. The conflict between the two soon degenerated into a violent feud, whose effects spread beyond the two printers, extending to all the Hebrew books being published in Venice. Meir Katzenellenbogen asked for the help of one of the highest authorities in the field of rabbinical interpretation, Rabbi Moses Isserles of Krakow. Isserles, having collected all the facts he needed to pass judgment, threatened to excommunicate anyone who bought Giustiniani's edition of Maimonides. Bragadin thus won the first battle, but the war was far from over. The enemy refused to concede defeat, and probably without realizing the consequences of his next move, Giustiniani turned to the pope in an attempt to get his competitor's book condemned. Each of the two printers, bent on damaging the other, claimed that the rival publication contained blasphemies and assertions against the Christian faith. The mutual accusations created an atmosphere of suspicion that considerably harmed the young publishing industry.

Certain apostates, namely Joseph Moro Zarfati (Andrea Dal Monte after his conversion) and Shlomo Romano, the grandson of the noted grammarian Elias Levitas, were especially virulent in denigrating the Hebrew books. Late in the summer of 1553, Pope Julius III issued a bull ordering all Hebrew books to be handed over or burned, especially the Talmud, which it was forbidden either to read or to own. In Rome, the Talmud was burned along with other Hebrew books in the Campo dei Fiori. A Jewish historian of the time, Joseph Ha-Cohen, author of *Emek ha-Bakha*,* relates: "They slandered the Talmud before Pope Julius III, maintaining that this book, so widely read among the Jews, was the cause of the customs that distinguished them from other peoples. In addition, they said that the Talmud slandered the Christian Messiah and that the pope should not tolerate its circulation. Julius III could barely contain his anger and immediately ordered that the Talmud be burned. The pope's wish was readily enacted by his gendarmes who began without delay to rifle Jewish homes, confiscating the books they found there and throwing them into the streets and alleys of Rome. The Talmud and other Hebrew books were publicly burned in Campo dei Fiori on the day of the Jewish New Year 5314, by our count, 1553 by theirs."

In Venice, after hearing the opinion of the Executors against Blasphemy (according to whom the Talmud contained blasphemies against God, Christ, and the Virgin), in October 1553 the Council of Ten ordered all the incriminated books burned in a great bonfire in St. Mark's Square. The papal nuncio of the time left an eyewitness account of the great fire that was kindled in the square on the morning of October 21: "Passing unannounced they confiscated all the Talmuds printed

---

*The Vale of Tears

by the gentleman, which were publicly burned at Rialto, and they likewise took all those of the Jews, of which they made a fine blaze this morning on St. Mark's Square; whereof the Illustrious Government sent me news by a secretary, so that it may be made known in Rome." Venice had been even quicker to enforce the papal bull than the rest of the papal domains, but fires were soon lit in many Italian towns.

The perverse mechanism triggered by the feuding Bragadin and Giustiniani had rapidly got out of hand.

Giustiniani, who in addition to the Talmud had printed eighty-five Hebrew books in his seven years of publishing, had been forced to suspend his operations in 1552, due to the heavy damages he had incurred. Bragadin closed up shop in 1553. The indiscriminate book-burnings went on until 1554.

In May and December of that year, the pope issued two decrees again authorizing possession of Hebrew books (with the exception of the execrated Talmud), subject to preventive censorship. The censors were zealous apostate Jews and new converts, who expurgated the books by scraping or cutting out the offending passages, or blacking out the words with ink. With the passing of time some of the ink has faded, allowing the obliterated words to re-emerge. Despite the gradual tapering off of the persecutions, the Venetian printers closed down in 1553, and printing shops began to appear in small towns like Sabbioneta and Riva di Trento, as well as in Ferrara and Mantua.

The sixties saw the institution in Venice of preventive censorship affecting all books, not only Hebrew ones. On religious and political grounds the government established rigid controls over the importing of books and appointed a permanent Inquisitor to the customs office. The Holy Office ordered the bookstores searched, and any forbidden book was summarily destroyed. These were the years of the Counter-Reformation and the war on heresy; the Three Sages on Heresy were placed in charge of censorship.

In 1563, the Venetian printers of Hebrew books resumed their activities after a pause of nearly ten years. Although their problems were not over, the commission that was to have compiled the Index of Forbidden Books at the Council of Trent had not yet reached a decision on the Talmud. In 1564, Pius IV once again allowed the reading of the Talmud and its commentaries, providing the word "Talmud" did not appear on the title page and the whole text were preventively censored. In 1564 and 1565, Alvise Bragadin's business improved thanks to the assistance of Meir Parenzo, already a well-known figure. According to certain sources, Parenzo had printed some books in his own right in the late forties. Other skilled craftsmen were encouraged by his success: between 1565 and 1567 Cavalli printed some codes of Jewish law (his trademark was the elephant—slow but steady). Between 1560 and 1567 Giovanni Griffio published eleven Hebrew books. The Zanetti family built a thriving business that flourished until 1608. Giovanni di Gara attempted to emulate Bomberg, whose printing shop he now possessed and whose style he imitated; his assistants included Samuele Archivolti, Leone da Modena, and Asher Parenzo. In 1565, La Bragadina published the first printed edition of the *Shulkhan Arukh** by Joseph Karo, a work describing Jewish ritual in minute detail and expressing the entire Sephardic culture. To make it acceptable to the Ashkenazic Jews, explanations by Moses Isserles of Krakow were printed in smaller type in the margins. From 1578 on, they always accompanied the original text.

Toward the end of the sixties, the heightening of international tensions again took its toll on Hebrew book publishing. In 1567 letters written in Hebrew were found, containing discussion of a plot against the Republic organized by the Jews of Venice and Constantinople. A year later, the life of the Venetian ambassador was threatened by a fire in Constantinople, and the Jews were accused of arson. In September 1568, the Executors against Blasphemy ordered the destruction of thousands of copies of Hebrew books, freshly printed, which lacked the authorization of the Council of Ten and violated the decree of 1559 because they had not been censored. The guilty publishers were heavily fined, but the Executors did not stop there: they began examining books printed earlier. They also fined many Jews for minor infractions such as the illegal importing, exporting, or possession of forbidden books. The judicial authorities of Venice were especially severe toward those who financed the publications, while the printers themselves, considered passive executors, were never heavily fined. Some eight thousand books are estimated to have been burned at that time. Many others, after extensive expurgation, were sold abroad. The economic damage was compounded by cultural and religious damage, such as the sudden loss of irreplaceable study aids, not to speak of the pain of those whose culture was being crushed and destroyed.

Censorship infractions were the most common charge, but it hardly seems plausible that there should have been so many deliberate transgressors. More probably, the climate within the city had deteriorated considerably, the international problems looming on the Venetian horizon seemed insurmountable, and the Jews were considered a fifth column in the service of the Turks and their diabolical adviser, the Duke of Naxos.

The smaller printers were soon forced to close: Cavalli, Griffio, and Zanetti closed down entirely, while di Gara continued on a much smaller scale.

The years from 1570 to 1573 were especially turbulent. The Venetian Senate again barred the Jews from the printing profession, as it had

---

*Table Prepared

done once before, in 1548. From that time on it was customary to find
the sentence "by permission of the superiors" printed on the first page
of each volume, attesting to the approval of the Inquisition. There also
developed an underground market in the printing and sale of Hebrew
books.

With the brightening of the international situation after the dark
years from 1570 to 1574, printing and publishing once more began to
thrive. Publishers who had survived the storm included Giovanni di
Gara, the famous Bragadin family, and the Parenzo heirs.

At the end of the sixteenth century the Venetian Jews began to adopt
a kind of self-censorship: each volume had to bear the stamp of approval
of the rabbinate, guaranteeing that the book contained no matter in
any way offensive to either Judaism or Catholicism. This precaution
enabled them to serenely confront the surveillance of the Council of
Ten, the Executors against Blasphemy, and the Cattaveri, each responsible, in its own way, for protecting the public morals.

De Medico Hebreo, a treatise on Jewish physicians by David De
Pomis, one of the most illustrious doctors of the day, and the *Discorso
sopra gli accidenti del parto mostruoso*,* an anti-Jewish pamphlet annotated by Giovanni Giuseppe Gregorio Cremonese, are two valuable
testimonials of the cultural and religious atmosphere that reigned in
the late sixteenth century.

The myth of the divine origin of Venice, nurtured by Isaac Abrabanel
earlier in the century, was elaborated in various forms by other Jewish
thinkers and intellectuals. Its magic did not fail to influence David De
Pomis, who was born in Perugia but left Umbria for Venice due to the
anti-Semitism of Pope Pius V, who had forbidden the Jews to practice
medicine. De Pomis was thus able to enjoy the tolerance of the Most
Serene Republic and won great renown both within the ghetto and in
the town.

De Pomis was the author of a book, since lost, on the divine origin
of the Republic; he also published in Venice an Italian translation of
Ecclesiastes, dedicated to Cardinal Grimani. In 1572 he published his
noted *Discorso circa l'humana miseria e sopra'l modo di fuggirla con
molti bellissimi esempi ed avvertimenti*,** written, as the subtitle
tells us, "by the Excellent Jewish physician David De Pomi for the
greater comprehension of Solomon's Ecclesiastes, translated and commented by this author." In 1577 his *Brevi discorsi et efficacissimi
ricordi per liberare ogni città oppressa dal mal contagioso*† was re-

*Discourse on the Birth of a Monstrosity
**Discourse on Human Misery and How to Avoid It with Many Fine Examples and
Much Advice
†Short Discourses and Highly Effective Reminders whereby to Liberate any City
Oppressed by Contagious Disease

ceived with great favor, and 1588 saw the publication, by Giovanni Varisco, of *De Medico Hebreo – Enarratio apologetica*. This book in defense of Jewish doctors emphasized the basic similarities between the way Jews and Christians practiced medicine, thus attempting to dispel deeply rooted prejudices so that Jewish doctors would be allowed to treat Christian patients. During the latter half of the sixteenth century, fear and mistrust had been approved and encouraged by Pope Paul IV and Pope Pius IV, who had repeatedly forbidden Catholics to call in Jewish physicians. Pius IV decreed that anyone seeking to obtain a university degree in any field had to make a profession of faith to the Catholic Church. Since he could not prevent Christians from associating with Jews, he tried to prevent the Jews from becoming doctors. The University of Padua, which, in a spirit of discreet tolerance, accepted students from all over Europe, became a favorite target for papal pressure.

Venice resisted such pressures. In 1593, as a mark of official recognition, the Republic authorized De Pomis to practice medicine among Christians. Another illustrious Jewish doctor, Giuseppe or Joseph De Dattolis, the protagonist of an action for defamation against his son-in-law before the Holy Office, received special honors from the Senate for the spirit of great sacrifice with which he had served the city. The Cattaveri conferred a coveted privilege on the sons of this doctor: two brokerages in the ghetto.

De Pomis, unquestionably the most famous Jewish doctor in Venice at the time, exemplified this climate of tolerance toward Jewish medicine. Following in the footsteps of Abrabanel, he offered a new Jewish contribution to the legend of Venice.

Unlike the Spanish philosopher, who wrote in Hebrew, De Pomis used Latin and Italian. Following the victory of Lepanto he sent a memorandum to the Venetian authorities, the doge, and the Senate, saying that the events of Lepanto had been described in the Bible. The memorandum was followed by a tract entitled *Tractatus de divinitate*, known to us only because De Pomis himself talks about it in his trilingual dictionary *Zemach David*,* dedicated to Pope Sixtus V.

De Pomis lost no opportunity to emphasize the divine origin of the city in every work he wrote. The preface to *De Medico Hebreo*, dedicated to Doge Cicogna, contains a eulogy aiming to demonstrate the similarity between Mosaic law and the Venetian constitution. According to De Pomis, the idea of a republic is implicit in the law of Moses as the only form of government that can effectively combat tyranny. This interpretation echoes the thesis espoused eighty years earlier by Isaac Abrabanel, who also drew an analogy between the ancient government of Israel and that of Venice, closing with an au-

---

The Shoot of David

dacious parallel between Moses and the doge. De Pomis ends his eulogy
with a glorification of Venice and its divine legend even more fervent
than Abrabanel's.

Another work of a totally different nature dates from the same pe-
riod: the *Discourse on the Birth of a Monstrosity to a Jewess in Venice.*
This was a piece of propaganda "discussing the future destiny of the
Jews," printed and annotated by Giovanni Gregorio Cremonese.

In the sixteenth century, any occurrence that seemed to violate the
laws of nature was considered an evil omen. Thus the birth of Siamese
twins to a Jewish mother in the ghetto caused a great sensation and
aroused the keen interest of doctors, astrologers, seers, and
theologians—a perfect example of the way in which science, religion,
and myth intermingled at that time. The whole affair, however, was
overshadowed by the anti-Jewish religious polemic unleashed, with
renewed virulence, by the event.

The freak was described as "two twins joined together where the
umbilicus should be, and they lie with their heads at each other's feet.
They have all the proper parts: four legs, four arms, etc., except the
privates, and instead of the place whence excrements should issue they
have a common hole in their belly which has the form of an umbilicus
and serves for excretion."

What meaning does the Christian polemicist offer for the monstrous
birth, after his dissertations on genetics and philosophy? "From these
accidents we may conjecture infidel conspiracies . . . or crimes being
plotted, the abduction of maidens or the taking of some grand personage
into slavery, or to death." His prophecy is laden with menace: "If these
twins live, it will mean the multiplication of infamous vices, and if
they die, vengeance on these scoundrels . . . It falls to you, unhappy
people of the treacherous and obstinate Synagogue . . . While this year,
through your false interpretation of the prophecy of the prophet Daniel
you awaited your Messiah, these monstrosities came to you."

Given the general tone, the conclusion cannot be optimistic. Addressing the Jewish nation, the author exclaims: "Perhaps a similar
thing will be born to lead you to the precipice . . . Devil and demons
will unite to possess you . . . Do you not remember what God says in
Deuteronomy? When the stranger in the midst of thee makes signs
and wonders, he shall mount up above thee higher and higher, and
thou shalt come down lower and lower. He shall lend to thee and thou
shalt no longer lend to him. He shall be the head and thou shalt be
the tail. He who pursues thee shall overtake thee, till thou be destroyed
because thou didst not hearken unto the words of the Lord thy God
. . . Do not despise this sign. Even Joseph took account of the offspring
of a cow in his sacrifice . . . Jerusalem, Jerusalem, convert to thy God
. . . Here I end, desiring the salvation of this people and my own grace."

The Siamese twins died, to the probable relief of all, Jews and Christians alike, who longed for a return to normality. When the "monster" died, a new prediction was addressed to the Jews, who had been unable to circumcise the twins according to their law: grave misfortunes would befall the ghetto.

CHAPTER EIGHT

Joao Micas, Giovanni Miches, Joseph Nasi, Duke of Naxos: A Man of Four Names and Many Identities

The feuds and adventures of the Mendes family — The abduction of young Beatrice — Gracia Nasi in Constantinople — The Jewish colonies at Tiberias

The Mendes clan was founded by the brothers Francisco and Diego, merchants who created a trans-European business enterprise, trading from Lisbon, the home of Francisco, to Antwerp, where Diego lived. Especially prominent in the spice and pepper trade, they built together a financial empire of international magnitude. They also may have been involved in clandestine transfers of capital on behalf of numerous Marranos who had moved eastward from the Iberian peninsula, toward Salonika or Constantinople, via tortuous routes through Europe and Venice.

In 1536, after the death of Francisco Mendes, his widow, Beatrice de Luna, determined to leave Lisbon for Antwerp, where her brother-in-law Diego lived with his wife, Brianda de Luna. Like her late husband, Beatrice was a Marrano, and her secret, original, name was Gracia Nasi. According to many historians, Brianda and Beatrice were sisters. Each had a daughter: the daughter of Beatrice was named Brianda, and Brianda's daughter was Beatrice. Francisco's widow, Beatrice de Luna, arrived in Antwerp accompanied by her nephew Joao Micas, a young man of keen intellect and noble bearing. In Antwerp the family lived in wealth and comfort at the court of the Holy Roman Emperor Charles V, but even in their new country, despite many powerful friends, the situation of the Mendes family was precarious because they were suspected of secretly being Jews. In 1532 Diego Mendes had been jailed on suspicion of heresy and in 1540 numerous Marrano associates of the Mendes company were arrested.

In 1544 the two Mendes sisters, Beatrice and Brianda, both widows by that time, were living in Antwerp with their two daughters Brianda and Beatrice and the young Joao Micas, when a new threat appeared on the horizon. Francisco of Aragon, a favorite of Charles V, aspired to the hand of the lovely Brianda de Luna, the daughter of Gracia Nasi alias Beatrice. Judging such a marriage incompatible with the family's Marrano condition, the widow of Francisco Mendes abruptly left Antwerp with her daughter, sister, and niece, leaving young Joao Micas alone at the helm of the powerful family business. Micas gradually and skillfully cut back his business in Antwerp and Flanders, diverting it toward Lyons, France, and Regensburg, Germany. He then joined his aunts, who by March 1544 had arrived in Venice under the protection of a special safe-conduct granted by the Council of Ten. The safe-conduct extended to the family's household and employees, no more than thirty people in all. The document ended with the words, "And let them be granted authorization in the customary liberal form, as is done for the other inhabitants of this, our city." Had the Venetians even remotely guessed what quarrels and troubles the Mendes de Luna sisters would stir up during their stay in the city, they would have avoided granting them any kind of asylum.

Beatrice was the administrator of the entire family fortune, a situation Brianda soon came to find intolerable. She applied to the Venetian authorities with a request that half the estate be adjudicated to her. The litigation went on for at least five years. The Venetian court enacted an initial decision in September 1547 and a second one in December 1548, both enjoining Beatrice to make over half the Mendes inheritance to Brianda, to be deposited with the Office of the Venetian Mint until the other Beatrice, Brianda's daughter, reached the age of eighteen. The Venetian nobility welcomed this ruling, for if young Beatrice married one of their sons the wealth would stay in Venice.

Gracia Nasi, alias Beatrice de Luna, the aunt of little Beatrice, no longer felt safe in Venice. One dark night in 1549 she fled to the liberal court of Ercole II d'Este in Ferrara. Shortly thereafter she was followed by her sister Brianda, for the climate in Venice was becoming much less hospitable after the July 1550 decree expelling the Marranos.

In Ferrara the two feuding sisters made peace. They returned temporarily to Venice and from there prepared to move to Constantinople for good. But the conflicts between the two, just barely appeased in Ferrara, flared up again as soon as they returned to Venice. The Venetian government, unwilling to lose the family's wealth, decided to prevent any sudden defections by confining them to obligatory residence. The affair was growing from a family feud into an international diplomatic incident. The Turkish ambassador requested permission to visit the sisters, which did not please the Senate and the Council of Ten, for although they could not refuse the ambassador's request, they would have much preferred not to be caught up in this complex quarrel.

The matter was not officially settled until June 1552, when Beatrice decided to deposit 100,000 gold ducats with the Office of the Mint in favor of her niece Beatrice. The agreement between the sisters had become an affair of state, to the point where the Senate felt it necessary to ratify the pact. Beatrice de Luna, alias Gracia Nasi, was finally free to leave for Constantinople with her daughter Brianda (alias Reina).

This ends the first chapter in the adventures of the Mendes family, but not the stories and legends concerning the family and its quarrels.

Joao Micas, alias Giovanni Miches, alias Juan Migues, alias Joseph Nasi, a man of many names and resolute character, was determined to intervene in his own way. In January 1553, he abducted Brianda's daughter, Beatrice. The abduction created a great stir and became a favorite topic of popular gossip, and in fact there are many conflicting versions of the story. The similarity in the names of the sisters and nieces was in itself a natural source of confusion; in addition, the future duke of Naxos was a typical Marrano whose life had been elusive and ambiguous, and the legends that grew up around him were equally so.

Some light, at least, is shed on the events by the ruling of the Council of Ten, a report from the Austrian ambassador Dominique de Gaztelu to his government, and the reports of the papal nuncios from Venice to Rome. According to the Austrian ambassador: "On a foggy night in January 1553, a boat slipped over the Grand Canal to the house of Donna Brianda. There it carried off Donna Brianda's daughter, with the consent of the damsel, and quickly escaped across the lagoon. In Faenza the two runaways were arrested and taken to Ravenna, where Nasi had numerous contacts. They were not imprisoned, however; on the contrary, they were married."

The Council of Ten ruled that Nasi must give himself up and stand trial. If he failed to do so (as indeed he did), a college of dogal councillors would be given carte blanche to use every means at its disposal, including torture, to discover the truth of the affair that had created such a scandal. Giovanni Miches alias Joao Micas (the first name is Venetian dialect, the second Spanish, and the third, Joseph Nasi, was taken later, in Constantinople) was sentenced to perpetual banishment from Venice and the territories of the doge and state. If captured, he would be hanged between the two columns in St. Mark's Square. No pardon or remission of sentence, even in the form of a safe-conduct, would be granted except at the joint request of six councillors and three leaders of the Council of Ten, in the presence of thirty council members.

The story, as told by the Austrian ambassador, did not end there. The young Beatrice was brought back to Venice and Nasi went to Rome.

There he petitioned the pope to recognize his marriage and intercede on his behalf with the Venetian government. And intercede he did, testimony to the power of the Nasi family. The papal nuncio to Venice was unable to placate the Venetians, however. Since they could not lay their hands on the miscreant, they were determined to identify and punish his accomplices. The feud between Donna Beatrice and Donna Brianda in Venice carried over into the court of the Inquisition with the trials of Odoardo Gomez and Augustino Enriquez, who worked for Donna Beatrice, and Licentiato Costa, in the service of Donna Brianda.

Another clear picture emerges from the document submitted to the Council of Ten by Donna Brianda, containing accusations against her sister and against Beatrice's employees Gomez and Enriquez. The two men had repeatedly tried to have her safe-conduct suspended. With great circumspection and delicacy, Donna Brianda stressed the value of that special permit granted by the Republic, and came to the defense of her employee Licentiato Costa, accused of behaving as a Christian although he was a Jew. She concluded, "I will keep him home, and present him at every request of your court, and if he does not appear I will pay 10,000 ducats." On August 21, 1555, the Council ruled that Donna Brianda could have her money back but that she was to leave town within a month, with her family and stewards, and not return to the city except by special permission.

Donna Brianda's adventures were not over. The next day, she requested a hearing before the Council of Ten. She declared that everyone in her household lived as good Christians and asked that anyone who had not done so be punished accordingly. That same day, the council again urgently summoned Donna Brianda and her daughter, Beatrice, interrogated them separately, and peremptorily ordered them both to drop all pretense and ambiguity. Young Beatrice unmasked, stating her wish to live as a Jew.

The following day, Donna Brianda poignantly addressed the court: "I left my home in the Emperor's domains to escape the Inquisition. I came here because I had a safe-conduct and to live in peace." She said she was a new Christian, forcibly baptized, but "had always lived as a Jewess in her heart and thus wanted to live." The government of the Serenissima informed the pope of the measures taken against the Mendes women, to the great satisfaction of Paul IV.

Unexpectedly, the French ambassador interceded on their behalf. The Council of Ten was hard put to resist such pressure and, in an attempt to lighten the tone of their refusal to grant the ambassador's requests, tried to illustrate, with a wealth of detail, the grave wrongs that had been committed. Donna Brianda Mendes and her daughter Beatrice, still in Venice in January 1556, finally fled back to Ferrara.

Meanwhile, Donna Beatrice had arrived in Constantinople from

Venice, sumptuously escorted by forty horsemen, with four magnificent carriages and a large retinue of servants. Her arrival caused a great sensation and kindled the imagination of contemporary historians.

There were no restrictions in Turkish society, and Donna Beatrice could live openly as a Jew. She untiringly came to the assistance of other Jews, and her concern for the plight of the Marranos grew constantly. Beatrice Mendes de Luna, now openly Gracia Nasi, was probably the most outstanding representative of this new Jewish community, and the subsequent arrival of Joseph Nasi contributed to strengthening the family's influence with the Sublime Porte* still further.

Nasi reached Constantinople a year later. He, too, made a splendid, triumphant entrance. He apparently had two bodyguards and twenty liveried servants, followed by a cortege of five hundred Marranos. Shortly after his arrival he openly returned to Judaism and was circumcised. He married Donna Gracia's daughter, formerly Brianda and now Reina. For a while the newlyweds lived with Donna Gracia, but later moved to Belvedere, a new house with a magnificent view over the Bosphorus, a true court with servants and soldiers. Joseph's political career in Constantinople was made possible not only by his financial influence, but thanks to a vast network of international relations branching out to all the Marrano communities of Europe. Suleiman the Magnificent, who met Nasi through the ambassador De Lansac, soon came to appreciate his dynamic personality. He was glad to make use of Nasi's services, for he had a keen interest in learning about the European affairs of which Nasi was such an attentive observer, with his acute powers of analysis and access to first-hand information.

Their influence at court gave Donna Gracia and Joseph Nasi the opportunity to intervene in certain delicate international affairs, including the events of 1556 in Ancona that culminated in the tragic executions. The boycott attempt organized against Ancona by the Marrano community of Constantinople lasted two long years before its failure was finally conceded.

In 1561 the sultan favored Joseph Nasi and his aunt Gracia in a manner highly unusual for the time: he gave them the city of Tiberias and the surrounding area and allowed them to found a Jewish settlement there. Nasi threw himself into the enterprise with passion, but although he poured large sums of money into it, the result was disappointing. The artificially created wool and silk industries never really thrived. Despite Nasi's appeals to the Jewish communities, including those of Italy, very few were motivated to move to Palestine, although they did often request to be buried in Jerusalem. After the death of Gracia Nasi, in 1569, Joseph Nasi abandoned his plan to found Jewish colonies in Palestine.

---

*the government of the Ottoman Empire

In 1566 Joseph Nasi reaped a new triumph. Selim II had succeeded his father as sultan, partly thanks to Nasi's support. He returned the favor by naming him duke of Naxos and the Cyclades, Joseph's moment of greatest glory and splendor. He had not forgotten the ill-treatment suffered at the hands of the great nations when he was a young merchant with no power or influence, and now he paid them back in full. His chief targets were the Republic of Venice and France.

His accounts with Venice were still painfully open: he was still under sentence of death by hanging between the two columns in St. Mark's Square. Daniele Barbarigo, the Venetian ambassador to Constantinople, reported to Venice on his conversation with Giovanni Miches, who now called himself Joseph Nasi. Nasi, he said, had shown him a letter from Sultan Selim II to the doge requesting a safe-conduct for Nasi. The request had been denied. Nasi reiterated his devotion to Venice and begged the doge to reconsider. He continued to press for reconsideration, and even sent emissaries to Venice. Despite evasive replies, the emissaries stayed on in the city, intent on obtaining satisfaction for their master. The matter, they were promised, would be brought before the Council of Ten. They sent encouraging messages to Constantinople, but time went by and no decision was reached. The emissaries tried again, insisting that Nasi was not requesting remission of the sentence for himself alone, but for all involved in the case. Considerations of political expediency led the doge to reluctantly support the request, despite the binding legal conditions attached to the sentence just for the purpose of making pardon more difficult. The man who had been Giovanni Miches in Venice was now a powerful adviser to Sultan Selim II; he was a feared and influential man, duke of Naxos and the Cyclades—islands the Venetians had lost. And now Joseph Nasi, the former fugitive, seemed to have no intention of backing down. By unanimous vote the Council of Ten repealed the sentence against Nasi. Such a quick and unusual decision did not escape the papal nuncio, whose comments were sarcastic. The perpetual banishment decreed against Miches-Nasi in 1553 was revoked in 1567.

A year later, Nasi turned his attention to France. In 1540 Henry II had borrowed 150,000 ducats from Nasi and on various pretexts had refused to pay them back. Backed by the sultan, the duke of Naxos had all the goods on French ships confiscated for the value of the sum owed him. France, too, was forced to yield; the treaty that put an end to the hostilities between France and Constantinople was actually written in Hebrew. France did not submit passively to this injury and attempted to sidestep Nasi by accusing him of one conspiracy after another. Nasi paid France back in kind by supporting the rebellious Flemish Calvinists.

A constant among Nasi's political projects was the possession of Cyprus. To achieve his aim, he planned to exploit his old friendship with Duke Emmanuel Philibert of Savoy, which dated from his years in Flanders. The Venetians were occupying the island on the pretext that Queen Caterina Cornaro had very special ties to Venice. But her husband, the king of Cyprus, was related to the Savoys, who could advance certain claims to the succession. In 1564 Nasi sent a business agent to Emmanuel Philibert, with two letters. The official letter was followed by a personal letter from the duke's old friend Joao Micas, now Joseph Nasi, with a reserved postscript to be delivered orally. The duke was flattered by Nasi's proposal, and there followed an exchange of letters, full of plans and promises. The reality, however, was clear: Venice, Spain, and France were strong and close at hand, while the Sublime Porte was very far away. After much hesitation Emmanuel Philibert abandoned the plan and informed the pope and the other Christian states of his secret relations with the Turks. But Joseph Nasi refused to give up. The Venetians knew and feared his extraordinary determination. In 1568, at the order of the Serenissima, the Cypriot government at Famagusta arrested Jewish and Turkish agitators "who are going about the island and sending false reports to Giovanni Miches." The match between Venice and Joao Micas, alias Giovanni Miches, alias Joseph Nasi, duke of Naxos, was yet to be played. It culminated in the most celebrated naval encounter of the sixteenth century: the battle of Lepanto.

CHAPTER NINE

Lepanto

*The question of Cyprus — The Holy League — The battle of Lepanto
— The expulsion of the Jews — Salomon Askenazi*

The contest between the Most Serene Republic and the Sublime
Porte had been a constant for nearly a century, and its natural
arena was the Mediterranean. Skirmishes, sneak attacks, and repeated
ambushes alternated with head-on clashes and open warfare from 1463
to 1479, 1499 to 1503, and 1537 to 1540. The thunder of battle was
often announced by sinister rumblings.

The battle of Lepanto was no different. During the 1560s, Cyprus
grew increasingly desirable in the eyes of the Ottoman Empire. To
stem the Turkish aggression, Venice sent new forces to the area: illustrious military architects built stronger defenses, and thirty new
galleys patrolled the region under the command of Gerolamo Zane,
captain of the fleet. Venetian counterintelligence brought alarming
reports of prodigious and detailed plans of attack, new instruments of
war for tearing doors off their hinges, and soundings in the waters off
Famagusta to find the stronghold's weak points. Venice ordered "most
diligent" investigations and commanded that all suspect persons be
removed from the area and the fortifications restored. At Famagusta
all Jews not native to the island, who might theoretically be in contact
with Joseph Nasi, were expelled despite the lack of concrete evidence
against them. Confusion was rife among the Venetian authorities: some
feared the worst and advocated arming at any cost, while others thought
there was still room for negotiation and that too aggressive a position

would compromise any possibility of peace. The situation in the city was made more critical by a grain shortage that afflicted the entire Italian peninsula.

The fire at the Arsenal in Venice in September 1569 was a dire premonition. Francesco Molin, a contemporary Venetian, relates: "I awakened at the first collapse and saw the windows break, the walls part and the beams burn, and such ruin that with all the fire I thought myself come to the last judgment, wherefore I commended myself to God and awaited the outcome. When the crashing abated, although it seemed that the air still burned, I arose with difficulty, being covered with stones, beams and ruins, and in attempting to leave my chamber I wounded my feet in various places and heard the frightened voices of many calling for help." Accident or arson? It was never known. But suspicion fell on Joseph Nasi, seen as a dangerous enemy, an able and astute man of iron will and capable of diabolical machinations. If Nasi had made up his mind to have Cyprus, with his obstinacy, his successes, and the aid of the powerful sultan, he might even win out. Turks and Jews alike were considered enemies, allied against the Most Serene Republic. The former threatened the Republic with their galleys, the latter with treachery and espionage. Nasi was perceived as representing both enemies, and he wanted revenge on Venice. Seen through the eyes of fear, his power grew into a legend.

Venice was experiencing a new time of trouble, and lived in perpetual fear of conspiracy and isolation. The Jews were seen as a threat, and their indecipherable language took on the sound of a secret code.

Early in January 1570, news reached Venice that two ships had been taken. From Constantinople, the Venetian ambassador Antonio Barbaro reported the curt words of a high Turkish official: "What do you want with that island so remote that it can bring you no profit and is the cause of such turbulence? Leave it to us who have so many provinces nearby. And in any case, our Lord is determined to have it."

Venice was nervous. Even the nuncio Facchinetti, who certainly had no tender feelings for the Jews, complained that traffic between Ancona and Ragusa was being hindered and the Jewish merchants disturbed. He was told that letters in Hebrew had been found: a clear case of espionage.

At the end of March, a Turkish ambassador arrived in Venice. Summoned before the Cabinet, he said that his sultan wanted Cyprus and that only by ceding the island could Venice avoid war. All the Turkish merchants in the city were arrested and so, naturally, were the Levantine Jews, whose merchandise was confiscated. In those particular circumstances, the protection of the Sublime Porte did them more harm than good.

In May 1570, while signs of imminent war continued to multiply, Doge Pietro Loredan died and Alvise Mocenigo was elected to succeed him. Early in July, the Turkish fleet disembarked at Cyprus. In September Nicosia fell. The head of Nicolò Dandolo, the commander of that post, was sent to Marcantonio Bragadin, the commander at Famagusta. When Famagusta fell after a long siege, Bragadin, too, was tortured and flayed alive. Cyprus had fallen to the Turks.

Faced with the threat of Ottoman supremacy in the Mediterranean, the Christian powers abandoned all hesitation and opportunism. Early in 1571, by dint of much effort, Pope Pius V succeeded in forming a Holy League to undertake a crusade against the Infidel, but its members all looked at each other with suspicion. Spain distrusted Venice because of her pragmatism and her intrinsic need for peace and trade. Venice did not wish to be crushed by the continental powers and tried to defend her frontier position, a junction between two different worlds. The pope distrusted both. Negotiations under these circumstances were slow and difficult.

On the one hand Venice went along with the idea of the league, but she maintained relations with the enemy to the last, in the hope of finding a compromise. Nor did all the Turks want war. The adviser to the sultan, Sokolli Mehemed, a friend of Salomon Askenazi and a fierce adversary of Joseph Nasi, tried to ease the tension between his country and Venice. Negotiations between the nations of the Holy League dragged on for seemingly endless months, from July 1570 to May 1571. The duke of Alba aptly summed up these problematical relationships with the remark: "These French would be happy to lose an eye if they could cause us to lose two."

After much vacillation, the league sent out a fleet commanded by Don Juan of Austria, the son of Charles V. The fleet sailed from Messina on September 16. The battle of Lepanto was fought between Christians and Moslems on October 7, 1571, with 230 Turkish against 208 Christian vessels. According to Fernand Braudel, "Lepanto was the most resounding military event in the Mediterranean during the sixteenth century. But this great victory of technology and courage is difficult to place in the ordinary perspective of history . . . It even appeared strange—as Voltaire observed with amusement—that the unexpected victory had such meager consequences. Lepanto was fought on October 7, 1571; a year later the allies were defeated outside Modone; in 1573 an exhausted Venice abandoned the fight; in 1574 the Turks triumphed at Goletta and Tunis. And thus all dreams of crusades were dispersed by the contrary winds."

Samuele Romanin tells of the Lepanto victory announcement: "Giuffredo Giustinian was dispatched in haste to Venice with the happy news, and with great diligence made the journey in only ten days. It was October 18, 1571, at midday, in a time of great affliction, when the galley appeared bearing such happy tidings, dragging enemy standards through the water, full of turbans and Turkish costumes, whence amid the bursts of cannon resounded cries of *victory, victory*. At that sight, at those sounds, the populace gathered from all round, and while Giustinian disembarked and presented himself to the Doge and the Cabinet, universal joy spread throughout the town, and those who met in the street embraced and congratulated one another. The populace in an excess of zeal rushed to free the prisoners, crying *liberty, liberty*, but only those imprisoned for debt were allowed to flee: the shops were closed with signs reading *for the death of the Turks*, no one left the square before evening, no one minded the shops: the Turkish merchants stayed locked in their Fondaco."

Doge Alvise Mocenigo went to St. Mark's church. The Te Deum was sung with full orchestra and brilliant illumination. The wave of emotion that swept the city at the news of the victory of Lepanto was followed, as usual, by renewed religious fervor. And the Jews paid the price. The idea of a Jewish plot, hatred of the renegade Giovanni Miches, and the need for catharsis all combined to arouse in the Venetians a burning desire for revenge.

The Council of Ten's secret reports from June 1568 read, "And we see the very great esteem in which the entire Jewish nation holds this Joseph Nasi especially since he was named Duke of Naxos; and he is considered the chief leader of those Jews, with whom he concurs in all things." It seems likely that the powerful Marrano would have been a popular figure in the ghetto, and even that he may have had contacts and supporters there; but it has never been proven that the Venetian ghetto sided with the Turks, nor does it seem reasonable. At all events, when the bill concerning the renewal of the Jewish charter came up before the Senate in December 1571, with terms not much different from those of 1566, very few were surprised by Alvise Grimani's countermotion advocating the expulsion of the Jews. We would have no knowledge of this debate, bound by strict secrecy, were it not for an account by the sixteenth-century bishop of Verona, Agostino Valiero, in his book *Dell'utilità che si può ritrarre delle cose operate dai Veneziani,* * printed in Padua in 1787.

Grimani recalled the great victory over the Turks, interpreting it as a mark of divine favor. He felt that Jesus Christ deserved a sign of gratitude—such as the expulsion of the first deniers of the Christian faith, those traitors to the State: the Jews. He maintained that the Jews had exaggerated the importance of the Arsenal fire and the shortage of grain in the city in order to fuel the hopes of the Turks. Through their financial activities, maintained Grimani, the Jews were the ruin of many patrician families, and they corrupted the young with extravagance and ostentation that grew worse day by day.

---

* *Of the Usefulness that may be Derived from the Actions of the Venetians*

Alvise Zorzi rebutted Grimani's countermotion by saying that there was "no need to drive so many people to desperation by a new policy that would destroy those who might one day serve God." If the Jews did not lend money, the Christians would have to, and that would be inappropriate. As for extravagance, would expelling the Jews put an end to it? Possibly to avoid laying himself open to accusations of complicity or corruption, Zorzi, too, attacked the Jews, whose faults were well known: they were sneaks, spies, usurers, and misers, but God desired them to remain among Christians as an example of an erring people.

Argument was heated and many orators took the floor with opposing motions. Grimani won, with two-thirds of the vote.

On December 18, 1571, the Senate ordained: "All the Jews, of whatever nation, rank, sex and condition, shall be obliged to leave this City at the end of two years' grace, granted them by their Charter. During that time they shall not lend money in any way, nor return, sojourn, dwell or transit, for either long periods or short, on pain of all the penalties contained in the Decision taken in this Council on 8 July 1550 against the Marranos." So the Jews could stay in Venice until February 1573. By that time, the Cabinet and the Senate would have to find a solution to the credit problems of the urban poor.

Four days after the motion was approved, the papal nuncio was informed that the Republic was willing to expel all the Jews from her territories if the pope would follow suit. For only if they were expelled from Ancona at the same time would Jewish merchants be eliminated from the Adriatic trade routes, thus placing Rome and Venice on an equal commercial footing.

Suddenly and for no apparent reason, there was a reversal. Two members of the Avogadori de Comun stated before the Senate that the law of December 18, 1571 concerning the Jews was illegal and could be neither proposed nor enforced, based on the Council of Ten's ruling of April 20, 1524. It must therefore be considered void to all effects. The law of 1524 forbade any talk of instituting *monti di pietà* in Venice unless such discussion were explicitly authorized by the Council of Ten. The Avogadori insisted that the expulsion of the Jews from the city was a surreptitious way of recalling to public attention the long-debated issue of the *monti di pietà*, and that it had all been done without the prescribed authorization of the Council of Ten.

The Senate sustained the objection of the Avogadori and just a few days later, on July 11, 1573, approved a new law very different from the first, one whose effects would be felt until at least the middle of the next century. The most important innovation was that the Venetian Jews, through their representatives Marcuzzo, Fricele, and Samson Pescaruol, promised to collect the sum of fifty thousand ducats with which to finance loans to the Venetian poor, against pledges, of "small sums of 2 or 3 ducats at a time, for a profit of one Bagattino* per lira per month to cover their expenses." The interest they could charge was lowered from 10 percent to 5 percent. The autonomy of the banks was limited still further: the Cattaveri were to ensure that they operated within the law and had the right to examine their accounts. The sale of pledges, which must be held on deposit for twelve months, remained the duty of the Sopraconsoli.

The old pawnshop, originally conceived as an independent business enterprise, was completely transformed. In its place arose a charitable institution financed as a losing venture with capital forcibly provided by the Jewish community and earmarked for the Christian poor. The result was a special new kind of credit instrument, entirely under government control. Its totally profitless management was in the hands of the Jews, who were legally bound to refinance losses and keep the endowment intact. The social benefits were similar to those conferred by the *monti di pietà*. Pawnbroking was thus no longer a profitable business; it had become servitude.

The singularity of the Venetian situation has not escaped historians. Leon Poliakov has observed that instead of transferring the money-lending operations to Christians, the Jewish banks were adapted to suit the times. An investigator sent from Paris during the Regency to study the operation of the Italian *monti di pietà* became extremely cautious when it came to talking about Venice, and wrote: "I have many reasons to fear arousing a just distaste for this report by describing a singularity that cannot, however, be overlooked. The Republic of Venice has realized, as have other Italian States, that it would be much more useful to the poor to find a place where, in exchange for their rags, they could receive what they need to relieve their pressing poverty. But it has made singular use of this realization, and I think that only in Venice does the *monte di pietà* live by means of the Jews."

How can this Venetian change of heart toward the Jews be explained? One might suggest that it was the result of momentary euphoria in the wake of the Lepanto victory, mixed with religious zeal and a desire for retaliation against the Jews, both Levantine and Venetian. Or perhaps pragmatic economic considerations were paramount. While there may be elements of truth in both these hypotheses, they are clearly only partial explanations.

After the battle of Lepanto, Venice needed to settle her differences with the Turks, but she had been strongly conditioned by the sluggishness of her allies. The Republic needed either peace or war: the three years of hostilities had blocked traffic for no gain. There was constant tension at the Istrian and Dalmatian frontiers. Cyprus and

---

*a small Venetian copper coin

several strategic Adriatic ports had been lost. The expeditions of 1571 and 1572 had been costly. Lepanto had been the end of a nightmare, but the hoped-for results had not become concrete. The negotiations were lengthy, and as time passed, the Venetians' desire for peace intensified while the Turks resisted all the more firmly, setting harder terms.

On March 7, 1573, Venice struck out on her own. She left the Holy League and reached a separate agreement with the Sublime Porte. Cyprus remained with the Turks, but Venice kept certain outposts in Dalmatia and Albania. The Turkish prisoners were returned without ransom and three hundred thousand zecchini were paid as war damages. The peace obtained by the Serenissima on those terms was a hard one, but she was able to restore the normal trade conditions in the Mediterranean that were essential to her survival. The author of the peace was the envoy Marcantonio Barbaro. A memoir published as an appendix to volume five of *Relazioni degli Ambasciatori Veneti** tells some little-known details. Barbaro maintains that after Lepanto, the Grand Vizier had tried for some time to weave a network of contacts with Venice. He was aided in these semiclandestine advances by a Jewish doctor influential at the sultan's court, a certain Salomon Askenazi, who was, according to Barbaro, "a native of Udine, with brothers and nephews at Verona and Oderzo, and as a subject of the Serenissima, he had been friends with the illustrious envoys Bragadin and Soranzo and had made himself known as such in all circumstances." Barbaro had found him "very well disposed toward this Most Serene Dominion."

Another version of the negotiations behind the peace appears in Joseph Ha-Cohen's Hebrew chronicle *Emek ha-Bakha*, which describes the persecutions suffered by the Jews in Europe up to 1576. An anonymous contemporary added an appendix bringing it up to 1606. That history clearly shows the important role played by Salomon Askenazi, who came to Venice with Barbaro and interceded on behalf of the Venetian Jews. The anonymous author of the appendix to *Emek ha-Bakha* colorfully describes the events of the time: "Following the expulsion decree, many Jews had already embarked with their wives and children, prepared to set out for other lands where they might find the possibility of a peaceful life, and were awaiting a favorable wind to fill the sails. It was at that very time that Senator Soranzo, the ambassador to Constantinople, returned to Venice where, upon disembarking, he heard the shouts of the small children on board and the cries of the infants. He asked those about him what the noise signified, and they replied that it came from the families of the Israelites whom an expulsion order had banished from the city. Hearing those words Soranzo was inflamed with anger and even before going home he went before

*Reports of the Venetian Ambassadors

the Doge, had the Council of Ten summoned and addressed them." Soranzo maintained that the Jews were useful to the State and that they, above all, were the only true allies of the Republic and not, certainly, the nations of the Holy League, who had made the victory of Lepanto meaningless by their conduct. The anonymous historian continued, "Those words of Soranzo's were a gleam of light for the Ten, who, persuaded that he had spoken the truth, met a second time and voted to annul their former decision, making an agreement of peace with the Jews who thus serenely returned among the Venetians."

Other historians have emphasized the importance of developments in the Venetian economy: on the one hand, the Senate was beginning to feel the adverse effects of having reduced the Jewish community, and on the other, the Jews were offering new and more advantageous terms in exchange for being allowed to stay.

Bishop Valiero, in his book, supplies hitherto unknown details about the debate in the Senate, pointing out that some senators owed large sums to the Jews while others were their creditors. In either case, cutting off all financial and commercial relationships would be detrimental to both parties.

All these factors probably influenced the tempestuous relationship between Venice and her Jews. As we have seen, two important Jewish figures were very deeply involved: Joseph Nasi at the beginning, and Salomon Askenazi when the conflict was over.

Although Salomon Askenazi, an important contributor to the peace, had not lived a life of adventure as had Nasi, like most Jews he had done his share of traveling. His ancestry was German, but he himself was born in Udine and was therefore a Venetian subject. His family was dispersed throughout the Venetian territories from Udine to Oderzo, Verona, and Candia. He had studied medicine at Padua and from there had gone to the court of Sigismund at Krakow, and finally to Constantinople. Here he had become friends with Mehemed Sokolli, who disliked Nasi, and had acted as an underground link between the envoy and the court vizier who, in time of war, could not openly expose himself to charges of conspiring with the enemy. Askenazi was arrested and interrogated on suspicion of engaging in clandestine relations with Venice. He was in serious danger, but Sokolli succeeded in saving him, and the envoy Barbaro was grateful to him as well. As a mediator between two enemy nations, Salomon Askenazi was not successful in overcoming the powers that wanted war. It was only later, when both sides began to feel the need for peace, that his loyalty to both Venice and the Sublime Porte, and his continuous efforts at moderation, bore the hoped-for fruit.

As attested by the envoy Barbaro, Askenazi almost certainly interceded on behalf of the ghetto Jews, suggesting that the condition of the Venetians in Constantinople might be improved if the expulsion order were repealed. And once peace was made, Venice needed to revitalize her economy. The Jews could be useful in implementing this new policy.

Askenazi won a highly significant personal victory when he came to Venice in 1574 as the ambassador of Selim II and was received with honor by the Senate and Doge Mocenigo. After this initial diplomatic mission, the sultan entrusted the Jewish doctor with other delicate international missions, including the signing, in 1586, of a treaty between Turkey and Spain in the name of the Sublime Porte. Askenazi is thought to have died in 1602. When his son came to Venice in 1604, bearing a letter from the sultan, Doge Grimani welcomed him with great honor, a sign of the Republic's lasting gratitude toward the Askenazi family.

And what of Joseph Nasi, the bold hero of so many adventures? Although Cyprus was now in the hands of the Ottoman Empire, his star was dimmed by the defeat at Lepanto. The last years of his life, consistent with his personality and history, are veiled in ambiguity. Some historians have expressed skepticism with regard to certain controversial documents referring to secret relations and correspondence between Nasi and Philip II, supposedly involving a petition to the Spanish king for a safe-conduct to return to Spain for himself and his retinue of seventy, including Turks and Jews. According to those documents Nasi implored "pardon for having practiced and professed the Jewish law for some time, having been constrained and obliged thereto." Truth or fiction? One last attempt to seek salvation or a banal historical counterfeit? Nasi's life of adventure was drawing to a close. Wealthy and respected, but relegated to the margins of political life, he died in Constantinople in 1579.

CHAPTER TEN

Daniel Rodriga
and the "Western Nation"

*The port of Spalato: the plan — Vacillation of the Senate and the
Five Sages of Commerce — The Charter of 1589 — The port of
Spalato: its realization*

Lepanto, a crucial moment in sixteenth-century history, had
certain paradoxical aspects. After the battle, Venice and her
traditional Turkish adversary became lukewarm allies. For Venice, this
was a way of countering the maneuvers of Austria, Spain, and the
papacy, who were attempting to cut her off from her customary Adriatic
trade routes. The Spanish influence had spread from the south, and
now extended as far as Albania and Istria. To the north, Austria maintained regular contacts with the fearsome Uskok pirates. From the
west the Leghorn-Ancona axis projected toward Ragusa, threatening
the steadily weakening Venetian monopoly. Venice still had bases on
the Dalmatian coast, but Spalato had lost its protecting fortresses.
Many contemporary witnesses attest to the ruin and poverty of those
sites: Sebenico and Zara were abandoned. The islands of Pago, Cherso,
and Lesina were all but uninhabited, their population having been
decimated on the galleys. The English, French, and Dutch appeared
more and more often in the Mediterranean, shuffling the cards in a
trading game whose players were growing in number. The oceanic
routes had made it necessary for the new seafaring countries to mod-
ernize their technology rapidly, building stronger ships and manning
them with well-trained crews. Venice and the Sublime Porte were now
threatened on the very seas they had once ruled uncontested. They
joined forces in an attempt to forestall an otherwise inevitable decline.

Venice also had problems at home. The war had drained the coffers of the Republic, political tension had heightened, and the nobility was beginning to abandon maritime trade, made riskier by the spread of piracy. Once again, the lifeline of Mediterranean commerce was the Jewish refugees, who had abandoned Spain and her possessions Naples, Milan, and Sicily and were turning toward the Mediterranean ports. Secure in their broad network of family relationships, easily adaptable, and clever in their dealings with merchants of every nation and kind, these new polyglot Christians of Marrano descent, once they had left their homeland, often revealed their secret, repressed Jewish identity and reverted to their original faith. The Venetian merchants in the Turkish capital now traded primarily with Jews "who set the price of the goods" and dominated international trade.

In describing the Mediterranean situation of his day, the famous seventeenth-century rabbi Simone Luzzatto remarked, in fact, that "the principal settlement of the Hebrew Nation was in the state of the Turkish Lord." Not only had Jews been living there for a long time, but new refugees continued to arrive from Spain. Many of them settled in the Turkish domains, for no religious or professional restrictions were imposed there, nor was there any prohibition against owning property. These conditions, much more favorable than those in many European countries, attracted a composite medley of Jewish refugees of all sorts to Salonika and other Turkish seaports. They were natural competitors of the Venetian merchants, who had been too long accustomed to enjoying a preeminent position in every corner of the Mediterranean.

Only after Lepanto did the situation change. In October 1573, a new idea for solving the thorny problem of Adriatic commerce was brought to the attention of the Venetian government. Possibly at the suggestion of a Marrano merchant (one Daniele Rodriguez, called Daniel Rodriga), a Bosnian official wrote to the doge advising the reassessment of land routes, as opposed to the traditional maritime ones.

A merchant by necessity and vocation, Rodriga had been trading in the Mediterranean since at least 1549. Ancona, Ragusa, Venice, and Dalmatia were all familiar to him. He knew their secrets, their problems, and, more important still, their prospects for development. As early as 1563, buying silks and woolens on the Venetian market, he had established business relations with Venice and Bosnia. Because he was on good terms with the Turkish *sanjakbeyi* (governors) in Dalmatia, in addition to being a confidential adviser to Venice, he was entrusted with diplomatic missions: in 1574 he journeyed to the Slavonic territories to "learn the minds" of the Turkish officials who were making trouble for Venice, and that same year he went to Cattaro, on the authorization of the Council of Ten, to recover certain strategic outposts over which the Republic wished to maintain control. Diplomatic and commercial missions were two sides of the same coin, each essential to the success of the other. Rodriga was backed by a company he had set up with his brother Petrus Dieghi, his brother-in-law Isaac De Castris, and Josef Hoef Falcon de Hispania.

In 1577 Rodriga addressed a memorandum to the Senate in which he proposed, among other things, "to create a port of call at Spalato, where merchandise coming and going from the Turkish countries may transit." In his judgment, Venice would sharpen her competitive edge, reduce the danger of her ships falling prey to pirates, and undermine the competitive force of the Ancona-Ragusa axis. At the same time Rodriga also requested privileges and freedom of transit for merchants who settled in Spalato with their families, in exchange for a small tax, half of which would be paid to him personally.

At the end of October 1577, the Senate approved the general outline of the plan, except for the privileges for foreign merchants. Venice was not yet willing to renounce her protectionist policies.

Rodriga had written: "I can confidently promise not only to increase trade in this glorious city, but to ensure the safety of the gulf and remove many hindrances which, owing to the Uskoks, trouble Your serenity . . . I offer to erect in your territory of Spalato a vast, rich port, taking upon myself the burden of working all about, fixing the roads, building inns, preparing houses and setting up commerce by establishing an important channel in this city . . . Through this very important port of call much merchandise will come to this city, for the commerce of Narenta and Castelnuovo will of necessity fail due to the Uskoks. With traffic diverted from the port of Ragusa, the port of Spalato will be of great help in transporting the riches of the Levant all entire into our city."

Rodriga's enthusiastic initiatives were opposed by those Venetian patricians who were afraid of being personally damaged by a policy of free trade, and those nobles of Spalato who feared being supplanted by the enterprising Jews. In June 1579, Rodriga asked the Senate for permission to bring fifty Jewish merchant families to Venice, each willing to be taxed a hundred ducats. The newcomers demanded no special terms, but they did request a guarantee of safety for their persons and property, as subjects of Venice.

In August 1579, the Senate postponed a decision yet again. Accepting fifty new families into the Old Ghetto was out of the question, and expanding the ghetto would have been a delicate issue to raise at that particular time. Just a year later, in August 1580, the Five Sages made a visit to the ghetto and ultimately had to agree with the resident merchants who were complaining about lack of living space and inadequate warehouse facilities.

The Senate at that time was involved with defending the positions gained by the Venetian merchants. Defensive measures against the

Uskoks in the waters off Spalato had to be decided on, and evaluating Rodriga's project required the gathering of much information. The governor general of Dalmatia, Alvise Loredan, sent an account of the hostility with which the plan for the port had been received at Spalato, partly because, as Loredan wrote, "It would be necessary, above all, to launch this enterprise with great expenditure, which we doubt Rodriga is in a position to undertake since on account of costs already incurred he cannot afford to spend a sou." And indeed, Rodriga had already spent large sums of money: he had dipped into his own pocket to build roads and send gifts to the Turks, tenaciously pursuing the realization of his project. His determination naturally provoked envy, doubt, and resistance.

In Venice, Rodriga, considered a "man of incomparable business acumen," was both respected and feared. But those who opposed him finally won out. Short of funds and obstructed on all sides, the audacious Marrano merchant found himself in serious difficulty. He left Spalato and returned to his private business in Ragusa. But he continued to weave his web with patient determination and in 1583 again asked the Five Sages of Commerce to grant privileges to the Levantine merchants, requesting that they be "guaranteed the freedom to live in the city and that there be no obstacles posed to commercial navigation."

A Marrano merchant in his own right, Rodriga thus intended to facilitate the immigration to Venice of Judaizing Christians from the Iberian peninsula, who wanted to reach Venice directly from the West without first passing through the Eastern ports. In addition to being a link with Turkey, Venice was a port where not too many questions were asked and where a Jew who declared himself such and lived in the ghetto would not be tormented with tedious investigations into his Christian past. Moreover Venice, whose policies on religious issues differed from those of the papacy, was assuming a position of autonomy.

This time, too, however, Rodriga's request was denied. In the words of the Senate, "If this were granted, it would give rise to many inconveniences, disorders and damages because there is no doubt that our citizens, who for various reasons do very little, would be completely excluded from trade if said Jews were permitted to freely navigate to the East and West, and the traffic would be concentrated entirely in the hands of these Jews." The Senate also feared the Jewish merchants might acquire a monopoly, which could pose a serious threat to the city should a new war break out with the Turks. It bears remarking that in this circumstance Venetian opposition to the Western Jewish merchants was motivated exclusively by economic rather than religious considerations.

Meanwhile, a new council of Five Sages of Commerce had been appointed. The new appointees, while recognizing the important role of the Jews in the economic development of the Republic, still refused to grant new concessions, and played for time.

Meanwhile the projected port of Spalato was still a live issue, one which addressed important commercial needs, and whose intrinsic value could not be negated by the Five Sages or the Venetian Senate as if it were a mere manifestation of Rodriga's personal ambition. The reports from the Venetian procurators in Dalmatia are illuminating in this respect. Nicolò Correr paints a vividly realistic picture of the situation. The dangers he describes include piracy, Turkish treachery, and the possibility of excessive Jewish influence. The almost inaccessible roads from Sarajevo to Spalato would have to be completed, warehouses and deposits enlarged, the surrounding regions pacified, the port structures reinforced. The guiding hand of Rodriga, a man of forceful energy and imagination, was sorely missed.

In a memorandum written in April 1586, Rodriga once again reminded the Senate that navigation had been eroded by competition from various nations and that Venice was risking isolation and suffocation. As a first and urgent measure, the galleys needed to be escorted. This time the Five Sages of Commerce agreed immediately, although for some time there were not enough armed galleys to escort every voyage and guarantee complete safety. Meanwhile, the permit for the Levantine Jews, which expired in 1586, was renewed without question.

Meanwhile, Daniel Rodriga continued to send authoritative suggestions: "It would be best that these galleys not touch the port of Ragusa, because that would be to the disadvantage of our trade; it would provide the opportunity to expand that port and detour diverse merchandise which would reach Ragusa without coming to Venice." Rodriga's plan was to block the Constantinople-Ragusa-Ancona-Florence axis, which would have cut out Venice irremediably. The Five Sages recognized the importance of Rodriga's role in the defense of Venetian trade and became the spokesmen for his ideas before the Senate. In 1585, the project for the port of Spalato was re-examined completely, first by the Five Sages and then by the Senate, which now found itself with no alternative. The Senate looked back to the decisions of 1577 and 1580, which had never been implemented "due to various accidents" (including tacit reservations), and decided that the merchants' galleys would have to dock at Spalato rather than Narenta "to avoid certain and manifest dangers." The investments needed to make the port operative and complete the customs offices were authorized, and the tax on merchandise in transit for Spalato, instituted eleven years earlier, was revoked.

Venetian diplomacy was fired with new energy by these operations. A Venetian consulate was established in Bosnia, and directives were conveyed to the administrators in Zara to have the new pasha of Bosnia authorize the widening of the road between Sarajevo and Spalato. The Five Sages, belatedly convinced of its usefulness, threw themselves into the realization of the project. They called Nicolò Bragadin, who had recently left his post as count of Spalato, and Daniel Rodriga. Not all went smoothly, however; the plan was opposed by the notables of Narenta, who stood to lose much of their merchant traffic to Spalato. It also became necessary to create a network of new, concurrent interests in that area that would involve the leaders of Bosnia and take Turkish needs into account. The right conditions had to be created for a new organization of the traffic, without traumas or "violent resolutions." In Spalato the Turkish merchants would be able to buy salt, rice, and soap more cheaply than in Ragusa or Narenta, but it would all have to follow a pre-established schedule, "without disruption or open ostentation," to avoid antagonizing anyone. The Turks further agreed to deforest certain areas along the road, in order to reduce the danger of ambush. All was in readiness for a permanent, exclusive link between Venice and Spalato, scheduled to become operative in 1590.

In anticipation of this new order of things, the Jewish merchants petitioned the Senate for confirmation of certain privileges. Rodriga, too, addressed a petition to the doge, emphasizing the advisability of increasing the number of Jewish merchants and their families in both Venice and Spalato. He submitted several clauses concerning privileges to be granted both to those who had been living in Venice for some time and to those who would be arriving. The memorandum was entitled: *Capitoli dei Privilegi presentati a piedi di sua Serenità da Daniel Rodriga per nome degli Ebrei mercanti Levantini Spagnoli et altri habitanti in Venetia con le loro famiglie.** The first clause asked "that all the aforesaid merchants may live in safety with their persons, families, merchandise and facilities, suffering no danger or disturbance, thus in this city of Venice as well as in any other city and locality of this Most Serene Dominion, both on land and at sea, whether coming, sojourning or departing, and let it be at their discretion, without any hindrance made, freely sailing to windward or to leeward as do the Venetian citizens." The second clause requested that the merchants "descending from Jewish families, of whatsoever Nation, be allowed to safely practice their religion, without inquisition by any office or magistrate, either ecclesiastical or secular, although they may have lived in another place under another guise or religion, but that after coming to this state, they be allowed to live freely as Jews." If the Most Serene Republic no longer wanted them they should be allowed to leave freely on ships, wagons, or boats, after eighteen months in which

---

*Clauses containing Privileges Presented at the Feet of His Serenity by Daniel Rodriga in the Name of the Levantine, Spanish and Other Jewish Merchants Living in Venice with their Families

to settle their debts and credits. The third clause tackled an issue that was still a sore point after the war with the Turks. In case of war, "either with the Turkish Lord or any other Prince," there would be no retaliation against the merchants; on the contrary, they would be given every assurance of safety and be allowed to carry on their business. The fourth point dealt with the relations between the new Jewish merchants and the German-Jewish pawnbrokers: "The merchants shall not be obliged by this Charter, that runs from the present time into the future, to contribute any tax or duty for the loans that the German Jews make in their banks, but shall be obliged only to pay ordinary Customs duties, remaining free of all other burdens." Finally, Rodriga's document discussed the port of Spalato: Jewish merchants, both in transit and in residence, were to enjoy all privileges, be authorized to lend money, and be treated like any other citizen of the city. They were to be given a place to live with their families, and a cemetery, and be allowed to keep a bank for residents and transients, at terms and conditions to be agreed upon between Daniel Rodriga, consul, and the Magnificent Community.

The Five Sages of Commerce debated the proposal on June 27, 1589. They saw that many of the questions had been raised before, but recognized that the conditions of commerce had changed. They decided, therefore, that a new settlement of Jewish merchants in town could only be a good thing. If their requests were not granted, these Jews would simply go east and return to Venice later as Levantines, and would benefit from the already existing privileges in any case. The Five Sages therefore suggested only a few revisions to the requests and judged the rest acceptable. They did recommend, however, that the newly privileged merchants be forbidden to lend their names to non-privileged merchants for business purposes, and asked that they themselves not be called upon to rule on questions concerning the merchants, since that would increase their work load.

This decision reflected the pragmatic attitude of the Venetian government: it was right to guarantee privileges only to those who did business with their own reserves and capital and could increase the Venetian revenues. And it was made clear that no Jew of any nation would be guaranteed any new privilege unless he had been accepted first by the resident merchants of the University of the Jews and secondly by the Five Sages.

So Daniel Rodriga's proposal was approved, and on July 27, 1589, the text, accepted by the Cabinet, was submitted to the Senate. This was yet another sign of the recent radical change in the Venetian attitude toward the Jews. "The circumstances of the present times give this Council cause to open the way to those wishing to come and live in this city and sojourn in our Dominion." The document reiterated the benefits to the commerce and economic growth of Venice that would result from this new charter.

In the final document, the principal requests were set forth and accepted: the merchants' right to live safely in the town with their families, freedom of worship, and immunity from prosecution for the past. The term of the concessions was set at ten years. The merchants would have to wear the customary yellow hat. No distinction was made between Spanish Jews, Marranos, and new Christians; they were all vaguely referred to as *ebrei ponentini*, or Western Jews. The Senate passed the document. After his long efforts and many struggles, Daniel Rodriga had finally won.

Needless to say, his tenacity had not been the only determining factor. No longer were Ancona and Genoa Venice's only competitors: the continental powers, France, Spain, Portugal, and Holland, were roving through the Mediterranean. The privileges granted to the Iberian Jews and the actuation of the Spalato project were intended, if belatedly, to reconfirm the role of Venice in commerce with the Levant—if not throughout the entire Mediterranean, at least in the Adriatic. There was a significant change in Venetian trading policy: non-Venetian merchants were assured trading rights analogous to those reserved for the select Venetian merchant class. As Ravid observed, this meant that the Western and Levantine Jews, most of whom were descended from Marranos, had rights to which more than 90 percent of the Venetian citizenry could not hope to aspire. But although they were favored in their trade with the East, the Jews were still barred from membership in trade guilds and associations, as well as from retail trade. Unlike other Venetians, who enjoyed hereditary rights, the rights of the Jews had fixed limits in time. A charter might run for two, five, or ten years, and it was always precarious. Nonetheless, it would be unfair not to point out that Venice was at that time the most liberal port in Christian Europe for Jews and Marranos of every description.

The charter of 1589 reflected important changes of attitude not only from an economic standpoint, but also from that of religious relations between Venice and the Jews. The Levantines to whom privileges had been granted in the past were Turkish subjects, formally independent of the Venetian state. Now, the Most Serene Republic was offering residence and desirable business privileges to a category denominated "Western Jews" whose identity was actually ambiguous and uncertain, and who were allowed to revert to Judaism in Venice with the promise that their former lives would not be investigated.

These liberal concessions take on still greater significance if we consider that they apply not only to the Levantines, who hailed from the ports of the Ottoman Empire and lived openly as Jews, but also to the Western Jews, who came directly from the Iberian peninsula where they had been Marranos, often for decades, and who now, in Venice, could safely revert to Judaism.

Following this success, Rodriga continued his preparations for perfecting and launching his project. The port was scheduled to become operative in July 1590. On Rodriga's recommendation, Venice negotiated the liberation of some citizens taken prisoner by the Uskoks and declared exempt from all taxation any Levantine or Western Jew who had left Spalato at least five years earlier and now wished to return. Among them were Daniel Rodriga himself, dubbed "inventor of the port," his brother Petrus and his brother-in-law Isaac De Castris.

This grand enterprise of commercial engineering caused a great sensation at the time. Forty years later, Simone Luzzatto wrote in his *Discorso circa il stato de gl'Hebrei et in particolar dimoranti nell'inclita città di Venetia,* * "The city of Venice will never forget the first inventor of the port of Spalato who was of the Hebrew nation, and who established contacts that brought a large part of the Eastern trade to the city, that port now being considered the most firm and solid foundation for traffic that the city possesses, prevailing over other routes since both the land and sea are much more stable and less exposed to the injuries of fortune."

The port had become a trump card for Venice. In 1591 the Five Sages decreed that all the merchandise should be loaded, in Spalato, onto the "merchant galley" which would leave for Venice under escort. In 1592 a second galley was built for the transport of "large objects," and an escort was also provided for the ships of merchants who did not want to wait at Spalato. This delicate mechanism was organized as Rodriga had so lucidly theorized: the Turks themselves agreed to broaden the roads and organize safe merchant caravans. In 1594 Daniele Da Molin, count of Spalato, reported on the success of the port: the Mediterranean and Adriatic routes had been shortened to reduce danger from the Uskoks, backed by the Holy Roman Empire and implacable enemies of the Turks. In just a few years, thanks to the port, the volume of trade coming through Spalato equalled that of Ragusa.

Rodriga continued to press for measures to guarantee the safety of the port. He asked for better defenses, proposed a new port at Durazzo to encourage the influx of merchandise from Albania, and urged the involvement of the port of Salonika. The Five Sages, convinced of Rodriga's ability, agreed with his ideas but balked at the thought of going as far as Salonika. The risk was too great, they thought. In October 1597, Rodriga began trading with Salonika, insisting that the Venetian supremacy in the Adriatic, against the historic Ancona-Ragusa axis, was at stake.

**Discourse on the State of the Jews, Particularly Those Residing in the Noble City of Venice*

The charter of the Levantine Jews was due to expire that year, and considering the fine results achieved, its renewal seemed a foregone conclusion. But even now, opposition was not lacking. Alvise Sanudo, for one, did not deny the positive side of the initiative but maintained that there were many good Christians capable of doing what Rodriga had done, and that the Jew could not be trusted. But his was an isolated voice. In 1598 the Senate approved a new ten-year charter. In 1602 new galleys were needed, to deal with the growing trade.

Rodriga also mediated in the quarrels between the German Nation, which was operating its banks at a loss, and the Levantine and Western Nations. As the representative of the Western and Levantine Nations, he asked the Venetian authorities to devise a new method of taxation.

This was his last public action. There is no further mention of Daniel Rodriga after 1602. Had he been alive, he would certainly have addressed some new appeal to the Five Sages, as he had been doing for nearly thirty years of his life.

CHAPTER ELEVEN

The University of the Jews in the Sixteenth and Seventeenth Centuries

Discord between Venice and the papacy — The new activities of the German Nation — The Cattaveri, the Five Sages, and the Sopraconsoli, and their attitudes toward "the Ghettos" — Doge Leonardo Donà and the Marranos — The Jewish merchants in the sixteenth and seventeenth centuries — The Interdict — Paolo Sarpi and the baptism of Jewish children — The charter of 1624

After the German and Levantine Nations had settled in Venice, the arrival of Jews from Spain and Portugal, who came to be recognized as the *Natione Ponentina*, or Western Nation, concluded the three consecutive stages of immigration that gave rise to the *Università degli Ebrei*, or University of the Jews, as the Jewish community of Venice was then called. In the years from the peak of the first plague epidemic, in 1576, to the next, in 1630, the presence of the Iberian Jews was explicitly, if controversially, acknowledged by the charter of 1589. This marked the beginning of a slow process of fusion among the various groups in the ghetto, who differed in their culture, language, and even their religious observances.

Almost a century after its founding, the ghetto was developing a definite physiognomy. After years of difficult adjustment, relations between the ghetto and the town were taking on unique characteristics of stability that distinguished the Jewish community in Venice from those of other settlements in the Mediterranean and the rest of Europe. At this time the strong tie between the destiny of Venice and that of her Jews appears clearer than ever before. S. Simonsohn, an Israeli student of Venetian history, points out the close parallel between the development of the Jewish community and that of the Venetian Republic. Jewish Venice represented the sum of many communities: German, Portuguese, Spanish, and Levantine. Each of these groups preserved its own religious traditions; they lived separately, enjoyed different privileges, and had distinct economic functions. They were often in conflict, even while they were joined in a single community organization. With the passing of time the differences waned but, owing partly to the strong, innate Jewish tendency toward individualism, they never disappeared entirely.

Toward the end of the sixteenth century, the political situation in Venice was characterized by forces pressing for change. The emerging power groups styled themselves "innovators" and were called *i giovani* —"the young men." They were the expression of a ruling class that felt the need for greater dynamism in both foreign and domestic policy and favored Venetian autonomy. Leonardo Donà, the chief exponent of the group, fought to reduce papal influence and the authority of the Inquisition in Venice, while considerations of economic and commercial strategy led him to support France and oppose Spain.

There were many reasons for conflict with the Church. In addition to the activities of the Holy Office, in themselves a delicate matter, there was also the refusal of Venice to side against the Turks after Lepanto, as well as differences of opinion over a plan for diverting the Po River and questions of control over agriculture and food production on the Venetian mainland. After centuries of reaching toward the sea, the Venetians were now turning inland, from choice as well as necessity, to exploit the agricultural resources that had become vital after the grain crisis of 1590–91. The strategic need of the Republic to control the food supply merged with the new agricultural vocation of many patricians, eager after generations of seafaring to avoid the perils of the sea and invest their capital in arable land and real estate. At that time much of the arable land was owned by the Church and clergy, and it is not hard to understand why the discord between Venice and Rome was fueled as much by conflicting and often irreconcilable interests as by abstract ideological dissent.

The Senate decisions of 1602 (rental of land to lay farmers who would pay a modest rent to the Church), 1604 (requirement of special authorization to build new churches), and 1605 (prohibition to bequeath real estate to the Church) created a state of tension between Venice and the Papal States that would soon lead to a rupture. Formerly united in the fight against heresy and the Turks, Venice and Rome now stood on opposite sides of a widening chasm. The Holy Office and the Executors against Blasphemy disputed jurisdiction not only over blasphemy, but also over sodomy and gambling. The Executors claimed jurisdiction over matters relating to polygamy, books, and clandestine marriages and also wished to shield the Jews from the jurisdiction of the Holy Office, which had proved so insensitive to Venetian relations with the Ottoman Empire. This issue was of prime interest to the Republic because of her trading activities, in which the Jews played an essential role. Venice attempted to recover her political supremacy, using every means at her disposal and relying especially upon her magistracies (the Executors against Blasphemy, the Avogadori de Comun, and the Five Sages of Commerce) and on the organs of the State (the Cabinet, the Senate, the Council of Ten, and the Administrators of the Mainland). To demonstrate their undisputed authority, the Venetian courts were more than usually severe at this time. In one instance, the Holy Office and the Council of Ten each claimed the privilege of trying a gang of men who had roamed through the city by night, singing curses and obscenities. The Council of Ten denied all jurisdiction to the religious tribunal and sentenced the defendants to death, even though some were patricians. On the mainland, however, where the ecclesiastical court was stronger, the friction was unremitting.

When Pope Paul V succeeded Clement VIII, the situation came to a head. And when, in 1605, Paul V issued an ultimatum against Venice, followed by an Interdict, he was opposed by that staunch defender of Venetian autonomy, Leonardo Donà.

The Venetian Jews, having survived the critical period after Lepanto, resumed their former activities, favored by the calmer international climate and the newly harmonious business relations between the Sublime Porte and the Most Serene Republic. They developed their natural role as business mediators and expanded their activities as small moneylenders and second-hand tradesmen.

After 1573, no further expulsions were discussed. On the other hand, the Jews no longer enjoyed a total monopoly on moneylending: the monti di pietà generally held sway in the major cities of Venetia, while small family-run Jewish pawnshops remained in the smaller villages. These were useful for agricultural credit but of very little significance for commerce on a larger financial scale. It is known that while the interest rate in Venice was 5 percent, banks on the mainland sometimes charged as much as 10 or 12 percent.

Especially in the Papal States, these were auspicious times for the Jews. Up until 1584, Gregory XIII had been very repressive, even attempting to keep Jewish doctors from treating Christian patients. Then in 1585, Sixtus V adopted the policy of certain of his predecessors, encouraging Jews to settle in the Papal States to set up banks and develop commerce there. This liberality was formally expressed in October 1586, in his bull Christiana Pietas. Between 1587 and 1605, the Apostolic Camera issued three hundred permits for new banks in various Italian states, with the exception of Venice. Jealous of her autonomy, Venice would ask no favors of anyone, least of all the pope.

Jewish moneylending in Venice was regulated by the Venetian authorities. The rate of 5 percent was no longer sufficient to defray the expenses of running the pawnshops, so the deficits that accumulated had to be covered by the revenues from other Jewish businesses in the city.

The Jews of the German Nation, the original nucleus of the ghetto at the time of its founding, whose chief activity had been pawnbroking, were finding new sources of income. In 1594, according to British historian Brian Pullan, groups of Jewish second-hand merchants owned thriving shops patronized by many aristocrats and leaders of the Republic. The Cattaveri, in charge of business activities in the New Ghetto, spoke of the brothers Abraham, Benedetto, and Nascinben Calimani, their cousin Isaac Luzzato, Orso Dalla Man, and Iseppo dalla Baldosa as merchants of "some esteem and good name." A year later, in 1595, these same merchants were named heads of the University. The second-hand tradesmen had warehouses whose doors opened onto the ghetto canal, for direct access to barges for loading and unloading. The keys to those gates, like those of the others, were kept by the Christian guards.

In addition to their trading activities, a new auxiliary profession had opened up for the Jews. They were now allowed to act as brokers or intermediaries for business transactions in the ghetto. During the 1580s there were at least twelve Christian brokers in Venice, but some Jews were also allowed to practice this profession in recognition of special merit. Simone and Mosè, two sons of the famous doctor Joseph De Dattolis, were awarded the privilege by special letter from the doge. They could either use their licenses themselves or appoint substitutes, who had to be approved by the Cattaveri. Competition between Jewish and Christian brokers often resulted in disputes and accusations: in the attempt to keep the Jews from moving freely through the town, the Christian brokers often reported them for one infraction or another and maintained that freedom of movement would facilitate illicit sexual contact between Jews and Christians. The Cattaveri then decreed that the Jewish brokers could not make business calls on commoners, but only on the nobility, merchants, and citizens, in the conviction that these classes would be less easily corrupted than the general populace.

Gradually, the Jews were finding their way into new commercial circuits. In 1597, the Senate and the Sopraconsoli agreed to let them take part in the Rialto auctions. The Venetian trade guilds resisted the arrival of these newcomers. The tailors, for example, were especially staunch in their opposition, citing the old rule that Jews were not allowed to manufacture goods even for their own use. Yet many documents attest to a strong trend toward integration of the Jews into the community between 1590 and 1610. Doctors, greengrocers, butchers, hatters, engravers, printers, dancers, and musicians are all mentioned. Special permits multiplied—or at least the requests for them did—

especially in the early seventeenth century. Business often made it necessary to stay out at night, and a special permit was required.

The Cattaveri had given the Jews permission to hire Christian porters and servants, providing they were elderly; the idea was to prevent friendships, intrigues, and love affairs.

Despite the exceptions, the official norm dictating segregation of Jews and Christians remained in force, and every now and then someone spoke up in support of it. Lorenzo Priuli recalled the teachings and concerns of Gregory XIII, according to whom the Jews might seduce Christian women, have children by them, and then take the infants into the ghetto to bring them up as Jews. The ghetto and the town should travel on separate if parallel tracks, especially at night: no Christians in the ghetto or Jews outside. And no Christians should be in the synagogues, especially during Passover. Any Jew who encountered the procession of the Holy Sacrament on Good Friday was expected to withdraw into a side street.

Although they were separate and segregated, the Jews enjoyed codified rights (albeit subject to periodic review) and an often enviable autonomy. The Venetian ghetto assumed an increasingly strong position of leadership among all the other Jewish communities of the Venetian dominions. In 1594, an assembly held in Venice to discuss taxation was attended by eleven representatives from nearly all the mainland Jewish communities and six leaders from the Venetian community alone.

The Cattaveri had appointed agents from the ghetto to collect taxes throughout the region; the sharing of the heavy tax burden was often a source of controversy not only between the Jewish community in Venice and those of the mainland, but also among the three Nations comprising the ghetto community itself. In 1596, the Levantines protested against the German Jews, maintaining that they, the Levantines, were in Venice "due only to the accidents of trade." They did not enjoy the same rights as the others, and therefore should not incur the same obligations. To settle the question a distinction had to be made between Levantine Jews who lived in Venice and were citizens of the Republic and "Transient Levantines subject to the Turkish Lord."

Around the turn of the century the ghetto Jews gradually began to integrate into the urban economy. More and more often, they worked at odd jobs of various kinds, and their role as pawnbrokers had become very different from what it was originally. In addition, the Marranos had acquired a more precise physiognomy, with the original small groups of individuals merging into an organized and respected community. At the beginning of the seventeenth century, this opulent Western Nation was becoming a reality to be reckoned with in the life of the ghetto.

Just at the time when the situation of the Marranos, now called

Ponentini, or Western Jews, was being legalized, the Holy Office was becoming less repressive, partly as a result of the profound discord between Venice and Rome toward the end of the sixteenth century and the beginning of the seventeenth. At a time when the politics of Venice and Rome were widely divergent, a conflict of jurisdiction was inevitable, with clashes between the Inquisition, the Executors against Blasphemy, and the Cattaveri. After the 1580s the Inquisitors rarely interfered with the ghetto. But the Cattaveri, whose job it was to maintain the distance between Jews and Christians at all times, often did step in, along with the Executors against Blasphemy, to prevent sexual relations between Jews and Christians. Only after 1641 did these two offices arrive at a somewhat singular division of labor: the Cattaveri were responsible for sexual relations between Jewish men and Christian women, and the Executors for those between Jewish women and Christian men.

In 1594 Ambassador Paolo Paruta, who had been under pressure from the pope in the past on account of the privileges granted to Levantine and Western Jews in Venice, pointed out that papal policy toward Ancona was no less lenient. Every means was used to encourage Levantine Jews to settle there. The Venetians had no difficulty finding a reply to the accusations of Rome and the party of papal supporters who deftly maneuvered in their city. Leonardo Donà, an opponent of papal influence, leader of "the young men," and later doge, frankly stated the Venetian position vis-à-vis the Marranos. Donà, having lived in Spain for some time, criticized the Spaniards' refusal to accept baptized Jews. As Donà saw it, in their desire for pure bloodlines they had encouraged the preservation of Jewish identity in individuals who, had they not been persecuted, would have assimilated with the Christians. When he became doge of Venice, Donà reminded the papal nuncio that the Marranos were Jews, saying: "At home and in their hearts they live as Jews, they have Turkish or Jewish names by which they are called at home, and outside they have Christian names, and if you ask the children they will tell you: they call me Abramo at home and Francesco in the street." Donà preferred dealing with Jews wearing yellow hats than with false Christians in black hats who attended church hypocritically. That kind of Christianity dishonored God and the city. The ideas of the new doge were consistent with the Venetian love of clarity.

The new agreements with the Western Jews had eliminated ambiguity once and for all and achieved the desired aim of encouraging new merchant forces to settle in the city. Somewhat paradoxically, the strongest opposition to the arrival of immigrants from the West had come from the ghetto Jews themselves, especially from the German Nation, of old Italian and German descent. The newcomers were different from these earlier residents. Their rituals, language, and experiences were different and their strange customs and bizarre behavior created thorny problems for the rabbis. Moreover, they enjoyed privileges and exemptions never granted to the original residents of the ghetto, and this was a source of jealousy and rivalry, felt all the more deeply because the newcomers refused to contribute to the burdensome maintenance of the banks. Many Jews therefore had little liking or sympathy for the Marranos. Housing in the ghetto was scarce, and with the newcomers there was even less room. It must be recognized, too, that for many Marranos, to declare themselves Jews would have meant exposing their relatives in Spain and Portugal to almost certain reprisal. Nor was it a simple matter to change their names and recognize themselves in a new Jewish identity, especially because so many different influences had been superimposed on their original Jewish background during their long travels.

But in Venice, an important possibility had been acknowledged. Anyone who so desired could revert to Judaism, living in the ghetto and wearing the yellow hat in accordance with the laws of the Republic. Once again, Venice was a city of dramatic choices, a city of encounters and conflicts not only for those vacillating between Christianity and Judaism, but also for those enclosed within the ghetto walls. And while the ghetto gained vitality from the new immigrants, the process of acclimatization caused it considerable discomfort.

It was many years before the Italian Jews came to accept these Sephardic Jews, the Marranos. And the Marranos, although they adhered long and tenaciously to their customs and language, finally did blend with the Jewish communities of Italy and conformed to the Jewish tradition. This process of aggregation continued through the entire seventeenth century.

The early seventeenth century was a time of rapid change—almost like the onset of spring, punctuated by clouds and thunderstorms. In Venice it was the season of the Interdict and thriving trade. In 1605, Camillo Cardinal Borghese was elected pope, taking the name of Paul V. He was known to be friendly to Spain, a traditional enemy of Venice. In January 1606, Leonardo Donà, a staunch upholder of Venetian independence from the Church, became doge. Even before his election, he had almost prophetically warned the papal nuncio to avoid excommunications, "because that might follow which would bring dire repentance to those who were its cause." The last straw, the "accident," as Paolo Sarpi called it, was the arrest, in the territory of the Republic, of two clergymen accused of various crimes. The Holy See interceded, demanding that the two be sent to Rome for trial before an ecclesiastical court and that certain laws unfavorable to Church rights be abrogated. The Senate denied the papal requests. After an ultimatum, which Venice ignored, Paul V excommunicated the Senate and issued an Interdict against the entire territory of the Republic.

In the words of Gaetano Cozzi, "It was a time of very difficult political and religious balance. It was said at the time that, taking advantage of the confusion caused by the Interdict, a new reformed Church was being established in Venice with the aid of rulers and reformed groups from across the Alps, a church that would find a champion in no less a personage than Fra Paolo Sarpi." It was an underground movement unknown to the government of Venice, which hastened to deny its existence when the Holy See demanded an account. In his *Trattato dell'Interdetto*,* Paolo Sarpi asserted that "no heresy has ever set foot" in Venice, not an entirely true statement since a large number of Protestants and heretics of other descriptions lived there and counted many followers and sympathizers. Venice, a meeting place for a wide variety of peoples and cultures, was also an ideal center for religious propaganda. According to Sarpi there were ten thousand Protestants in Venice, but most of them were foreigners. There were twelve thousand Greeks. These colonies far outnumbered the Jewish community, although the latter was much more closely intertwined with the history of Venice.

The discord that culminated in the Interdict left a deep rift in the relations between the Most Serene Republic and the papacy. A key figure in that period was Fra Paolo Sarpi, deeply religious but strongly opposed to Church interference. As a theologian and adviser to the Senate, he influenced the policies of the city at the crucial junctures of her conflicts with Rome. The atmosphere was so highly charged that in October 1607 an attempt was made on Sarpi's life: he was critically stabbed near the Santa Fosca bridge in the Cannaregio district.

Sarpi was especially fervent in defending Jews and Marranos from the repeated attacks of the Inquisition. The principles that inspired his political position emerge from analysis of the consultations on issues submitted to the friar's attention by the Venetian government in the years from 1614 to 1617. Sarpi made a clear distinction between heretics, subject to the Inquisition, and Jews, who were considered infidels but came under the jurisdiction of the secular magistracy. As for the Marranos, they could not be considered Christian, and therefore subject to the Inquisition, since their ancestors had been baptized by force. No steps could be taken against them if they reverted to Judaism, even after several generations. Moreover, the Marranos enjoyed a safe-conduct that permitted them to live in the dominions of the Republic, wear the yellow cap, practice their religion in safety, and leave whenever they liked, taking their property with them. They were guaranteed this

---

Treatise on the Interdict

permit for the public good of Christianity, so that they could "bring much wealth and industry from the Turkish lands." These words not only sum up Sarpi's politics, but underlie the concepts that inspired the charters of 1589, 1598, and 1611. Sarpi saw an advantage for the city in her policy toward the Marranos, and justified it by citing the papal actions that had preceded the Counter-Reformist attitude: "And the granting of the safe-conduct is legitimate under the law. It cannot be condemned, since many popes have allowed the Marranos to live in Ancona with privileges even greater than those guaranteed by Venice."

The Serenissima Signoria* abided by the opinion of its trusted theologian and systematically created obstacles for the Inquisition every time that court tried to institute criminal proceedings not only against Jews, which happened fairly seldom, but against Judaizing Marranos. Sarpi himself interceded in more than one instance. In a written opinion dated December 1616, he denied the legitimacy of proceeding against a Portuguese refugee, one Simon Gomez, who was living as a Jew in the Venetian ghetto but who, according to a report from the Inquisition of Pisa, had lived as a Christian there. "To investigate him for things that occurred in other States," wrote Sarpi, "would be to subvert the privileges which for just and necessary reasons have been accorded by the Republic to that nation for many decades, as likewise they are elsewhere by other religious princes, and which cannot be violated without breaking our word."

One especially important opinion by Sarpi is dated June 1616 and refers to the case of a Jewish baby who was baptized in secret, against the will of its mother. Cozzi has stressed the apparent ambiguity of the theologian's opinion, the first part of which ends with the assertion "that it is an act of injustice and a sin deserving of punishment to baptize an incapable child without the consent of its father or mother," and notes that secret baptism has never been considered a valid sacrament. At the same time he notes that the Church, mindful of the forced baptisms performed in overseas missions, was inclined to hold valid a baptism conferred *pro bono religionis.*** Further on, however, having told certain members of the Cabinet what they wanted to hear, he concludes that in this particular case there was no concrete evidence of the baptism actually having taken place. Cozzi emphasizes the calculated ambiguity of Sarpi's rhetoric, which on the one hand fulfills the Cabinet's formal requirement of respect for the Church, and on the other, by virtue of his formidable skill as a debater, extols independence of judgment and concludes with an opinion favorable to the poor Jewish mother. Confirming his interpretation of Sarpi's view,

---

*This supreme organ of government, presiding over the Maggior Consiglio, consisted of the doge, six dogal advisers, and the three heads of the Quarantia al Criminal.
**for the good of the faith

Cozzi writes, "Anyone subsequently referring to that opinion—in practice all legal counsel called upon to deal with similar cases up to the end of the eighteenth century—would interpret it broadly as affirming the principle of the invalidity of forced baptism, which is not incontrovertibly expressed in Sarpi's opinion."

Following Sarpi's lead, Venice introduced into the clause renewing the charter of the German Nation (December 18, 1618) an article remanding to the judgment of the Avogadori de Comun all controversial cases regarding the baptism of Jewish children. "The Avogadori," notes Cozzi correctly, "were not just an ordinary magistracy; their institutional mandate was to defend against anyone, in favor of anyone, the correct enforcement of the laws of the Venetian State. In the exercise of this duty they had grown to symbolize the defense of State prerogatives against the demands of the Holy See."

A dogal letter from the Senate to the administrators of Padua in 1619 clarifies the position of the Republic: "Having received the report on what our law provides (concerning the baptism of Jewish children), we have determined to commit to you, our two representatives, the task of putting an end to all such traffic, in which we charge you not to allow the vicar or any other ecclesiastical bodies to intervene in any manner. Rather, you shall resolve it absolutely, and shall return to the hand of the father who so desires, any minor Jewish children, the judgment to be yours alone; and we further commit to you, in execution of our laws, to resolve it yourselves without any intervention of clergy."

Problems of a religious nature were compounded by those of the patrician oligarchy. Jealous of their time-honored privileges, the nobles were having difficulty adjusting to the new commercial and industrial situation. The Five Sages, consulted by the Senate, had advised continuing the open policy that in 1589 had culminated in concessions to the Western Jews. Not until the summer of 1610 was there an open debate in the Senate on a proposal to modify the laws on the granting of Venetian citizenship *de intus et de extra*—from within and from without. Nicolò Contarini and Nicolò and Antonio Donà spoke in favor of citizenship. With great eloquence, they reminded the Senate of the Venetian tradition: "Foreigners, albeit of different religion and customs, have never been abhorred by this state; dwellings and storehouses have been permitted for the Germans, Turks, Jews, and Marranos." Their adversaries, including the patrician Duodo, feared the supremacy of the Dutch and English, who boasted superior technological strength, and they also feared that greater economic laissez-faire could lead to unpredictable social consequences. They won, but the victory was short-lived.

Change was the sign of the times. The free trade ideology was gaining ground, propelled by an irresistible inner force. The seventeenth century, the age of heresy, was fast approaching, and Venice with her galleys was no longer the unrivaled queen of the seas. Vessels from northern Europe were sighted with increasing frequency in Mediterranean waters. They might be unwelcome, but if Venice wanted to survive she would have to be a reed, not an oak. This widespread feeling of inevitability could not help but arouse strong feelings and stimulate bursts of pride. All the foreign merchants—Dutch, Spanish, French, and English, not to speak of the Turks—were feared, with good reason, not only for their valor, but because they were backed by foreign powers of which they were the "long arm." The Jews of Marrano descent, the Iberian Jews, and the Levantines, dynamic, efficient, and useful intermediaries, may have been mistrusted on religious and social grounds but they gave no cause for political concern. They were, at bottom, the most acceptable and the least to be feared because they had no great powers behind them.

This does not mean the Jews were loved, or even accepted without resistance. In 1603 Alvise Sanudo, acting as spokesman for a group of Venetian merchants, opposed the granting of monopolistic privileges to the Jews "because Venice having invited every Levantine and Western Jew to come to this city with the promise that, regarding customs duties and navigation, they will be treated like Venetian citizens and will never be harassed by any magistrate on account of their religion, so many of this treacherous people have arrived that now the Rialto square at the usual hour is reduced to such a pass that the yellow hats are more numerous than the Christians, to the great amazement of the many nations that come to this city, and there will be still more when, as we expect, those Jews arrive that have left Spain." Sanudo also remarked that formerly, out of a hundred merchants in Constantinople, seventy-five were Venetian and twenty-five were Jews, but that now the ratio was inverted. He may have been exaggerating, but he had certainly touched on a sore point: Venice no longer had a merchant class of her own and needed to rely on foreigners. This problem, which was becoming increasingly acute, heightened the discord between the Venetian magistracies in charge of the ghettos: the Cattaveri, responsible for the New Ghetto, and the Five Sages of Commerce, in charge of the Old. They had already clashed several times in the past over the issue of possession of the keys to the gates of the Old Ghetto.

In 1609 the Levantine charter was nearing its expiration, and this occasioned a new conflict between the Cattaveri, on the one hand, who wanted to extend their influence to the Old Ghetto, and the Five Sages and the Levantine Jews on the other. The Levantine Jews were still unwilling to share their privileges with anyone, refused to contribute to the expenses of the banks, and wanted to remain under the jurisdiction of the Five Sages, who had proved more sensitive to the specific demands of trade.

In 1611, the question of trade once more came up for discussion.

One of the Sages again pointed out the role of the Levantine Jews in the wool and silk trade with Spalato and Constantinople, insisting that Venice needed to keep offering privileges that would attract merchants from the Netherlands as well. At this point the German Nation requested permission to engage in trade with the Levant, a request reiterated more forcefully in 1618 when the Five Sages considered expanding Venetian trade in Flanders.

The Senate was well aware of the valuable service performed by the Jewish merchants. In 1620 it acceded to repeated requests to abolish the taxes on brokerages. In 1622 Moise Israel and Davide Navarro proposed new trade toward the West, with ten thousand ducats' worth of merchandise to be exported to Tunisia and Algeria over land routes through France and Spain. The Five Sages and the Senate voted in favor, and even agreed to reduce the red tape entailed in the authorization for such commerce. These minor changes attest to the victory of a more liberal and less protectionist policy. A little customs evasion was a small price to pay for a larger volume of trade.

By 1621 the number of Jews in Spalato had grown from the original two or three households to some two hundred people. Their activity caused jealousy, and reports reached Venice of "the disorders that ensued from the Jews being scattered throughout the town" and of the need to confine them to a ghetto and impose on them "some tax for the public good."

In Corfu, too, a Jewish community prospered, buying real estate and renting baronies and estates. In November 1622, Giust'Antonio Bellagno, the public prosecutor in Dalmatia, observed that there were seven hundred Jews on Corfu. Of these, only a hundred were natives and the rest were Spanish.

A century had now passed since the founding of the Venetian ghetto in 1516, and the ghetto had lived through three distinct phases.

The first phase, with the arrival and settlement of the German Nation, had led to the founding of the ghetto. These were the years of Jewish pawnbrokers and heavy taxes levied on them to finance investments for the Arsenal, the strengthening of the fleet, and other pressing expenditures. The banking operations were explicitly requested by the Republic, and the Jews enjoyed a fair degree of autonomy in the management of their business.

The second phase, beginning in 1540, culminated with the settlement of the Levantine Nation. At that time Venice attempted to reduce the wealth of the Jewish community by exerting stronger fiscal and religious pressures. The Christians, who had formerly deposited large sums in the banks in the expectation of healthy earnings from their lending activities, withdrew their money and their confidence.

After Lepanto, which marks the opening of the third phase, and from the acceptance of the Western Nation in 1589 up to the great plague of 1630, the Venetian Jews were obliged to run banks for the poor. The banks had by now become a sort of secular *monte di pietà*, operating at a loss for the most part, for which the Jews were forced to provide the operating capital and cover the deficits. In the face of a declining economy, the new Jewish merchants, both Levantine and Western, contributed to revitalizing the Levant trade and, despite their many protests, to covering the chronic deficits of the ghetto pawnshops. By the end of the sixteenth century, the Venetian Jews were no longer bankers in fact but only in name, employees of institutions that had no administrative autonomy and were shackled by rigid government controls.

By the beginning of the seventeenth century, the German, Levantine, and Western Nations were settled and firmly ensconced "in the Ghettos of Venice." From now on the history of "the Ghettos" would be that of a single ghetto, a melting pot of many worlds and cultures.

CHAPTER TWELVE

The Ghetto of Venice a Century Later: Society, Religion, and Culture

The etymology of the word ghetto — *The environment* — *The synagogues* — *How the ghetto was organized* — *The rules of the Italian School* — *The cultural debate* — *Jewish doctors in Padua* — *The* Great Book — *The notaries' documents* — *Population figures*

A hundred years of tormented history had forged for the Jewish ghetto a well-defined role in Venetian life. Zaccaria Dolfin, the Venetian patrician whom Marin Sanudo quotes in his *Diarii* as having said "the Jews are ill-placed on the earth," and who recommended that they "should all be sent to live in the New Ghetto which is like a castle, and build drawbridges and wall it in," could never have imagined the far-reaching consequences of his demands, or the fortune the term *ghetto* was to enjoy the world over, with historians and linguists hotly debating its etymology. The commonly accepted opinion is that *ghetto* is a Venetian word denoting an enclosed area where the Jews were obliged to live. In earlier times, the site occupied by the ghetto was the site of a foundry, called *geto* in Venetian dialect (from the word *gettare*, meaning to cast). Early in our century, Emilio Teza, basing his opinion on data found in Tommaso Temanza's *Antica pianta dell' inclita città di Venezia*, confirmed that the term *ghetto* had been in use for many centuries in Venice, and in the fifteenth and sixteenth century was written *geto* or *getto*.*

Temanza writes: "The large island that is now home to the majority of Jews, called the New Ghetto, adjacent to the Rio di San Girolamo, was a swampy lowland. The neighboring island, toward Cannaregio,

---

*The Italian "ge" is pronounced "je" as in "jet"; therefore: "jeto" or "jetto"

called the Old Ghetto, was dedicated to the Public Foundries, and was the seat of the Magistracy that governed them. The place was therefore called *getto*. There were twelve furnaces there, whence waste products and flakes were strewn, time and again, over the nearby swamp. In this manner little by little the island was reclaimed, and the houses seen on it today were later walled up, which before the Jews set foot there in 1516 were inhabited by numerous Christian families."

Giuseppe Tassini, in his *Curiosità veneziane,** cites Temanza and says that those foundries had been in existence since the fourteenth century: "As we read in a document dated May 29, 1306: *Cum tempore quo diminuta fuerunt salaria, fuisse diminutum salario Nicolao Ajmo qui est officialis ad ghettum.*"** Tassini also says that the foundries "had ceased to exist, however, since the dawn of the fifteenth century, for in 1418 a certain Gasparino de Lon, forty years of age, cited as a witness in a lawsuit between the parish priests of San Geremia and San Ermagora e Fortunato, said that the place *'ideo vocabatur el getto quia erant ibi ultra dodecim fornaces'*† adding that he had seen them in his youth." Tassini is referring to the Old Ghetto, to which the New Ghetto was probably added later as a deposit for waste matter from the foundry. The Jewish settlements followed the reverse itinerary: first the New Ghetto, then the Old.

In *Venetia città nobilissima e singolare*, Francesco Sansovino spells the word *ghetto*, adding, "For as this site was frequented by many peoples of every language and country, there also came the Jews, who had first lived on Spinalunga whose name was later changed and called, after them, Giudecca." In the second edition of Sansovino's book, published in 1604, Giovanni Stringa says the word *getto* is associated with the foundry, but this remark was deleted from the 1663 edition.

The origin of the words *ghetto* and *giudecca* was a source of uncertainty for many illustrious scholars, Venetian and otherwise, including Muratori and Vettor Sandi.

In our century, Ravid has pointed out that the original documents establishing the ghetto in 1516 contain the spellings *geto* and *getto*, and that after 1541 we find *ghetto, gheto, geto,* and *getto*. He therefore feels that the origin of the word is clear and that any remaining doubts must concern the connection between *getto* and the verb *gettare*.

In October 1984, the Venetian historian Marco Morin brought to light certain documents in the Venetian State Archives that would seem to dispel any doubt: on September 2, 1360, the Cabinet ruled that

---

*Venetian Curiosities

**Since at the time when stipends had been cut, there had been a cut in the stipend of Nicolaus Ajmo who was an official in the ghetto.

†is called *el getto* for this reason, namely, because there are more than twelve furnaces there

all copper brought to Venice should be taken to the "geto" for refinement[1] before being sold, and that a foundry worker was to supervise the operation: "*Constitutus fuit affinator geti Raminis per collegium.*"[2]* In a ruling by the Cabinet on March 2, 1414, the word appears spelled with an *h*: "*Quod auctoritate huius collegij Raminis datur libertas provisoribus nostris et officialibus ghetti raminis.*"[3]**

The word *ghetto*, theoretically of Venetian origin, soon spread to many cities of Italy. In 1562 Pope Pius IV refers to it in his bull with the meaning of an enclosed place, where the Jews were obliged to live. In his famous bull *Cum nimis absurdum*, dating from the 1550s, Pope Paul IV refers to the Jewish enclosure: the word *ghetto* is not yet used.

In the 1570s, the word *ghetto* is used with its modern connotation in public documents in Tuscany, and in the eighties we find it in Padua and Mantua.

Further evidence is provided by a letter written at the end of the sixteenth century and published in 1890. The Modenese ambassador to Venice writes that since 1516 the Jews had been confined in a part of the city where artillery was cast, called *gietto* and, later, *getto*.

Despite the copious documentation, the origin of the word *ghetto* has been debated even in our own time. One of the most subtle interpretations is that of Joseph Baruch Sermoneta, who has based his re-examination of certain questions on the identification of a new literary source. Sermoneta, aware of Dolfin and Teza's use of the word as well as of its early use in the official documents of the principal sixteenth-century States, advances different hypotheses: namely, that *ghetto* derives from the Hebrew *get* (repudiation or divorce), from other early Germanic words, or from Syrian or Yiddish. He recognizes the plausibility of the generally accepted theory, but, as a student of linguistics, he comments that "for the latter [the linguists], the interpretation of the word *ghetto* as having evolved from an original word *getto* or *geto* leaves a residue which is obscure and, above all, phonetically difficult to credit." Sermoneta concludes, "In other words, the historic event that marked the birth of the word *ghetto* as a well-defined socio-cultural institution was unable to satisfy with equal facility the rules of phonetics, which do not generally admit the passage from the palatal *ge* to the guttural *ghe*." This was precisely the opposite of Teza's theory, as stated in his article: "Etymology, whether it succeeds in its aims or merely attempts to do so, should remain the servant of history, not

---

[1]Venetian State Archives: Collegio Notatorio Reg. 1 31V
[2]Venetian State Archives: Collegio Notatorio Reg. 2 135 V 16 febbraio 1388 mv
*He was appointed as the refiner of the copper foundry by the Cabinet.
[3]Venetian State Archives: Collegio Notatorio Reg. 5, 1R
**By the authority of the Cabinet of Venice a franchise is given to our provosts and to the officials of the copper foundry.

the tyrant." But Sermoneta advances a new theory, based on a source according to which the word *ghetto*, as an enclosed place where the Jews were obliged to live, appeared twenty years prior to 1516.

In 1536, a collection of responsa by David Ha-Cohen, the rabbi of Corfu, was printed in Hebrew in Constantinople. It contains an interesting description of the Jewish exodus from Spain in 1492. At a certain point we read, *"V'lakechu otham, ha-malachim b'ghetto v'horidum mechutz l'ir,"* meaning, "The sailors took them [or put them] into the ghetto, making them disembark outside the city," where *ghetto* could mean dike or jetty. All Sermoneta's observations are based on the hypothesis that the text dates from 1492 or shortly thereafter, and on the equivalency between "pier" and "ghetto" from the Latin *jectus* (stone dike or jetty). The phonetic transformation would then be justified by the distortion of the words as pronounced by Judeo-Spanish refugees and incorrectly understood by the Italian Jews.

More recently, in 1961, S.A. Wolf attempted to demonstrate that *ghetto* is derived from a Provencal word, *gaita*—meaning guard, for the four sentinels that guarded the ghetto. Jews from Provence could have imported the word to Venice. But the Jews themselves, in Venice and in cities of Italy, called their ghetto *chazir* (which in Hebrew means "enclosure"), and in Venetian it became *hasser*.

In reviewing these various theories, we should emphasize that most historians favor the Venetian origin of the word *ghetto*. Linguistic, historical, and etymological questions aside, it was amidst the canals and narrow streets of Venice that the tiny ghetto grew to its final complex form, incorporating economic, cultural, social, and religious aspects unique in their relationships with the Most Serene Republic of Venice and with the entire known world to the east and west.

Life in the Venetian ghetto during its first hundred years was never static. It changed constantly, sometimes violently, not only because of the alternating immigration and emigration of small groups, but also owing to the influx of larger masses that brought the three most important groups in ghetto history, the German, Levantine, and Western Nations, into close proximity, despite their own wishes. The three Nations differed widely in all their cultural characteristics, as well as in their legal status under the jurisdiction of the Venetian magistracies, who distinguished them not only according to their economic roles as moneylenders or merchants, but also with regard to the privileges the Republic granted—greater privileges went to the new arrivals, while the pawnshops sank under the weight of continual taxation.

Isolated and marginal with respect to the city, the ghetto was the Jewish space, the scene of all Jewish life at that time. The New Ghetto, where the pawnshops were, was entered through long porticos, narrow passageways running beneath buildings sometimes as tall as nine stories, as we can see from certain eighteenth-century cadastral records. The *"campo,"* or square, was a broad circle with all the windows of the houses facing inward. The "Campo del ghetto novo" is still circular today, but on one side the old houses have been replaced by the nineteenth-century Jewish Rest Home for the elderly, and part of this picturesque stage set, the side toward the canal called Rio di San Girolamo, has thus been lost. The tall structures probably stood out even more then than they do today, for there were fewer buildings in the area, which was a district of gardens, convents, and monasteries, with unpaved, muddy roads. The public staircases in the buildings were made of wood. To avoid excess weight, all the partitions and structures separating the rooms were also wooden, as were those dividing the garrets and covered roof-terraces and separating the small flats with their low ceilings and common lavatories.

A variety of tongues was heard in the ghetto. Hebrew chants and Mediterranean dialects were superimposed on the colorful tones of Spanish, Turkish, Portuguese, and Greek, along with the argot spoken by some of the Polish and German refugees and with the many Italian dialects: a true Babel of people and tongues, where adventurers and ambiguous Marranos stood out, different in everything, even to the color and style of their garments, living testimonials to the customs of far-off lands.

The rhythm of daily life was marked by the traditional morning, afternoon, and evening prayers, and at night by the closing of the gates and the boat making its rounds on the canals. The great square, a center of Jewish and Christian life during the day, after dark became a sort of independent Jewish republic in the heart of Venice. At night the stage of the New Ghetto emptied, leaving outside its gates the buyers of second-hand clothing and those who by day lined up outside the pawnshops. All was still in the Old Ghetto, a long street intersected by tortuous alleys: Calle Storta, Corte del Moresco, Corte dell'Orto, Calle Barucchi, Campiello delle Scole, Scale Matte. Further on, joined by a narrow little bridge, was the Ghetto Novissimo (the Newest Ghetto), established in 1633, with elegant small buildings but no shops or synagogues, a residential quarter for the latest arrivals. Each of the three ghettos was unique, and their physical proximity masked a conflict of ingrained habits.

In the trapezoidal New Ghetto, the first synagogues had been built, squeezed in and almost hidden among the houses. Here were the *scola grande todesca*, the Great German School, built in 1528, the *scola Canton* (1531), and the *scola italiana* (1571).

The German School is still recognizable from the outside, with its five large arched windows, two of which are now walled up. Inside, the plan is asymmetrical; the women's gallery, close to the ceiling, attenuates this irregularity in a twisted ellipse. The pews date from the Renaissance, in contrast with the pomp of the gilding on the walls, added later. On the walls are commemorative and celebrative inscriptions. The *aron*, or ark, flanked by two large windows, rests on four pink steps bearing the name of the donor. The *bimah*, or pulpit, is stylized but well suited to this dynamic structure, which creates the illusion of a regularly proportioned room.

The Canton School, another Ashkenazic synagogue, has undergone many restorations, as recorded on the marble plaques inside. The name Canton could be that of the family that financed its construction, or it might be derived from the position of the building on the corner (in Venetian dialect the word *canton* means corner), or the synagogue might have been built by German Jews of French origin, in which case the word would mean "canton," or district. A seventeenth-century map published in Paris in fact defines the ghetto as "Canton des Juifs." The present *bimah*, after much restoration, dates from the seventeenth century. Five wooden steps raise it above the level of the hall, and it is framed by a semielliptical arch supported by a double pair of openwork columns in the form of intertwined branches.

The Italian School is recognizable by its five large windows surmounted by a coat of arms bearing the words "Santa Comunità italiana 1575," and by a small cupola over the pulpit. A small plaque on the wall commemorates the destruction of the Temple in Jerusalem.

The two largest synagogues, and the last to be built, are the Levantine School and the Spanish School, which face one another in the Old Ghetto across a small square called "campiello delle Scole."

The Levantine School was built at about the same time the Levantine merchants were granted permission to reside in the city. It is identifiable from the outside by the polygonal structure projecting from the facade, a characteristic element of Venetian architecture known as *diagò*, or *liagò*. Inside is an evocatively beautiful wood pulpit with richly carved floral motifs and high twisted columns, attributed to the famous Bellunese sculptor Andrea Brustolon. On the opposite wall is the simple marble *aron*. The structure of this synagogue is typical of the Renaissance, even though the interior was restored a century later.

The Spanish School, the largest of the Venetian synagogues, dates from the second half of the sixteenth century. Its congregation consisted of Jews and Marranos who had come to Venice from Spain. According to tradition, it was completely restored by Baldassare Longhena in 1635. Subsequent restorations in the nineteenth century partially altered its earlier harmony. The simplicity of the exterior is in contrast to the refinement of the furnishings, brass chandeliers, and gilded wood. The *aron* and *bimah* face one another on the two short sides of the rectangular hall. The polychrome marble and the decoration of the oval matroneum bannister are fine examples of Venetian Baroque.

The Spanish School in the Old Ghetto.

The Italian School in the New Ghetto.

A corner of the old Jewish cemetery, on the Lido.

In the New Ghetto were the famous pawnshops, black, red, and green, and at ground-floor level, all round the square, were the second-hand shops. In the Old Ghetto the Levantines had their warehouses and there were a few greengrocers and kosher butchers. All the ground floors in the New Ghetto were probably used for business; of the estimated sixty thousand square meters available at that time, at least twenty-five thousand must have been shops and public facilities, including synagogues. If it is true that the population reached five thousand in an area of thirty-five thousand square meters (a maximum figure, which would have lasted for only a short period of time), we can calculate the average space per capita as seven square meters. Even allowing a considerable margin for error, it is clear that the space was very cramped. Such overcrowding contrasted strangely with the spaciousness and opulence of the prayer-houses, attesting not only to the generosity and commercial success of the latest arrivals, but also to the importance of the synagogue as a gathering place in the daily life of the Jews. In discussing the population density in the ghetto, one source says that "eight or ten individuals lived squeezed into one place, and with a great stench." One result of this intolerable situation was the building, in 1633, of a new block adjacent to the two earlier areas but reached by crossing a canal. This was the Ghetto Novissimo, the Newest Ghetto, which completed the urban development of the Jewish quarter.

The houses in the ghetto were not owned by the Jews, who were forbidden to own real estate. But Jews were granted a special privilege known as the *Jus gazakà*, an expression combining Latin and Talmudic Hebrew. It had various connotations and indicated the presumption of a legal relationship. The term took on the meaning of "having the right to a specific place and a specific house"; that is, not a right of ownership, but a right to guaranteed rental conditions valid for a specific person. The right could be inherited, bestowed as a dowry, given away, or sold.

By the end of the seventeenth century, after the completion of the three Ghettos, the Most Serene Republic recognized the leaders of the University, the body that united the three component Nations, as their regular interlocutors.

The leaders, or *parnassim*, were elected by a general assembly called the *Kahal Gadol*, whose numbers varied, as did its proportional representation of the different groups. In the latter part of the sixteenth century there were twelve leaders. In 1585 the assembly reduced the number to six. These six formed a small executive council, the *Va'ad Katan*, which could pass a motion only by a majority of two-thirds. To be elected a leader of the Jewish community was of course a mark of esteem, but it was also a moral obligation. Caught between the pressing demands of the Republic, which frequently amounted to blackmail, and the criticism and quarrelsomeness of their constituencies, the leaders often found themselves in an embarrassing position. In 1585, as Pullan relates, certain eminent Jews firmly refused to assume this burden and threatened to emigrate if an attempt were made to force them to accept it. They committed considerable sums to proving that their threats were serious.

At the beginning of the seventeenth century, the University of the Jews was governed by the Va'ad Katan, the executive council, elected every two-and-a-half years by the Kahal Gadol. This general assembly was presided over by a *parnas*, or leader, and included anyone who could afford to pay a tax of twelve ducats. In 1594, according to Pullan, the assembly comprised about seventy Venetian Jews, plus the six leaders of the Jewish community and eleven Jews from the mainland who represented most of the rural settlements. In the seventeenth century, the Kahal Gadol consisted of sixty Western, twelve Levantine, and forty German Jews, just over a hundred people. Given the population of the ghetto, this assembly could hardly be said to represent the entire community.

Anyone could be elected *parnas*, but no more than twice, and the proportional representation of the different Nations always had to be taken into account within the general assembly. Each Nation also had its own assembly: the Germans and Levantines called it *Kahal*, and the Western Jews *Talmud Torah*. The business of each group was discussed in these separate assemblies, which were concerned not only with economic and legal issues, such as relations with the various magistracies that controlled the community, but also with ritual and religious questions according to the traditions of the different groups. The general assembly was concerned with more general matters such as hygiene, kosher butchers, the Christian guards, and subsidies for the neediest families. The University thus enjoyed considerable autonomy within the confines of the ghetto, with far-reaching responsibilities concerning taxes, expenditures, synagogues, cemeteries, and so forth. Under no circumstances, however, could they engage in any political activity.

It was difficult to ascertain exactly how much tax each person owed on capital and income. Such taxes were seen primarily as a moral obligation and paid for this reason alone. Some of the tax money was used to defray the current expenses of the ghetto and to support its permanent personnel: the *shochet*, or ritual butcher, the *chazan*, or cantor, and the *shammash*, in charge of synagogue services. But most of it went to pay the taxes due the Venetian government under the charters. The issue of taxation, which had always colored the life of the community and its relations with Venice, was of vital importance, and tax collection in the ghetto was organized with special care in an effort to distribute the excessive demands of the Republic fairly among the members of the community. To avoid resentment, the tax collectors, called *tansadori*, were always carefully selected. In the synagogue, they solemnly swore on the scrolls of the Law to carry out their task with exemplary diligence. In 1589, 200 out of 1,700 Jews were reported to have been subject to taxation in Venice. The *tansadori* were sometimes escorted on their rounds by the Cattaveri, who were responsible for protecting them. In some cases the Cattaveri requested the collaboration of the Jews in their attempts to find out whether stolen goods were being sold in the ghetto.

By 1663, the various groups in the ghetto were already fairly well integrated. The executive council, the Va'ad Katan, consisted of seven members: three German, three Western, and one Levantine Jew. The Ashkenazim, or German Jews, still had a numerical majority in the ghetto, but the system of taxation reduced their representation in the Va'ad Katan. Interpenetration among the different groups of Jews was accelerated by an increasing number of mixed marriages, and gradually the differences between the groups began to fade, although they never disappeared entirely.

The rabbis, whose positions had for years been distributed among the Nations according to criteria of influence, were later elected as the spiritual leaders of the entire community on the basis of reputation and personal merit. The rabbis' role, too, changed with time. Once teachers, they had become preachers and judges, authoritative interpreters of the Law. The increased significance of their role and the importance of their interpretations of doctrine may themselves have been the result of the lower general level of Jewish culture and the consequent need for more cultivated and capable guidance. The rabbis were paid by the community, and their contracts ran for a limited term. Supervisors and scribes assisted them in their everyday duties. Being a rabbi in Venice was of course a privilege, given the influence that the University of the Jews in Venice exerted over the other Jewish communities of Venetia, with the direct encouragement of the Senate. Jealous of their autonomy, the Jewish communities of Verona and Padua more than once attempted to shake off this paternalistic and interested guardianship of their religious as well as their fiscal affairs.

The pawnshops, whose losses were charged to the University, were not run directly by the general assembly, but were sublicensed to Jewish bankers, subject to surveillance by both the University and the Venetian State through the Sopraconsoli. But it was the University that bore the primary responsibility for their smooth operation and the accuracy of their financial management, in observance of detailed regulations laid down by the Venetian Senate.

A set of regulations for the Italian School, dated 1664 in the Hebrew register, or *Pinkes,* is an important document of ghetto society. The manuscript, found by Rabbi Riccardo Pacifici a few decades ago in the library of the Talmud Torah of the Italian School, unfortunately disappeared a few years later and has never been found. The register contained *regolationi,* or statutes, and minutes of the assembly of the Italian Jews in Venice, as well as a statute enacted in 1644 with a list of the names of the Italian *Kahal,* minutes of earlier discussions, since lost, and a list of the *parnassim* from 1650 to 1763. It is reasonable to suppose that other groups also drew up documents of the same kind, which have subsequently been lost. The statute remained in effect for ten years; the *Kahal* would renew it when it expired, appointing legislators to make any necessary changes.

Among the Italian Jews, as we see from the statute of 1644, the Va'ad, or council, consisted either of permanent members, who attended the Italian School and paid their taxes regularly, or members elected by the council with a quorum of at least 75 percent. The sons of former members were admitted after their thirtieth birthday (as ruled later, in 1654), upon approval by the council. Anyone who had transferred to another synagogue, or had not attended services on the major holidays or for ten consecutive sabbaths, was considered a nonmember. To be considered fully legitimate, the council had to have a quorum of at least two-thirds.

The *parnassim* relied on the *shammashim* to urge the members to participate. Anyone who was late or absent was fined half a ducat, and anyone who failed to vote was fined five ducats. Voting by proxy was not permitted, and no outsiders were admitted to meetings. Half of the fines went to the Cattaveri, and the other half was used for running the synagogue, under the supervision of the three *parnassim,* who served for a year and swore on the Torah to fulfil their duties faithfully. They had the honor of distributing Torah and Tefillah readings. The public Tefillah readings often provoked heated discussions; anyone whose lot was drawn for a public reading and refused to officiate was heavily fined. The *parnassim* were also in charge of administering donations and taxes: anyone who failed to pay was publicly denounced on the eve of Yom Kippur. At the end of their term, they had to present a detailed statement of accounts.

Other honorary posts were held by the *gabbaim,* who acted as secretaries, the *parnas* of the Shèmen La-Maor, that is, the person who supervised offerings of oil and money for the illumination of the synagogue, and the *parnas* in charge of collecting contributions for the poor Jews who lived in Palestine. The offices of *chazan,* or cantor, and *shammash,* the beadle of the synagogue, were salaried posts assigned by public competition.

Later fragments of regulations from the Italian School were found some years ago by Rabbi Abramo Piattelli. These, too, stress the prohibition against members' attending other synagogues, on pain of heavy fines.

Within the ghetto, the synagogues were not the only places where people gathered to pray or study. There were also the *midrashim* and the academies, schools funded and supported by groups of individuals, or by those families to whom scholarship was most important. The *midrashim* of the Luzzatto, Vivante, and Meshullam families were among the most illustrious.

There were a great many charities with picturesque names, such as "For Marrying Maidens," "For Ransoming Captives," and "For Assistance in Childbed." Each and every aspect of Jewish life came under the aegis of a specific organization. Events of special importance in Jewish society were circumcisions, visits to the sick who lived alone, and preparations for funerals.

Many trades were practiced on a small scale in the ghetto, in addition to the sale of second-hand clothes. There were craftsmen, small tradesmen, and dyers. Printing and tailoring, however, were prohibited, as was any profitable occupation that might have encroached on the territory of the Venetian guilds. Without ever being printers in their own right, many Jews worked as typesetters, proofreaders, and bookbinders in the publishing houses owned by Venetian aristocrats. Others produced oil and kosher foods, distilled wine, or kept inns for Jewish travelers.

A society like that of the Jews, with its insatiable thirst for learning, was bound to produce illustrious humanists, writers—many of whom, then as now, worked for publishers—artists, and physicians. Medicine was an especially popular profession among the Jews, affording not only material advantages but, given the precarious condition of Jewish life, a measure of security not to be underrated, thanks to the privileges the medical class had always enjoyed.

From 1517 to 1721, two hundred and fifty Jewish students graduated from the University of Padua, and many more attended its courses without attaining a degree. Many of their names are known to us: Josef Del Medigo, Josef Hamuz, Tobias Cohen, David Nieto, Isaac Contarini, and Salomon Conegliano are a few. The University of Padua was subordinate to Venice, and the special conditions of freedom that allowed the admission of Jewish students are yet another aspect of Venetian policy that so often distinguished it from the contemporary norm. Not all the Jewish students came from the ghetto of Venice; they hailed from all over Italy and the Eastern lands, where many returned after graduation. The university was renowned throughout Europe, and its medical school taught philosophy in addition to medical subjects, for the degree conferred was in Medicine and Philosophy. Not until the seventeenth century was there an increase in courses more specifically pertaining to medicine.

Jewish students in Padua were never segregated. On the contrary, they were assimilated into the university environment. A Jew who went to study at Padua underwent a traumatic experience of integration, thrown from his closed ghetto into an open student community, where he encountered difficulties of language, culture, and religion (observance of the Sabbath, kosher food), and was charged higher fees than the other students. To preserve his Jewish identity, the student needed a great capacity for adaptation.

The experience of the Jewish students in Padua, with its benefits and its problems, foreshadowed the more widespread Jewish intellectual revolution in Europe that would accompany first the Age of Enlightenment and later the emancipation of the ghetto, when Jews, free at last, were obliged to compete with the world beyond the ghetto walls.

In April 1616, the Venetian Senate, on the strength of Paolo Sarpi's opinion, examined the question of the degrees earned by Jewish and Greek students at Padua. Because such degrees did not entail a profession of faith to the Church, they constituted one of the many as yet unresolved problems in the relations between Venice and the papacy. Sarpi wrote: "Those who need the authorization of Your Holiness for the validity of their doctorates will not refuse to receive them in the manner that you wish. But those to whom a show of dependency on the Roman court, by swearing an oath that they consider bondage, would constitute an impediment, will be in no way damaged by any annulment Your Holiness might decree."

The Jewish students at Padua of Polish and Levantine origin showed a special inclination for kabbalistic ideas. In the 1570s, a critical period in the history of the ghetto, the Kabbalah exerted a strong fascination, and study of the Zòhar was widespread. Violent controversies broke out between Kabbalists and Talmudists. German and Levantine Jews united in a bitter polemic against the book *Me'or Enayim* by Azaria de Rossi, a scholar accused of yielding to the seductions of the Zòhar. De Rossi at first resisted, but he finally agreed to make numerous changes in his book and to add an appendix that softened its polemical edge and contributed to placating his adversaries, including Rabbi Samuel Judah Katzellenbogen, one of his most ferocious critics. This episode marked the culmination of Ashkenazic influence on the religious life of the ghetto.

Toward the end of the sixteenth century, Azaria da Fano, known for his strong kabbalistic leanings, was the protagonist of a radical transformation of the public ritual through the publication of a prayerbook reflecting the Italian tradition, in which even the Kaddish for the dead, one of the masterworks of Hebrew religious poetry, was revised. This growth of kabbalistic influence and ritualism in the sphere of daily prayer, which had always been dominated by Talmudism, may be considered a true moment of transition in the Jewish culture of the time. A century of continuous immigration had transformed the once monolithic Venetian Jewish society into a model of pluralism. Once static, with the repetitive clockwork rhythms of its shops and banks, it had become dynamic with the comings and goings of the Levantine merchants.

This marked fragmentation and ethnic pluralism within the ghetto was visible in the different positions taken by its various groups with respect to the Christian society outside. The Germans and Italians, more deeply rooted, were more open to dialogue, while the latest arrivals from the West were more introverted and mistrustful. The Ashkenazim were divided among themselves: on the one hand were the Germans, who had lived in Venice and Venetia for decades; on the other, the more recent immigrants from the East. The Sephardim, both Levantine and Western, also bore the marks of their more or less remote experiences in Spain and Portugal, alongside those of a certain superficial Turkish influence. The Hebrew language, spoken with many different accents, may well have been the only element common to the different groups in the ghetto and was the only idiom in which individuals of disparate origin could converse, until they all eventually absorbed the singsong cadence of the Venetian dialect. For a long time, the Sephardim spoke Ladino (Judeo-Spanish), while the Ashkenazim used various forms of Yiddish. The latter soon fell into disuse, however, and had almost disappeared by the end of the seventeenth century. But in the early years of that century Yiddish (a language combining elements of German and Hebrew) was still used by the Ashkenazim in the ghetto, as attested by Leone da Modena in his *Historia de' Riti Hebraici*. The learned rabbi complains, among other things, that the Venetian Jews knew too little Hebrew. Little by little, a Judeo-Venetian idiom evolved, of which very few traces remain today, and only in the memory of the oldest Venetian Jews. It resulted from the introduction of Hebrew words or expressions into the Venetian dialect and the formation of words that were part Hebrew, part Venetian. This idiom never became a full-fledged dialect or a language like Yiddish, but remained at the level of a private jargon, used primarily to keep the Christians from understanding.

Leone da Modena and Simone Luzzatto, members of the ghetto's original nucleus, often criticized the customs and attitudes of the newcomers. But Joseph Ha-Cohen reproached the Ashkenazim, perhaps a bit too harshly, in his *Emek ha-Bakha*, blaming their misfortunes on their own vices. The Marrano Sephardim continued to be a thorn in everyone's side for many years: they posed new and disconcerting questions, and their religious and cultural backgrounds contained the seeds and echoes of heretical philosophies.

This composite environment was a fertile terrain for the birth of original ideas. The complexity of its rituals and customs is exemplified by a *Haggadah* with translations into Spanish, Italian, and Yiddish, so the Passover tale would be accessible to all, and prayer books translated into many different languages. The three Nations, living together in such cramped quarters, set down detailed and rigid rules: the internal organization of the ghetto was so meticulous that more than one student has called it a "republic within the Republic."

If we give credence to the official decrees repeatedly enacted by the Venetian magistracies, Jews and Christians should have been almost totally segregated. In actual fact, Jews and Christians had frequent contact in the course of their daily lives, and their habits were, after all, not so very different. Like their Christian neighbors, the ghetto dwellers often gathered to chat and to practice various sports; in fact, the rabbis more than once debated the question of whether ball-playing should be allowed on the Sabbath. Like many Christians, the Jews believed in supernatural forces, and some rabbis complained that they prayed too little and placed their faith in amulets. Some rabbis also pointed at the ghetto as an example of lax morals, a den of sinners. Indeed, like most Italian Jews, the Venetians were not very orthodox, liking their comforts and eager for ways to participate in Venetian activities and festivals. Leone da Modena himself, obliged to be absent from Venice for a while, wrote a letter in which he asked a friend to reserve him a place from which he could comfortably watch a certain regatta, despite the fact that the regatta was scheduled for one of the days of penitence preceding the fast of Tisha b'Av. To justify his request, the rabbi writes that on such a happy occasion it is permissible to overlook the period of mourning.

Ovadia da Bertinoro remarked that the Jews treated their faith as the Christians their saints, forgetting their monotheism for superstition, vows, and belief in spirits and demons. In the early seventeenth century, kabbalistic religious leanings once again gained a foothold in the ghetto, encouraged by the preaching of Menahem Azaria da Fano.

Christian culture and study of the classics also filtered in past the ghetto gates. Novels, poetry, and essays in Latin and Italian gradually supplanted Spanish and Yiddish literature, and integration between the two neighboring worlds continued to grow. The works of Leone da Modena, Simone Luzzatto, and Sara Coppio Sullam, popular figures in the seventeenth-century ghetto, reflect the strong interaction between the Jewish and Christian worlds.

On the feast of Purim, in emulation of the famous Venetian Carnival, the Jews dressed up in masks and disguises. Jews and Christians met at weddings and other festive occasions. The Venetians loved music, theater, and dancing, and the numerous proclamations and prohibitions are themselves the best evidence of the constant contact between Venetians and Jews. Especially famous is the edict of 1592 prohibiting the Jews from teaching voice and dance. Gambling, too, was widespread in the ghetto, and Leone da Modena is a unique example of its pervasiveness.

Not even the synagogues were immune to non-Jewish influence, for their walls were painted with birds and flowers. Rabbi Archivolti, Leone da Modena's teacher, protested against this introduction of images, which he feared would distract the congregation from its prayers.

The holy books were always finely decorated with drawings and engravings of great beauty. An edition of the Pentateuch was marvelously illustrated by Mosè da Castellazzo, one of the ghetto's most celebrated painters and engravers.

The ghetto was very fond of theater. A play by Salomon Usque, entitled *Ester*, was performed in the New Ghetto in 1531. Marin Sanudo wrote of the premiere, "This evening in the Ghetto a fine play was given among the Jews." Revived in 1559 and again in 1592, it was revised by the versatile Leone da Modena sixty years later. At the beginning of the seventeenth century a singer named Rachele was famous in the Venetian salons, and during this same period Leone da Modena wrote his pastoral drama *Rachele e Jacob*, which we know about only because the author, in need of money, pawned his only copy with a friend.

The orthodox, always hostile to theater, which they considered overly promiscuous, also vigorously opposed the use of music in the synagogues. In 1605 the dispute sharpened when an uncommonly fine male choir sang in the great Spanish School. Rabbi Leone da Modena, combative as always, answered the scandalized protesters with a formal rabbinical responsum in which he maintained that there was nothing wrong with using the human voice to sing God's praises. His defense of music went further: in his preface to *Shir ha-Shirim*, by Salomone De Rossi, and in a subsequent responsum, Leone da Modena mantained that the joining of words and music posed no danger to the integrity of the Jewish faith, and that there was no blasphemy in pronouncing the name of God in song.

Giulio Morosini, alias Samuel Nahmias, is an excellent witness of the times: "Well I remember what occurred in my day in Venice, around 1628, if I mistake not, when Jews who had fled from Mantua because of the war came to Venice. And at that time, when study of every kind was thriving in the Community of Mantua, the Jews had also applied themselves to music and instruments. When these people arrived in Venice, a musical Academy was established in the Ghetto of that city, where there was regular singing twice weekly, in the morning and in the evening, and there congregated only certain leaders and wealthy men of the Ghetto who supported it, myself among them, and my teacher Rabbi Leone da Modena was the Kappellmeister." That year, he relates, passages in Hebrew and numerous psalms were sung in the great Spanish School, "with solemn music that lasted some hours into the night, and there gathered many noble Gentlemen and Ladies, with great applause, so that many Guards and Police Officers had to be stationed at the gates to maintain order among those passing through. Among the other instruments, an Organ was brought to the School, which however the Rabbis did not allow to be played because it is an instrument which is normally played in our Churches. But alas! All this was but a brief spark, the Academy and the Music were short-lived, and we soon returned to our former state."

The ghetto musical association was called the Accademia degli Impediti. It also had a Hebrew name, Bezochrenu et Zion, inspired by the opening verses of Psalm 137: "By the rivers of Babylon, there we sat down, yea, we wept, when we remembered Zion. Upon the willows in the midst thereof we hanged up our harps."

Liturgical and synagogue music, which made its first appearance at the dawn of the 1600s, did not become common until the middle of the century. Especially interesting is a Hebrew cantata in dialogue form by Carlo Grossi, a Venetian composer and a Gentile. It is the only musical composition of this type in the latter half of the seventeenth century. Under the influence of the legendary Kabbalists of Safed, a brotherhood called *Shomerim L'boker*, or "Watchers of the Dawn," had been formed in Venice toward the end of the century. The cantata was commissioned from Grossi for the anniversary of its constitution, which coincided with the feast of Hoshana Rabba. On stage, a nocturnal traveler observes a group of men singing the praises of God with intense joy. They are "the watchers of the dawn," who on a night of many years past, in the ghetto, expressed not only their religious devotion, but a very special bond with the great starry sky of distant Safed.

All these social and cultural manifestations were dominated by religion. The study of the Torah was a constant, a refuge in adversity. The Ashkenazim accepted the teaching and commentary of the celebrated, undisputed Rashi, and were considered unrivalled in *pilpul*, a method of studying and discussing Talmud. We also know of a private academy established by Caliman or Calonimos Belgrado in 1594, in which Leone da Modena, once again, was a prominent figure.

All the prerequisites thus existed for the development of a strong cultural dualism, for the ghetto walls were a permeable barrier. The Jews studied both the Torah and Latin; their studies encompassed Jewish and non-Jewish subjects.

But Jewish culture remained primary, and a man could achieve no greater recognition than the title of rabbi. As Leone da Modena wrote: "In Italy the elder rabbis ordain a new rabbi and they call him, both orally and in writing, '*Haver di rav*,' associate rabbi, if he is young or insufficiently trained. If instead he is sufficiently trained they call him '*moreno o rav*.' " Many young men in the ghetto aspired to these titles and honors, while the Sephardim were critical of what they considered Ashkenazic foibles. In the early sixteenth century Don Isaac Abrabanel remarked sarcastically: "When I came to Italy I found that the custom of indiscriminate ordination was very widespread, especially among the Ashkenazim. They all ordain or are ordained rabbis. I know not whence comes such license, unless they are envious of the Gentiles who give doctorates to everyone, and want one themselves." Be that as it may, being considered a rabbi was a distinction among the Jews, and there are documented cases of bribes offered in an attempt to gain the longed-for recognition.

An event that occurred in May 1631, at a dramatic juncture for the plague-ridden city, sheds light on the internal autonomy of the ghetto and provides a wealth of documentary evidence for historians. An Avogador de Comun was informed of a conflict between the association of ghetto shopkeepers and the leaders of the University, who had severely admonished the shopkeepers to settle any squabbles or controversies among themselves, without involving the Venetian magistracy. Upon learning of this directive, which he suspected of subverting the sovereignty of Venetian law, Avogador Morosini summoned one of the University leaders, Isaach Levi, who denied that any such admonishment had been made, and Leone da Modena, who according to Morosini's information had communicated the University leaders' decision to the shopkeepers' association. Isaach Levi admitted that it had indeed been decided, long ago, that anyone who did not resolve his own controversies would be punished by excommunication, but insisted that this principle had never been intended to sidestep the Venetian authorities. Another leader, David Baseve, known as Abram the Jew, confirmed that none of the leaders had authorized Leone da Modena to threaten excommunication, but said that just a few days earlier the learned rabbi, who at the time was working as a scribe in the Italian School, had consulted the section of the *Libro Grande* (the Great Book) that discussed the ancient custom of excommunication. The Avogadori instructed Leone da Modena and Jacob Levi to make two separate translations of the chapters of the *Libro Grande* that had caused the trouble. A few months later, in September 1631, the Senate decided that the entire *Libro Grande* should be translated. The resulting translation, a gold mine of information not yet exhaustively examined, has been preserved in the collection of the Ufficiali al Cattaver in the Venetian State Archives. It contains numerous annotations that shed light on the everyday life of the Jewish groups, with information on rituals, taxes, the appointment of rabbis, *shammashim*, and *shochetim*, internal quarrels (especially regarding the excavation of the canals surrounding the ghetto), and all manner of major and minor decisions taken by the general assembly of the Jewish community. The original had been written in Hebrew by the leaders of the three Nations comprising the University, and had been translated by Sebastiano Venier, permanent interpreter to the very reverend Prime Inquisitor, "by order of the Most Illustrious Ser Zuane Morosini Avogador di Comun." The Senate now called on Fra Fulgenzio Micanzio, who showed little enthusiasm for the task, claiming that he considered himself a consultant with "talent consisting more in an ardent will to serve than in the ability to do so." Cozzi has pointed out that Micanzio, while stating his conviction that the sovereign powers of the Most Serene Republic should extend to the ghetto, and despite having written countless pages of opinions upholding the full exercise of Venetian state sovereignty, did not actually feel he could invoke the literal enforcement of those principles against the University of the Jews.

One of the many curious documents in the *Libro Grande* is an ordinance against luxury dated 5377 (22 December 1616). The leaders and functionaries of the University of the ghettos, "in view of the extraordinary and superfluous pomp in use among the Jews, and considering that owing to the intolerable expense many poor men cannot wed, nor marry off their daughters, moved by just zeal and fear of God, and in the general interest, have resolved to regulate the matters described hereunder to obviate the scandals that could ensue from such arrogant luxury: let no woman, of whatsoever condition or quality, dare leave her house dressed in velvet, plush, velveteen or lace of any sort, excepting some strips of velvet on her skirt, but within doors they may visit their neighbors dressed however they please." Forbidden to all were garments of gold and silver, or even with gold and silver embroidery. "Only one slim cord of gold and silver" was allowed, "and out of doors they will wear it under their clothing, and not otherwise." Elaborate headgear was not allowed, "nor may they wear over their faces drooping headdresses made of hair, wool or silk, nor of any other imaginable material, and when they go out of doors they must go with their bosoms covered so they cannot be seen." The ghetto leaders also forbade the women to bleach their hair blond or wear excessively high heels. Children, too, were not to be dressed too showily. Furthermore: "And because in the feasts given at weddings . . . extraordinary expense is incurred, it is ordered that at these banquets no more than twenty people, including men and women, may be seated at table, and in addition to these, five . . . paupers." These clauses were due to take effect in March 1617, but were revoked the month before.

The *Libro Grande* also contains an order from the leaders of the executive council: each Jew was to contribute to the salary of the man who blew the *shofar* every Friday at sundown to announce the beginning of the Sabbath. Dated Friday, August 27, 1604, it reads: "Having seen the great usefulness resulting to all the inhabitants of the Ghetto from the trumpet that every Sabbath eve toward sundown sounds to warn all Israel and especially to advise the women that they should prepare everything needed to honor the Sabbath, kindling the Sabbath lamp to differentiate the working days from the feast day, and it being necessary to pay the aforesaid trumpeter, let a faithful man go about once a week with an alms-box through the two ghettos and collect from the blessed among the people, who will each put in the aforesaid box however much he pleases to help pay the aforesaid player."

Cozzi has emphasized that the question of civil justice constitutes an important element in tracing the evolution of the life of the Venetian Jewish community, in its relations between Nation and Nation and with the Venetian State. The autonomy of the ghetto, a "republic within the Republic," may be the most striking aspect to have emerged from the *Libro Grande* "affair," but it was in fact always present in one form or another as long as the ghetto existed, with the differences in sovereignty and jurisdiction between the ghettos that we have discussed earlier.

Another source of hitherto unpublished details on ghetto life is the records of the notary Bracchi, preserved in the Venetian State Archives and containing sixty-six Jewish wills. The collection has already been studied in depth, and certain essential facts have emerged. The notary lived just outside the ghetto, in the adjacent San Marcuola quarter, and his collection supplies information about personal, financial, and religious conditions in the ghetto. Nearly all the documents are in Italian, but there are a few exceptions, written in foreign languages with attached translations. Some of the wills are very interesting from a linguistic standpoint. Rachel, the widow of Samuele Namias, for instance, spoke in a mixture of Spanish and Italian which, through the notary's simultaneous transcription, provides a vivid example of the kind of language spoken by the Iberian immigrants in the ghetto. If we take into account the limitations set by the particular sample of the population they represent, the testaments seem to indicate a considerable level of culture, for nearly all of Bracchi's clients wrote correct Italian. The fact that the Christian witnesses from districts near the ghetto, such as the Fondamenta degli Ormesini, San Girolamo, and Ponte del'Aseo, were boatmen, greengrocers, or weavers attests to a certain integration with the world outside the ghetto. Certain testators describe their tombstones in detail, give instructions for the reciting of the mourner's Kaddish, and arrange the details of charitable donations to brotherhoods and collections for the ransoming of captives, aid to relatives in the Holy Land, and the dowries of poor girls. Religious books, too, were important bequests.

Given the almost total lack of real estate, which the Jews were not allowed to own, bequests of precious objects and the rights of *jus gazakà* took on especial importance. We also find certain curious details, such as the case of the Jew who left his only daughter permission to choose one of two cousins for her husband. The other cousin would be left a sum of money.

Concerning the population of the ghetto in the first hundred years of its history, certain official statistics are supplied by Contento, in *Il censimento della popolazione sotto la Repubblica Veneta,* * and G. Beloch, in *La popolazione di Venezia nei secoli XVI e XVII.* ** According to Beloch, there were close to 1,000 Jews in Venice in 1500; from 1556 to 1563 the number increased from about 923 to 1,424, due to the immigration of Roman Jews expelled by Pope Paul IV in 1559. The figures of Contento and Beloch, in substantial agreement, are generally accepted.

The Venetian census of 1586 estimated the ghetto Jews at 1,694, about half the number living in Rome at the same time, where they were 3,500. The total in Padua and Verona was about 400. In Venice in 1640, after the tragic plague, the Jewish population was estimated at 2,600. In Verona in 1599, there were about 300 Jews and in Padua, in 1615, about 665—2 percent of the total population. In 1630 there were 590 Jews before the plague and 300 afterwards.

Other historians have observed that in 1555 there seem to have been 932 people living in the Venetian ghetto, and that by 1646 the number had risen to 4,870, despite two terrible plagues. This increase, they theorize, may have been due not only to continuous waves of Iberian immigration, but also to an influx of those escaping persecution in the eastern countries.

One statistic of especial interest counts the total Jewish population of the Venetian Republic toward the end of the sixteenth century at 3,000, in a state numbering 1,500,000.

Ravid takes the figures of Beloch and Contento as his point of departure, but feels that the conclusions of A. C. Harris, a historian who has analyzed the demographic aspects of the Italian ghetto with particular care, should also be taken into account. He therefore accepts the following figures:

*Census of the Population under the Venetian Republic
**The Population of Venice in the Sixteenth and Seventeenth Centuries

Year	Jews
1516	700
1536	1,424
1581	1,043
1630	5,000
1642	3,300
1655	4,870

It is unclear whether these figures include the transient Levantine merchants, semipermanent residents of the city. Note that in 1642, certain sources number the Jewish population at 3,300, while others talk of 549 families; the correlation is not automatic.

D. Beltrame, the author of an extensive study on Venetian demography, has fixed the figure for 1642 at 2,671, too similar to that given by other sources for 1766. The figure 4,870 for 1655 may seem excessive: Beloch seems to favor a much smaller number: 1,870.

There are no data between 1655 and 1766 to use as controls. C. Roth has spoken of immigration to Venice from both East and West.

Two additional sources are worth mentioning: Thomas Coryat, an English traveler who visited Venice in 1608 and described his impressions of the ghetto in his *Coryat's Crudities* (London, 1611), speaks of a Jewish population numbering somewhere between 5,000 and 6,000. And Menasseh ben Israel, in *Humble Addresses*, writes admiringly of the ghetto and speaks of 1,400 inhabited houses there. Rather than houses in the literal sense, they may have been families: multiplying this figure by four would give us a population of 5,600.

In concluding we should note that Harris puts the Jewish population in sixteenth-century Venice between 0.6 percent and 1.2 percent of the total population, in the seventeenth century between 2.5 percent and 3.3 percent, and in the eighteenth century at 1.2 percent, with a presumptive maximum of 5,000 Jews out of 150,000 inhabitants in 1630 and 4,780 out of 159,000 in 1655. Harris has derived some of his data from Beltrame. In 1630, there were 1,015 Jews per hectare in the two ghettos, Old and New (the population density in the rest of the city was 236), and in 1642 there were 897 per hectare in the Old, New, and Newest Ghettos.

The problem of space remained unresolved throughout the seventeenth century. In 1659 the patrician Loredan, addressing the Senate in favor of the Jews, said: "Where twenty Jews live, there would not live more than four to eight Christians ... Excepting three or four, they all mind their shops, living therefore in the small enclosure of the ghetto where they hold their services and where some rabbis explain the religious dogmas, inciting to penitence, fasting, abstinence and charity; the populace tolerates them, bound by necessity and certain special interests; they are without correspondence, without strength, without help, spirit, heart and will."

DENSITY PER HECTARE
IN THE COURSE OF THE SIXTEENTH AND SEVENTEENTH CENTURIES

	1581	1586	1633	1642
Old Ghetto	502	826	1,127	568
New Ghetto	420	662	903	1,023
Newest Ghetto	—	—	—	1,100
Average	461	744	1,015	897

For the Serenissima, troubled on so many other fronts, the terrible plague of 1630 did more damage than the loss of a fierce battle. At the request of noblemen Pietro Soranzo and F. Morosini, as well as of the procurator Gieronimo Corner, a Jewish doctor from the ghetto named Joshua Chabiglio presented a report to the Venetian authorities, assuring them that he wished only to act "for the useful benefit of this noble City, and with no other aim than to render it a service, as my homeland of sixty years." He also said, however, that "in this cruel and poisonous contagion learning and culture can be of no avail." Under the circumstances, the Venetian doctors worked miracles, but long practice and the experience of many years would have been needed to cure this disease. "In long and various journeys," continued Chabiglio, "I have seen and frequented many places where there was plague, and have seen an infinity of people treated by diverse methods according to the nature of the patients, time and place." Within forty days, said Chabiglio, he could bring to the city twelve men over fifty years of age, and assured them: "The virtue of these twelve is miraculous in that when they see a sick man from afar, and all the more so when feeling his pulse, they can tell simply by looking at his urine if that man has plague, or if he will get it, and in short they are men highly expert in this disease, serving as physicians, surgeons and barbers. If bleeding is required, they will do it immediately, for the life or death of the poor invalid often depends on dilation, inasmuch as that tainted blood, if not let immediately, will be his ruin." These doctors, Chabiglio assures the authorities of the Republic, "can also recognize carbuncles, abscesses and pimples and the differences between them, distinguishing each of them by special names and which are malignant and poisonous and which are not, and treat them with great success and propriety according to their type. They also know when to give the patient aperients and lubricants, or antidiarrhetics, and this is very important, as life and death are often determined by evacuation."

Further testimony on the plague is provided by Jews in the ghetto who testified against one Iseppo Ferach, called Benceze the Jew, who lived in the Old Ghetto "near Cannaregio and who, afflicted by the plague, neglected through guilty indolence to obey the orders of both the Venetian authorities and the Ghetto leaders who insisted that all infected articles be sent to the Lazaretto."

The Venetians, noticing that the Jews successfully protected themselves from the disease by following strict rules of isolation, eventually emulated them. Despite all precautions, however, not even the ghetto was spared. According to Abraam Catalano, a contemporary chronicler, 454 people died in Venice, and some 2,000 left the city.

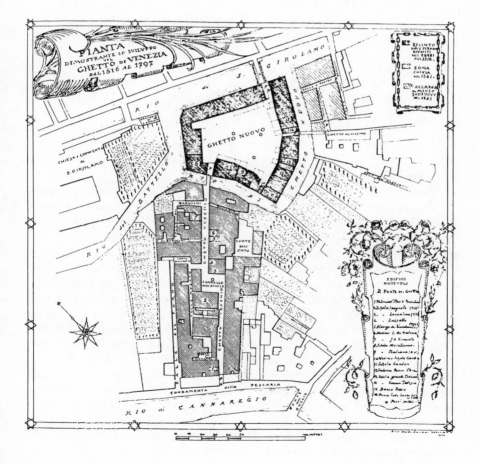

Map of the ghetto (New, Old, and Newest) drawn by architect Guido Sullam.

CHAPTER THIRTEEN

Leone da Modena, or On Contradiction

Early works, dreams, and marriage — Gambling obsession and preaching career — The study of alchemy — Diffesa da quello che scrive Fra' Sisto Senese — The University leaders' edict against gambling — The Historia de' Riti Hebraici — The Kol Sakhal

"Ever since my childhood I have been concerned with investigating all fields of knowledge, and even if I have not been able to learn any more than a man who attempts to drink all the water in the sea, I have never hindered my intellect from seeking to understand anything I wished. For this reason I have always been opposed to the views of Rabbenu Asher, who thanked God because he had no secular learning, which, in his opinion, leads people away from God. For myself, I say: would Heaven that I were able to thank, exalt and glorify God so that He might help me to acquire all the knowledge in the world. I have become master not only of the teachings . . . of the Torah, but I have studied, day and night, the books of the heretics and unbelievers, and of the exponents of other religions, to learn how to refute the heretics, and therefore I have studied books of magic and sorcery not, God forbid, in order to practice these arts, but to understand, teach, and be capable of distinguishing [between good and evil], and to be more careful [to do justice and avoid evil]."

Thus wrote Leone da Modena (in Hebrew Jehuda Aryeh mi Modena), the most famous and controversial of all Venetian rabbis, in a paragraph that demonstrates his modern and open-minded world view. This moral testament is part of his most biting and most problematical anti-Kabbalist

and antiheretic work, *Ari Nohem*,* also known as *Shaagat Arieh*.* *
Only a few fragments remain of this book, written in rebuttal of the
ideas contained in a presumably anonymous work entitled *Kol Sakhal*,† which attacked rabbinical power and the Oral Law.

Leone da Modena was born in Venice in April 1571 of a family,
originally from Ferrara, that had come to Venice as temporary refugees
from an earthquake. After a period of residence in the ghetto just around
the time of Leone's birth, the family returned to Ferrara, but in 1578
Leone's father, Isacco, found himself embroiled in a conflict with Cardinal Alvise d'Este over matters which are unclear.

Leone was a precocious child: at the age of two and a half, he was
reading the Haftarah, and at three he was said to have been able to
translate some simple passages of the Torah from Hebrew into Italian.
His teachers were illustrious scholars, rabbis Finzi and Samuele Archivolti, and Mosè della Rocca, related to the rabbi of Ancona, Mosè
Basola.

One of Leone's early works is a piece in dialogue form, *Sur Merah*,‡
written with the intention of combating the passion for gambling that
had seized two of his stepbrothers. Yet, full of contradictions in his
life as well as in his thoughts, Leone too was caught up in the vortex
and succumbed to the fever, gambling desperately for the rest of his
life.

Leone's *Autobiography* is a treasury of information about himself
and his environment, the ghetto. He recalls some difficult times and,
especially, certain dreams to which he attributes great premonitory
importance.

In 1589 Leone returned to Venice with his mother, who had arranged
a marriage between Leone and her sister's eldest daughter. Leone was
introduced to his cousin Ester, whom he found both beautiful and wise.
"After Shavuoth we went, happy and joyful, to Venice." There they
found the promised bride ill. It was thought she would soon recover,
but instead the poor girl got worse: "Every day her illness worsened
until she was at the point of death, but her heart was courageous like
that of a lion, and she never let fear overcome her. At death's door she
sent for me and embraced and kissed me, saying she knew that at any
other time such behavior would be unseemly. But the Lord knew that
during our year's engagement we had never so much as touched one
another even with our little fingers, and it was only now as she lay
dying that death granted her this freedom." Shortly thereafter, Ester
died. Leone assuaged his sorrow by marrying her sister Rachel only
fifteen days later. The next day Rabbi Salomone Sforno, after a short

---

*The Roaring Lion
* *The Lion's Roar
†The Voice of the Fool
‡Turn From Wickedness

sermon in the synagogue, called him "chaver" (companion, assistant to the rabbi), a much-prized title for so young a man.

But there was no peace for the young scholar. The year 1591, which brought dire famine to Venice, was a year of illness for Leone's entire family. Leone himself, his wife, and his father, Isacco, all fell ill. In September a son, Marco, was born, but in December Isacco da Modena died at the age of seventy-two. In his autobiography, Leone tells of a dream in which he saw and spoke to his dead father. Like many of his contemporaries, he considered dreams as messages to be interpreted, premonitions or contacts with the beyond that influenced the lives of men.

In 1593, on the Saturday after Tisha b'Av, Leone addressed a large congregation in the great German School, and that marked the beginning of his long career as a preacher in the Venetian ghetto, a career that lasted over forty years. Authoritative testimony reports that men of all descriptions came to hear him, including Venetian nobles, ambassadors from other European countries, priests, and monks. Within the ghetto he enjoyed great intellectual prestige, and he was asked to head the yeshiva founded by Calonimos Belgrado.

His family life during those years was much less fortunate. He lost his mother and two sons (the second born in October 1593). Perhaps to forget his sorrows, he abandoned himself to his passion for gambling, which he had so detested in his youth. "And at Chanukkah, 5355 [1595], the devil mocked me and harmed me not a little, for I lost 100 ducats." From that time on, gambling became a way of life for Leone, a disease continually and painfully alternating between remission and relapse. "And in the days of Chanukkah, they urged me to play, and between that time and the feast of Shavuoth I lost more than three hundred ducats. From that time, therefore, up to the end of the feast of Chanukkah I threw myself into my studies and studied for 18 months and paid all my debts." Shortly thereafter, he succumbed to gambling again, by his own admission, losing 300 ducats in six months. Meanwhile, however, his literary activity was as intense as his desire for the thrill of gambling. He also developed a keen interest in alchemy, partly through his acquaintance with a young doctor, Abramo di Camis, who was squandering his health and fortune in a tireless quest for the philosophers' stone.

Leone went for some time to Ferrara, where his preaching won the admiration of all. To support himself he worked as a private tutor for the Zelman family, but he was homesick for Venice and when Zelman died in 1607, he decided to return to his beloved city in search of his former students and luck in gambling. In the spring of 1609 he was called to Florence, but he could never stay away from Venice for very long and returned in the autumn of that same year, obtaining a salaried post with the Talmud Torah Brotherhood of the German Jews. Around that time his daughter Diana married, and his son Marco, for reasons unclear, left Venice.

In May 1615, Marco returned and set up a small chemistry lab in the Old Ghetto where he and his father conducted experiments in the attempt to transform nine ounces of lead and one of silver into ten ounces of silver. Leone da Modena had no doubt whatsoever about the validity of the experiment, and wrote, "Twice I myself have seen this happen, and I myself and no other sold the silver after having assayed it in the crucible." He was convinced that he had found an inexhaustible source of wealth, which he estimated would bring in a thousand ducats a year.

Naturally his hopes were dashed, and his son fell suddenly ill, "with frequent hemorrhages caused by the arsenic salts and other substances used in his laboratory." Marco was forced to drop his study of alchemy, and in the two years he lived after his illness, his poor health made it impossible for him to engage in any serious occupation.

In the autumn of 1616, Leone's friend and mentor Rabbi Salomone Sforno died, leaving a marriageable daughter. During a sermon which has become famous, Leone da Modena succeeded in collecting five hundred ducats as a dowry for the girl. The news spread beyond the ghetto, and a priest in the church of San Geremia, while telling his congregation with admiration of this feat, saw Leone da Modena himself among the listeners, and pointed him out.

Leone wrote and preached incessantly during those years, during which he was entrusted with the ambitious project of preparing a new Bible with a Chaldean translation. He remarked with satisfaction, "By my words I succeeded in collecting 500 ducats for an orphan, and the Lord has caused me to earn as much again." But he was always beset by financial problems. When he had wanted to marry Ester, he had had no money for her dowry and had had to return to teaching at the Talmud Torah. *Ester*, his only play, was published in 1619. Although he spent many hours each day teaching at the Germans' Talmud Torah, Leone felt sad and oppressed. "I am a prisoner," he wrote, "and no human strength can break my chains."

For despite his success and recognition, Leone's private life was far from serene. Marco had died and the rabbi was left with two surviving sons: Isacco, who lived a disorderly, roving life, and Zebulun, also called Marino, who had a quarrelsome nature. In 1620, when Isacco returned from the East, the poor rabbi had to pay the captain a ransom to let him off the ship.

In April 1621, despite his intensive teaching, the family was again in debt. In May Leone's daughter Diana gave him a grandson, Isacco, but this happy event was followed by one that caused him great anxiety: his son Marino was arrested and jailed by order of the Magistrato dei Cinque.

Study was his natural refuge: in 1622 he worked on the Talmudic tract *Ketubot*, dealing with marriage contracts, and that same year he preached eighteen sermons to large congregations in the great German School, accompanied by a choir of young cantors. Even Marino, who was far from assiduous in attending synagogue, took his turn at singing. But a new family tragedy befell the house of Modena that very year. Marino had an enemy, one Sabbatai Benincasa, with whom he had often quarreled. Benincasa had even chased him outside the ghetto walls with a butcher knife, and young Marino had miraculously succeeded in saving himself by pushing his assailant into a canal. Leone da Modena had attempted to settle the conflict and had even involved the noble Alvise Giustinian, who tried to mediate but to no avail. One March evening in the ghetto, Sabbatai Benincasa and his brother were in the company of Isacco, the illegitimate son of a woman nicknamed La Spagnoletta, and one Abramo known as Ciompo, the spurious son of a woman called La Bella. With them were four young Spanish Jews, Davide Mocato, Mosè Emmanuele Giacobbe, Isacco Montalti, and Elia Muciacion, Marino da Modena's rival for the favors of a certain "immodest" woman. Marino was spending the evening at the home of some Levantine frends when the group of youths staged a brawl. With shouts and cries, they made it sound as though they were being attacked by non-Jews. The unsuspecting Marino rushed down the stairs and was surrounded by the hoodlums, who treacherously murdered him. The funeral in the Jewish cemetery was heartrending. Dolfin, a young aristocrat who attended, was so deeply moved and prostrated by it that "he took to his bed and died." The old rabbi fell into a state of deep depression, and mused on the prophetic words of Senator Lorenzo Sanuto: "If your son does not moderate his excesses, they will soon kill him." Leone appealed to the Council of Ten, who summoned the guilty youths before the Court of Blasphemy and sentenced them to ten years' exile.

Now that he was alone, Leone's daughter Diana and his son-in-law Giacobbe Levi insisted that he move in with them and his little grandson, Isacco, in the Old Ghetto. The rabbi agreed.

But his adventures were not over. In May 1623, while accompanying a young bride to Mantua for her wedding ceremony, with an escort of thirty-six harquebusiers, his group was attacked by a troop of guards. In the midst of the fighting and confusion, he escaped through the fields with the terrified bride.

One day a few years later, in 1625, as told by Moisè Soave, who takes his information from Leone's autobiography, Rabbi Leone da Modena of Rialto was on his way to the district of San Cassiano. Since he was late, he turned off his usual route and took a shortcut. He had gone only a few steps when a chimney, torn off by a strong wind, fell with a great crash into the street that he had not taken. So it is, thought the wise rabbi, that a man's life often depends on the most insignificant things.

In 1626 the directors of the Talmud Torah again hired Leone as a teacher and paid off his gambling debts. But they withheld six ducats a month to settle an outstanding debt of 152 ducats. In the presence of two witnesses, Rabbi Leone promised not to gamble again for twenty-five months.

Early in May 1627, Rabbi Leone da Modena completed his *Diffesa da quello che scrive Fra' Sisto Senese nella sua Biblioteca Santa*.* Fra Sisto had led an adventurous life. Apparently born a Jew, he converted in adolescence, becoming first a Franciscan and later a Dominican friar. Whatever his order, he was always a zealous convert and proponent of the superiority of the Christian religion. In his apologetic treatise, Fra Sisto denigrates the Talmud, maintaining that it contains instigations to incest, anti-Christian blasphemy, and deception against Christians. Moreover, he says, the Talmudists oblige other Jews to consider Christians *bruta animalia*, and the Talmud contains precise legal provisions to the detriment of Christians and promises even worse, such as immunity for anyone who kills a Christian or destroys churches and books of Gospel. Leone da Modena felt a protest should be made, although he was well aware of the serious risk incurred in publicly refuting such an authoritative figure. He wrote a twenty-three-page manuscript and requested the Venetian authorities' permission to publish it. According to custom, it was passed on to the legal adviser for his opinion on the work's suitability for publication. The opinion was negative, and the manuscript lay in the State Archives until modern times.

Leone da Modena writes that his intention was to refute "the false and contrived calumnies of a certain Fra Sisto Senese." He confesses that he had often thought of "replying with a few lines to confute these infamies." Bitterly realistic, he adds, "had it been granted me to have them appear in print . . . men, who hold sacred that which they see in print, might compare one with the other and clear up the question once and for all. But this is not the first obstacle encountered by the poor Jew in all his defenses."

Fra Sisto accused the Jews of inciting to incest, to which the rabbi replied in shocked consternation: "Now when has it ever been heard of any Jew taking his daughter or sister to wife, or having carnal knowledge of them with or without marriage?" He accuses Fra Sisto of having distorted the Talmudic passage, to "vomit out against it his venomous and poisoned thought." In rebutting the accusation of deception against Christians, Rabbi da Modena displays all his power as a polemicist: he denies all accusations of deception, but acknowledges that, in speaking of usury, his defense touches on an extremely delicate issue. "When

---

Refutation of what Fra Sisto Senese Writes in his Holy Library

the Talmud discusses whether it is permissible to defraud the Gentile, the conclusion in any event is no . . . and many others say that it is a greater sin to deceive or cheat the Gentile than another Jew, because the Jew attributes it to the dishonesty of the particular Jew who cheats him, but the Gentile is scandalized by the entire Hebrew nation and law, which he believes allows it, and when God said in his Commandments: *non furaberis,* * he excepted no nation. Now if many Jews may be found who try to cheat and deceive Christians, it is not the law that permits it, nor commands it . . . but it is true that the law is not observed by this Jew or that; both because in every nation there are many of little conscience, and also because need and poverty, in which the Hebrew nation finds itself in this long captivity, intrinsically give it a certain freedom (albeit neither just nor legitimate) to act against conscience for survival's sake."

At this point in his eloquent defense he cites a personal experience he had in Ferrara, in 1605. "A Jew was claiming repayment of a large debt from a gentleman of Ferrara, which included hundreds of ducats of interest, and that gentleman alleged it was illegal, even according to his own law, for the Jew to take interest from a Christian. And a rabbi had written him an attestation, which had been presented in court in favor of the Christian: and other rabbis had written the opposite, in favor of the Jew. The most illustrious Cardinal sent for me and asked me whether or not I thought it was legitimate for a Jew to take interest from Christians. My answer was, 'No, sir, and yes, sir.' 'Explain yourself,' said he. 'I believe it is legitimate,' said I, 'for the text in the previously cited chapter of Deuteronomy says: *non fenerabis fratri tuo usura pecunia usura cibi etc.; extraneo fenerabis, et fratri tuo non fenerabis, etc.* ** And by *foreigner,* certainly no other is meant but those seven nations. The others are considered brothers, and all the more so in that the Talmudists at times take the Christians for Edomites and earlier in that same chapter it is written: *non abominaberis Idumeo quia frater tuus est etc.*† So the Christian is a brother and cannot be lent to at interest. And therefore I said: no, Sir; but if the Christian treated us as brothers and let us live as his citizens and subjects, and did not forbid us familiarity in all dealings, the purchase of real estate, many trades and, in certain places such as Venice, even the mechanical arts and infinite other prohibitions, we would be equally obliged to acknowledge him as a brother. But if he treats us like slaves, we, as slaves, would feel it legitimate to do what should not be done, for the sake of survival, which is to lend at interest. And therefore I

---

*thou shalt not steal

**thou shalt not lend to your brother at interest, whether the interest is on food, etc.; you may lend to foreigners, but to your brother thou shalt not lend, etc. (Deuteronomy, 23:19)

†thou shalt not hate the Edomite because he is your brother, etc.

said yes.' The most illustrious Cardinal, with a grave laugh, placed a hand on my shoulder and, dismissing me, ruled in favor of the Jew."

In 1627, Leone's son Isacco came home again, but stayed only eight months. The poor old rabbi could not help complaining: of his three sons, one had been poisoned, one murdered, and the third was in exile.

The year 1629 was no better. Leone's sermons in the great Spanish School were attended by Venetian nobles, clergymen, and European diplomats. His public life was a triumph, but his family life was a torment. His son-in-law Giacobbe died and his daughter Diana, widowed and pregnant, gave birth to a daughter who died shortly thereafter. Now he had only Diana and his young grandson Isacco Levi.

The following year the learned rabbi, who had defended the Jews against the insidious propaganda of Fra Sisto Senese, was obliged to defend himself. The leaders of the community had issued an edict against gambling and threatened severe penalties for disobedience: "As many and diverse games of cards and dice have been introduced into our Nations, causing the ruin and extermination of families, the Leaders of the University order that any Jew living in Venice, man or woman, young man or maid, boy or girl, is forbidden on pain of excommunication to gamble in or outside Venice with a Jew or any other person, nor may he ask others to gamble on his behalf . . . and on anyone who disobeys shall fall all the excommunications, anathemas and curses written in the Holy Scriptures, and by order of the Leaders of the University his excommunication shall be publicly announced in the synagogues of the ghetto, nor shall he be pardoned until he shall have accomplished that which is commanded him by the Leaders of the University."

Cut to the quick, the learned rabbi replied in his usual polemic tone, taking a firm position. He insisted that the majority constituted in the assembly, comprising those hundred individuals who paid twelve ducats each, probably also including fourteen-year-old boys, could not be considered an absolute majority of the community. Would it not be more logical to broach the problem with the six hundred family heads who had been excluded from the assembly merely on financial grounds? How did seventy-one people dare excommunicate two thousand? "Can such abuses possibly be pleasing to the Excellent Almighty God?" In his *Autobiography*, Leone writes, "I took this stance not to justify gambling, but to show them that they had neither the power nor the right to forbid it." Speaking of his own mad passion, he implies that the stars are responsible for his human fate: "I had always been convinced that no one can elude them or flee their force and anger . . . and thence derives a fierce conflict that makes us struggle in need and adversity, and this has been the cause that has constrained me, all the days of my life, to err in gambling."

In defending his fragile thesis, which he takes greatly to heart, the rabbi resorts to every possible device; he points out that in Venice, more than in any other Italian city, the Christians spend thousands of zecchini on gambling, and that gambling afforded Jews and Christians frequent opportunities for contact. "In fact it often happens that the former have need to speak with the latter in places where men gamble, or in the gaming halls, or even in the aristocrats' palaces, where they are gambling. In all such cases the Jew is invited, and even obliged to play, and if he refuses he risks harsh words or the loss of his clientele . . . Is there not the court of Blasphemy which through wise and appropriate laws punishes gamblers in certain cases? Why must we Jews be judged by two different courts and serve two sentences? Where is the justice?" In this circumstance the learned rabbi denies the independent jurisdiction of the ghetto, which the Jews repeatedly and jealously claimed, resulting in frequent controversies with the Venetian magistracies. Not the least of these was the affair that had resulted in the translation of the *Libro Grande*, personally involving Leone da Modena. In this case, however, departing from the rabbinical tradition of autonomy, he finds it more convenient to shield himself behind the Venetian laws, even though we must acknowledge that his criticisms were not addressed to either the rabbis or the Torah, but to the secular leaders of the University, the elected heads of the small council. "I can only state that respect for human dignity, which they [the University leaders] gravely offend, moved me to write this protest. It has been 38 years since they chose me as preacher to the Community, granting me freedom of speech, and sometimes in my sermons I translate the verse from the Proverbs in the following manner: 'You pay me to give you good counsel, and then you do not want my reproaches.'"

Tragedy still more dire loomed over the city and the ghetto. Leone da Modena relates: "And from that time the plague began to spread everywhere, and over the people of Israel. The hand of the Lord was very heavy in all Italy because of war, hunger, and epidemic . . . the plague arrived here in Venice before the days preceding the great Jewish holidays . . . the first victim was Moisè Sarfatti and in the days of Sukkoth Giacobbe Kohen died. It spread so fast that, up to this day, which is the first of Adar 5391 (autumn, 1631) 170 people have died."

In Venice the plague was a true scourge. The epidemic, claiming 50,000 lives out of 150,000 residents, wreaked havoc upon the life of the city, including the ghetto. The pawnshops accepted only pledges of metal, and much of the merchandise in the Levantines' warehouses was destroyed to avoid contagion. A special tax of 120,000 ducats ordered by the Senate further increased the ghetto's economic hardships. Leone bitterly remarked, "Those who were rich descended to the ranks of the middle class, the middle class became poor and the poor no longer found anyone to take pity on them, for there was no more money."

The plague ended in the winter of 1631. In all the synagogues, the end of the danger was celebrated with fasting and penitence, and the offerings were used to buy silver utensils for the religious services. Leone's household had not been touched by the plague: he and his family were spared. Indeed, the emergency had had a paradoxically beneficial effect on the gambling rabbi, who wrote unstintingly during that time and earned five hundred ducats, enabling him to live comfortably and without his usual dependence on the charity of friends and supporters. His daughter Diana was remarried to Mosè Fano òf Padua, whose wife had died of plague, leaving Leone with the responsibility of bringing up his grandson, Isacco. And arour.d the same time the other Isacco, Leone's wandering son, came home from Leghorn in answer to the insistent appeals of his father, who wanted him close at hand.

By now the old rabbi was feeling the weight of his years. He concentrated more intensely on his writing, almost as though he knew his time for self-expression was drawing to a close. The publication of *Beth Yehuda*, a collection of moral teachings permeated by reformist spirit, caused him no end of trouble. A certain Jew filed a complaint with the Cattaveri, as a result of which the Vendramina printing-shop was closed for six months and the typesetter of the book, his own grandson, Isacco, who had been left in his charge by his daughter, Diana, was arrested. It was two months before the Quarantia al Criminal acknowledged the young man's innocence and ordered him released. On the subject of the book that had aroused such controversy, Leone writes in his *Autobiography*: "I had never desired or longed for anything in all the days of my life, so much as to see it printed and distributed and disseminated in the dispersion of Israel, because I was certain that I would thence reap merit, honor and lasting fame . . . The printing-shop was sealed and remained shut for about six months . . . Wednesday, 6 Iyar (May 16, 1635) government officers suddenly entered the printing-shop seeking my grandson Isacco with two of his friends, and they took him to a dark prison and again shut up the printing-shop. I was much upset because despite my efforts I could not settle the affair and have him released . . . until God was merciful . . . he was released without punishment."

By Purim of 1636, an atmosphere of gaiety once more reigned in the ghetto. The plague had been a grievous trial for everyone and people now felt like having fun. Moisè Soave describes this climate, on the basis of information from Leone's *Autobiography*: "Relatives, friends and acquaintances exchanged gifts consisting chiefly of sweets, confections and other delicacies. Women with happy faces greeted one

another from the windows, chatting with enviable innocence of presents given and received, the good dinner awaiting them, the happy
evening to follow, etc. Youngsters happily roamed through the ghetto
dressed in their holiday best, with drums and trumpets that would stun
even the deaf, with swords, pistols and dolls, tiny chairs and cupboards
and mirrors, the delight of that innocent age . . . Those three streets
teemed with people and smiles, handshakes and kisses; nothing was
wanting. A foreigner would have thought himself among people content with their fate, and enviable in many respects. And that morning
they were."

But a sad surprise was just around the corner. Sudden awareness of
their ever-precarious situation would soon replace the general gaiety.
Soave, again inspired by Leone, describes it eloquently: "The noonday
bell was ringing when numerous police officers, fully armed, suddenly
ordered the ghetto gates shut, and with the delicacy that has almost
always distinguished the police, set to searching through all the houses,
none excepted, and arrested one Sabbadin Catalano. A great robbery
had been perpetrated in the Merceria, against a rich merchant called
Brigonzi. The stolen goods, bales of silk, silk garments with gold brocade and other precious objects, amounted to the considerable value
of seventy thousand ducats. A Jew in the confidence of the magistrate
asserted that Catalano and a certain Scaramella, who had succeeded
in making his escape, were the guilty buyers and holders of the stolen
goods, and he told the truth. It was all found in a room indicated by
Catalano who, arrested, as we said, and threatened with torture, confessed his crime and that of his accomplices." Even poor Leone was
indirectly involved in the affair. From his prison cell Scaramella, possibly out of a simple desire for vengeance, accused two Jewish family
heads of bribing two judges of the Quarantia al Criminal. Feeling un-
safe, Leone da Modena's son-in-law fled to Ferrara with some other
men. For the whole of the following year Leone lived in fear and anxiety; although he himself was not guilty, the air was charged with
tension: "The merest suspicion was enough at that time to cause even
a man of honor to be dragged up as guilty before the courts. Isacco
Vigevano of Rovigo was detained in prison on the serious accusation
of having, with money, bought some votes of his city's Magistrates,
for the purpose of obtaining an extension for the Jews of the city."

Leone da Modena found out that Vigevano had mentioned his name
to the judges. Among the nobles accused of bribery in that affair was
a personal friend of his. In his initial panic, Leone considered leaving
Venice for Padua and seeking refuge outside the territory of the Serenissima. But flight might be construed as an admission of guilt and
would result in perpetual exile not only for those directly involved,
but for their families as well. So he decided, with pride and courage,
to remain in his beloved Venice. But a new surprise awaited him.

Leone da Modena. Engraving from the title page of his Historia de' Riti Hebraici.

In his *Autobiography*, Leone da Modena mentions having compiled, in 1616–1617, a collection of Jewish rites, customs, and regulations at the request of the English ambassador to Venice, Sir Henry Wotton, who intended to present it to his sovereign, King James I. The work was read in manuscript and greatly appreciated by many, including the English diplomat Sir William Boswell. He presented it to the jurist John Selden, who mentioned it in his treatise *De Successonibus*, calling Rabbi Leone by the name of "archisinagogus." One of the few existing manuscript copies came into the possession of the Frenchman Jacques Gaffarel, who wrote to Leone da Modena in 1637: "Later, perhaps, than I should have, I send you the history of your people, finally printed under my supervision." When the rabbi received Gaffarel's letter, he rushed to reread his manuscript, almost with a feeling of foreboding. Possibly he had forgotten to delete something that might carry undesirable consequences not only for his position as a rabbi but, indirectly, for all the Jews of the ghetto, especially at such a stormy time.

Concerning the *Historia de' Riti Hebraici*, as the book was entitled, Leone wrote: "I was not very careful to avoid writing against the Inquisition, because this work was a manuscript that was not to have been read by anyone connected with Papal influence ... I did not concern myself with correcting and removing all those passages that might sound damaging to the Inquisition if it were published in Italy ... The second Monday of Passover, 5397, a man came bearing a message from the Frenchman, informing me that he had printed the book in Paris. He did not tell me to whom he had dedicated it or whether he had changed anything ... I rushed to consult a copy ... and in it I noted four or five remarks against the Inquisition that I should not have made. Because of this I felt ill, tore my beard and was numb and dispirited for I knew that, when this book reached Rome, it would harm all Jews ... Where can I go, since I cannot flee to Ferrara nor to any other place in Italy?" Beside himself with anxiety, as he recounts, "with none among my friends to console me," he went of his own free will, and by divine inspiration, to the censor, who treated him kindly and advised him to present a copy of the manuscript to the court of the Holy Office, accompanied by a written statement in which he volunteered to delete any word or sentence that might be considered damaging to the Christian religion. As it turned out, the rabbi's fears were justified. Fra Marco Ferro of the monastery of San Giovanni e Paolo found a great deal of incriminating material in the text, especially in the sections on metempsychosis, the thirteen articles of faith, and the incorporeity of God. *"Ipse esse abolendum,"** peremptorily sentenced Fra Ferro. And Leone continues, "I, however, imagined a greater

---

*That must be obliterated

danger than there actually was, for in the final analysis, what I had written was not even that dangerous to say."

A month after his spontaneous presentation of *Historia de' Riti Hebraici* to the Inquisition, wrote Leone, "that Frenchman arrived in Rome, and sent me thence a copy printed in Paris and I saw that he had been astute and intelligent, and had deleted those four or five insertions that had caused me such anxiety. At the beginning of the book, he had also written an introduction in which he praised me highly; the work was dedicated to a noble ambassador of the French King who had come to live in Rome. This man personally sent me a letter saying that the work had greatly pleased both himself and the King. Then my fears were calmed."

The Venetian edition of the *Historia de' Riti Hebraici vita e osservanza degli Hebrei di questi tempi di Leon da Modena rabbi hebreo da Venezia, già stampata in Parigi et hora da Lui corretta e riformata** came out in Venice shortly thereafter, in 1638. In the foreword, Leone says his motivation for writing the book was to satisfy Christian curiosity about Jewish rituals. "My being easily persuaded by my friends," he observes, "and willing to obey the majority, as has always been my nature, easily disposed me to satisfy them. I have divided it into five parts, corresponding to the five books of the Law written by Moses. In writing, I truly forgot I was Jewish, imagining myself to be a mere neutral narrator."

Leone's *Historia* is a concise book, written in a clear narrative style. He points out that not all the rituals are equally important: there are 613 *mitzvoth*, or legal commandments—248 affirmative and 365 negative. There are precepts that must be respected, handed down by the wise men in the Oral Law, and simple customs called *minhagim*. The precepts of the Written and Oral Law are the common heritage of all Jews, including those "different among themselves," observes Leone, thinking of his own ghetto. He points out that the differences among Levantine, German, and Italian Jews are primarily in matters of custom. In speaking of the synagogues, or schools, he says, "There may be one, two, six, ten per city, depending on the number of Jews living in that place, so that they may understand, and according to the diversity of the Levantine, German and Italian nations, for they differ more in their prayers than in any other aspect, and each wants one after his own fashion." He emphasizes that the different nations have different styles of praying: "In chanting, the Germans sing more than any others; the manner of the Levantines and Spaniards resembles the Turkish, the Italians are simpler and more relaxed." Always thinking

---

**History of Jewish Rites. Life and Observances of the Jews of These Times by Leon da Modena, Jewish Rabbi from Venice, Previously Printed in Paris and Now Corrected and Revised by Him*

of his own Venice, the rabbi continues: "In the large cities there are diverse Brotherhoods for many charitable works such as those that care for the sick or bury the dead, mostly called Gemilut Hassadim; or for simple charity, called Tzedakah, for ransoming captives, called Pidyon Sevuim, for marrying maidens, called Hassi Betulod, and many others, more or less, according to the number of Jews living in that place." He places special emphasis on the charities and aspects of modern social welfare within the ghetto.

Given the rabbi's argumentative nature, criticism could obviously not be lacking. "Few are the Jews today who are able to speak an entire discourse in Hebrew, or in the holy tongue, called Lashon Ha-kodesh, in which the twenty-four books of the Old Testament are written, or in Chaldean either, called Targum, which they used to commonly speak . . . because they have learned and are brought up in the language of the land where they are born, if in Italy Italian, if in Germany German, if in the Levant or Barbary, Turkish or Moorish or the like. In fact they have appropriated these tongues to such a degree that many who have emigrated from Germany to Poland, Hungary and Russia have continued to use and teach their descendants German, and most of those who have gone eastward from Spain have used Spanish. In Italy, they speak one or the other language depending on the origin of their fathers; therefore the plebeians are concerned only with conforming to the people of the land where they live, mixing a few corrupt Hebrew words into their speech. The learned have a somewhat greater knowledge of Scripture, but except for the Rabbis, those who know how to speak a continuous, elegant discourse in Hebrew are rare. And in the pronunciation of this Hebrew language, there are such great differences among them that the Germans are barely understood by the Italians and Levantines, and none speak more clearly or conform more closely to the rules of the true Grammar (which they call Dikduk) than the Italians."

Study, which was considered an essential aspect of Jewish life, is described in great detail. Some studied Kabbalah, others Talmud. "Academies are established for this purpose, called Yeshivoth, where Rabbis and disciples meet and dispute, shouting in disorderly confusion, for it seems that these subjects are conducive to it; and they usually stay until morning, after prayers."

The customs surrounding Jewish weddings, in Venice and elsewhere, are evocatively described: "At the arranged hour, the couple is led into a room or chamber, beneath a canopy . . . and some are attended by children, singing, with lighted torches in hand. The people gather round, and one of those square mantles with fringes, called Tallit, is placed over the head of bride and bridegroom together. The Rabbis of that place, or the cantor of the School, or the closest relative, takes up a chalice or carafe of wine and says a blessing to God who has created man and woman and ordained their marriage, and offers some of the wine to the groom and bride. Then the groom places the ring on her finger in the presence of two witnesses, usually the Rabbis, saying, behold, thou art wed to me according to the law of Moses and Israel . . . And then with another vessel of wine they chant six more blessings, seven in all, and once more offer wine to both bride and groom, then they pour the wine on the ground as an omen of happiness, and the empty vessel is given to the bridegroom who hurls it to the ground and breaks it as a memento, in his happiness, of death that breaks and shatters us like glass, lest he become too proud. Then everyone cries Maazel Tov, which means good fortune, and they depart."

The *Historia de' Riti Hebraici* was widely acclaimed. It was printed and reprinted in several different editions and translated into a variety of languages including French, Italian, English, Dutch, Latin, and, in the mid-nineteenth century, Hebrew.

It was inevitable that a man like Leone da Modena should arouse controversy and debate within Jewish circles, and the nineteenth-century historian Graetz, author of a monumental study on Jewish history, was severely critical of the *Historia de' Riti Hebraici*.

Another fascinating and as yet largely unresolved debate concerning Leone da Modena stemmed from the publication in 1852, in Gorizia, of a book entitled *Bechinat ha-kabbalah*,* under the supervision of Rabbi Isacco Reggio. The work contained two hitherto unpublished pamphlets, both of which Reggio attributed to Leone da Modena on the basis of numerous points of formal and conceptual agreement between them and between both pamphlets and other writings by Modena.

The first pamphlet, *Kol Sakhal*, is a criticism of the Talmudic tradition; the second, *Shaagat Arieh*, the refutation of *Kol Sakhal*, has not come down to us complete. It is the ideal continuation of the philosophical journey undertaken in *Beth Yehuda*, an earlier work by Leone da Modena. The personality of the learned gambling rabbi, and the conflicts raging within his soul, seem expressly designed to feed curiosity and polemic. Was this defender of rabbinical power actually a heretic in disguise? Did he choose to hide behind an anonymous author in order to more freely propagate his most secret, subversive ideas?

In the early seventeenth century, the ghetto of Venice, thanks to its consolidated fame and cultural tradition, took on a role of leadership in the eyes of many European Jewish communities, such as Amsterdam and Hamburg, where the influx of heterogeneous groups with different life experiences and no uniform tradition had provoked sharp conflicts on matters of religion. The rabbis considered those thinkers, often Marranos, who questioned such fundamentals of Judaism as the valid-

---

*The Study of Tradition

ity of the Oral Law to be true heretics. Baruch Spinoza and Uriel da Costa are two famous and exemplary cases. In the attempt to diminish the impact of the often disruptive Marrano dissidents, the leaders of many European Jewish communities appealed for help to the learned rabbis of Venice. In 1618 they excommunicated those who denied the Oral Law.

Kol Sakhal is a work emblematic of this period dense with suspicion and charged with religious tensions. Its mysterious author attacks the Oral Law, demanding a return to the original teachings of the Bible and elimination of the power of the rabbis. Down through the centuries, he maintains, the rabbis had invented hundreds of precepts that distorted the meaning of the biblical text. According to the anonymous author, the Jewish religion should be the fruit of a new encounter between Religion and Revelation.

Was the *Kol Sakhal* the product of Leone da Modena's genius? In his brief introduction to the book, the rabbi tells us his own version: "In the month of Sivan 5382–1622 in Venice, about three months after the cruel murder of my son Zebulun, I was sadly walking along the banks of the city's canals, lamenting my sad destiny and the misfortunes that have befallen me from the day of my birth to this day, when a learned man, an acquaintance, came up to me." This friend handed Leone the anonymous text attacking rabbis and the Oral Law, which resulted in the answering pamphlet, *The Lion's Roar*. Is this statement a satisfactory answer to the accusations of Reggio, who considered Leone the author of the *Kol Sakhal*, or is it, rather, a convenient expedient which only serves to sharpen our suspicions? Can Leone da Modena be the author of this book? Could he have written it and been sorry later? Could he have been afraid of the ideas he had expounded? Did he adopt this ruse in order to express himself freely and with impunity? Was this why he never finished *The Lion's Roar*? Jewish commentators are understandably divided on this unresolved dilemma, so modern, so engaging, and so emblematic.

In a later work, *Magen v'zinnah,** compiled at the request of the leaders of the Spanish and Portuguese Nation in reply to the eleven theses that the heretic Uriel da Costa sent to the Jewish community of Venice in 1616, the rabbi used reasoning rather than invective, showing a certain flexibility in the face of certain of Uriel's observations and defending the validity of Oral Law with special zeal. In brief, he maintained that the text of the Torah is written without vowels, such that its words would have been impossible to decipher had they not been handed down through the Oral Law. The Torah is short and concise, and if there were no tradition of commentary and examination, the Jews might lose their way among the difficulties of its text. Each

---

Shield and Defense

generation, thanks to its sages and teachers, can confront the meaning of the obscure and unexplained passages in the Torah. The Oral Law, then, is a necessary interpretation and a cautionary rule. Despite centuries of exile and dispersion, the words of the masters have changed very little, and all Jews the world over have followed the Oral Law. This basic homogeneity is, in itself, proof of truth. The differences in prayers and rituals are unimportant, concludes Leone da Modena. The rabbi is bent on convincing his reader and attempts to give the discussion the tone of a debate within the Jewish community, without making accusations. His aim is to reaffirm rabbinical power and the value of the Oral Law.

Could he have possibly been so dissociated and paradoxical, so torn between orthodoxy and heterodoxy, as to uphold in the *Kol Sakhal* exactly the opposite of what he asserted in the *Magen v'zinnah?*

Some commentators have identified the *Kol Sakhal* as the lost work of Uriel da Costa, *Examen des tradicoens phariseas,** possibly reworked and adapted by Leone da Modena. Da Costa, born in Oporto in 1581 to a Marrano family, had been a religious Catholic before reverting to Judaism. When he did revert, he was excommunicated for his heretical books and committed suicide in 1640, after an act of public contrition. Did Leone da Modena sympathize with some, if not all, of his nonconformist ideas?

In his will, Leone asked the man who would deliver his elegy to point out "that he was not a hypocrite, that his heart was the same inside as out, and that he went in fear of God and fled evil more in secret than in the open." Once again, to his very last salutation, Leone maintained his ambiguous character. In his *Autobiography,* for that matter, he called himself a living anachronism. He was a Jew of the Renaissance, born too late and at odds with the dominant Counter-Reformation. From the sixteenth to the seventeenth century, he witnessed profound changes.

The seventeenth century was an age of rapid economic expansion, accompanied by an intellectual progress that changed the ideological and religious outlook of the old society, still tinged with medieval attitudes. Man's relationship with God also changed, and at the risk of being schematic we can say that, in keeping with the air of the times, a new concept of a "constitutional" God, bound by the laws of nature, began to replace the idea of an omnipotent deity, the arbitrary master of human life. Spinoza, according to the Jews, had the guilty audacity to take an even longer step forward, eliminating the personal God of the Jews and replacing Him with a pantheistic view of harmony in nature.

Seventeenth-century Judaism, the product of ancient Talmudic

**Examination of Pharisaical Traditions*

teachings, surrounded by defenses and protections called "hedges," as taught by the rabbis, was forced to meet the challenge of the new ideas. At the same time, the very nature of the ghetto made it resistant to novelty, especially coming from outside. The attack on the official rabbinate, representing conservatism, was in the natural order of things. And it was not by chance that the strongest centrifugal impetus came from Amsterdam, the dynamic center of the new capitalism. The new arrivals opposed the authority of the Oral Law which had been codified in the Mishnah and Talmud, representing the accumulation of rabbinical debate through long generations.

In Italy, too, heretics attacked the Oral Law and rabbinical supremacy, threatening to topple the consolidated orthodoxy of the native Jews. The words of the edict mentioned above, promulgated in 1618 by the leaders of the University, are eloquent: "And now the terrible sound is heard from these men who insult the messengers of God, the sages, the interpreters of the word of God by authority of the verses of the Scriptures . . . Both in our land and abroad . . . there are a few evil men and common sinners who deny the words of the sages and their allegorical interpretations and consider their words as nought. If this leprous scab were to spread through their houses and only among them, we could preserve our peace, for it would strike them alone, saying may their soul and their spirit end, for the punishment reserved to them in the present world and in the future world would be sufficient. But we hear a terrible sound from their mouths, their voices hiss like serpents . . . like a band of prophets . . . they go about the city to convince men by their words. They think they are highly placed in Israel . . . considering the Torah a fraud and the man wise who mocks at the words of the sages . . . they throw down the gates placed before the Torah. They consider the words of the sages as words that count for nothing. They believe they are the sole possessors of salvation." We can see from this excerpt that the problem of identifying the author of the *Kol Sakhal* was, at that time, more than a mere curiosity or academic problem. If Leone had been proven to be its author, the scandal would have been overwhelming.

Whether the author of the *Kol Sakhal* was indeed unknown and anonymous, or whether the book was an adaptation by Leone da Modena, whether he wrote it to combat rather than to encourage heresy, or whether it was the sign of an unconfessed and unconfessable ideological deviation, the work remains a fierce attack on official Judaism. In his reply, Leone da Modena harshly rebuts the author of the *Kol Sakhal* (himself?). He says he can accept a polemic on general principles, but not the accusation against the rabbis of distorting the meaning of the Torah. The Torah is not a human document, but comes from God. Every letter has meaning and needs an Oral Law to accompany it. For centuries rabbinical study has been devoted to this.

Albeit with uncertainty and from different positions, the scholars of the nineteenth century, Isacco Reggio of Gorizia, Abraham Geiger of Breslaw, and Libowitz who, like Geiger, wrote a biography of Leone da Modena, have always believed that the two works, *Kol Sakhal* and *Shaagat Arieh*, were complementary, and present much evidence for this thesis, based on both style and content. Reggio even interpreted the writing of such an explosive work as the *Kol Sakhal* as a way of goading the rabbinate to action without risking repercussions.

The American scholar E. Rivkin, on the contrary, whose book *Leon da Modena and the Kol Sakhal* was published in the United States in 1952, propounds a thesis diametrically opposed to Reggio's and is unconvinced by the latter's interpretation of certain ambiguous words which, correctly interpreted, would read: "My refutation of the heretical work *Kol Sakhal*, entitled *The Lion's Roar*, is not a refutation, because I only seem to roar in that work. The voice you hear in the *Kol Sakhal* is not the voice of a fool, but the authentic voice of Leone." The title would seem to contain two falsehoods: the denial is not a denial, and the heresy is not the creation of a fool.

Did Leone da Modena, involved in the writing of two contradictory works, support and attempt to establish that which he wished to destroy? Does this represent extremely modern thinking on the part of a seventeenth-century man, or the character of a confirmed gambler, a dual personality always in violent conflict with himself? Rivkin, who has attempted to put up a fence between Leone da Modena and the anonymous author, identifies many contradictions between the two texts—but are formal inconsistencies (regarding liturgy, ritual, and choral prayer) enough to decide the question?

Leone da Modena may have been the first Jewish scholar more concerned with divulging than interpreting the rules of Jewish life. This desire transpires not only from his writings, but from his intense relationships with exponents of the non-Jewish world: prelates, noblemen, ambassadors, and Catholic intellectuals. He showed a special preference for two Christian students: Giovanni Vislingio and Vincenzo Noghera, theologian to Cardinal Sacchetti, the archbishop of Bologna. Rabbi Leone certainly knew the illustrious Hebraist Giovanni Argoli and Jean Plantavit de la Panse, bishop of Lodève, Jacques Gaffarel, and John Selden. In a letter to the bishop of Lodève, Leone lamented: "My unhappy state forces me to say what I otherwise would not, but at any rate paper does not blush . . . I am old, ill and poor, abandoned by children and relations, and well known but poorly recognized by this University of my Jews, so that I live in no little want."

Moisè Soave describes Leone da Modena's last years: "Suffering from asthma he changed lodgings frequently; he was tormented night and day by his wife, whose tongue being the only healthy part of her body used it mightily, causing the poor old man great annoyance and distaste for life; twice he thought his end was near, and he was 74 years old when he was obliged to journey to Ferrara for several weeks to quarrel with the in-laws of one of his daughters for the restitution of her dowry, which he obtained with difficulty."

In February 1648, he wrote his last will, sold some books, and gave others to his grandson Isacco and to certain relatives. He died at the end of March 1648, at the age of seventy-seven, after four months' illness, with catarrh and fever. In his *Autobiography* he reports having practiced twenty-six professions in his lifetime: 1) Teaching Jewish students, 2) Teaching non-Jewish students, 3) Teaching writing, 4) Preaching, 5) Writing sermons for others, 6) Serving as cantor for the entire community, 7) Writing on various subjects, 8) Carrying out rabbinical duties, 9) Issuing religious sentences, 10) Serving as judge, 11) Teaching in the Yeshiva, 12) Granting the title of *chaver* to rabbis, 13) Engaging in foreign correspondence, 14) Composing music, 15) Writing poetry for weddings and gravestones, 16) Writing sonnets in Italian, 17) Writing plays, 18) Teaching how to perform them, 19) Drawing up documents, 20) Translating, 21) Printing his own writings, 22) Proofreading, 23) Studying and interpreting amulets, 24) Selling books and amulets, 25) Mediating and doing business, 26) Arranging marriages.

He wrote a Hebrew epitaph, to be carved on his tombstone. In translation, it reads:

"Words of the dead / Four ells of earth in this enclosure / With right of possession for eternity / Were acquired of the Highest for Yehuda Leone / da Modena. Be merciful to him (o Lord) and grant him peace."

In one passage of his will, Leone wrote: "Today, Tuesday, 3 Sivan 5394, both my head and my limbs are very heavy, and I feel a weakness upon me that fills me with fear of what may happen to me . . . The base of my coffin must be rectangular, and not grow wider at one end. They will put upon it only those books I have written myself, both printed and manuscript, and care shall be taken that the manuscripts not fall into the hands of non-Jews, so they shall take care to put only large, well-bound books. The Chazanim shall not follow the coffin with chants of admonition to others, but only a passage from the book of Psalms, 'I will lift up mine eyes unto the mountains . . .', or 'He who dwells in the mystery of the Lord,' a musical composition by my grandson Isacco Levi . . . Seek also to recite some of my original interpretations of biblical verses and some of my writings, and bury me opposite the entrance to the cemetery, on the side of the exit toward the square near my mother, my son, my grandfather and my uncle. Let them walk around my coffin according to the Levantine custom. Let my son Isaac come to the Italian Synagogue all year long to recite Kaddish."

The inventory of Leone's property has survived. According to historian Clemente Ancona, it is the only such document we know of from a Venetian Jew of that period. It was published by Leone's daughter Diana, possibly to forestall the claims of her creditors, and was preserved in the Venetian State Archives. In addition to listing the humble objects used by the rabbi, such as an old iron bedstead, "two mattresses, a few sheets, and three used men's shirts," the inventory is especially interesting because it contains a list of the rabbi's books, in Hebrew as well as in other languages: books of doctrine, Kabbalah, Jewish precepts and rituals, in addition to books on watches, the sermons of Savonarola, a copy of Boccaccio's *Decameron*, and texts on cosmography, to mention just a few.

Leone da Modena was, and remains, a controversial figure, polemic by nature and vocation, gifted with great talent and vast potential that he never fully tapped, exhausting and wasting it, to a large extent, in gambling. He taught for years, but found no joy in teaching. Proofreading was a nuisance. His only real love was writing.

Many of his contradictions were the fruit of his environment. Burning with intellectual curiosity, he opposed the Kabbalah but believed in amulets and astrology; he showed a strong attachment to Judaism, but kept an open mind toward the outside world and had a keen interest in Christianity. He often attempted to reconcile the Jewish tradition with the culture of Venice, a city he loved and left only when obliged to, but to which he always returned. The very diversity of his interests made him tolerant. He was intelligent, irreverent, and sarcastic. And he was never afraid to contradict himself.

CHAPTER FOURTEEN

Sara Coppio Sullam, Poetess

Correspondence with Ansaldo Cebà — Controversy with Baldassare Bonifacio on the immortality of the soul — The Codice of Giulia Soliga

"Sara was a great beauty, with blond hair and gentle glance . . . but of delicate constitution and afflicted by frequent illness." Thus did Emanuele Antonio Cicogna, a famous nineteenth-century student of Venetian history, describe Sara Coppio Sullam, an extraordinary woman, poetess, and intellectual, who lived in the ghetto of Venice in the late sixteenth and early seventeenth century.

Sara, who married Giacobbe Sullam in 1612, became well known, even more than for her exemplary personal qualities, for certain literary polemics that accurately reflect the culture of her time, and not merely that of the ghetto.

One especially curious aspect of Sara's literary life was her exchange of letters with Ansaldo Cebà, a nobleman of Genoa, himself a poet, translator of the classics, and author of an epic poem entitled *La Reina Ester* (1615). The correspondence lasted for four years, but the two never met.

It was Sara who initiated the exchange. Her first letter to Cebà, in May 1618, expressed her interest and admiration for the author of the poem, and her wish to correspond with him. Cebà immediately accepted, urging Sara to read Canto XIX of his poem, reflect on the words of Queen Esther, and convert to Christianity.

Cebà sent Sara a sonnet:

When to the limit of my long life
Already my foot draws nigh,
A woman, who hopes and who does not believe,
Attempts to make me sigh and moan for love.

Fresh is her grace, and her beauty supreme,
Wherewith she kindles and calls forth my desires,
But she harbors neither piety nor Faith
Wherefore I fear not the bonds of her dominion.

Still in the darkness of Hebraic rites
She sees no Latin torch, nor Greek
That might discover to her eyes what it reveals to mine.

But were it not that Heaven shields me,
Vainly would I combat the arrows
Shot by a little boy for a blind woman.

A few months later, Cebà sent her a portrait, with more poetry. Sara replied with a portrait of herself, accompanied by a sonnet that begins:

This is the image of one who in her heart
Bears only thy image carved,
Who pointing to her bosom tells the world,
Here I wear my idol, let all adore him.

In answer to the appeals of Cebà, eager to teach her the way of Christianity, Sara wrote, "He who leaves the old way for the new is often mistaken and later feels anguish." After four years of vain attempts, Cebà wrote to Sara, "If you do not mean to convert, lay down your pen; for without this I cannot use my own." And the long exchange of letters (Cebà had written fifty-three) came to an end. Contact between the young Venetian Jewess and the elderly Genoan nobleman, separated by all aspects of their lives, including a thirty-year age difference, was broken off. A year later, in Genoa, the publisher Giuseppe Pavoni printed a volume entitled *Lettere d'Ansaldo Cebà scritte a Sara Coppio e dedicate a Marco Antonio Doria.** There is a copy of this rare collection in the Library of the Correr Museum in Venice, but of Sara's letters no trace has remained. Cebà may have destroyed them all.

This correspondence between the elderly, infirm Catholic nobleman from Genoa and the blond young Venetian Jewess is a singular testi-

---

*Letters of Ansaldo Cebà Written to Sara Coppio and Dedicated to Marco Antonio Doria

mony of a singular relationship, and indeed, of the times. Although such a correspondence was not unusual in the literary culture of the day, it could not fail to arouse the interest and curiosity of historians. Who helped young Sara hold her own against the expert Cebà? A friend of hers, Fra Angelico Aprosio, did not credit her with such an acute intellect, and Cicogna thought the secret mind behind her wisdom might be that of Numidio Paluzzi, a poet and prose writer often seen at her literary salon in the ghetto. Moisè Soave had no doubts on the matter. The inspiration for Sara's ideas, her prudent but lively answers, must have been none other than the famous Leone da Modena, an expert polemicist and Talmudic scholar, and a friend of Sara's. Actually both Cebà himself and another priest, Baldassare Bonifacio, suspected the presence of a learned rabbi behind the bold, blond Sara. We know for certain that Leone da Modena frequented Sara's salon, and that when he published Salomon Usque's tragedy *Ester*, with extensive modifications, in 1619, he dedicated it to Sara Coppio.

In 1621 Sara Coppio Sullam found herself engaged in a difficult contest with another man of letters, Baldassare Bonifacio, archdeacon of Treviso and later bishop of Capodistria. Although he had originally been a frequent guest at her salon, he later became one of her harshest critics. In his *Discorso sull'immortalità dell'anima*,* published in 1621 by Antonio Pinelli in Venice, Bonifacio accused Sara of heresy and of denying the immortality of the soul. Since the Holy See posed a threat to all, at the time, Sara was obliged to answer promptly, and did so in a *Manifesto di Sara Copio Sulam Hebrea nel quale è da lei riprovata e detestata l'opinione negante l'immortalità dell'anima, falsamente attribuitale dal Signor Baldassare Bonifaccio, da lei dedicato alla memoria di Simon Copio suo dilettissimo genitore.***

We learn more about the life of Sara Coppio Sullam from Fra Angelico Aprosio. A Frenchman, having arrived in Venice and "hearing about the fame of Sara and her Academy, desired to be presented there." Her teacher and preceptor, Numidio Paluzzi, saw that Sara was much taken with the foreigner, and thought he could turn this to his own advantage. He had a forged letter delivered to Sara, in which the Frenchman revealed his love "which he said he had kept concealed," and requested a prompt reply which would be conveyed to Paris by magic in just a few hours. The poetess took the bait, Fra Aprosio tells us, and followed Paluzzi's advice, giving him four hundred gold scudi to buy gifts and pay for a portrait of herself commissioned from the painter Berardelli. Paluzzi assured her that it would all be delivered to Paris

---

*Discourse on the Immortality of the Soul
**Manifesto by Sara Coppio Sullam, Jewess, in which she condemns and deprecates the opinion denying the immortality of the soul, falsely attributed to her by Signor Baldassare Bonifacio, dedicated to the memory of Simon Coppio, her beloved father

"by an airborne spirit that would take no more than three hours to travel from Venice to France." The story is also told in a manuscript called the *Codice di Giulia Soliga,* formerly the property of the Venetian bibliophile Cigogna and now in the Correr Library.

The identity of Giulia Soliga is still a mystery, and the reason for her impassioned defense of Sara is unknown. But certainly this miscellany, a valuable example of Baroque literary style, offers more than one curious tidbit and supplies the background for the whole Paluzzi affair. Paluzzi, dismissed from his post as secretary to a Venetian nobleman on account of his arrogance and ignorance, was aided by Sara who, seeing him dressed in rags, got him some new clothes, a place to live, and a monthly salary of six zecchini. She also sent him "morning and evening, sumptuous provisions both for himself and for the page who served him." Soliga tells how, six years later, Paluzzi suddenly abandoned his post and went to Friuli, but not before he "quietly emptied the house of everything the Jewess had lent him and, not without first making her pay him three months' salary, and without saying goodbye, he took flight: a fraud worth a hundred ducats and more." His adventure in Friuli proved a fiasco and he returned to Venice "more wretched than ever." The poetess took him in, cared for him, and for two years gave him "a room near her own," entrusting him to the care of her favorite maid Paola, a woman from Friuli whom she considered "as a mother." But Paola conspired with La Mora, a black Marrano woman from Granada, and they soon began to rob Sara systematically, accusing an imaginary ethereal spirit of the thefts. Paluzzi, who had taken up residence in Paola's house, joined with the two women "and, thinking this was just the work for him, made a third in the infamous concert, eagerly welcomed by the two women who hoped, by virtue of his authority, to accomplish some grand things, as indeed proved true." The poor poetess, who trusted those she had helped and was keenly interested in all magical and supernatural phenomena, fell into the trap, which spread even wider when the painter Berardelli and Paola's three children joined the conspiracy. Soliga relates: "And singing to this melody, with the seven voices tuned as one, they brought that poor Lady to such a pass that she went nearly out of her mind . . . The thefts continued ad infinitum, nor did they stop while there was anything left to steal; there was no jewel-case left intact, no strongbox unforced, no arms-cupboard not thrown ajar; every lock was open to the airy spirit, every door unlocked . . . the bracelets were not safe on her arms nor the necklaces on her neck, the girdle at her waist, the rings on her fingers." The deceptions grew and multiplied, partly because the scoundrels had such an easy time of it. They stole jewelry and household goods, and finally, because the poetess showed no sign of suspicion, went on to steal gold and jewels under the guise of an exchange of gifts with the French nobleman, as we learn from Fra Aprosio.

Soliga writes, "As God willed, this vile treachery was finally discovered, and having ascertained the extent of her loss the Jewess appealed to justice, and complained both in private and in public, with the result that those dastards published opprobrious writings against her innocence." In fact, after Sara denounced them to the Signori di Notte al Criminal, Paluzzi and Berardelli retaliated by distributing defamatory satires about her, entitled *Sarreidi*, in the ghetto.

Paluzzi, who had long been suffering from syphilis, died shortly after Sara's denunciation and the outbreak of the scandal. In July 1625, his friend and accomplice Berardelli, in an attempt to defend himself against Sara's accusations, collected Paluzzi's papers and had some of his poems printed, under the title *Rime del signor Numidio Paluzzi allo illustre ed eccellentissimo Signore Giovanni Soranzo.* * In the preface to the *Rime*, the painter accused Sara of having deliberately dominated and manipulated Paluzzi.

The central chapter of the *Codice di Giulia Soliga* describes Paluzzi's imaginary trial in the Court of Appeals on Mount Parnassus. Before the court, presided over by Apollo and populated by eminent literary figures and statesmen, the spirit of Paluzzi is summoned to account for his misdeeds. He is called to defend himself against the accusation of offending the reputation of a virtuous and honored gentlewoman with supreme ingratitude and extraordinary deceit. The hearing is conducted by Vittoria Colonna, marchioness of Pescara, and Veronica Gambara di Careggio, assisted by Sappho and Corinna. Having examined the records, letters, and documents taken from the "authentic originals of the Signori di Notte al Criminal," they summon the preceptor Paluzzi, who stands up before the court, "that blackened face, that hermaphrodite's voice, that assassin's leer . . . to be examined by the actress Isabella Andreini." After a moment's hesitation, the man confesses his crimes and describes his deceptions in detail, but swears he had nothing to do with disseminating the slanderous satires and accuses his accomplice the painter. Then the public prosecutor stands up, in the person of Pietro Aretino, a poet known for his licentious verse as well as for his witty pen. He delivers a severe summation, and Paluzzi is ultimately found guilty of the entire intrigue and sentenced to have a mark branded on his forehead. Berardelli is also convicted, but since he has not yet arrived in the kingdom of the dead on Parnassus he is symbolically branded in effigy, chained with other convicted felons to the peak of a high mountain, and handed over to the populace,

---

* *Verses by Signor Numidio Paluzzi Addressed to the Illustrious and Most Excellent Signor Giovanni Soranzo*

who tear him to pieces. The final banquet is attended by the whole cast of characters on Parnassus, over five hundred in all, and many clever sonnets are recited.

Sara Coppio Sullam died "of fevers" in March 1641. On her tombstone is engraved a Hebrew epitaph dictated by Leone da Modena. It was translated into Italian in the nineteenth century by Moisè Soave, and in English reads:

THIS IS THE STONE OF THE DISTINGUISHED
LADY SARA, WIFE OF THE LIVING
JACOBBE SULLAM.
THE EXTERMINATING ANGEL LOOSED HIS DART,
MORTALLY WOUNDING SARA,
WISE AMONG WIVES, THE SUPPORT OF DERELICTS.
THE WRETCHED FOUND IN HER A COMPANION AND FRIEND.
IF NOW SHE IS GIVEN IRREPARABLY IN PREY TO THE INSECTS,
ON THE PREDESTINED DAY THE GOOD LORD WILL SAY:
RETURN, RETURN, O SHULAMMITE.
SHE PASSED AWAY ON THE SIXTH DAY (FRIDAY)
5 ADAR 5401 OF THE JEWISH ERA.
MAY HER SOUL ENJOY ETERNAL BEATITUDE.

CHAPTER FIFTEEN

Simone Luzzatto, or On Consistency

Luzzatto and the legend of Venice — *The* **Discorso circa il stato de gl'Hebrei et in particolar dimoranti nell'inclita città di Venetia** — *The success of the* **Discorso**

In the course of nearly a century and a half, the Venetian Jews who contributed most to creating the myth of Venice were Isaac Abrabanel, David De Pomis, and Simone Luzzatto. Abrabanel arrived in the early sixteenth century, before the establishment of the ghetto, having wandered through all the ports of the Mediterranean. De Pomis, driven from Perugia by papal intolerance, found hospitality and honor on the lagoon at a time when the memory of Lepanto was still keen. It is understandable, therefore, that they felt a debt to the new home that had welcomed them. But Luzzatto was a member of the German Nation, the group that had founded the ghetto, and although he, too, contributed to promulgating the Venetian myth, in the early decades of the seventeenth century he was quick to sense the symptoms of impending decline. Working out an original theory of economics, he sought to revitalize the ideal view of Venice in a synthesis that would emphasize the city's indissoluble tie with its Jews.

The myth of Venice, to which Abrabanel and De Pomis had attributed metaphysical connotations, was interpreted by Simone Luzzatto in terms of the commercial reality of the time, based on historical and political considerations. Luzzatto was a man of Renaissance culture, and his writings contain frequent references to Machiavelli, Paruta, and the theory of the reason of state; they also abound in classical echoes, with references to such authors as Plato, Aristotle, and Tacitus.

Luzzatto, whose political ideas and economic theories were formulated with both passion and rationality, wrote the *Discorso circa il stato de gl'Hebrei et in particolar dimoranti nell'inclita città di Venezia* in an effort to convince his readers of the usefulness of the Jewish presence in Venice by presenting them with concrete facts.

Luzzatto gives political significance to the messianic idea by interpreting the dispersion of the Jews in the light of the Machiavellian concept of necessity, and by emphasizing that man's life is not shaped by free will alone, but is subject to the struggle for survival. Echoes of Machiavelli emerge, also, in an acutely humanistic analogy in which Luzzatto asks that what remains of the Hebrew nation be granted the same respect as would be accorded to an archeological finding, say a statue by Phidias.

Abrabanel and De Pomis were content to point out the parallels and affinities between the Mosaic and the Venetian law. Luzzatto, who reflects the new commercial demands of the seventeenth century, presents not a static, unchanging view, but a dynamic picture in keeping with his time. Economics and politics are the true protagonists of the city's greatness, he says, and of its decline. Luzzatto emphasizes the Republic's special capacity for stability, its exemplary administration of justice, and the firmness of its laws in contrast with the uncertainty of the times, but he attributes that state of well-being not so much to metaphysical ideals as to a strong economy and good government. In explaining the greatness of the Most Serene Republic, the symptoms of its decadence, and the possible remedies, he deductively demonstrates the importance of the Jews in the city. Herein lies the novelty of his work, and in this respect Luzzatto shows himself to be a man of the seventeenth century, a man of the new age and the new science.

What motivated Luzzatto to write the *Discorso*? Was it some particular circumstance affecting the life of the Venetian Jews? John Toland, in supporting British naturalization for Jews in 1714, hinted that the Jews of Venice had found themselves in some difficulty around the late 1630s. Leone da Modena wrote of incidents occurring in 1636: "All the residents of the city, the noble citizens and all the common people, assailed the Jews as was customary, for if one man commits evil they are angry with the entire Community." Luzzatto echoes this when he writes, "Every nation produces bad individuals, and the whole group must not be judged on the basis of their bad conduct."

An anonymous chronicle entitled *Storia delle disgrazie che hanno colpito gli ebrei d'Italia*, brought to light by Schulwass in 1949, helped solve the mystery and clarified many heretofore obscure details. The work, written in a flowery style, probably between 1640 and 1663, was meant to be read in the Italian synagogues on Tisha b'Av. In September 1635, a large lot of merchandise was stolen in the heart of the city. The event caused a great uproar and when some of the loot was traced to the ghetto, the scandal intensified. The thieves were arrested, and some of them were Jews. Some high-ranking patricians and judges were also involved in the scandal, suspected of having taken bribes. Between vendettas and unexpected turns of events, the case took on the proportions of a full-fledged affair of state, with disputes and tensions involving the entire University of the Jews. The whole ghetto felt threatened. In an attempt to prevent the seemingly imminent expulsion of the Jews from the Venetian territories, reduce the widespread agitation in the city, and calm the troubled waters, the Council of Ten and Doge Francesco Erizzo appointed three mediators. Shemuel Meldola, a personal acquaintance of the doge, was called from Verona, the University designated Simone Luzzatto, head of the Kahal Kadosh Yeshiva in Venice, and the third was Israel Conegliano, a close friend of the minister Marco Giustiniano.

At that time Simone Luzzatto was the chief rabbi of Venice. Born in 1583, he was already a well-known personality in the early years of the seventeenth century, and his responsa on various religious matters were widely respected. His great culture was not limited to Jewish subjects; Joseph Del Medigo praised his profound knowledge of mathematics and Giulio Morosini, alias Samuel Nahmias, mentions in *Via della fede* that he was known and esteemed inside and outside the ghetto for both his learning and his eloquence.

The *Discorso circa il stato de gl'Hebrei et in particolar dimoranti nell'inclita città di Venezia* was printed in Venice "at the shop of Giovanni Colleoni" in 1638. A subtitle on the cover indicates the existence of an appendix to the work, but this additional tract, probably in manuscript, has since been lost.

In his preface, Luzzatto sets forth the essential lines of his apologia, and expresses his sorrow at the fact that "the Jewish nation, in past centuries celebrated and illustrious, is now in disgrace" and that it "suffers from lack of those doctrines and disciplines that it would have needed in order to reveal and manifest itself to the sincere judgment of the more prudent, severing those stigmas of infamy and mendacity that the condition of the times has woven about it." Luzzatto's intention was to emphasize "certain benefits that the Hebrew nation living in the Noble City of Venice brings to it," not to overrate it "but only to show that this nation is not a totally useless member of the general population of this city," and "also with the intent to show those less well versed in worldly affairs the reasons and impulses that led this most prudent and just Republic to annex our nation in safe domicile, with paternal protection, and defend it from this latest injury."

Alluding to the recent hostility against the ghetto, he writes, "If in accordance with the condition of human frailty some agitators and scoundrels have been found within this nation, this is no reason why the sincere affection held by the University of the Jews for its Most

Clement Prince should be obscured and denigrated." Even a well-tilled field produces some weeds along with a good harvest, he continues, but the peasant does not abandon his field for this reason. In his defense of the Jewish role in the life of the city, Luzzatto states, "The crimes of a few among our nation are exaggerated, by some, as intolerable disgrace and insupportable calamity; but the ordinary benefits, conveniences and profits that derive from our people are overlooked and neglected as imperceptible and unknown things." The Jews bring considerable wealth to the noble city of Venice and should be considered "an integral part of its common populace."

Recalling the ancient Greek concept of the world, our author writes: "Thus it is legitimate for the Jewish nation to compare itself to the atoms of Democritus . . . The Kingdoms are like the Milky Way that appears to our eyes as a conglomeration of tiny stars, with each one invisible by itself, but together giving light and brilliance, and thus do great empires result from the minuteness of diverse populations." The Jewish population in Venice is one of these minuscule stars, but its importance in the economy of the Serenissima is great. The many duties it pays free the Venetian people from the harassment of constant taxes and levies to meet the urgent needs of the State, for "civil experience teaches that in cities which thrive on copious trade, their people are to a large degree relieved of extraordinary levies and exorbitant taxes." He praises the greatness of Venice in "taxing only the industry of men and not their lives, punishing their vices rather than profiting therefrom, which has ensued principally through her moderate government; but aided in part by the abundant revenues brought in by the merchant traffic and maritime trade."

In the first of the eighteen "considerations" into which the text is subdivided, Luzzatto emphasizes the "utility of trade; the human consortium is nothing but a union of mutual needs or pleasures, and alternating negotiations between abundance and penury and what the Moralists call superfluity, luxury and vain objects of our greed." The Venetian rabbi, who requests tolerance in the name of economic expediency, then writes, "Coming to the particular treatise proposed, I say that among the benefits and advantages that the Jewish nation brings to the city of Venice, the primary one is the profit resulting from trade . . . whence the city derives five important benefits." Paraphrased, these are: the increase in public customs duties; the conveying of merchandise from distant lands, not only for the needs of the people, but as ornaments to civil life; the supply of raw materials, wool and silk for example, to Venetian craftsmen (and this means that those who work live in peace and quiet without commotion and rioting for lack of food); the exporting of finished products and the sale of many goods processed and manufactured in the city; and commerce and mutual trade, which constitute the foundation of peace and tranquillity between neighboring peoples. The Jews contribute to all this, notes Luzzatto, through "the industry of individuals and the use of their assets."

Some say the Jews are not importers of merchandise, but that they occupy spaces that do not belong to them, thus damaging the Christian citizens of Venice. They add that the Jews are not the ones responsible for the flourishing Venetian commerce, but that conditions favorable to trade already exist in Venice by virtue of its excellent position with navigable rivers nearby, convenient access to other cities, the freedom and safety of its life, and the perfection of the arts. Luzzatto takes all these observations into account, but in his second consideration offers an explanation for why so much of Venetian trade is conducted by foreigners. Trade, useful to those who engage in it and profitable for the city, is laborious and involves great danger to both merchants and merchandise. After so much risk and anxiety, the merchant looks forward to security and a peaceful life, and it is therefore no wonder that so many sumptuous palazzi with rich furnishings are built in trading cities. The richer a city grows, the less willingly its citizens go to sea; they prefer to leave trade to newly arrived foreigners who are fleeing lives of poverty elsewhere. Venice is no longer living in the age of Quirini, Da Mosto, Barbaro, and Marco Polo, whose bold voyages in all directions took them to the remote reaches of Muscovy and Tartary. Today the Venetians prefer the farms and countryside of the mainland, and are no longer willing to expose themselves to the ocean winds and the tricks of fate. Their place in the Levant trade, from Dalmatia to Constantinople, has been taken by the French, English, Flemish, and Genoans.

The growth of a city can be compared to that of a body that feeds and grows, then stabilizes at a certain stage and slowly begins to decline. The citizens in their opulence are concerned with consuming rather than producing wealth, and this is when the foreigners come in, first accumulating wealth and then returning home to enjoy the fruits of their trading. And this is very harmful as it means the loss of energy and wealth for the city. What to do? It is not always easy, or even possible, to assimilate foreigners into the city. They miss their distant homelands and want to die where they were born. If Venice wanted to permanently attract Frenchmen, Germans, and Genoans, she would have to offer them the opportunity to buy houses and land at the same terms accorded Venetian citizens. This is not feasible in Venice, surrounded by the lagoon, marshlands, and land unsuitable for agriculture. The wealthy merchants would not be satisfied with simple possession as an incentive for staying in the city, but would demand additional privileges entailing titles, property, and public office to make their position more prestigious.

The Jews represent a solution to these problems, "having no Country of their own to which they aspire to transfer the property they amass in the city, nor do they have the faculty or the ability to acquire real estate anywhere, nor, if they had, would it be in their interest to do so, tying up their assets, since they do not aspire to dignities, titles, or power, for once accepted in a city they firmly resolve not to leave . . . in addition to which, since the Jew living in Venice has no craft of his own except for trade, it would be difficult to leave, with no hope of supporting himself by any art or profession that could be practiced in any city . . . And there is no doubt that of all the States and places in the world, the Hebrew Nation prefers the most benevolent Government of the Most Serene Republic for its stable form of Rule, which does not alter owing to the vagaries of a sole Prince." Given their natural traits, then, the Jews are more useful to Venice than other foreigners. And because of this special bond with Venice, they bring merchandise to the city which, were it not for them, would probably go no further than other ports in the Tirrhenian Sea better suited to trade with the nations on that side of the Mediterranean, "wherefore the abundant Merchandise brought by the Jews causes rapid turnover and consumption, whence derive Customs revenues for the Prince."

But are the Jews "fit to engage in trade"? In the fourth consideration, Luzzatto buttresses his thesis with psychological and anthropological observations. He points out that "indigence and need are the true stimuli and incentives to the invention and discovery of the most vital and excellent arts," and adds that "the Jews, more than any other nation, have been educated and instructed in the school of hardship, under the rigid discipline of need, since they own no real estate, do not practice mechanical Trades, are barred from urban employment and are for the most part burdened with families since their law forbids Celibacy . . . Where the Jews find a home, traffic and commerce flourish, as Leghorn can attest, and Venice herself will remember that the founder of the Port of Spalato was a Jew, and from that time henceforth the Port has been an anchor point for all trade toward the East." The political stability of the Republic favors the influx of capital from relatives of Venetian Jews living in other cities who are looking for a safe place to invest their money. The Jews cultivate no land, they own no ships, and are channeled into trade by the very condition of their lives: the Venetian Jew, goaded by need, feels more than any other man the necessity for moving his capital around the world, not only "in ports accessible to the Venetians," but especially in those out of the Venetians' reach, where the Jews can go not by virtue of their greater willingness to incur risk, but because they have contacts with other Jews under Turkish rule, who can be trusted, but only by themselves.

Luzzatto offers an overview of commerce at that time and of the ascent of the new trading classes, first among them the Portuguese, Flemish, and English, who did business in the ports of Lyons, Antwerp, and Amsterdam. Concluding that certain aspects of commerce are the prerogative of the Jews, actually "conjoined to their persons," and that "flourishing industries depend on them," yet aware that such statements may prove to be a double-edged weapon, he hastens to play down their importance and diminish their potential danger. The fifth consideration, in fact, deals with the Jews' readiness to obey: "The Hebrew Nation is scattered and dispersed throughout the world with no leader or protection, and always conforms with ready flexibility to the Public Command, and when special taxes are imposed is never heard to complain or voice even the simplest protest." Again praising the Venetian Republic, "the best governed of all," Luzzatto points out the beneficial effects of its inflexible stratification and the rigid divisions between common people, citizens, and nobility, and between the city's numerous trades and guilds: the trades maintain their high quality, improving from father to son with increasingly refined specialization. There is peace among the people because everyone knows his place, one person does not usurp another's trade, and jealousies and resentments are thereby avoided. Since the people are divided they more readily obey the commands of their leaders and are less given to conspiracy and rioting.

How, then, can a potentially foreign body, such as the ghetto Jews appear to many, be incorporated into an orderly structure like that of Venice, so insistent on perfection, unity, and obedience? The Jews, too, says Luzzatto, have a profession different from all others. They, too, are separate from the artisans and citizens; moreover, they are not authorized to own real estate and cannot convert their capital, which, all other considerations aside, they have to keep for their travels "whence derive great Customs revenues." Luzzatto compares capital investment in real estate with investment in trading journeys, and concludes that real estate, while less risky, is also less remunerative. Trading journeys are fraught with unknown dangers, but they bring in profits which benefit all the Venetians in peacetime and make it possible to create a reserve of well-equipped ships ready to put to sea at any time in case of war.

"In the body civil," writes the rabbi, "the Jew may be likened to the part of the foot that treads the ground, which being inferior to all the other members is a burden to none, but indeed supports them." He goes on, "And I say that, since the Jew is forbidden any profession except Trade, he harms people of no condition, neither Artisans, nor Foreigners, nor is he a great burden even to Merchant Citizens." The risks of sailing are many and unpredictable. True, there are wealthy merchants, but many of them experience sudden bankruptcy and yet, over the past hundred years, not one of them in time of good fortune has ever left Venice. Luzzatto repeatedly stresses the fact that the Jews have no political authority, and in support of this statement he lists some reliable figures: "I estimate the Jews to number close to 6,000." He calculates that the duties paid on food imports amount to 48,000 ducats (8 ducats per capita). He also feels that the Jewish presence has an indirect influence on the city's economy and calculates that four thousand people are indirectly affected, with customs duties amounting to 32,000 ducats. The Jews themselves pay direct duties of roughly 70,000 ducats. This commerce, observes Luzzatto, creates oblique duties (on materials for the processing of raw materials): the compound duty may be calculated as two-thirds of the direct duty, or 47,000 ducats. To this must be added taxes on the banks, special taxes, the obligation to provide lodging for ambassadors, and "certain minutiae could be added, hardly worth mentioning, such as the consumption of Salt which I believe to be four times that of the Christians, through their ritual of salting meat to extract the blood which is forbidden to them." Luzzatto arrives at a sum of 205,000 ducats and then, almost as though alarmed at such a large figure, softens its impact: "Nor would I make bold to say that the above calculation is faultless and unimpeachable; Political matters are full of uncertainties." Albeit with this reservation, he does not back down. To the above sum he adds a special tax and again "the tax of one-fourth of the rents, which the Jews find very heavy, since the houses are appraised in proportion to the small size of their dwellings; confined in the cramped enclosure of the Ghetto." The rents on houses in the ghetto were three times higher than those in other parts of Venice, plus an additional tax of a thousand ducats. The sum of approximately 220,000 ducats, collected at no expense, was clear revenue in the coffers of the Republic.

Ravid, analyzing Luzzatto's calculations, has observed that the sum of 220,000 ducats was higher than the net revenues of any mainland city, at least in 1633, and drew the conclusion that the net revenue produced by the Jewish community was much higher than the analogous net revenues of the individual dominions, either on the mainland or in the Levant and Candia. The colony in Candia and the vast "maritime state" would in later years prove to be a burden to Venice because of the increasing military expenditures they necessitated. The net revenue of 220,000 ducats produced by the ghetto required no special supervision: "The Ghetto Enclosure needs no praesidium to guard it, nor fortress to defend or restrain it, no armada to patrol its coasts against sudden attack by Corsairs, nor can it be surprised by Princely rivalries, nor agitated by fear of internal sedition; there is no danger of flood from the sea nor impetuous rivers to submerge it; no necessity for the continuous repair and restoration of ramparts or for provision of war materials, there need be no concern for the lack of victuals, nor is there need of a Ruler to govern it, nor Quaestor nor Chamberlain to collect revenues; the Hebrew nation is in itself submissive, subject and obedient to its Prince, placed in the center, it might be said, of the diligent city, and itself industrious in observance and strict compliance with the dues and payments it owes to the public." Moreover, adds Luzzatto, the Jews would like permission to bear arms, being willing to shed their blood for the Serenissima just as they are ready to pour out their money.

Luzzatto's *Discorso* attracted attention and interest far beyond Venice. Many scholars have found points of agreement with the *Discorso* in a work by Menasseh ben Israel, a famous rabbi of Amsterdam, published in London in 1655. Written in Latin with the title *De fidelitate et utilitate Judaicae gentis libellus anglicus*, it was translated into English as *To his Highness the Lord Protector of the Commonwealth of England, Scotland and Ireland, Appeal in Favor of the Jewish People.* In his book Luzzatto defended the right of the Jews to stay in Venice, while ben Israel was arguing in favor of readmitting the Jews to England after 350 years of banishment. Their basic intention was the same, however, and the arguments they both used are amazingly similar. In fact, nearly identical passages appear in both texts, although Luzzatto's influence is never mentioned explicitly in ben Israel's work.

Luzzatto also influenced James Harrington, an English nobleman who visited Venice in the 1630s. His book *Oceana*, printed in 1656, deals with the Venetian Constitution, the surprising political stability of her Republic, and her unchangeability through the centuries.

Although he does examine problems relating to the microcosm of the Venetian ghetto, Luzzatto was strongly influenced by the cultural climate in Europe, expressed by illustrious visitors to Venice.

In addition to Harrington and ben Israel, Isaac Cardoso and ben Zion Frizzi (a seventeenth-century figure) were also influenced by Simone Luzzatto. John Toland, who in 1714 advocated the naturalization of the English Jews, used the same arguments as the Venetian rabbi, which had so impressed Harrington.

Simone Luzzatto was a freethinker and nonconformist. He did not believe in the survival of the Ten Lost Tribes and spoke skeptically and with small esteem of the Kabbalah and mysticism in general. The originality of his religious convictions is reflected in a long treatise called *Pessak*, in which he maintains that the Talmud permits traveling by gondola on the Sabbath, given the special nature of Venice. The Va'ad Katan, the small council of the Jewish community, while appreciating the rabbi's acumen, ruled in favor of caution and denied the validity of such an extraordinary concession.

In 1651, two years before his death, Luzzatto published another work in Italian, *Socrate o dell'umano sapere*,* dedicated to Venice and the

---

Socrates, or On Human Knowledge

doge. This highly erudite philosophical treatise is a curious work which, as more than one historian has observed, contains absolutely nothing that would reveal its author's Jewish identity were it not explicitly stated on the title page—a reflection of the degree to which the ghetto and the illustrious rabbi, its highest representative, were sensitive to outside influence.

CHAPTER SIXTEEN

Giulio Morosini Alias Samuel Nahmias: His Uncertain Identity and Anti-Jewish Polemic

Via della fede: *a spiritual journey suspended between rejection and nostalgia — Leone da Modena: former teacher and imaginary interlocutor — Circumcision, the feast of Simchat Torah, Purim, kosher wine, and the Sabbath.*

V ia della fede (Derekh Emunah) mostrata a'gli ebrei da Giulio Morosini veneziano scrittore della Biblioteca Vaticana nella lingua ebraica e lettore nel Collegio di propaganda fide, opera non meno curiosa che utile per chi conversa o tratta con gli ebrei o predica loro* is the title of a book printed in Rome on August 1, 1683, and considered one of the most fertile sources of information on the Jewish life and customs of the time, especially with regard to the ghetto of Venice.

Morosini, whose real name was Samuel Nahmias, adopted the name of this patrician Venetian family at the time of his conversion in 1649. *Via della fede*, a 1,500-page tome, is unquestionably a detailed anti-Jewish attack, but it contains a number of apparent contradictions, as though Morosini-Nahmias had never quite succeeded in resolving the dilemma of his identity and remained wavering unconsciously between Christianity and Judaism.

The introduction explains the official purpose of the book. Having converted to Christianity, the author intends to show incredulous Jews that he will not change his mind and means to die a good Christian.

---

*The Way of Faith (Derekh Emunah) shown to the Jews by Giulio Morosini, Venetian writer in the Hebrew language at the Vatican Library and reader in the College of propaganda fide, a work no less curious than useful for those who converse or associate with Jews, or preach to them

He considers this public profession of faith of value to his readers, for the Jews say that all converts to Christianity die with the law of Moses in their hearts. He hopes, moreover, that the book will serve to illuminate some Jews and show them the benefits of the Christian religion. His third reason for writing *Via della fede* was to describe the Jewish rituals "for the use of those who preach the Gospel."

Morosini-Nahmias recalls the Marrano origin of his family. His great-grandfather David, unwilling to be baptized and live as a secret Jew, left Castile at the time of Ferdinand the Catholic and set out for Albania. Once there, he decided to revert openly to Judaism, have himself circumcised, and go to Salonika, where he made his living as a merchant for forty years. Isaac, the son of David, came to Venice as a traveling Levantine merchant and made a fortune, which he left to his heirs. Morosini stresses this fact, emphasizing that his conversion was not dictated by need or opportunism. To lend his writings greater authority, he boasts a thorough knowledge of the Hebrew language, and indeed we must acknowledge that his Hebrew culture, as reflected in these intense portrayals, was both vast and profound.

He converted simply because, living with Christians, he came to the realization that theirs was the true faith. He also points out, in a statement typical of the anti-Jewish polemicists who attempted to sow discord within the Jewish community, that Leone da Modena himself spoke of the Christian religion in flattering terms. Knowing Leone's free spirit, it is quite possible that he may have spoken in favor of the dominant religion. But Morosini clearly had an interest in emphasizing the importance of Leone's words, and thus distorted their meaning.

The words of another celebrated Venetian rabbi, Simone Luzzatto, seem to have been similarly skewed. Morosini tells of a dispute between his brother and himself, both of Marrano origin. At the time of the argument, however, one was Jewish and the other Christian, each convinced of the superiority of his own choice and eager to convince the other. They had argued at length without reaching a conclusion and finally decided to seek the answer in an interpretation of the prophecy of Daniel, agreeing that the loser would adopt the religion of the winner. Morosini's brother went to the ghetto's most illustrious rabbi, Simone Luzzatto, asking him to bring all his eloquence to his aid, and Luzzatto instructed the rabbis of the community to examine the question. "The day of the contest, the contenders quarreled among themselves," relates Morosini, who goes on to say that, since the Christian seemed about to win, Luzzatto suddenly clapped his hands and said, "The text we are discussing throws all the rabbis into such a state of perplexity and bewilderment that they know not whether they are in heaven or on earth." Placing his finger on his lips, he declared that if they discussed Daniel's prophecy any further they might as well all become Christians. Our author also attributes far more compromising words to Luzzatto: "It cannot be denied that it is clearly shown therein [in the Catholic religion] that the Messiah has come, whose time is already past. If this be Jesus of Nazareth, I do not wish to venture my opinion." Both Nahmias brothers therefore decided to convert to Christianity with their children.

Giulio Morosini lived in Venice for ten years, after which he moved to Rome where he met popes Alexander VII, Clement IX, and Clement X. Under their influence he became a Capuchin friar and undertook to write a complete testimonial of his spiritual itinerary: *Via della fede.*

The interest of the book lies in the fact that it is an attack "from within," by a person who refutes facts and beliefs which he formerly observed. He also provides a minute portrayal of ghetto life. The passages of criticism, except for certain chapters of anti-Jewish propaganda in the traditional style, are so closely interwoven with the descriptions that it is impossible to separate them.

In discussing "the cessation of the Mosaic law due to the coming of the Messiah Christ our Lord, whose mysteries are proven," Morosini maintains that the sins committed by the people of Israel are the cause of their long dispersion and present servitude.

At a certain point in his discussion of the Jewish precepts, he attacks his former teacher Leone da Modena. The purpose of the *Historia de' Riti Hebraici,* says Morosini, was to make Jewish customs acceptable to the Christian world by emphasizing only those devotional passages that would inspire "respect and decorum, hiding those which are truly subjects for derision." His old affection for his teacher, however, has not entirely faded. Morosini writes: "Because I was for so long his disciple in error, I have excellent knowledge of his qualities and sincerely believe that he did not like many things that please the others of his race ... In his familiar discourses he told us, his students, that the Christians were virtuous and even said that Christ was a good man and probably the promised Messiah, since too much time had passed since the date indicated by the prophets, and said that his only difficulty was in believing him to be the true God incarnate. These words, repeated by him many times, were one impelling reason among the others that led me to embrace the Christian faith." Morosini-Nahmias concludes, "For my part, I will not, like Leone da Modena, tell only the good things, but also those that are less good, and I am no liar for I lived 37 years as a Jew."

Aware of the importance of the daily, informal tie between the Jew and his rituals, Morosini attempts to break this bond in the conviction that only then will the Jew convert. This conviction was shared by many rabbis who maintained, arguing from the other side, that the strength of Judaism consisted in its daily practice, and that the substance and form of religion were two sides of the same Jewish coin.

To demolish this concept, Morosini analyzes the many rituals that accompany Jewish life—circumcision, the redeeming of the children, the manner of observing feasts and fasts—in order to show their superstitious aspects. "The true faculty of superstition is that of being an unlawful cult. You are superstitious because you observe ceremonies of the Pentateuch and the Old Testament that are extinct. You are superstitious because your judicial ceremonies or ceremonials depend on a Temple you do not have and a government you do not have . . . God no longer demands these things from you. You do not understand that the requirement of the Law has ceased for you . . . you are guilty of having added to the sacred precepts ceremonies of your own through obligation and habit. This contradicts the teachings of Deuteronomy."

One memorable passage describes the ceremony of circumcision. On the eve of the eighth day after birth, when the child is to be circumcised, friends and relations are invited to visit the child and his parents at their home. The godfather who is to hold the child during the circumcision and the *mohel*, who will circumcise him, are also there. They keep watch over the child to guard him from the evil eye. The mother sits in the ghetto, dressed up in her best finery, holding the child between her thighs, with only the closest relations about him who let none approach except the dearest friends. To ward off sleep, they make as much noise as possible, singing and bringing gifts, each according to his means, eating sweets and drinking wine. "The next morning, which is the eighth day after birth, before the child is sent to the circumcision he is usually bathed with various perfumes and after bathing they dip him three times in another basin of clean, warm water and then wrap him in fine embroidered bindings with a little mantle of brocade and silk . . . placing him in the arms of the matrons they carry him to the circumcision. In the Synagogue or at home, or wherever the ceremony is to be held, two chairs are set at some distance, one for Elijah, with an open Bible, and in placing it they say: 'This is the chair of Elijah. No one else may sit here.' This they do in their firm belief that the Prophet always invisibly attends all circumcisions in all parts of the world. In the other chair sits the godfather who holds the baby on his lap while they circumcise him. At the hour of the circumcision many people of both sexes gather, and while the child is being made ready the cantors in their usual tone chant the appropriate prayers. At this moment the Circumciser arrives, and behind him another man carrying a basin or cup containing all the instruments needed for the solemn rite, that is to say a sharp razor, a silver clip that is placed as a mark of how much prepuce to cut, a powder-box full of Dragon's Blood and other constricting powders to stem the bleeding, and two small cups or bowls, one with specially cut little bandages annointed with oil of Balsam or Roses to medicate

Top: The Circumcision.
Bottom: The Wedding.
(Engravings on colored copper by Antonio Baratti after sketches by Antonio Novelli, second half of the eighteenth century)˙

the cut and one with earth or sand wherein to bury the piece of circumcised prepuce ... All cry 'Barukh Habba' which means 'Blessed be he who is come.' Nor do they take the words simply at their face value, but imbue them with mystery, which I shall explain. The Kabbalists maintain that the word Habba, he who is come, contains virtually three others, which are Behold Elijah is come, for taking each letter of habba as a word they spell Elijah is come. They believe that Elijah has taken part in the entire circumcision."

Of the synagogues, Morosini writes: "In Venice there are seven Synagogues, of which one of the most famous is that of the Spanish and Portuguese, and another that of the Levantines whose customs resemble those of the Spanish. Of the other five, some are Italian and some German, and they follow the customs of their countries. In Constantinople, Salonika and such other cities, there is the Greek school, and in others there are the schools of the Aragonese and the Lisboans. The differences among them are in non-essentials, as we have said, and depend on the whims of the rabbis of the Nations. Each nation, at its own expense, maintains a Talmud Torah or Doctrine of the Law, with National Teachers to teach and interpret the Holy Scriptures in their language, and they are paid by the congregation of that Nation."

In the section devoted to the study of the holy books and prayers, Morosini talks about the Sefer Torah, the Book of the Law, which, he says, "contains the entire Pentateuch on many sheets of paper made from the skin of a sheep or some other clean animal, one alongside the other, so that it comes out to a great length and breadth, and about one arm's length in height. The book is not made in the modern fashion but in the old way, that is, rolled into a scroll." In meticulous detail he describes how, to enhance the beauty of the Torah, the Jews make two round, well-turned rods the same height as the scroll, which they roll from one side and unroll from the other "with a ring of the same wood, one finger thick and wide enough to contain the scroll ... as an ornament outside the Sefer Torah they hang a taffeta cover of green or some other bright color, so that in opening it the bare parchment on the back will not show, and another smaller one inside, big enough to cover the opening of the book when it is not being read or shown to the people, since they consider it unlawful to keep the Holy Book open without reading it. When the Sefer is rolled, it is bound with an embroidered tie, the beginning being tucked between one turn and the other and then winding it around until the end, when it is tied with long ribbons ... And left thus, it is robed in a long mantle."

Almost as though attempting to exorcise the impetuously thronging memories through detailed exposition, Morosini describes the Jewish holidays one by one.

About the feast of Simchat Torah, the Rejoicing of the Law, Morosini writes: "And if indeed there is joy among the Jews, it appears on this day. The reason for rejoicing is that in this week they finish reading the whole Pentateuch called Torah, that is Law, since they have divided the five books of Moses into so many Parashot, that is to say Sections, as there are weeks in the year, reading one each week in the Synagogue so that by the end of the year, that is to say in 12 months' time, they finish reading all five books. And since they keep careful count of these Parashot, noting them on their calendars or Almanacs ... when they come to the end they celebrate a very special feast for having completed the reading of the Torah, which they then begin again." In each synagogue two Jews are chosen, one of whom has the honor of reading the first and one of reading the last "Lesson of the Pentateuch." These men are called *hatanim* or bridegrooms: the bridegroom of the Law and the bridegroom of the Bereshit, or Beginning (because the first lesson or Parasha begins with the word Beginning, or Bereshit). On the two Sabbaths, the one when the reading ends and the one when it begins, they are most highly honored and revered in the synagogues, surrounded by friends and relations who treat them with the greatest respect. Then all the Books of the Law are removed from the Ark and displayed one alongside the other, all richly garbed in silk mantles and gold brocade, adorned and enriched with gold and silver crowns and pyramids, and with quantities of magnificent bells and jewels. The bridegrooms of the Torah are honored repeatedly: "When they go to the synagogue they are welcomed by most of the people there. At the hour of the principal prayers, the leaders and Rabbis leave the Synagogue followed by those who wish to honor the Bridegrooms with their friends and relatives and go to the homes of the aforesaid bridegrooms and escort them to the Synagogue, each separately. On these two days they take first place near the books, taking precedence even over the Rabbis in their seating. The same is done at the end of the prayers, when they are accompanied home by all, up to the doors of their houses, led by the Cantors chanting hymns and Psalms, and their closest friends and relations go into their houses, as is customary in the Levant, where they are all welcomed and entertained with sweets and strong drink, and many stay to dinner."

What is striking about Morosini's writing is his extraordinary photographic memory and a vitality that refuses to be dampened. Sometimes his religious attacks take on harsh tones that soften only when the author feels the stronger, almost irresistible urge to describe. The pages seem to reflect a tremendous inner conflict, a state of profound dissociation that the Marrano convert never succeeds in resolving and carries with him like a curse. So effective are his descriptions that even today, hundreds of years later, the reader feels as though he were attending a slow-paced Jewish ceremony. Here is an example of this easy narrative cadence: "After this the first bridegroom is called by name, by the Cantor, to great applause, and invited with diverse praises and honors to come up to the pulpit and read the last portion of the Pentateuch. As he goes up he is followed and accompanied, as a sign of the reverence due to the dignity he has on that day, by all the Rabbis in the synagogue, and by friends, relations and others who wish to honor him. While he walks with great solemnity and slow stride, he is constantly praised in song by the Cantors. When he arrives at the pulpit, one man strips of its binding the book, carried by the bridegroom, who approaches this book, placed upon the Pulpit, and reads all the aforesaid lesson (if he knows how) with all its notes and accents; unless the Cantor does it in his place. When the reading is over, the Cantor with further hymns and chants applauds and praises the bridegroom, and blesses him again . . . The Bridegroom then offers money for the synagogue, for other alms, for the confraternity and for charities in accordance with his means and liberality. And taking up his book again, he returns to his place accompanied by the same group of people, with more hymns. After this the same is done with the other Bridegroom of the *Bereshit*, or in the Beginning, who reads the first lesson of the Pentateuch."

And here is a wonderful description of the ceremony of Simchat Torah, one of the holidays best loved, even today, by the Jewish children of Venice because on that day they receive sweets and gifts. Centuries later, the ceremony is still celebrated in the Spanish synagogue in the Old Ghetto, much as Morosini described it: "In the afternoon they go to the usual Mincha service, which is the same as on the other solemn days . . . During this service, an auction is held and the honor of carrying the scrolls, which as we mentioned are 8 or 10, is given to whomever offers the most, except for the two most important which the two bridegrooms carry, one each. With all these scrolls they then march in procession several times around the synagogue and each bridegroom may lend his scroll to his friends to carry for a few steps, and so they receive some of the honor. Meanwhile this ceremony, which does have its serious side, is not performed without jubilation, with the Cantors and singers leading in the company of many plebeians who, believing themselves to have good and sweet voices, all join together in great confusion singing hymns and verses, most of which contain God's praises, praying for the restoration of the Temple of Jerusalem and for the coming of Elijah with their Messiah. They do not, however, allow these holy chants to be accompanied by the music and verses of secular Spanish or Turkish songs, which for brevity's sake I shall not relate. I will say only that in seeing the noise that is made (for Rejoicing of the Law, they say) anyone can see the distance between this and the true worship of God, for nations of all kinds take part, Spaniards, Levantines, Portuguese, Germans, Greeks, Italians and others, each singing according to his own custom, and since they use no instruments, some clap the palms of their upraised hands, others clap against their thighs, some snap their fingers, others play the guitar by scratching at their tunics, in short they accompany those sounds with leaps and dances, with confusion of faces, mouths and arms, and make such display of all their limbs that it looks like a Carnival prank. At many places in the Levant I have seen the timbrel played, but the above manner is the most common. In this way they parade around the Synagogue at least seven times, and the Books of the Law are kissed again and again by all, with great show of joy, but with great affectation. After the seventh turn, the Cantors go up to the pulpit followed by all the books of the Law, placing them about in sight of all, and after several hymns and chants the Cantor raising his voice as loud as he can blesses the Prince, since in the city of Venice many of our Christians come out of curiosity, and he blesses him . . . in the vulgar tongue calling him by name, the Most Serene Prince X . . . with all his Most Serene Signoria." Morosini says that in those cities which have a ghetto, the synagogues are open day and night, lit by lamps, candles, and torches. "Likewise in many places, especially in the city of Venice, that evening is almost like Carnival, in that many maids and matrons mask themselves to avoid being recognized, and go see all the synagogues. At this time Christian ladies and gentlemen come to the synagogues out of curiosity almost more than on the other holidays, to see the outfitting and wealth of the synagogues thus illuminated, and the silly happiness of the Jews on that day."

Another colorful passage is the description of Purim: "Now let us look at another celebration at Purim, held outside the synagogue with rejoicing and festivities. The young people play at Bullfighting, using oxen and other animals, and in the evening married men too, and married and unmarried women don masks and go visiting their friends and relatives, where they dine and dance. This is how they do in Venice, and it is called the Jewish Carnival, and indeed there is not much difference, for our own Christians also celebrate Carnival there, although it does not end on the same day. The day before Purim, that is the 13th of the month of Adar, which comes in February or March, the Jews fast in the usual way . . . in memory of Esther's fast during the persecution of Haman, which ended with his tragic death as we fully read in the sacred Book, to the eternal praise of the aforesaid queen, the glorious liberator of her people. In some places certain women may be found who, in order to seem more pious, fast continuously for three days and three nights, without eating or drinking either much or little."

In his sometimes harsh, sometimes nostalgic attack against Jewish law, Morosini repeatedly cites his teacher Leone da Modena. Recalling the Jewish prohibition against eating blood, he describes the custom of salting meat: "And they let it sit an hour before putting it in the pot or pan to cook, so all the blood may drain off; otherwise they may

Ketubah, or marriage contract.
(Illuminated parchment, 1708. Correr Museum, Venice)

only eat it roasted, and therefore liver, which is all blood, may never be cooked unless it has first been well roasted on an iron grill or over wood embers. What think you of this fine doctrine? Liver which . . . is all blood may be eaten after roasting. Why, then, may meat not be eaten with its blood, while a roasted piece of congealed or hardened blood may be? And can the Divine commandment be eluded by such a bizarre invention? Either liver is blood, or it is not. If it is blood, God forbids it at many points in the Mosaic Law. How then can the Jewish people avoid transgression by eating roasted liver? If it is not blood, why does Leone da Modena say that it is all blood? And certainly if he said otherwise he would be speaking falsely, since the substance is not changed by being adapted in one or another incidental manner. In fact the transgression of eating blood is compounded with superstition, through believing it to be God's will that it be eaten in this way."

The Jewish dietary laws, a frequent topic for discussion and polemic, both within the Jewish community and between Jews and Christians, provides fertile ground for Morosini. He particularly emphasizes the fact that the Jews are obliged to have two sets of dishes and cookware, one for dairy foods and one for meat. Again, he challenges his teacher Leone da Modena: "And if the Jews were content to wash their dishes, or break them when they become unclean due to one of the above things, this could be tolerated because the Law prescribes breaking vessels and washing them, but they do it at the least shadow of suspicion, as Modena himself attests." If the vessel is of earthenware, and has contained hot food, continues Morosini, they throw it away in their concern that the food contained may have been forbidden and seeped into the pores. If it did not contain hot food, but was used by others, in doubt they throw it away all the same. "Vessels used for milk cannot be used for meat. Those used for Passover, either in the kitchen or at the table, cannot be used at any other time. I do not attribute to you, Jews, doctrines that are not yours; it is your very own Modena who has published all this. But tell me, for courtesy's sake, how wretched and impoverished you find yourselves? And because of those rules, which are not Scripture but the vagaries of the Rabbis, you are obliged to incur heavy expenses if you wish to follow them."

His dispute with Leone da Modena is an underground stream ready to surface at any moment. In his *Historia de' Riti Hebraici*, the Venetian rabbi discusses drinking. Morosini comments: "There are some who by order of ancient Rabbis hold that the Jews are forbidden to drink wine made and touched by non-Jews, and this is observed by the Levantines and the Germans. But in Italy they do not have this reservation." The Jews, says Morosini, will not drink wine touched by Christians. Surely they consider the Christians and Turks equally idolatrous; yet in the Levant, where this rule is strictly observed, they do not mind at all if their kosher wine is touched by the Turks. Morosini says the Levantine Jews tell their children, "If you ever want to change religion, better turn Turk than Christian." He then writes: "The above Rabbi Leone teaches that in Italy they do not have this reservation, and that it may have been decreed by those Rabbis who lived among the idol-worshippers, to prevent commerce with them. I know not, nor can I conceive for what reason or on what grounds this great Man speaks thus against his country, when he knows very well that there is no City in Italy where kosher wine is not made by the Jews either in public or private, if only for use at the holy functions, as we shall now describe. And in the Ghettos of the City of Venice, for example, a large storehouse of Kosher Wine is continuously kept, made with great diligence by the Jews themselves, for their own use, nor can it be sold to Christians, but only to Jews. And to supervise this, each year that University elects Leaders or Governors, that is two from the Levantine Nation and Synagogue, two from the Spanish and Portuguese, and two more from the Germans and Italians, who are called Parnassim de' Mezonoth, Heads of Governors over foods and provisions. With the utmost vigilance and diligence they supervise not only the Kosher Wine and cheeses that are made, but also other foods sold cooked or raw."

Morosini's account continues in the tone of an Eastern fable: "When I was in the City of Constantinople around 1635, the noble Lord Amurat, who ruled at that time, decreed banishment for life against whomever kept or drank wine within the City of Constantinople, but it could be drunk outside the city: and so the Jews, whenever they wished to drink Kosher wine, had to go to Peraea or elsewhere across the sea, where there are many Jews that keep inns and storehouses; and for their services and ceremonies they secretly smuggled it in by bribery and endangering their lives. Therefore they resolved, after holding many meetings and assemblies, to go before the Grand Vizier with rich and precious gifts, and petition him saying that they had been accepted in Constantinople by the Antecedent Kings with the privilege of observing their Laws and Rituals according to their custom, but that since His Majesty King Amurat had forbidden wine, with which they celebrate their most important functions, they knew not how to perform them; and that most of them would therefore have to move to other States. The Grand Vizier, seeing the rich and precious gifts, sent an order to the city gates that if a Jew passed through carrying wine, as long as the wine were covered so it could not be recognized as such, they should let it through without asking questions. This order was obeyed for a few months, and then by virtue of greater and richer gifts, they were granted the free use of wine by the Great Lord himself. Before that free dispensation, it was curious to see the tricks and stratagems devised by the Jews to bring their wine secretly into Constantinople, for drinking or for their holy services."

From Constantinople to Venice, between attacks on the Talmud and appeals to convert to Christianity, Morosini's itinerary winds through scholarly passages teeming with biblical and theological references, and lively descriptions of life in the ghetto of Venice. "On Friday afternoon the Rabbis or other men go about making certain the shops are closed and knocking on the doors so the people will stop working, light the candles and greet the Sabbath. In Venice, moreover, they have a Christian trumpeter come to a house in the midst of the ghetto, whom they keep on salary, who plays the trumpet two hours beforehand for a goodly time in three blasts, with a half-hour between one call and the next, and at the end of the third call he plays a sort of air, as if he were saying Good Evening, Good Evening, whereby all know that the Sabbath has come and all the women light their candles, each in her own home; and they greet the Sabbath; and they cease working. This trumpet call is very convenient for the Jews so they will not overlook the hour, and for observing their ritual, since those who are away from the Ghetto, when they meet another Jew coming from the Ghetto, ask him if the first or second call has sounded, so that they may be in time to stop their work at the third . . . The women with great diligence, since this is a law commanded especially to them . . . prepare the lamps and candles . . . On Friday evening at the beginning of the Sabbath they prepare the table, sumptuously set with a clean cloth, salt cellar in the middle, and at least two loaves . . . They keep these loaves covered with another cloth in memory of the Manna that came down from Heaven each day, except the Sabbath, covered with dew above and below. When all this is done, early in the evening the men go to 'greet the Sabbath, or Kabbalat Shabbat' . . . Then they say their prayers, including the hymn 'Come my beloved to meet the Bride,' which is the most appropriate for greeting the Sabbath. Instead of Good Evening, they say Good Sabbath. The children go to their Father and Mother, and to their elders, kiss their hands and receive their blessing. On returning home they find the table adorned, illuminated in the manner described, and they dine heartily, first observing a ceremony with a glass of wine in hand, reciting the first three verses of the Second Chapter of Genesis, and others called Kiddush, meaning Consecration or Sanctification, blessing God who created the fruit of the vine and sanctified the Sabbath."

Few Jews could paint such a fond and idyllic picture; yet Morosini seems not to realize that he is reliving childhood memories, or that he is moved by them.

His tone becomes severe, however, when he criticizes Rabbi Simone Luzzatto, for whom he apparently did not feel the same deep respect and affection as he did for his teacher Leone da Modena. Luzzatto, he recalls, said that a farmer does not give up cultivating his field just because he finds an occasional weed in it, and used this metaphor to stress the benefits that the Jews bring to the Christian community even though there may be a few among them who do not obey the laws. But, says Morosini, the Jews are all bad and should all be punished. In fact many rulers have expelled them entirely, for this reason. The Jews have shown themselves to be very foolish, for if they were the least bit clever they would convert to Christianity. They should not be compared to weeds, as Luzzatto does, but to a bituminous swamp that gives rise to noxious rivers. Luzzatto, in one of the last considerations of his *Discorso*, wrote that the kindness with which rulers treat their people can be measured by the way they treat the Jews. Morosini, pointing out that many illustrious kings had gone to a great deal of effort to drive out the Jews, replies that for this very reason he considers them virtuous kings, and that in any case, every city and country has a different way of doing things and each makes its own laws, "nor can a rule be derived from examples, or from authorities; for if this were the case it could be inferred that since the very wise and prudent Republic of Venice keeps the Jews, others should keep them too; but even the Republic of Venice keeps them in Venice, but not in Brescia, Bergamo, Crema and other cities of the State."

Toward the end of his book Morosini touches on a classic theme: "On the Commandment of not lending at Interest, contained in the very Eighth Commandment; and how it is observed by the Jews." He begins: "The whole world knows that the commandment against lending at interest is not obeyed by the Jews; money may not be borrowed from them, who possess it, except with pledge in hand. They think they are not violating the Commandment against stealing, as we say. But let us examine it. If this be the case, why do they practice it among themselves, while permitting (like other sins) the one, they forbid the other? O great privilege of this people, to be able not only to interpret the holy books at your whim, but reform them." This is the beginning of a long, severe tirade: Morosini recalls that Simone Luzzatto observed that the Jews had no other means of support since they were barred from "mechanical arts, farms, and real estate, and . . . are burdened with duties and taxes. But prostitutes say the same, that they cannot live otherwise, and yet they are not excused. Evil must not be committed for gain." Morosini's attack against Luzzatto reiterates the traditional commonplaces of anti-Jewish criticism. He does not see the originality in Luzzatto's argument and neglects to consider the importance of the Jewish community in the Venetian economy.

Anti-Jewish books continued to be published up until the second half of the eighteenth century, the most famous being *Riti e costumi degli Ebrei** (1746), by Paolo Sebastiano Medici, a Florentine Jew. But none of them can compare in size, wealth of detail, or color with the work of Morosini.

Jewish Rites and Customs

CHAPTER SEVENTEEN

Venice and the Ghetto in the Seventeenth Century: From Opulence to Decadence

The German, Levantine, and Western Nations and their relations with the Sopraconsoli, the Five Sages of Commerce, and the Cattaveri

T he plague that racked Venice in 1630 killed a third of her 150,000 residents and profoundly altered the socioeconomic conditions of the city. Among those most severely affected were the Jewish merchants, who had previously benefited from the favorable international economy and enjoyed good relations with the Turks. Suddenly they found themselves obliged to suspend their import-export business to and from the plague-ridden city. They lost large quantities of merchandise (a thousand bales, according to some estimates), burned because it was considered contaminated, in addition to which they and the German Nation had to pay a special tax of over 120,000 ducats.

After that terrible year the ghetto seemed doomed to rapid economic decay and gradual depopulation, owing both to the deaths from plague and to the emigration of those who had fled to other cities. Unexpectedly, however, it rallied, for Venice still preserved the extraordinary capacity to attract and absorb peoples of all kinds. Many Jews from East and West, driven by continual persecution, turned their steps, and their hopes, toward the lagoon.

This new state of affairs is clearly documented. In March 1633, the Western and Levantine Jewish leaders informed the Five Sages of Commerce that certain Jewish merchant families from other states would move to Venice if they could find comfortable homes there and new storehouses for their wares. The Senate consulted the Five Sages, and "there being a number of houses near the Ghetto, behind those at Ca' Zanoli, as recollected by the Jews themselves, with the convenience of easy communication by a bridge over the canal while remaining closed and incorporated," asked the Sages to find twenty suitable houses for twenty Jewish merchant families, on condition that they "have not been in this city for two years and are therefore new residents and have not had a domicile, again for two years, in our State." The Senate also decreed that for three years no ghetto dweller could "move to the houses in this new annex" and that only thereafter would the old and new families be allowed to freely exchange houses "as they see fit."

"But because it is necessary to join the new Houses of the Ghetto with an Enclosure before any Jew goes to live there, the Sages of Commerce must establish the way of so doing, as they deem best, with rules and orders, as are now in effect for the rest of the Ghetto, and also as to the building of a bridge over the Canal" with no public expenditure. The Levantine and Western leaders were responsible for bringing in the twenty promised families. If they failed to do so they would have to pay a fine of 3,000 ducats "or less in proportion to the number of families that fail to arrive." The Five Sages of Commerce were held as guarantors for the entire transaction. The motion passed by a large majority, and the last section of the ghetto, the Newest Ghetto, thus came into being.

This attempt to attract a few families to the city is an indication of the acute economic hardship endured by the Republic, which was losing ground in Mediterranean trade. The patricians who governed the Serenissima were well aware of these problems and attempted to implement severely protectionist policies against all the other Adriatic ports. In this delicate situation the Jewish merchants proved useful. The Five Sages of Commerce admonished the Venetians "not to disturb the port of Spalato which always brings good trade" and advised that Joseph Penso, who had replaced Rodriga and had always been very loyal to the Republic, be compensated with two houses and a license to sell in the ghetto, as an example of how the Republic would show her gratitude to those who faithfully served her.

In late December 1634, the Senate consulted all the magistracies involved and decided to renew the German Jews' charter for five years "with conditions and clauses" identical to those of the earlier charters of 1624 and 1629. The Jews protested against their obligation to supply materials and labor for the building of houses for ambassadors, princes, and illustrious visitors to the city. They insisted that they had been required to supply a "number of rooms in excess of those needed, which are then assigned to menials." The Senate admitted the justice of their claim and ordered a more scrupulous supervision of the situation.

Certain sections of this resolution are especially interesting because they indicate a change in attitude on the part of the Venetian authorities, who had always stressed the distinctions between the different Nations in the ghetto, on the principle of "divide and conquer." Now those distinctions were fading. "The Five Sages of Commerce may and must grant the German Jewish merchants permission to trade in the Levant as do the Levantine and Western Jews, according to their petition, and with those good rules and precautions regarding the capital that must be their own and not of others, and they are reminded and advised by these same Five Sages that this cannot otherwise result than to the benefit of the Customs and the advantage of our government." The document also contained a new glimpse of light in a field where the Jews had always encountered obstruction: they were formally permitted to "freely revise any books needed to be printed for their rituals . . . in accordance with the provisions of the Inquisition, the Reformers of Study of Padua, and the Cattaveri."

German, Levantine, and Western Jews had also finally agreed on a thorny subject that had always been a source of tension: the amount of tax to be paid proportionally by each Nation, and its collection. The Senate was also called upon, that year, to consider a petition from the city's jewelers and diamond merchants, who felt their guild was being threatened by competition from Jewish artisans who worked with "mills," not so much in Venice as in Padua. The resolution prohibited all manufacture and sale, especially in the very central Ruga degli Orefici near Rialto, to anyone not a member of the guild, from which, obviously, the Jews were barred.

The Senate acted on the opinion of the Five Sages, who insisted that the Levantine and Western Jews, already heavily taxed, could not support a further increase. But the aristocrats who were newly elected to the office of Sages of Commerce shortly thereafter were more sensitive to the interests of the Venetian patricians, who were eager to penalize Jewish business, which was flourishing again after the critical plague years. The patricians again proposed a tax of "a third of the brokerage fees," which the Five Sages had formerly abolished. The new Sages, in their nearsightedness, probably exaggerated when they wrote: "We must bear in mind that the Jews have ensconced themselves in the shops, that they have taken over we might say everything, stripping bare the houses of the citizens, and how this Nation has expanded since Your Excellency has permitted the enlargement of the ghetto." This hyperbole refers to the arrival of twenty families in the Newest Ghetto. "It is well known that for all practical purposes most of the Levant trade is in their hands, and the same is true of the Western trade."

The Levantine and Western Jews resisted, and submitted many formal protests, but they were not on an equal footing with the Serenissima. This had been clearly emphasized by Asher Meshullam on moving into the ghetto in 1516: "When will struggles with power, power wins."

Excluded from almost all productive crafts, the Venetian Jews often tried to find loopholes. In 1638, the patrician Bembo acted as the mouthpiece for new complaints from the Venetian jewelers, proposing new steps to reduce the Jewish influence in that trade. Bembo acknowledged that the Jews were not the only ones creating problems for the Venetian goldsmiths, since an increasing number of other countries was beginning to make and sell jewelry, but he felt that the Jews were only making things worse. The Senate listened to Bembo, and in May of that year approved a law that made it illegal for the Jews to sell jewelry, in order to "restore the trade and commerce of jewels to its former grandeur." The issue came up again in 1671, when the local craftsmen once again appealed to the authorities for protection, in an attempt to eliminate the competition and to reduce the Jewish interest in "the commerce of unfinished jewelry." The Five Sages accepted the protests, holding that the Jews had cornered an excessive quota of the market. Only one of the Five Sages, the aristocrat Gritti, objected. "Restricting trade is totally counterproductive . . . If jewelry ceases to arrive in Venice, there will also cease the introduction of the other goods brought from those same countries; the sale of silk cloth will also cease, as it happens most often that this merchandise is bartered for jewels." But the Senate accepted the opinion of the majority, limiting the Jewish trade.

The ghetto, meanwhile, was becoming increasingly cramped, as evinced by Nachman Giuda's request to the Five Sages for permission to move his chemical factory outside the ghetto. His request was granted, albeit with some limitations.

The influence of the Five Sages was not limited to the city proper, but extended to controversies throughout the Venetian domains. In 1639, the Five Sages intervened to settle a quarrel on the island of Zante between some Levantine merchants and the local Venetian governor, who had committed an abuse of power by confiscating their merchandise. This far-reaching influence sharpened the traditional rivalry between the Five Sages and the Cattaveri, who often arrested Jews caught outside the ghetto after curfew. The Jews protested and requested exemptions on the basis of their need to supervise their businesses. In September 1639, the Five Sages went to battle in their favor, asking that the ghetto curfew not be too severely enforced. In addition to the difficulty of doing business under such conditions, they said, "The laws establishing the times when the Jews must stay in the ghetto date from 1516, when there were no Levantine and Western Jews, but only Germans." This amounts to an implicit recognition of different paces of life in the ghetto. The merchants worked on an irregular, unpredictable schedule, as opposed to the uniform routine of the moneylenders.

As had happened so often in the past, hostilities between Venice and the Turks were announced by numerous signs. The Mediterranean was infested by pirates, and navigation was a risky business. Traces of this uneasy situation appear in the surviving reports of the Five Sages of Commerce. In September 1641 they expressed an opinion in favor of granting a request for help from Jewish merchants who had lost the cargo of a vessel captured by Maltese pirates. But in March 1643, to avoid creating a precedent, they refused a request to load merchandise onto military ships to protect it from capture.

The renewed tension between Venice and the Turks upset trade in the Mediterranean. The Jewish merchants tried to encourage the conveyance of merchandise over land routes and devised ingenious ways of bypassing the gaps in the sea routes, such as loading eastbound merchandise onto English ships in Leghorn or Ancona. That trick was short-lived. The ambassador in Constantinople very soon found out that Venetian merchandise was arriving from Leghorn on English ships, and informed his government.

In 1645, Venice and the Turks, again struggling for supremacy in the Mediterranean, found themselves face to face; this time the hostilities lasted twenty-five years, with alternating periods of greater or lesser asperity and a long sequence of battles and skirmishes, culminating in a fierce defense of the island of Candia, under Turkish siege for twenty years. With the advent of peace in 1699, the island was ceded to the Sublime Porte. For Venice the loss was more than a defeat: it was the end of an entire historical cycle.

This long crisis had a profound effect on Venetian economy and commerce, as well as on her ghetto. Heavier taxes and duties were levied on the Jews, while their role as commercial mediators weakened with the decline of trade. Poverty was on the rise, and pressure on the pawnshops increased.

The pronouncements of the Council of Ten in December 1659, just a few years after the Senate rulings on the sixth clause of the German Nation's charter, and those of the Sopraconsoli in September 1665 and May and July 1666 were somber in tone. With the weakening of the Venetian economy, the operation of the pawnshops became an increasingly problematic issue. The Levantines and Germans offered the Republic an immediate payment of fifty thousand ducats, in exchange for which their charters would become perpetual rather than requiring renewal every ten years and the annual payments of three thousand ducats would be abolished. A small group of Iberian Jews, four families in all, offered a large sum of money in exchange for exemption from contributing to the maintenance of the banks, permission to wear black hats, and exemption from certain customs duties. The first request could be considered consistent with the policy of stability pursued by the various Jewish groups from the time the ghetto was founded. But the second has all the appearance of being an expression of family opulence, with no immediate political motivation. The Five Sages reasonably considered that accepting this latter proposal "could create serious discord among the ghetto communities who would find themselves hard put to support the banks and pay their taxes without the contribution of those families which are among the wealthiest; and in fact it is thanks to the assistance of one of these that the University has been able to continue operating a bank." They added, furthermore, that granting a privilege to a small group of Western Jews might subvert the rules of free competition, resulting in more problems than benefits and creating confusion among those excluded. Such discussions are evidence of the existence, in the ghetto, of a few especially powerful families.

In February 1681, the Sage Treasurer of the Cabinet and three Deputies for the Provision of Money received instructions from the Senate to "summon before them the leaders of the University and other wealthy Jews with the form and expressions that appear most appropriate" and demand a loan of 150,000 ducats within three months, in addition to the 150,000 ducats of the loan already decreed in 1669. The Senate's ruling again stressed the Jews' "devotion to Public Service, the opportunity to acquire new benifices by further pleasing the public." And in 1686, the Venetian authorities graciously addressed the leaders of the University, again "with the form and expressions that prudence deems best," to demand yet another loan of 150,000 ducats.

The coffers of the Republic were draining rapidly. In 1684, after having joined the Holy League with Austria, Venice declared a new war against her traditional Turkish enemy. Heightened fiscal pressures and the dangers of seafaring crippled not only the Venetian economy but the finances of the ghetto as well. The tensions accentuated existing controversies between the Western, Levantine, and German Nations, who were having increasing difficulty collecting the capital demanded by the Republic. The situation was approaching emergency status, and Venice faced it with her usual pragmatism—by milking all her citizens. A title of nobility would be conferred on every Venetian willing to contribute 100,000 ducats. Forty-seven families accepted.

The most pressing problem in the ghetto was finding a fair system of taxation. The method used up to that time (the taxpayers elected the tax collectors and agreed to abide by their decisions) was replaced in 1685 at the recommendation of the Five Sages. The total tax was first divided among the Nations, each of which then established the amount owed by each individual. This method was chosen in the belief that a smaller group would have greater control over collection and a better chance of dividing the burden fairly.

The number of proclamations issued by the Sopraconsoli concerning the ghetto pawnshops may give some idea of the growing economic malaise. In 1682, that Venetian magistracy examined complaints by people who had pawned objects and found them changed when they went to redeem them. The bankers were then forbidden to "switch said pledges on any pretext"; in fact, "at the time of collection they must open the parcels in the presence of the interested parties and list, piece by piece, the objects being redeemed." The Sopraconsoli issued new proclamations in October 1683, November 1684, and September 1685.

In 1688, the three Nations appealed to the Senate for confirmation of the seven new clauses purporting to facilitate tax collection. After the ritual consultation with the Sages and the Cattaveri, the Senate instructed the latter to make sure the money they collected was first used to defray the "Public Tributes," and later to pay other debts.

A year later, on July 27, 1689, the Senate granted a safe-conduct "for ten years to all Levantine and Western Jews" who wished to come "live with their families in this city and stay here freely, wearing the yellow cap and living in the New Ghetto with the other Jews." The former concessions were maintained: "They may freely navigate, as do currently the traveling Levantine merchants. In case of war with any Prince, none of said merchants may be held or their property seized in retaliation or their families harmed. But they shall rest in safety, buying, selling, negotiating, and bringing merchandise by land or sea." These privileges were limited to Levantine and Western Jews approved by the Five Sages of Commerce; they had to be permanent residents of Venice and members of the University.

The pressing need for funds created by the war with the Turks spared neither Venice nor the Jews. In May 1691, the Senate charged the Sage Treasurer of the Cabinet and the Deputies for the Provision of Money with determining appropriate ways of obliging the Jews to lend the Republic 100,000 ducats.

In November 1696, the Five Sages and the Cattaveri, in their usual report to the Senate, emphasized that the continual levying and collection of taxes was becoming an increasingly difficult problem. The Senate ruled that tax collection in the ghetto should be delegated exclusively to Jews, the only ones to have "certain knowledge of the fortune and business" of each taxpayer. It also decided not to change the customary method, but that "this method must be inviolably observed, by means of secret books, by the Western and German Nations." It looked as though the economic hardships of the University would gradually lead the Jews to abandon Venice and the ghetto, but according to the decrees of 1630, 1669, and 1695, authorization to leave was contingent upon paying to the leaders of their Nations "the ordinary and extraordinary taxes," or coming to an agreement on specific terms of payment, with appropriate guarantees.

By now the end of a difficult century was in sight. In December 1696, the charter of the German Jews was renewed for five more years, on the basis of the clauses set forth in 1658 and updated in 1668. In 1697, the leaders of the University were Moisè Coen, formerly Simon dal Medico, Jacob di Samuel Baruch, "the excellent Doctor" Salomon Conegliano, Mosè Alfarin, Isach Mugnon Soares, Emanuael Levi Dal Banco, and Emanuel Lunel. On 6 Adar 5457 (February 1697), they held a meeting, of which we have the minutes, in the Chapter General of the University. "The decline in trade and the scarcity of profits in this market, the considerable debts to which our University is subject and the supreme command of the most excellent Senate for the punctual collection of the many current taxes, as well as making up for past omissions, which taxes having to be shared among a small number of taxpayers, since many families have unfortunately declined or have departed this city, make our burden very heavy and almost intolerable. These are reasons to call upon the vigilance of everyone to moderate the luxury and superfluous expense introduced into our Ghettos and restrict their excesses, to use their most flourishing substances, which are heedlessly wasted, by putting them to a more fruitful use which is to serve our Most Clement Prince and benefit themselves by the payment of their taxes and the settling of debts, and in compliance with the venerable public commands practice the moderation and temperance characteristic of our nation and also prevent many scandals."

Convinced that greater moderation was appropriate "to the straits of our Nations," the leaders of the University, on pain of excommunication, forbade "any Jewish person of whatever sex, age or condition to wear embroidery all of gold, silver or silk, no one excepted, or to dress in costume or pierce or cut their garments or to have all their trimmings of silk, or silver and gold of any sort under any name by which they may be called, whether braiding or lace or galloons, fringes, frogs, bows, or any such, being allowed to place only one cord of spun gold or silver, or silk to attach buttons, and in the seams and false eyelets of gold or silver, either spun or braided, or to reinforce the hems of any garment with gold, silver and silk as they like, as long as the trim does not exceed a finger's breadth, all which embroideries and trimmings are forbidden on all clothing as well as on girdles and straps, by clothing being meant mantles, bodices, bibs, skirts and overgarments, undergarments, house dresses, hooded coats, furs, vests, frockcoats, capes and overcoats, as well as stockings, shoes, aprons, sleeves, undersleeves, camisoles, bonnets, caps, hats, gloves, muffs, shirts, and veils." This ordinance was to be made known throughout the ghetto in an attempt to contain luxury and make every effort to settle their debts "in order to leave our children free of such great burdens."

In 1699 the Senate mobilized the Sage Treasurer of the Cabinet and three adjunct Deputies for the Provision of Money, and in the usual courteous but categorical terms ordered the Jewish community to lend the city 150,000 ducats. Peace had just been signed with the Turks, but there was still a financial emergency in Venice. The fifteen years of war ending in 1699 had been hard ones for the city, and the conquest of Morea was the swan song of her ancient splendor and the beginning of an inexorable decline.

CHAPTER EIGHTEEN

Hell, the Messianic Hope, and a Newborn Baby

Mosè Zacuto, the Jewish Dante — The Venetian Jews await the Messiah — An infant abandoned in the ghetto

The early seventeenth century was, as we have seen, a time of intense economic and intellectual productivity in the ghetto. The Levant trade was thriving, and the Jewish cultural circles, boasting prominent figures such as Leone da Modena, Sara Coppio Sullam, and Simone Luzzatto, were sophisticated and lively.

In the latter part of the century the atmosphere gradually changed, as a result of the many long and exhausting battles with the Turks. The Venetian treasury was drained, and the ghetto merchants suffered from the interruption of their traditional trade routes in the Levant. The Jews also labored under the increased tax burden placed on them by the Republic, in support of its military efforts. The cultural and religious climate, too, was adversely affected by the new financial hardships.

The conflicts between Venice and Rome had become less acute, and the closer ties between these two states were not favorable to the Jewish community of Venice. The Western Jews, whose numbers had rapidly increased, were experiencing a period of opulence, and the Spanish School was the wealthiest, most luxurious synagogue in the ghetto. Surviving documents testify to the growth of the Spanish and Portuguese community: the curate of a neighboring parish categorically stated that, in 1651, many of these Western Jews had been Christians in

Portugal. Just a few years earlier a Spanish Jew, whose identity is unknown but who apparently had a taste for malicious troublemaking, had scandalized a Venetian monk by telling him that the Church in Spain was penetrated by secret Judaism, that many religious rites were being conducted by Jews disguised as priests and friars, and that many baptisms were invalid, having been administered by Jews. He ended by saying, "These are maladies and disorders that come from the desire to make us Christian by force and deprive us of our freedom of conscience." Reversions to Judaism were often sensational events, for men in the public eye, honored at the Spanish court, would come to Italy, change their identity, and move into the ghetto. Duarte Pereira took the name of Jehuda Lombroso, Andrea Falliero became Emanuele Aboab, Daniel Ribeiro Enriques changed his name to Samuel Mocatta, and Alonso Nunez da Errera became Abraham Cohen Errera.

Among the new arrivals was the Caravaglio family, who soon became as well known in the ghetto for their quarrelsome nature as for their wealth, the brothers Abraham and Isaac Cardoso, and Roderigo (Jacob) Mendes da Silva. Isaac Cardoso, a prominent figure, wrote *Excellentias de los Hebreos,* * one of the most interesting apologias of the late seventeenth century. Cardoso observed that every community in Venice was a small republic, governing itself according to laws handed down to it by God. Roderigo Mendes da Silva, official historiographer at the court of Spain, came to Italy at the age of sixty. He was circumcised and converted to Judaism, taking the name of Jacob, married a girl of eighteen, went to synagogue very infrequently, and held modern ideas on the Bible. His ambiguous behavior puzzled the ghetto residents, for he doffed his hat every time he heard the name of Jesus or Mary, and he even kissed the robe of a monk who was a friend of his, causing no little scandal among the more observant Jews.

Among the most illustrious Marranos living in Venice at that time was Mosè Zacuto, who has been called the Jewish Dante. Born in Spain in 1625, he was a scholar of Kabbalah and studied under Benjamin Levi, a disciple of Chaim Vital of Safed. He lived in Amsterdam for some time but made his home in Venice from 1645 to 1673, when he moved to Mantua where he died in 1692. He wrote *Yesod Olam* ** and *Tofteh Aruch,* † both published posthumously.

Tofteh Aruch, a work of his maturity, is a poem describing the condition of a sinner who dies and goes to hell. The title is taken from a verse of Isaiah, and it was this work that won him the nickname of "the Jewish Dante." In 1819 it was reprinted with the title *L'inferno*

---

* *Virtues of the Jews*
** *The Foundation of the World*
† *Hell Prepared*

preparato, poema ebraico del rabbino veneto Moise Zacuto trasportato in versi italiani da Salomone Isacco Luzzati di Casal Monferrato. *
There are two characters in the poem: the deceased sinner and a demon he meets in hell. The sinner wakes up in his bed, not realizing he has already died. He inveighs against the doctors, reproaches his uncaring relations, complains about the hardships of life, and hopes death will release him from suffering. He begins to be aware that he is dead when they bury him. The poor sinner is greeted by a terrifying vision. He meets a maleficent devil who tells him he is now a man with no hope, in hell. Zacuto forcefully delineates the human condition of a person who had no awareness of his life while he was living and meditates on his destiny only after death. An asymmetrical dialogue takes place between the sinner and the devil, who first answers with a few eloquent words—"vain," "dust," "nothingness," "zero"—and then, after letting the sinner talk, replies with a long sequence of verses that remind him of his past, forever lost, by beginning with the word "yesterday" set in opposition to the word "here," to stress the tragic present. There is also a description of hell taken from the Zòhar:

> *These are the seven rooms of hell*
> *Whose sight wounds the heart of every man*
> *The deep caverns underlying them*
> *Human thought vainly strives to follow;*
> *Minds and brows tire in describing them,*
> *Full of desolating wonder.*

The evil demon describes each room, illustrating the different ways in which the wicked are tormented.

Zacuto's poem is an unusual synthesis. On the one hand, it is a gloomy, pessimistic view of the afterlife clearly influenced by the seventeenth-century Catholic, and especially Spanish, conception, with distant echoes of Dante; on the other, it reveals influences of the Talmud, Zòhar, and Kabbalah, with overlying Marrano and Spanish influences evocative of Calderon de la Barca.

Zacuto was one of the ghetto personalities most closely involved in the affair of the false Messiah Sabbatai Zevi and the visit to Venice of his trusted disciple, the prophet Nathan of Gaza. Sabbatai Zevi, from Smyrna, proclaimed himself Messiah in 1665 and gathered many loyal followers about himself, giving rise to a religious movement that took his name. The movement was nurtured by a renewed hope in the imminent coming of the Messiah and was opposed by the exponents of rabbinical orthodoxy. It became very popular throughout the Med-

---

Hell Prepared, a Hebrew Poem by the Venetian Rabbi Moise Zacuto Translated into Italian Verse by Salomone Isacco Luzzati of Casal Monferrato

iterranean region and did not die even when Sabbatai converted to Islam. As on so many other occasions, the rabbis of the Venetian ghetto played an important role in the affair, which was charged with tension and irrationality. The messianic movement insisted on the need for stricter moral and religious conduct, practiced penitence, and exalted piety and asceticism.

During the 1660s a number of messengers came to Italy from Jerusalem and from Safed, the most important center of mystical culture in Palestine, renewing the hope of the Messiah's coming and, with it, ambivalent feelings of enthusiasm and agitation, for although the idea of the Messiah was a constant element of Jewish culture, many people were incredulous or hesitant. Throughout the Mediterranean region, however, new religious fervor was kindled.

In 1666, according to the testimony of a traveler, this reawakening of religious consciousness in Venice took concrete form in the renunciation of Purim. Festivities, costumes, pageants, and plays were abolished. The rabbis had no wish to discourage genuine religious zeal, which, though uncustomary, was consistent with their teachings; nonetheless, they acted with caution. They forbade the publication of books announcing the redemption, of the sort printed in Amsterdam and Leghorn. In Venice, the affair of the false Messiah served to rekindle the disputes, never wholly extinguished, between the lay leaders of the Jewish community and the local rabbis. The latter, though divided by fierce conflicts, were united in their desire to maintain their control over a conservative and aristocratic community, now seething with excitement at news of imminent redemption. The ghetto population did not react unanimously and deep rifts developed, exacerbated by the enthusiasm of some and the skepticism of others.

According to Baruch d'Arezzo, a contemporary follower of Sabbatai, the majority believed that God had visited His people to bring them the bread of salvation. For Jews living in a ghetto, this must have been an attractive proposition. Baruch d'Arezzo writes that the lay leaders and elders of the community, meeting in joint session, decided to proclaim a great penitence of a kind never before seen in the city, which had always been known for its gaiety. The Jewish authorities encouraged manifestations of zeal and repentance, but attempted to prevent extremes. Rabbi Samuel Aboab, a learned and esteemed polyglot of Marrano origin, maintained a cautious stand. He did not believe in the false Messiah, nor in the many miracles proclaimed, but he refused to commit himself fully in either direction. He believed that a mass act of penitence would in any event benefit the people of Israel. To Sasportas, the rabbi of Verona, who asked his opinion, Aboab expressed his concern about possible anti-Jewish uprisings, advised discretion, and stressed the need to use every possible means to calm the excited Jews, because that state of mind, fed by unrealistic expectations, was dangerous and could provoke an adverse reaction on the part of curious and irritated Gentiles. Remembering the excesses caused by other false Messiahs, he recommended a prudent silence. When summoned by the Venetian authorities, the officers of the Small Council of the University followed just this line of conduct, minimizing the affair and denying any specific knowledge. Aboab was unwilling to wage a war against the false Messiah; he did not want to see the ghetto irreparably divided, and he expressed this concern to the rabbi of Verona, who had written him a poignant letter asking for advice and illumination. In his view, time would heal all excesses, and perhaps this new zeal would really bring the day of redemption closer. Even a mistaken cause could have a positive outcome.

The prudent position of the Venetian rabbis, combined with the lack of definite information from Constantinople and Jerusalem, only heightened expectations, which grew increasingly spasmodic. The apparent immobility engendered all kinds of gossip and inference. The rabbis wrote to and consulted one another, with very little constructive effect. Rabbi Saraval of Venice wrote to his colleague Israel Isserles in Prague, asking him to please keep him informed, even if the news was bad. Mosè Zacuto joined with ghetto rabbis Jacob Mosè Treves, Salomone Hai Saraval, and Josef Valensi in writing letters that, while not always in perfect agreement, expressed reservations and good sense. But Aboab signed no letters and awaited the events. Zacuto, who was considered the leader of the Kabbalists in Italy and who believed in the coming of the Messiah, refused to speak out in support of certain ritual changes proposed by Sabbatai's followers, and declined to become the leader of Sabbatai's acolytes in the ghetto.

The caution of the rabbis was in direct contrast to the wild hopes and expectations surging among the lower social strata of the Jewish population. Testimony of these confused times comes to us from Rabbi Isaac ben Jacob de Levita, the grandson of Leone da Modena. He was a staunch opponent of the messianic movement and wrote an autobiographical essay that contains passages devoted to the affair of the false Messiah, whose name he does not even deign to mention. De Levita, not one of the ghetto's most influential rabbis, but steadfast in his convictions, tells of having often spoken to his congregation, but without being heeded. He also describes a stormy meeting between the Small Council and the rabbis, on July 2, 1666, in which the main topic of discussion was a letter in code from Constantinople speaking in favor of Sabbatai. The elders wanted the letter kept secret, but the news leaked out. Among the reasons for dissent was a request by Sabbatai's followers to abolish the fast of 17 Tamuz and the renewal of poisonous polemics between the leaders of the University and the rabbis. The former thought the rabbis should concern themselves exclusively with religious matters, while the latter claimed total autonomy and, consistent with this, issued a proclamation "in the name of the Yeshiva," which was publicly read on 2 Tamuz (July 4) at the hour of closing of the ghetto gates. The proclamation, addressed to the Jews of the ghetto, expressed Aboab's concerns; it called for silence, discretion with the Christians, and time to reflect.

Any silence was only on the surface. In actuality, everyone was talking, writing, arguing. Aboab himself realized that the proclamation was ineffective. How was it possible to pretend nothing was happening when everyone was talking about the Messiah? The Christians were curious and uneasy: what was going on in the ghetto? And what if Sabbatai was a true messenger of redemption and not an impostor?

The rabbis and community leaders went on fighting furiously. The leaders annulled the rabbis' proclamation and issued one of their own, threatening excommunications. The presence of a possible, however improbable, redeemer did not dissuade people from their vices. Isaac de Levita, who describes these events in his book, says that the discord between believers and nonbelievers had evolved into a dispute between the religious and secular forces, which had already been divided for centuries.

Meanwhile a letter arrived in Venice from Samuel Primo, Sabbatai's secretary. Its contents only fueled the conflict: the alleged Messiah, imprisoned in Constantinople, had signed it himself, and in it he arrogantly gave orders, suggested ways to punish the nonbelievers, and added various political and spiritual considerations. If his aim was to inflame the ghetto, he succeeded. There were incidents and riots, but Sabbatai's true adversaries, including Jacob and Emmanuel ben David, orthodox and fiercely opposed to the false Messiah, reacted to these excesses by openly expressing their views.

The news that Sabbatai had converted to Islam fell like a cold shower on the heads of the poor Jews in the ghetto and froze their enthusiasm, although there were a few die-hards who, amid the general tumult, thought the Messiah might be a Marrano (especially some Spaniards who saw the affair in the light of their own experience). Others, with admirable loyalty, thought back to the example of Esther who had pretended to be a Gentile to save her people. But Sabbatai deserved no such confidence and the rabbis, albeit belatedly, realized that the time had come to regain control of the situation. They suspended the penitences which they had so fondly advocated and decided to burn all the documents pertaining to the case, with a zeal that clearly reveals their embarrassment and their desire to erase, in a single stroke, any commitment they may have made. The sad reality of once more being Jews without a Messiah was comforted only by the eternal hope that sooner or later real redemption would come. Samuel Aboab, in a responsum delivered eight years later, wrote that everyone recognized the error. He confirmed that all relevant documents had been burned in an attempt to heal the wound inflicted by Sabbatai.

Sabbatai's prophet, Nathan of Gaza, arrived in Venice in 1668, just before Passover. As might have been expected, his visit heightened the discordant feelings. Nathan's followers accused his adversaries of not wanting to let him live in the ghetto, and it was only through the intervention of certain Venetian aristocrats that the matter was settled. Baruch d'Arezzo tells in his chronicle that the rabbis attempted to create a desert around Nathan of Gaza, threatening to excommunicate anyone who spoke to him or offered him lodging. Only the authoritative and moderate Rabbi Samuel Aboab went to Nathan, telling him he would be barred from the ghetto to prevent the eruption of violence. His words apparently carried little weight with Nathan, who continued to proclaim himself "a divine wanderer." Baruch d'Arezzo, one of Nathan's supporters, states that the prophet agreed to stay out of the ghetto if he was unwelcome there.

Mosè Zacuto's visit to Nathan the day before Passover, and his subsequent statement that even after studying the Zòhar for thirty-eight years his knowledge of the Kabbalah was inferior to Nathan's, clearly reveal the deep differences between the rabbis, which Sabbatai's conversion had masked but not obliterated.

Nathan did succeed in gaining entrance to the ghetto, however, after two Venetian magistrates ordered him admitted. He stayed there for two weeks, during which time he was an object of widespread curiosity, and despite rabbinical opposition, his contacts with the inhabitants of the ghetto were numerous and frequent. The rabbis published a tract, in essence an appeal to the sons of Israel, stating that they had required Nathan to take an oral examination and that he had failed. Nathan himself signed the record of that interrogation but maintained, in a letter to Caleb Coen, that he had signed under duress. The rabbis considered the battle won, and the people awaiting the messianic era lost their charismatic leader. In April 1668 the rabbis, although still concerned about the threat of heresy, belatedly congratulated themselves for not having agreed to variants in the ritual.

We have no record of how the faithful reacted, but their probable sarcastic comments and criticisms can easily be imagined. Now the religious authorities were distributing consoling letters and smiles, and seeking obedience, but the shock had severely weakened their position.

Aboab, Treves, and Saraval had no easy task to regain the ground they had lost, both with the ghetto and the Gentiles. Nathan of Gaza had to be discredited. On April 8, 1668, therefore, shortly before the prophet left Venice of his own volition, the rabbis and the ghetto leaders decided to take a major step. They summoned Nathan, verified his lack of knowledge on religious subjects, and his embarrassment, and induced him to state that he had been led astray by an evil spirit and that all his visions were the product of his distorted imagination. His errors were the fruit not of malice, but of a diseased mind. They decided not to punish him severely, showing themselves clement to the last, and concluded, "May God forgive those who could have raised their voices against him from the beginning." They were not alluding to themselves, of course, but to the rabbis of Jerusalem who had abetted Nathan by their silence. They did not excommunicate him, satisfied with having annulled his charisma.

The meeting between Nathan and the rabbis was seen from opposite vantage points by the two sides involved. Nathan propagated a different interpretation of his words: "They asked me for a miracle, but I said I had not the power to work one." Baruch d'Arezzo and Mosè Zacuto confirmed all the ambiguities of the interview. The rabbis' proclamation attacking the prophet was answered by his followers, in particular Meir da Mestre, who exhorted the faithful, disappointed by the false Messiah, to continue their acts of penitence. He gave the dispute the character of a controversy on religious doctrine rather than a polemic between individuals. Mosè Zacuto, who had waited until Sabbatai's conversion to break off relations with the false Messiah's followers, did not escape Meir da Mestre's attacks. As a Kabbalist, Zacuto instinctively sympathized with the religious fervor of these new believers, but he differed from Nathan in his conservative outlook, at the opposite pole from the strong innovative force of the prophet, which had conquered the ghetto of Venice. Shortly thereafter, Zacuto moved to Mantua. The rabbis remained.

Aboab lived in Venice until the eighties. An undocumented persecution forced him to seek refuge on the mainland, and it was only after several years that the doge granted him permission to return to Venice. In the summer of 1694, at the age of eighty-four, Samuel Aboab felt death approaching. He called his children about him and gave them his last counsel. He advised them not to take the name of the Lord in vain, to be honest, to educate their children, and to attend synagogue often. When he died on August 12, 1694, all the ghetto mourned. All the shops were closed, and a solemn funeral was held.

At the end of the seventeenth century, the University leaders and the Cattaveri were involved in a curious case. The story is of no historic importance, but provides another example of the interaction between Venice and her ghetto. We learn about it from a document in the records of the Cattaveri and preserved in the Venetian State Archives in the collection entitled *Magistratura dell'Inquisitorato sopra l'Università deli ebrei.**

---

*Magistracy of Inquisitors over the University of the Jews

On the afternoon of July 5, 1691, in the Old Ghetto, a middle-aged woman named Simcà, the wife of Manele Todesco, was on her way home. Here is her statement to the Cattaveri four days after the event: "At around three o'clock last Thursday afternoon, I was going home to my house opposite the Levantine School, at the top of the Scala Matta. At the entrance, after leaving my son-in-law who sells in the ghetto, I took up a candlestick with lighted candle, intending to go buy bread and then come home to dinner with my husband, and in passing under the portico I saw nothing at all. When I came back with the bread, I saw at one side of that portico a basket covered with a cloth. I said 'Shema Yisroel, what's that?' Aboaf, who was on the mezzanine floor, heard me and came out, and when we lifted the cloth we saw a baby in a basket. Said Aboaf, 'You uncover it, I'm afraid to.' When we had uncovered it, we decided, Aboaf and I, to go find a Nanny, so the child would not suffer. And when we unswaddled it we found a passage from our Law and the time of birth written on paper, the Law on parchment and the time on white paper." There were other witnesses too, she told the magistrate, two porters whom Aboaf sent away and another man, also named Aboaf. The Cattaveri called one witness, Isaach Almeda, son of the late Salomon, who stated: "Last Thursday afternoon at about two-thirty, while in answer to a call of nature I happened to be under the portico leading from the Scala Matta, which is in a courtyard opposite the Levantine School, Simcà Todesca comes in carrying a lighted candlestick, and she was going up the Scala and I went after her. There was nothing in the portico, and as I said I went four steps up the alley of the first staircase, and at the top of that staircase there are about five steps leading to Calle Sporca, where I went to relieve myself, and the aforesaid woman went up the other way, where her house is. A little later, while I was doing my business, I heard someone coming down and at the same time I heard a voice saying 'Shema Yisroel, a baby!' I went down as soon as I finished my business . . . and I heard Jacob Aboaf and that Woman who were arguing: 'You uncover it, you do it, I'm afraid,' Aboaf was saying to that Woman, and so I saw a baby, and then the Woman and Aboaf went into the New Ghetto and I went home." Isaac Aboaf, another witness, told how, at about three o'clock that Thursday afternoon, he had been in a shop near the Levantine School and saw Simcà Todesca and Jacob Aboaf carrying a basket "in a place called Scala Matta." All three then went behind the staircase of the Italian school. Ricca da Bolzan, the wife of Mosè Coen Tedesco, confirmed to the Cattaveri that Simcà and the two Aboafs had asked her to keep the child for that night and nurse it. They would look for its parents the next day.

On July 6, 1691, after hearing the opinion of the seven leaders of the University on the baby abandoned in the Old Ghetto, the Cattaveri decided to place it in the temporary custody of a Jewish wet-nurse, and to open an investigation.

Israel Lamno, the guardian at the Cannaregio gate, testified on July 13. On the afternoon of the fifth, he said, the gates at Cannaregio were locked before two o'clock. He was asked whether "anyone passed through those gates after two o'clock," to which he replied, "No sir, unless it be poor ghetto people going for oil or other necessities."

The University leaders addressed a petition to the Cattaveri, requesting custody of the infant. Among other things they wrote: "But why, among 3,000 souls of every age and sex, is it inconceivable that there be spurious births, obliged to be hidden out of regard for reputation . . . in this case the charity of the Ghetto Leaders has always provided, and infants abandoned at or near their houses have always been taken up and nurtured at the expense of the University. Many illegitimate men live in the ghetto, not knowing their fathers and raised by the charity of the Leaders; there always have been and there still are today; and if deprived of this asylum the worst may occur: mothers may strangle their children, throw them into the mains; it may be that a violated maiden, a married woman having committed adultery . . . will take her own life rather than expose herself . . . Let Your Excellencies suppose that a Jewess has fallen into error, what more could she do to cover herself and save her child for her Religion . . . than what this woman did? She places the child in a basket at night, when the Ghetto is locked, at the top or at the foot of a staircase in the Ghetto, near the rooms of two Leaders; she attaches a Paper called Mezuzah, with a Jewish prayer; she writes a note in Hebrew slipped among the swaddling clothes that says this child was born on Wednesday the 7th of the month of Tamuz, and that is for the purpose of Circumcision . . . And can there be any doubt the child is Jewish? If the Father were a Christian he would have taken it freely to the foundling home; he would not have left a note, or a Hebrew prayer . . . why leave a child in the Ghetto, in poverty, who could be placed in comfort? . . . The Father is therefore certainly a Jew. There can be no doubt that the mother is also Jewish. Could the mother be Christian and the father Jewish? Know Your Excellencies that just as the Jew is diligent in observing his religion, likewise he has no interest in propagating it to strangers. But if the mother is Christian, even though the father be Jewish, the child would not be in a state to be received among Jews, and this decides the controversial point and removes even the most remote doubt that the child may have been transported . . . for according to our laws, a child procreated with an alien Woman is excluded from our Religion and remains in the Religion of the mother . . . This child is of the Ghetto . . . There is no evidence to the contrary."

In an effort to learn the truth, the ghetto rabbis published a notice

of excommunication against anyone in a position to provide information leading to the solution of the case who did not come forward
to testify. A few days passed and news of the event spread to all the
small towns of Venetia. A Jew from Castelfranco, a town near Treviso,
finally came before the head rabbi of Padua, Salomon Pancieri, and
confessed: the father was a Jew by the name of Rieti, from Castelfranco
Veneto. The rabbi of Padua sent a messenger to the Venetian rabbis
with his deposition. On July 19 Cattaveri Nicolò Bolani and Alvise
Mocenigo summoned the messenger, who told them what he knew:
the child was born in the house of Ercole Zaccaria Rieti, a Jew from
Castelfranco, and the mother was named Corona Levi. Ercole Rieti,
called to testify, confirmed that he knew Corona Levi and told them
some further details: "A step-brother of mine, called Sansone Sacerdote
da Nomi, wrote to me around April 24, asking me to go to Strigno, 40
miles away, which I did. There I met this Sanson Sacerdote of Nomi,
which is 21 miles away, and he asked if I would do him the favor of
taking into my house a servant, a Jewish girl, whom he had made
pregnant, and he said it would cost me nothing, for he would pay the
expenses; I said that seeing it was he, he was the Master . . . and after
all these words the next morning he delivered her to a Nephew of his
who accompanied her, with me, to my house in Castelfranco." According to Ercole Rieti, Sacerdote had secretly confided his intentions
to him: he planned to take the infant to the ghetto in a basket "bought
at the women's market in Castelfranco." The witness admitted that
his confession had been motivated by the threat of excommunication
"obliging anyone who knew something to inform the Rabbis."

Anzola, the wife of Gregorio Bellotto from Castelfranco, signed a
notarized affidavit on July 20, 1691, saying that Ercole Rieti had asked
her, as a favor, to take a newborn child to Venice, to the house of a
woman who would nurse it. Anzola knew the child's mother, whose
name, according to Regina, the wife of Ercole Rieti, was Corona. Regina
confirmed this in her own deposition before the notary of Castelfranco:
Corona Levi of Mantua had been at her house for three months, "to
protect her virtue."

Corona Levi of Mantua, the involuntary protagonist of the story,
was finally called to testify before the notary. She said she had come
to Castelfranco to work as a servant in the home of Sanson Sacerdote.
Eight years had passed since that day. "Unluckily for me I became
pregnant by Sanson, and to prevent my family from finding out they
took me to Strigno, where the relatives of the aforesaid Sanson live,
and from there I was taken on horseback to this place by his nephew
and Signor Ercole Rieti." She admitted being the mother of the child,
born fifteen days earlier. She said they had given her to understand it
was a girl and only later had told her that it was a boy. What had
become of the baby? "On the evening of the day I gave birth, Signor

Sanson, the baby's father, came and the next day, which was Thursday
... his Father took him away, nor do I know what he did with him
... I've prayed and prayed to know where he is, but I hope to God to
find out; then when Signor Sanson came back I asked what he had
done with the baby, and he answered in anger ... 'I did what I pleased';
and I know nothing more." Why did Corona keep crying? "How could
I not cry, when they took away my baby ... let God do Justice." Did
she recognize the swaddling and the basket? The bonnet? "Yes, because
I sewed it myself, and the swaddling was a white striped cloth with a
little string on one end of the band ... yes, these are his things, I
recognize them, he had them when they took him away."

Gregorio Bellotto, who had accompanied Sacerdote to Venice, testified: "Sanson went to buy a basket in which he placed the child and
... we went to a place in the Ghetto, to a blind alley opposite a Church
of those Jews and he put the baby under a portico in that basket. I said
to him, 'Take care, Sanson, that no harm come to the child,' and he
said no, because there are doors here and someone will find it, and we
placed the child close to the wall, and left immediately, and went to
visit a brother of mine at San Cascian."

On July 24, 1691, Cattaveri Bolani and Mocenigo closed the case.
Their judgment reads: "The Most Illustrious and Excellent Cattaveri
Nicolò Bolani and Alvise Mocenigo, having reviewed the Investigations
conducted on the case of the newborn male found in the ghetto on the
5th of the current month and year, and having maturely reflected thereupon, have ... both in unanimous agreement determined that the child
shall remain in the Ghetto, in the custody of the appropriate persons."

CHAPTER NINETEEN

The Bankrupt University: From 1700 to 1750

The debts of the ghetto — The Cattaveri and public morals — The tax problem—A new magistracy: the Inquisitors over the University of the Jews — Plans for rehabilitating the ghetto finances — The new charter of 1738

The long and costly campaign against the Turks, from 1684 to 1699, which to all appearances ended with the Treaty of Karlowitz, guaranteeing Morea, brought no great benefit to Venice. Her finances had been drained by the war, and the hoped-for revival did not come. Venice remained dominant only in the Adriatic, by now a peripheral sea cut off from the new trade routes. The inexorable decline of the Most Serene Republic also affected her long-standing Ottoman enemy, while England, Austria, Holland, and Germany were increasing their influence and commercial strength. Even her primacy in the Adriatic was soon challenged: the Turks attacked Venice in 1714, conquering her last outpost in the Aegean and giving her no choice but to join forces with Austria. The peace of Passarowitz, signed in July 1718, sealed the defeat of Venice, her disappearance from the Aegean, and her abandonment of Morea and symbolized the eclipse not only of Venice, but of her enemy the Sublime Porte. From that day on the Republic slipped into a golden decline, removed from the great European crises, but increasingly isolated. Lord Chesterfield prophesied that the freedom of Venice would last as long as the great powers maintained their balance in Italy.

The destinies of Venice and her Jewish community once more intermeshed and traveled a common road for nearly another century, until the ghetto itself ceased to exist.

Between 1669 and 1700, in compliance with the decrees of the Senate, the University paid into the Venetian treasury the enormous sum of 800,000 ducats.

On January 6, 1700, the Senate, in dire need, having verified the "ready and devoted resignation" of the University leaders, acknowledged that their last loan dated from only a year earlier but decreed that the University should immediately contribute another 150,000 ducats to the Venetian treasury.

This marked the beginning of a new cycle in the relationship between Venice and the Jews. One of the most visible characteristics of this cycle was the stream of laws, provisions, decrees, injunctions, and resolutions issued by the various magistracies and government organs of the Republic. This copious legislative output increased in proportion to the inefficacy of its enforcement.

The financial crisis, affecting both the pawnshops and the University as a whole, which had already been heavily bled by massive loans during the last three decades of the seventeenth century, would be a constant in Venetian politics for many decades to come, creating situations unthinkable just a few years earlier. The Jews, laden with debts and owning no real estate, were no longer in danger of expulsion; on the contrary, they were better protected by their debts than by all their past riches.

The usual discriminations remained in force, and the Executors against Blasphemy continued to issue edicts regarding public morals. On pain of the most severe penalties, "all Christians under sixteen years of age were forbidden to enter the homes of Jews." A proclamation posted at the ghetto gates especially forbade "Christian girls and women not only to stay overnight, but to perform any service in the ghetto for any Jewish man or woman." A warning was issued to Jews "after becoming Christians": it was severely forbidden "to enter and frequent the ghettos of this city . . . or to enter the homes of any of the Jews on pain . . . of Strappado, Prison, Galleys, Whip, Pillory."

The greatest problem for the Venetian authorities, however, was the precarious financial situation of the ghetto.

In October 1706 the leaders of the German Nation petitioned the Senate for permission to admit non-Venetian Jews to the ghetto for limited periods of time. They would be required to pay an annual tax, to be established by the leaders of that Nation. The proposal was judged worthy of further examination and submitted to the Avogadori de Comun, the Five Sages of Commerce, and the Cattaveri, all of whom presented detailed and substantially favorable opinions.

Although the finances of the University, as a public organism, were not representative of those of the individual families living in the ghetto, whose fortunes were in a better state than those of the community, it could nevertheless be observed that it was primarily the wealthiest families that tended to emigrate, to avoid having to assume the debts of the entire ghetto. The Senate tried to prevent this. In 1630 it resolved that only those who had paid their quota of ordinary and special taxes would be allowed to leave the ghetto, after having obtained the authorization of the University leaders and the Senate. In 1669, as we learn from one of the University records, the Senate again intervened: anyone wanting to leave would have to obtain permission from the leaders of the University, "it being fair and just that all members of the University be responsible for paying the debt." In 1695, 1696, and 1697, senatorial resolutions on this subject increased. The Senate reiterated its opposition to emigration as a general principle, but authorization could be granted for those who guaranteed not only the payment of their taxes, but the payment of the individual quota of debt, by now considerable, established by the leaders of the University. In the early years of the eighteenth century, the Senate assigned a magistrate to investigate the "true causes that can motivate families to take this decision." The tables were turned. Once continuously threatened with expulsion and forced to pay heavy taxes in exchange for being allowed to live in Venice, the Jews were now being kept there on any pretext and their departure obstructed.

These financial problems had many consequences. Not only did they exasperate the latent discord always present among the nations in the ghetto, they also caused quarrels between individuals, who were constantly protesting against the decisions of the group to which they belonged, the University as a whole, or Christian creditors who were trying to recover money lent to the University but that had found its way into the coffers of the State through the huge taxes paid by the University over the previous ten years. One emblematic dispute involved the University and the Gentili family, who wanted to leave and encountered the opposition of the leaders. The Gentilis promised to pay 4,300 ducats in taxes. Later documents show that the issue dragged on, amid injunctions and resolutions, until 1731 when Anselmo Gentili, who had stayed in Venice, stated that he was willing to pay, but asked that his family be allowed to return to Venice on payment of only 500 ducats, and that the exemptions established in 1723 be honored. He also asked "to be considered a non-Venetian Jew."

The Cattaveri were in charge of issues involving public morals, and reported a "damned scandalous abuse in the ghettos of this city, consisting of the introduction of a number of Christians of every age and sex into the homes of the Jews, eating, drinking and doing other things contrary to the Public Religious Decrees, and violating the rules established in the charter." A document enacted by the Five Sages of Commerce a few years later shows that the day-to-day relations between Jews and Christians were probably closer than the authorities

PROCLAMA
PVBLICATO
D'ordine dell' Illuſtriſsimi Signori
Sopra Conſoli.

1647. Adì 17. Agoſto.

In materia de Banchi, e pegni di Ghetto
à Sollieuo della Pouertà.

Stampato per Gio: Pietro Pinelli,
Stampator Ducale:

A proclamation by the Sopraconsoli, one of the many attempts to bring order to the administration of the pawnshops between the mid-seventeenth and the end of the eighteenth century.

Nota degl'Esborfi fatti dall'Vniverfità degl'Ebrei dopo l'accomodamento 1736. fino io prefen-te ad' eftiozione de' Debiti , e ciò oitre il pagamento de Prò Vitalizj , Publiche Gra-uezze, fpefe de' Banchi, e del Ghetto.

Per affrancati a' Creditori ad Eredes per faldo del re-ſto de loro Capitali in ſumma di D. 321000. in ordine al Decreto dell'Eccell. Senato 22. Genna-ro 1755., & altri ſuffeguenti con Capitali nel De-poſito alla regolazione del Ghetto, & inveſtiti nei Banchi del Ghetto—— ————D. 150000:—

Per eſtrazione delle 4. Grazie annue , dall' anno 1737. 31. Luglio ſino 28. Settembre 1776. in ordine all' Accordo 24. Maggio 1736. del Conſeglio Seren. di 40. al Criminal , ſono anni 40. in ragione di D. 2000. P. V. all'anno—— ———D. 80000:—

Per pagati alli N.N. H.H. Labia in ordine all'Accor-do 27. Maggio 1736. ; oltre il rilaſcio di porzione de' Prò fatto con altro Accordo per anticipazio-ne —— —— —— —— —— ——D. 141722:—.

Per Capital di Duc. 13333:8. repriſtinato in Zecca di ragione del Legato Carauaglio , di cui ſono par-tecipi li Neofiti in ordine a Terminazione · dell' Eccell. Inquiſitorato 21. Marzo 1764.——— ——D. 7600:—

Per pagati alla Dita Aron Vxiel in ordine all' Accor-do 6. Giugno 1774. approuato dall' Eccell. Inqui-fitorato li 7. detto—— —— —— —— ——D. 17599:19

D. 406921:19

"Note of the payments made by the University of the Jews after the settlement of 1736, up to the present, in discharge of their Debts, in addition to Life Benefits, Public Taxes, Expenses of the Banks and the Ghetto."

would have liked. On September 18, 1720, they asserted that "wine made according to the Jewish law and custom" was a product to be sold exclusively to Jews, and prohibited its sale to Christians.

Forbidding Christians to buy kosher wine or visit Jewish homes was ineffective in segregating people who lived elbow to elbow. Venice was a city of temptations, especially in the eighteenth century. One night during Carnival in 1720 a small group of Jews, in innocent search of amusement, defied the edicts and proclamations and mingled with the festive crowd, hoping their transgression would go unnoticed under cover of darkness and disguise. They were unmasked, arrested, tried, and convicted.

In 1716, when the war with the Turks was at its peak, the Quarantia al Criminal was called upon to deal with the "grave disorder of the Pawnshops." New articles were issued and posted "above the door of each bank, for the clear understanding of all."

Despite repeated efforts by the Sopraconsoli and the Quarantia al Criminal, the administration of the banks was a constant problem from 1718 to 1721. In June of 1721 the Senate authorized an increase of half a percent in the interest rate for a short period of time, but the financial difficulties of the University, which were becoming increasingly acute, compelled its seven leaders (Josef Pincas Calvo, Abram Abenacar, David di Salomon Valenzin, Isach Hai di Moise Baruch Caravaglio, Aron di David Uziel, Haim Hai di Bignamin, and Baruch Alfarin) to unanimously take on greater responsibilities and discretionary powers in the management of the pawnshops, "to meet the emergency . . . with special authority of our University to stipulate Contracts both public and private, underwriting them in the name of the above University."

The financial situation did not improve. A document issued by the Five Sages of Commerce, almost certainly dating from August 4, 1722, and preserved in the State Archives, shows that the Sages attempted an analysis of the general state of the ghetto finances. They summoned the University leaders and the heads of the individual Nations and asked for all possible information on costs, revenues, and *mas* (taxes). The Sages' report discusses, in particular, the methods used for collecting taxes, including the one in use up to 1685, with "universal and national tax-collectors" authorized to tax each inhabitant of the ghetto according to his condition and means, and the later method (1698) involving secret tax books. According to this original and elaborate scheme, a number of small bags was prepared, corresponding to the number of registered taxpayers in each Nation. Each bag contained a sealed book. Each taxpayer received one bag, and was supposed to consider himself a tax officer. Each person was to fill out his own book, attributing to each taxpayer the amount he considered fair.

Only seven books, indicated by a secret mark, were actually used to determine the taxes to be paid; the others were ignored. But every registered taxpayer was personally involved in the distribution of the tax burden, the purpose being both to increase each person's sense of responsibility and to ensure that the names of the seven real tax officers remained secret. The books were to be returned to the bags, the bags sealed and handed over to the "confidential tax officers," who then opened the bags, found the seven marked books, eliminated the two with the highest and lowest taxes, took an average of all the taxpayers in the five remaining books, and thus came out with the tax liability of each Jew in the ghetto for the period of thirty months.

This complicated procedure was abandoned in 1720, when a new system was adopted successively by the Western, German, and Levantine Nations.

The Five Sages of Commerce were very disturbed by the results of their analysis of the University accounts. They noted that, while the old debts were indeed being settled, new ones were being incurred. The operation of the banks was expensive, and the debts of the individual Nations had to be added to those of the University, amounting to just under 600,000 ducats. The total came to more than a million ducats—1,200,000 according to some estimates.

In September 1722, the Senate heard the reports of the Cattaveri, the Five Sages, and the Deputies for the Provision of Money informing it "on a matter of grave importance, that is, making known the great disorder in which the University of the Jews in this city, and the three nations Levantine, Western and German, find themselves," and released to the public the news that the ghetto was deeply in debt. The situation called for extraordinary measures, so a super-magistracy was created: the Inquisitors over the University of the Jews, to whom all the other organisms in charge of the ghetto would be answerable. Three noblemen, already senators, would be appointed to this office for a one-year term. The Jews would be accountable to them for every detail of the situation, and the Inquisitors, after an overall examination of the ghetto's debts, taxes, tax collection, and operation of the pawnshops, would establish the registry as previously recommended by the Five Sages and find a notary for the ghetto. By virtue of their broad and special powers, they would attempt to lay the foundation for a permanent recovery.

The Inquisitors proposed an austere and complicated maneuver for rehabilitating the ghetto economy, but it may already have been too late. The harder the Republic and the University tried to repair the delicate machinery, the more fruitless their efforts appeared. On the one hand the Venetian patricians were becoming increasingly uneasy at not seeing the expected returns, while the Jews themselves, convinced that the University was a burden too heavy for their shoulders, tried to weave their way through the forest of privilege in search of personal gain.

The rules on foreign Jews in the ghetto, which had originally seemed a good way to attract new residents and capital, did not bring the hoped-for results, and indeed, introduced new conflicts and broadened existing fractures within the ghetto community. One example of the weakness inherent in that mechanism is a petition to the Ma'amad, or decisional body, of the German Nation, submitted by Isaac di Mandolin Treves. Treves, originally from Padua, requested that the rules on foreign Jews be applied to himself and his family, allowing him to establish his taxes for three years at a time. Being foreign—or pretending to be—had become another legal tax-avoidance scheme.

In their search for new blandishments, the Inquisitors distributed exemptions and privileges. Even the presiding magistrates of the Quarantia al Criminal stepped in with a number of rulings, but their indecisiveness clearly betrays the uncertainty and tension of this period. On August 13, 1723, they issued an order calling for the intervention of the Cattaveri, and annulled it on September 11. On September 16 and 26, they issued two new ordinances.

The situation was no better in 1728. In March the Senate was forced to acknowledge the inefficacy of its experiments in financial alchemy. It convened the major creditors and decided to freeze the funds of the University in order to prevent their dispersion. In July, while acknowledging the difficult nature of the issue, it expressed satisfaction with the agreement reached between the University and its lifetime creditors, which brought hope of a gradual reduction of the debt.

The disorderly administration of the pawnshops was made evident once again in August 1729 by the intervention of the Quarantia al Criminal, which issued a lengthy proclamation revising and reorganizing all the regulations pertaining to their operation. But the communication from the Senate in May 1730 is more eloquent than any comment: "Let the Presiding magistrates of the Quarantia al Criminal be charged with expeditiously providing information on the present capital of the pawnshops, how they are managed, who are the outside arbiters of said banks, and whether excessive usury is practiced, suggesting such compensation as their prudence deems most salutary." Despite all their efforts, in other words, the situation was serious and the Senate had no clear idea how to handle it, despite all the inquiries and examinations.

Throughout the 1730s, the already intricate situation grew more and more complicated, as witnessed by the many reports from the Inquisitors to the Senate. With increasing frequency the Jews changed their formal status from members of the University to foreign Jews in order to avoid paying the debts that continued to be huge, despite the Republic's best efforts. This tendency exasperated the creditors, fueling their justified suspicions, and placed the entire weight of the debt on the remaining Venetian Jews.

In April 1732, the Cattaveri stepped in. In a report to the Most Serene Doge they pointed out that the Hebrew nation, once very obedient and orderly, had managed, with the passing of time, to gain concession after concession. "We see with amazement at this time that there is no longer any distinction between Christian and Jew." According to this report the Jews eluded segregation, were no longer "without possessions or landholdings or leases," and had Christian servants of tender age. The Cattaveri also recalled that where printing had once been forbidden, there was now "a printing establishment publicly open to the Hebrew language" suspected of freely printing books on their religion, and the papacy had drawn the attention of the Venetian authorities to this violation. According to the Cattaveri, the censor Benetelli, who had been in office up to 1724, had been replaced by one Serafin Serati, a convert, possibly chosen by the Jews themselves. The magistrates had always trusted Benetelli; he had been a scrupulous supervisor, and the Cattaveri had approved his decisions. But they were suspicious of Serafin Serati. "He is of very lowly station," they wrote, "not clad by any learning." They did not trust his work and did not know whether the books he censored were offensive to the faith. They felt he was open to bribery, and thus concluded: "The Print-shop is a patrician house, the Typesetter is a Jew and the Editor has been one . . . God only knows what scandals have arisen or may arise." To their admonition Serati replied that the Jews could write anything they pleased. They therefore concluded that a new censor was needed, because "the Hebrew language lends itself to deceit, malice, and the outpourings of that impious nation."

In August of that same year, Jacob Levi Muia, the scribe of the University, sent a document from the ghetto leaders to the Inquisitors over the University. The document contained a circumstantiated plan for reducing the hereditary debt of 900,000 ducats, proposing, among other measures, new forms of public deposit for a sum of 600,000 ducats at 2 percent. This appeared feasible, despite the difficulties caused by the Jews that were leaving; the recovery program also involved the Jewish communities of Verona and Padua. The Senate approved the plan, after consulting all the magistracies, especially the Avogadori de Comun and the Deputies for the Provision of Money. Expressing the apprehension of those who had entrusted their precious capital to the Jews, the Senate decreed a six-month suspension of all pending claims and outstanding accounts, in order to clarify the situation and actuate the plan.

This painful step was taken with the intention of untangling the situation, identifying creditors and debtors, and establishing the amounts owed. By obtaining the consent of two-thirds of the creditors, and covering two-thirds of the sum, it would be possible to attempt a process of true recovery, with the remaining creditors being obliged to accept their loss. Once these questions had been tackled, the Inquisitors brought the agreement to the attention of the Quarantia al Criminal. The operation was ratified. Among the most important creditors to approve it were Francesco Labia, Marc'Antonio Venier, and Nicolò Bembo. Over 600,000 ducats were reimbursed, as predicted.

In September 1736, the Inquisitors issued a series of technical regulations intended to finally bring order to the management of the banks.

In March and April 1737 the Senate examined reports from the Quarantia al Criminal and the Sopraconsoli on the ghetto finances, in addition to an appeal from the ghetto requesting that at least one pawnshop be closed. The Senate refused, feeling that this was merely a palliative measure and concerned about possible congestion in the other pawnshops and tensions among the city's poor.

In September, the Inquisitors issued an important ruling intended to restore the ghetto to normalcy, reducing the earlier privileges and exemptions and introducing a gradual return to uniformity for all Jews in their relations with the University and the Venetian magistracies. The Inquisitors stressed, however, that "they poorly interpreted the intelligence of the Public Mind, who settled their debts, pretended to leave and then remained in the city passing themselves off as foreigners in order to enjoy special privileges." Anyone who stayed, despite such subtle tricks, would be considered a member of the University. The proclamation was approved by the Senate twelve days later. The government of the Most Serene Republic recognized that the population of the ghetto had decreased and that it was becoming more and more difficult to enforce taxation, and expressed its deep concern about the financial situation in the ghetto. Despite the profusion of laws, in fact, the results had been poor.

In April 1738, the Senate approved a revised charter for the University of the Jews, in sixty-six clauses. Thirty-three clauses related to the financing of the pawnshops, and the Senate hoped that this would settle the situation once and for all. For the first time since its founding, the structure of the ghetto changed. The charter annulled all differentiation in the treatment of the three Nations: the University remained responsible for the support of the pawnshops, and "all the Jews composing this ghetto of Venice, and those that live or have come to live in the mainland state, are obliged to contribute to the maintenance of said banks."

In 1739 the long-dormant question of establishing a *monte di pietà* surfaced again, primarily due to the precarious health of the pawnshops, now considered beyond recovery. The Senate assigned the presidents of the Quarantia al Criminal and the Inquisitors over the University

IL SERENISSIMO PRENCIPE
FA' SAPERE,
Et è d'Ordine degl' Illustrissimi, & Eccellentissimi Signori
CATTAVERI.

CHE restando per più Leggi a loro Eccellenze comessa la sovraintendenza nelli Sanseri del Ghetto, commandata perciò con Decreto 1563. Primo Zugno à loro Precessori l'elettione di dodeci Sanseri Ordinarij nel Ghetto stesso, quali Carichi benche in forza di posteriori ordinazioni venduti al Publico Incanto, & esercitati in parte da Proprietarij, & in parte da Sostituti con il peso delle Decime annesse, e dovute, mai però possano da veruno essercitarsi senza un Mandato di Sue Eccellenze, & essendo a questi tempi invalso gravissimo abuso, che molti Ebrei si fanno lecito di far li Sanseri in pregiudizio delli dodeci, che con titolo legittimo s'esercitano, e soccombono a suoi aggravij, e che oltre a questo alli stessi dodeci Sanseri non vengono corrisposte quelle Utilità, che dalle Leggi, e da Publiche Tariffe sono permessi; il che causa la desolazione delli dodeci Sanseri stessi; & è contro la Publica intenzione. Perciò

Fanno Sue Eccellenze publicamente sapere, & intendere, che non vi sia Persona alcuna così Ebreo, come d'altra condizione che ardisca di far il Sensale nel Ghetto, e molto meno, che da chi incombe, non siano corrisposte l'Utilità tutte legittime, e particolarmente espresse nell'ultima Tariffa a stampa esistente nel loro Eccellentissimo Magistrato gia formata dagl' Illustrissimi, & Eccellentissimi Signori Inquisitori sopra le Tariffe alli dodeci Ebrei Sanseri Ordinarij nel Ghetto, come è di tutta Giustizia, e ciò sotto quelle pene, che a Sue Eccellenze pareranno in conformità delle trasgressioni che si rilevassero.

Il presente per la sua essecuzione sia stampato, e publicato, e resti pur affisso ne luochi più cospicui nel Ghetto ad universale notizia; Ne sia anco consignata Copia alli Capi di Strazzaria acciò non se ne finga in tempo alcuno ignoranza per la sua essecuzione.

Dat. dal Magistrato Eccellentissimo di Cattaver li 26. Gennaro 1732.

(Lunardo Querini Cattaver.
(Iseppo Minio Cattaver.

Gio: Maria Marinoni Nod.

Adi 30. Gennaro 1732. M. V. Publicato nelli Ghetti di questa Città.

Stampato per Z. Antonio, & Almorò Pinelli Stampatori Ducali.

Proclamation by the Cattaveri against abuse of brokerage privileges at the expense of legitimately licensed brokers.

IL SERENISSMO PRENCIPE
FA' SAPER,

Et è per deliberatione degl' Illuſtriſſ. & Eccellentiſſ. Signori

CATTAVERI.

HE eſſendo diſpoſto con varij Decreti dell' Eccellentiſſimo Senato, e ſpecialmente di 18. Settembre 1683., e 23. Decembre 1712, e Capitoli delle Condotte, che ſia prohibito à cadaun Ebreo il tener Caſe, ò Poſſeſſoni ad Affitto nella Terra Ferma, oltre quelle del loro Ghetto per quel giuſti, e religioſi riguardi, che ben ſpiccano dai Decreti ſudetti, & eſſendo peruenuto à publica notitia, che ciò non oſtante vadano ſerpendo le transgreſſioni, che meritano opportuni compenſi, perciò gl'Illuſtriſſimi, & Eccellentiſſimi Signori Cattaueri, riſſoluti d'eſtirpar vna volta abuſo ſi pernicioſo, che può produr qualche graue ſconcerto alla religione, fanno con il preſente Proclama publicamente ſapere.

Che non vi ſia alcun Ebreo, ſia di che grado, ſtato, ò conditione eſſer ſi voglia, che ardiſca ſotto alcun color, ò preteſto, ne per ſe, ne per interpoſte perſone tener Caſe, o Poſſeſſioni ad Affitto, Liuello, ò per qualunque altro modo nella Terra Ferma, oltre quelle de loro Ghetti, ne meno habitar in cadauna Villa del preſente Sereniſſimo Dominio ſotto tutte le pene loro cominate dai Decreti dell'Eccellentiſſ. Senato 18. Settembre 1683., e 23. Decembre 1712., e Capitoli delle loro Condotte in tal Materia diſponenti.

In caſo poi, che foſſe alcuno ſi ardito di contrauenire, ò haueſſe contrauenuto à coſi ſalutari, e neceſſarie preſcrittioni, ſarà da Sue Eccellenze proceduto con le forme più valide, e vigoroſe, per il qual effetto ſi riceueranno anco denoncie ſecrete, ſecondo il rito del loro Eccellentiſſ. Magiſtrato, & il Denontiante, oltre eſſer tenuto ſecreto, conſeguirà la quarta parte della pena pecuniaria cominata à delinquenti.

Et il preſente ſia ſtampato, publicato, & affiſſo ne luoghi più coſpicui della Città, e traſmeſſo alli Rettori di fuori per la ſua pontual, & inuiolabile eſſecutione.

Data dal Magiſtrato di Cattauer li 16. Gennaro 1712.

[*Andrea Moroſni Cattauer.*

[*Antonio Lazari Cattauer.*

[*Lunardo Querini Cattauer.*

Gio: Maria Marinoni Nod.

Adi 26. Gennaro 1712. Publicato ſopra le Scale di S. Marco, e di Rialto.

Stampato per Pietro Pinelli, Stampator Ducale.

A proclamation by the Cattaveri reiterating the prohibition against Jews' renting homes or land on the mainland or anywhere in the Venetian domains, except in their ghetto.

to conduct the necessary inquiries and surveys. Every possible means to solve the financial crisis of the University and the pawnshops was examined; the Inquisitors even confiscated the funds of the charitable Company for the Ransoming of Slaves in December 1742, obliging the leaders of the three Nations to deposit 2,500 ducats withdrawn from that fund into the pawnshop reserves. This unprecedented operation occasioned bitter protest, for it deprived the charitable organization of all possibility of rescuing captive Jews.

Although the Inquisitors and the Sopraconsoli played the major role in the history of this period, the pawnshop crisis was not the only problem to concern the authorities, who did not lose sight of the necessity of safeguarding public morals. The Cattaveri frequently intervened in episodes that are of minor significance in themselves, but which give an idea of the prevailing attitude: David Jacob Choloa of Rovigo had been granted permission to wear the black hat for eight days, but he had abused the privilege, arousing the wrath of the defenders of the public order. A woman named Luceta Dorsi, who had lived for about fourteen months with Costantino Cona, an oil merchant from Zante, in a house on the Riva del Vin, and had sworn to the judges that she had had no idea the man was Jewish, was tried in court. In 1749 the Cattaveri indicted Jacob Alpron and Abraam Posteler. The former was arrested on the charge of having opened a dyer's shop in the district of Piove di Sacco. The latter had allegedly seduced a young woman with promises of marriage, and when his religion was found out had decided to convert, but had then disappeared from the House of Catechumens.

In December 1750, the Senate answered the request for renewal of the charter with the traditional consultations of the competent magistracies, maintaining the "need for some valid expedient if this University is to subsist." It expressed its intention to renew the charter, at the same time reiterating the need to finally devise ways of equitably distributing the taxes owed by the Jews for the privilege of living and working in the Venetian state according to the individual means of the Jewish taxpayers.

The following January, a ruling by the presiding magistrates of the Quarantia al Criminal made the Senate's resolution executive, listing thirty-three articles of a technical nature pertaining to the banks. Several days later, a new ruling dealt with the remaining issues relating to the life of the ghetto. Among other things it prescribed the institution of a book entitled *Haebreorum*, in which all matters concerning the business of the ghetto Jews would be recorded.

CHAPTER TWENTY

Mosè Chaim Luzzatto and Simone Calimani: Two Rabbis Compared

Mystical visions and rabbinical invective — The life of a Venetian rabbi in the eighteenth century

"For the Jews of the peninsula, the eighteenth century was an age of stagnation, if not of actual retrocession, with regard to universal culture and the study of their native tongue," wrote Lelio della Torre, a Venetian student of Jewish affairs, in an 1866 article for the Jewish periodical *Corriere Israelitico.* He also observed that the rabbis, who in earlier centuries had distinguished themselves as scholars and writers in the Italian language, had entrenched themselves in the study of Jewish ritual, less out of aversion to Italian literature and science than from a fear that new ideas might tempt them from the path of righteousness. The rabbis continued writing Hebrew verse and studying the Bible and Talmud, and their Italian sermons were couched in an obsolete and redundant style of oratory, teeming with absurd metaphors, puerile devices, and pompous words. Despite this, writes della Torre, "Italy may never have had Rabbis so worthy as in this period, lucid spirits who stood out above the crowd and always supported a wise and moderate religious education."

Venice and Venetia boasted two especially celebrated rabbis. The most illustrious, and a highly controversial figure, was Mosè Chaim Luzzatto. Born in Padua in 1707 to a Venetian family, he died in Palestine at the early age of thirty-nine. He had two excellent teachers: Isaac Chaim Cohen Cantarini, a mystic and a scholar of Kabbalah, and Isaia Bassan, a Talmudist. Reb Luzzatto, called Ramchal from the initials of his name, soon became known as a poet and dramatist, and devoted himself with great zeal to the study of the Zòhar. About him gathered faithful disciples and admirers, including Israel Treves, Isaac Marini, Jacob Israel Forti, Shelomoh Dina, and Jacob Chaim Castelfranco. The members of this symposium drew up a statute establishing that the Zòhar should be studied uninterruptedly, and they took turns covering the twenty-four hours of the day. Their mystical purpose was to cure the evils Israel suffered and establish divine harmony in an imperfect world. Their rules were strict: after a formal greeting, absolute silence was observed. They promised always to tell the truth, fast every ten days, and live an ascetic life. They used daily Kabbalistic formulas that were supposed to favor a return to lost cosmic unity through a mystical marriage of heaven and earth.

In this atmosphere of great spiritual tension, Luzzatto thought he heard strange voices and wrote of his experience to Rabbi Benjamin Coen in Sivan, 5487 (1727): "While thinking of a Kabbalistic formula, I fell asleep. When I awoke I heard a voice that said to me in Aramaic: 'I have come down to reveal the hidden secrets of the Holy King.' I sat there trembling, but then I felt encouraged and the voice continued to reveal mysterious things. The next day, at the same hour, I took the precaution to be alone in the room when the voice came down and revealed to me another celestial secret. Until one day it told me it was a *maggid* sent from Paradise and gave me certain formulas to remember until he returned. I did not see him, but I heard his voice speaking from my mouth. Then he gave me permission to ask him some questions. About three months later he gave me more formulas to say in my head every day, to make me worthy of being visited by Elijah, and he ordered me to write a commentary of the Kohelet according to the Kabbalist explanations of each verse revealed to me by him, and then Elijah came and told me the celestial secrets. And after so doing he said that Metatron, the great prince of Paradise, would come. I knew it was he because Elijah told me so. Since that time I have learned to recognize each of them. There are also some holy souls that come, whose names I do not know, and they tell me new things that I write down. I do these things lying face down, and meanwhile I see the holy souls in human form in my dream." This kind of vision was not new to Jewish mystics. In Safed, a center of mystical studies, Josef Karo, the author of the *Shulkhan Aruch*, Isaac Luria, and Chaim Vital had had similar visions.

Naturally Luzzatto told his disciples all about his mystical experiences in the years from 1727 to 1730. One of them, Jequtiel Gordon, who graduated in medicine from the University of Padua in 1732 and on that occasion was named "*dominus Jequtiel Sperodeum Gordon hebreus, filius quondam domini Leonis de Civitate Viena in Lithu-*

*ania,"** let the secret out. He wrote of it to the rabbis of Vilna and also to Mordechai Yaffe, a follower of Sabbatai Zevi, who lived in Vienna. His indiscretion caused an enormous uproar.

The letter fell into the hands of the rabbi of Jerusalem, Moshe Hagiz, who was temporarily living in Altona near Hamburg. He was the son of that Moshe Hagiz who had fought against heresy during the Sabbatai Zevi affair. Hagiz lost no time in writing to the Venetian rabbis: "You, mountains of Israel, my teachers and followers, wise men, rabbis and leaders of the Community, it is your duty, after rending your garments as a sign of mourning, to investigate and find the roots of this evil company before it propagates its evil in the mass of people, and condemn all the members of this movement as enemies of Israel. But I have saved my soul. Thus humbly speaks Moshe Hagiz of Jerusalem. Please inform us of further developments." The scandalized rabbi sent the Venetian rabbis a copy of the incriminating letter, convinced that it was their responsibility, by authority and territorial jurisdiction, to restrain this ambiguous fervor, which he saw as very dangerous. Wanting more information, the Venetian rabbis sent Hagiz's and Gordon's letters to Rabbi Bassan, who had meanwhile moved from Padua to Reggio Emilia. They were anxious to keep knowledge of the affair from spreading lest it provoke the Christians, for they had not yet forgotten the bitter and disappointing experience of the Sabbatai Zevi heresy. In a letter to the rabbi of Venice dated January 24, 1730, Rabbi Bassan defended his disciple Luzzatto, vouching for his purity of spirit.

At the beginning of the campaign against him, Luzzatto resisted firmly and was not unduly upset. He carried on the regular lessons and meetings with his disciples, despite his youth: he was only twenty-three. Evil, he was fond of saying, exists as long as God permits it, and if I am suffering its consequences, that means it was meant to be. Retraction would be unthinkable. To Rabbi Katzellenbogen of Hamburg, a friend of Hagiz's, he wrote that he considered himself neither Messiah nor prophet. He sent another, similar letter of the same gist to Hagiz, couched in humble terms, explaining that his disciple Gordon's letter was strictly private and had not been meant for publication. He expressed respect for the rabbis and their teachings, and asked only to be granted a minimum of autonomy. Far from having the desired effect, his defense provoked stronger reactions. He was finally convinced to accept a compromise and send his writings to Rabbi Bassan. But he continued to study in secret, and wrote a text criticizing Leone da Modena's attacks on the Zòhar.

Determined to punish his obstinacy, the Venetian rabbis excom-

---

*Master Jequtiel Sperodeum Gordon, the Jew, son of the late Master Leo from the City of Vienna in Lithuania

municated him in 1734, and Luzzatto signed the document in acceptance. It was his firm belief that every Jew must obey his teachers
"even if they say left is right and vice versa." He agreed to write his
works in Hebrew and not to print them until they had been approved
by his friend and teacher Rabbi Bassan. And he sent Bassan, in a wooden
case, all his earlier works, chiefly Kabbalistic writings, which were
entrusted to one of the most influential figures of the Jewish community of Padua.

The excommunication and other misfortunes forced Luzzatto into
exile, first in Frankfurt, then Amsterdam. He had also accepted two
other hard conditions: he would be allowed to study the Zòhar again
only after the age of forty, and then only in the Holy Land.

The exile found many friends in Amsterdam, where he was much
respected, and he set to work with new enthusiasm. He wrote *Dialogue
Between a Philosopher and a Kabbalist*, a defense of esotericism, and
sent the manuscript to Rabbi Bassan who approved it, but not without
many reservations.

Polemics and accusations against the mystical rabbi grew again with
renewed vigor. The Venetian rabbinate was convinced that he should
be kept on a tight rein and categorically forbidden any type of esoteric
study. He was asked to commit himself, on oath, to not publishing
any book until it had been examined by the rabbinate. This time Luzzatto refused to accept their restrictions, denying that the Venetian
rabbinate had the right to exert control over a Jew from Padua. The
rabbis then accused him of practicing magic and exorcism, and ultimately his excommunication was announced in all the synagogues of
Venice, in the name of the rabbis of Italy, Germany, Poland, Holland,
and Denmark. Luzzatto learned of this grave decision on his arrival in
Amsterdam. Here again, despite the tempest, he was warmly welcomed
by the community of Portuguese Jews, who lodged him and his family
and allowed him to continue his teaching and his beloved studies.
During this period Luzzatto wrote his *Mesillath Yesharim,** considered
his most important work. It enjoyed widespread popularity and was
praised by even the great Elijah, Gaon of Vilna, a Talmudist and adversary of the Kabbalah.

Groups of Polish and Lithuanian Chassidim named their study clubs
after the *Mesillath Yesharim*. Even the most famous Hebrew poet of
our day, Chaim Bialik, thought well of Mosè Chaim Luzzatto and
likened his name to a mezuzah that should be affixed to the glorious
doorpost of the temple of Jewish creativity.

As he approached forty, Luzzatto decided to move to Palestine where
he would be able to devote himself to mystical meditation in keeping

---

The Path of the Righteous

with his promise, with no further restrictions. But a bare few months after his arrival, he and his entire family perished in a plague epidemic.

From Tiberias, the appalling news spread to Venice and Italy. At hardly forty years of age, one of the most controversial and colorful figures of the eighteenth century was gone.

Lelio della Torre, despite his generally low opinion of the level of Jewish culture in the eighteenth century, acknowledged that it was not uniformly poor. "From time to time, certain flares brightened this overcast sky. Some chosen spirits not only appropriated the Italian literature generally neglected by their coreligionists, but they also won renown as writers." Della Torre mentions, in particular, Giacobbe Saraval, a Venetian rabbi who died in 1782, and Simone Calimani, who died in 1784. In their youth, the two rabbis collaborated on the first Italian translation of the *Pirke Avot*,* which remained the only translation available in Italy up to the mid-nineteenth century.

Critical judgment on Simone Calimani is not unanimous. Historians agree that he was a dedicated scholar and pedagogue, but are less enthusiastic about his poetry.

Little is known about his life. He was descended from an Ashkenazic family that probably settled in Venice in the early sixteenth century, shortly before the establishment of the ghetto. Simone, a poet, author, and rabbi, was born in 1699 and died in Venice at the age of eighty-five. He taught at the community Talmud Torah and devoted his major efforts to the writing of books for use in the schools and for guidance in bringing up Jewish children. Outside the ghetto, Calimani also taught non-Jewish youths and several Venetian noblemen (the historian Gallicciolli was one of his pupils). He wrote numerous poems for weddings and other happy occasions, which he signed Kol Simcha, literally, "The Voice of Joy," a play on words based on the translation of the name Simone into Hebrew as Simcha. Other elegies were signed Oté-Sak, where Sak stood for Simone Calimani.

Untouched by ideological and existential ferments of the sort that inflamed Luzzatto, Calimani was a cultivated rabbi of moderate habits, who spent his entire life in the ghetto with no extravagances and no polemics, but with great learning. He supervised a critical edition of the Bible and published grammar books and poetry.

If Luzzatto was irresistibly attracted by mysticism, Calimani, while never failing in his strict observance of rabbinical orthodoxy and his attention to *mitzvoth* great and small, felt a keen interest in the new movement of enlightenment that was sweeping Europe, involving the Jewish as well as the Gentile world—especially in Holland, where its

---

Sayings of the Fathers

major exponent was David Franco Mendes. Calimani wrote an explicitly anti-Kabbalist book entitled *Tokhachat Megulla*,* a dialogue between two enlightened citizens named Kalkol and Darda', who discuss such vices as hypocrisy, arrogance, and malice, rife in the society of their day.

Calimani's *Esame ad un giovane israelita*,** a dialogue in ten sessions between teacher and student, was written in 1782, two years before his death. On the one hand it reflects the eighteenth-century atmosphere of the Venetian ghetto, and on the other clearly expresses the almost constant pedagogic concerns that characterize all Simone Calimani's work, providing a synthesis of the essential ideas and crucial moments in the religious training of a Jew.

The entire work reveals the desire to protect himself from prejudice, typical of rabbis who write for Jews but know that many if not most of their readers will be non-Jews. Calimani displays this awareness when he explains, for example, why Christians are called *goyim*, and the difference between this and *arelim*, another name for them.

Although the *Esame ad un giovane israelita* provides first-hand testimony of how teachers communicated with their students in the late eighteenth century, there are other documents no less useful in providing an understanding of the educational climate in which Simone Calimani lived, in harmony with its tenets and with no special existential traumas, quite unlike Mosè Chaim Luzzatto.

The statute of the Talmud Torah Brotherhood of the German Nation contains a set of rules dating from 1714, which clearly illustrate the requirements for the typical religious education of a Venetian Jew in the early part of the century. As his family had for generations, Simone Calimani lived his entire life in the ghetto and adapted to it completely. Like every other Jewish boy, he studied at the Talmud Torah. The product of an age-old debate, the statute of the Talmud Torah organization devoted special attention to the mental and cultural training of children, in an effort to provide the young Jew with a complete religious education that would answer his every question, forming and fortifying him so that, as a member of a minority group, he could maturely confront pressures and attacks from the outside world.

The educational model is uncompromisingly rigid, and highly codified in its meticulous attention to the seemingly most banal details. The statute reveals a rigidly formal discipline governing the conduct of all members of the school, applying to teachers of all ranks as well as to the students. The punishments prescribed for students were commensurate with the severity of their misbehavior, with expulsion the ultimate penalty. The work of the lower-ranking teachers was super-

---

*Manifest Warning
**The Examination of a Young Jew

vised by those of higher rank, whose duties were strictly established, and this hierarchy strongly conditioned relationships within the academic microcosm. Duties and authority were all precisely set; the schoolmasters were obliged to attend synagogue every morning and supervise the group prayer of their charges. School and religious education were one and the same thing. Among the many subjects studied were Italian, Hebrew, geography, and arithmetic, but Bible, Mishnah, and Talmud were paramount. In the upper classes the curriculum was more specific, including the *Pirke Avot,* the Haggadah, Jewish holiday rituals, and the Talmud with its commentaries.

The concern, so clearly evinced in these regulations, with giving the children a secure Jewish identity and enabling them to defend themselves from attack and criticism by non-Jews bears witness to the fear engendered by the increasingly close contact between the Jews and the other citizens of Venice. The ghetto walls were developing their first cracks.

GRAMMATICA
EBREA
SPIEGATA IN LINGUA ITALIANA
COMPOSTA
DA SIMON CALIMANI
RABBINO VENETO

*Con un breve trattato della Poesia antica;
e moderna di essa Lingua Ebrea.*

IN VENEZIA.

NELLA STAMPARIA BRAGADINA MDCCLI.
Con licenza de' Superiori, e Privilegio.

Title page of a Hebrew grammar by Simone Calimani (1699–1784).

CHAPTER TWENTY-ONE

The End of the Ghetto: From 1750 to 1797

The economic crisis of the University — The conflict between physiocrats and mercantilists — The charter of 1777

At the beginning of 1751, the "great disorder" in the administration of the University and its pawnshops was still the object of constant attention on the part of the Senate and the Quarantia al Criminal. The University's patrician creditors were still trying to recover their ducats, but this reasonable necessity clashed with the reality of the situation: the Jews, by order of the Venetians themselves, owned no real estate and had only liquid assets. There was nothing to confiscate, and the Republic could take no stronger action. Further measures would be unpopular, create even greater disorder, and might serve to kill rather than cure the patient, to the detriment of all. There could be no benefit in intransigence. A turn of the screw would mean the irrevocable loss of all the outstanding credits, and would virtually eliminate any hope for the future. Moreover, the closing of the pawnshops would create severe difficulties in handling the problem of poverty.

The Senate, though probably aware of its own impotence, continued to enact one law after another in an attempt to arrive at a compromise. Such a compromise, though difficult, might even have been successful had the fortunes of the Republic been better in the eighteenth century, but her relentless decline further complicated matters.

In August, a number of the ghetto's creditors were reimbursed two thousand ducats. The lucky ones were chosen by the drawing of lots, a method established by previous agreements.

In March of 1760, the senators ordered a new detailed investigation into the financial health of the University and expressed some optimism for the first time in many decades, giving directives for the clauses of the future charter. Among other things it was thought the Jews could be authorized to engage in trades other than that of second-hand clothing merchants without damaging the Christians. The revised charter was ratified in August, for a ten-year term. On that occasion the Senate, for perhaps the first time in decades, expressed its satisfaction with the general progress of the ghetto economy and with the restoration of a modicum of order in place of the chaos that had reigned for so long. Naturally the controls were still very rigid.

Convinced that the University would be strengthened by an increase in population, the Senate persisted in seeking new financial mechanisms to encourage foreign Jews to come to Venice, stressing the benefits the Republic granted to Jews, as well as their favorable living conditions. In this context, the "well-meaning Christian Piety of snatching their sons and daughters from the breast and from their fathers' tutelage, to bring them to Baptism," was strongly censured. Long ago, in 1502, it was recalled, the Republic had ruled that no Jew under the age of fourteen could be baptized, and the delicate matter had always been regulated by copious legislation. With particular solemnity and emphasis, the Jews were once more assured of the "free, peaceful and undisturbed observance of their Rites and their religion, for both themselves and their children."

The revised charter of 1758 had introduced several changes, including further facilitations concerning navigation, trade, and religious matters, and new rules governing the hours for opening and closing the ghetto. Some exceptions were even made in the regulations for hiring Christian servants, but only in situations of urgent need.

The question of permitting the practice of professions other than that of used-clothes dealer had been passed to the Five Sages of Commerce for examination.

On December 9, 1760, the University issued a memorandum for circulation in the ghetto. The document dealt with foreigners, the taxes due from the two privileged groups, the Jews from Corfu and the transient Levantines, the schedule of taxation, penalties for noncompliance, and the duties and privileges of the leaders, including the use of excommunication.

But the Senate's optimism was short-lived. When a further analysis of the ghetto finances was published in September 1761, the senators realized that the situation was far from rosy. They therefore decided to extend the leaders' mandate for two years, so that there would be no discontinuity of authority at this delicate time of attempted economic recovery. The established lottery for the repayment of outstanding debts continued.

In 1762, the Sage Treasurer for the Provision of Money and the Inquisitors drew up a balance-sheet of the ghetto's debts, which amounted to three thousand ducats, and reached the conclusion that no more money could be demanded of the University.

While the precarious financial condition of the ghetto was the government's major source of concern at that time, it was not the only one. Fires, for example, were frequent in Venice, especially in the densely populated ghetto where the houses, very tall and built mostly of wood, were crowded into an inextricable tangle. Frequent inspections were conducted to prevent catastrophic fires. In February 1764, the presiding magistrates of the Quarantia al Criminal reported to the Senate on the results of one such inspection, and the Senate, concerned about the safety of the ghetto in case of fire and possible insurrection, required the Governors of the Arsenal to consign to the University leaders a hydraulic machine with an adequate number of tubs and hoses for the use not only of the ghetto but of the neighboring areas as well.

The general decline of Adriatic trade was causing severe problems for Venice, especially with regard to the commerce of food products and oil. Certain aristocrats, including Francesco Tron and Zuan Alvise Emo, insistently argued that the Jewish merchants should be prevented from buying products, especially oil, in Corfu and within the state, and be allowed only to export. The Senate accepted this protectionist thesis and planned to implement it starting in January 1771. This left the Jews only a few months, until December 1770, to wind up their affairs. At the last moment extensions were granted. The market greeted the Senate ruling first with disorderly protest, and subsequently by abrupt price increases.

In August 1772, the Jewish merchants having been barred from the trade, there was a widespread and flourishing traffic in contraband oil. At the same time problems arose among the farmers of Corfu. Superintendent Andrea Querini had predicted these consequences several months earlier and had been quick to point out that the sudden discontinuation of the subsidies traditionally granted by the Jewish merchants to the local farmers would give rise to a great "disturbance." He had also denied there ever having been a Jewish monopoly in the region.

The Senate instructed the Five Sages and the Superintendents of Oils to examine the question in depth. That discussion resulted in two conflicting reports. Superintendents Vincenzo Barsiza and Agostin Sagredo and the two Sages Prospero Valmarana and Sebastian Zustinian opposed the anti-Jewish measures, spoke in favor of free competition, and, in line with the physiocratic concept of economy, considered it harmful to separate trade from consumption, especially in the case of oil. In their opinion, Jewish dynamism was well-suited to filling the gaps left by the Venetian merchants, who were increasingly unwilling to incur risk and had no real initiative. Superintendent Zuan Alvise Emo and the three other Sages, Antonio Zulian, Andrea Giulio Corner, and Lorenzo Alessandro Marcello, were in favor of the decisions taken in November 1770 and June 1771, convinced that the price hikes could be blamed chiefly on the illegal traffic and the Jews. And although they accepted the concept of free trade, they observed that protectionist measures had been adopted at other times in the past. Among the most recent, they recalled, was the ban on the sale of grain, intended to favor the Venetians and obstruct the Jewish merchants. This clash among the authorities heralded the still more bitter one that was to take place within the Venetian aristocracy in 1777 and 1779, when the subject of free ship-owning and the granting of licenses to Jewish vessels came under discussion.

Caught between the rising price of oil and the agitation of the farmers on Corfu, the Venetian Senate again found itself in a tight spot. Tron and his followers, aiming to confirm the recent rulings, submitted a proposal stating, among other things, that it was not "in the interest, the dignity or the justice" of the Senate "to alter the established policies." They were defeated. The Senate, recognizing the inefficacy of its 1770–71 decrees, conducted a sort of self-examination, as a result of which the entire question was submitted to the opinion of the adjunct deputies. Late in 1772, the latter finally delivered their reply, suggesting that the Jews and other foreigners be granted freedom of trade, but that strict regulations be imposed to contain prices.

The seventies promised to be turbulent. In April of 1771, a "determination" by the presiding magistrates of the Quarantia al Criminal underlined, in harsh tones, the grave and persistent disorder in the pawnshops; and in August 1773 the magistrates stressed the irregularities of the ghetto bankers, who were violating not only the laws of the State but even the agreements signed with their own University. Appropriate sanctions were ordered. On the question of trade, discord had been increasing within the aristocracy. Tron continued to uphold his protectionist plan, fundamentally hostile to Jews and foreigners, while Pesaro, Memo, Sebastiano Foscarini, and Gabriel Marcello tenaciously opposed this attitude, which they judged shortsighted, and advocated a more flexible policy.

Available documents have enabled us to make an overall estimate of the Jewish impact on trade during those years: judging by the customs revenues (both entering and exiting), from 1770 to 1775, shortly before the restrictions, the Jews accounted for about 6 or 7 percent of the total volume of trade.

In January 1776, the Senate urged the magistrates to submit their reports with their proposals and clauses for the revised charter. That year, owing to political discord between the progressive and conservative wings of the aristocracy, contradictory signals were registered.

Foglio, che dimostra il Dazio fatto alla Dogana da Mar in Anni

Samuel Benetto Pincherle
Benetto Luzzato
Marco di Abram Malta
Alessandro Vital
Abram Vita Angeli
Emanuel Jacur
Salamon e Isach Treves
Daniel Bonfil e Figlio
Sabbato Alteràs
Aron Uziel
Isach David Sarde
Menachen Vivante
Angelo Valenzin
Isach Valenzin
Moisè Vital
Isach Levia
Anselmo di Leon Gentili
Jacob e Josef Bettilies
Jacob Curiel
Abram d'Isach Levi
Memo Curiel
Mandolin di Salamon Levi
Elia Vita Todesco
Vita Levi
Vita Calme
Abram di David Almeda
Emanuel Cigogna
Alessandro Abeaf Fonseca
Samuel Hua
Samuel Menavia
Emanuel Dies
Lustro Morpurgo
Abram e Benetto Fedore
David Bassan
Leon Serena
Caliman Bassan
Lustro Levi
Jacob Consigli
Moisè di David Soliani
Jacob di Simeon Mortera
Asdrael di Mandolin Levi

Tottale delli sudetti Anni due d 34282 : 23.

Marzo 1777. sin tutto Febbraro 1778			Da p͞nc Marzo 1778 sin tutto Febb.° 1779.			
Ponente	X.° p c.°	In Tutto	Leuante	Ponente	X.° p c.°	In Tutto
255 . 10	139 . 23	2719 . 9	1157 . 10	103 . 10	180 . 18	1400 . 14
	3 . 8	181 . 22	249 . 9		5 . 23	255 . 4
		196 . 8	66 . 22	9 . 20		70 . 18
	18 . 14	278 . 9	969 . 11	135 . 17	125 .	1230 . 4
33 . 6		215 . 6	417 . 7	150 . 2		567 . 9
7 . 81 . 15	261 . 22	1283 . 20	333 . 20	257 .		590 . 20
17 . 8275 . 21	93 . 18	9963 . 8	2088 . 5	534 . 21	1030 .	3659 . 2
15 . 2443 . 1		2783 . 10	925 . 10	640 . 14		1272 .
10 . 97 . 9		170 . 19	644 . 18	53 . 23		698 . 17
8 .		23 . 8	14 .			14
16 .		468 . 16	318 . 8			318 . 8
16 . 16 .	6 .	800 . 14	1296 . 3			1296 . 3
12 .		18 . 12				
6 .		48 . 6				
15 .		64 . 13				
17 . 622 . 14		624 . 7	4 . 5	321 . 14		325 . 19
21 .		337 . 21	447 . 7			447 . 7
18 .		249 . 18	411 . 18			411 . 18
21 . 117 . 8		152 . 5	17 . 18	39 . 19	49 . 15	157 . 4
20 .		12 . 20				
8 .		19 . 8	26 . 19	6 .		27 . 1
17 .		3 . 17	38 . 4			38 . 4
19 .		89 . 19				
		173 .	151 . 21			151 . 21
9 .		81 . 9				
7 .		55 . 7	89 . 11			89 . 11
13 .		1 . 13				
25 . 17		25 . 17				
	6 .		38 . 1			38 . 1
19 . 20	19 . 20					6
			1 . 20			1 . 20
			7 . 13			7 . 13
			2 . 16			2 . 16
			30 . 4			30 . 4
			7 . 6			7 . 6
			18 .			6 . 18
			6 .			1 . 2
			1 . 2	6 . 22		0 . 22
				6 .		6
			161 . 10			161 . 10
19 f 11952 f 21	537 . 21	20970 . 13	f 9454 f 10	f 2451 f 16	f 1406 f 8	f 13312 f 10

Giacomo Marchetti Quad.

Table showing the maritime customs duties paid from March 1, 1777, through February 1779, by the listed companies.

On the one hand the progressives obtained a short-lived victory with the abolition of the anti-Jewish legislation and the beginning of a new economic policy open to foreign participation; on the other, the Cattaveri issued new proclamations stressing the inviolable boundaries of segregation that the Jews were not to overstep.

In March, the University leaders, convinced that new measures were being prepared against the ghetto, wrote a second petition in an attempt to parry the blow before it fell. The five leaders of the ghetto asked for a preliminary hearing on the details of the new charter before the Senate instructed the relevant magistracies to draw up their reports. The request apparently produced no immediate effect.

In February of 1777 the Senate reiterated "the desire of the public not to grant the Jews the right of citizenship," explicitly confirming that any permission to reside in the Venetian domains was temporary, governed by the conditions set forth in the charters. In addition, it established that since the "outstanding debts of the University remained the exclusive responsibility of its present members, let the law on the imposition of a line of discipline and annual taxation be equal for all."

Physiocrats and mercantilists, the two opposing economic factions of the Venetian aristocracy, clashed again with greater force when the time came to renew the charter in August of 1777. Commercial and economic considerations played a more important role in this conflict than did the unequivocally anti-Semitic edict issued in 1775 by Pope Pius VI. The assembled magistracies, despite months of meetings and postponements, were unable to agree upon a draft to send to the Senate. In fact the assembly came before the Senate on August 8, 1777, split in two, with two separate reports, each signed by eight magistrates. On one side were three Cattaveri, two Sage Treasurers, one Inquisitor over the Jews, one Sage of Commerce, and one Adjunct for the Provision of Money, all of whom demanded an immediate decision with no further vacillation or delay. On the other side were ranged the other four Sages of Commerce, two Deputies and one Adjunct for the Provision of Money, and an Inquisitor over the Jews, who insisted that no resolution be made without first consulting the assembly of "returned envoys," that is, the senators who had represented the Republic in Constantinople. This convocation of the assembly of envoys had all the appearance of a delaying maneuver to prevent Tron, at the time a powerful voice in the Senate, from winning the debate.

On August 23 the Senate took the bull by the horns, instructing the Cattaveri to organize the assembly to draw up the clauses of the new charter. In great haste, on September 19, two reports were again submitted to the Senate; one contained ninety-six articles, the other, violent protests. "We were surprised and dismayed by the new and unusual form whereby the conference has been convened to discuss and rule on the immense volume of ninety-six clauses," wrote the adversaries, in protest against the pressure to which they had been subjected. They continued: "The proposed clauses . . . invariably and without alterations, should have been submitted to the most excellent Senate, and they should have either been signed by each, or the bases for opposition presented in a separate document within three days." The Cattaveri had, in fact, submitted a prepared text and had it approved without leaving any room for changes, in essence a true sleight of hand. The minority not only was alarmed by the substance of the dispute, but expressed its uneasiness about the unorthodox and disconcerting method resorted to by the Cattaveri. The Senate must be alerted: the very content of the law was potentially dangerous and could bring "greater decadence to what remains of the languishing commerce of this marketplace, and its pernicious effects would not afterwards be so easily or quickly remedied."

The report of the assembly that was to prepare the clauses for the new charter of 1777 not only set limits for the Jews in maritime and overland trade, but specified restrictions on the merchant-manufacturers (who contracted to manufacture products which they then sold directly) and on the factories that "exist in Venice and in the State in the name and on behalf of Jews, either arbitrarily or by public concession." The assembly ruled that all unauthorized factories be torn down within two years: "As for the factories existing by public decree, these must close as soon as their license expires, or within two years." An exception was made, however, for privileged plants "that did new work not practiced by Christians," the validity of whose permits was conceded as long as they were approved by the Cabinet and a four-fifths majority of the Senate. Because they were also exporters and retailers, the Jewish manufacturers could sell at highly competitive prices, to the detriment of the Venetian guilds.

Piero Emo, an Inquisitor over the Jews, dissociated himself from the action of the Cattaveri and went over to the opposition along with the Deputy for the Provision of Money Sebastiano Foscarini. Although the clauses of the new charter were voted down by the assembly (10 to 7), they were approved in their entirety by the Senate on September 27, 1777, with 98 favorable votes out of 160. The Cattaveri made the contents public the next day. The intention of the legislators was to create an organic corpus of rules (nearly forty pages) which would constitute an adequate precedent for years to come. "All Jews of every order, who wish to reside for the future period of a Decade in Venice must be equal before the Laws of Discipline and in annual taxation, and they are all considered equal Members of the new united and reformed Body of the University of Venice." This is an excerpt from the first article of the charter. The first sixty-three clauses were devoted to the banks and their administration, and to regulations governing life in the ghetto (cemetery, houses, customs), obligations concerning the decoration and adornment of the buildings, and methods for paying taxes. This first part of the charter, devoted to taxes and ways to improve "the management and discipline of the pawnshops," brought no special reaction from the Senate.

Clauses sixty-four to ninety-six concerned the Venetian Jews, living in the state "on land and sea," except for those in Corfu who enjoyed special privileges. Several patricians opposed them firmly. "When these clauses were read at the assembly, we were surprised at the contention of some that they ought to be burned," because "if the Jews were barred from participation in manufacturing, the people would remain at the mercy of the guilds."

The restrictions on Jewish trading and manufacturing contained in the new charter, motivated more by economic than by religious considerations, were rooted in a social view of which Tron was the chief advocate. In accordance with a long-standing Venetian tradition, he felt that society should be divided into classes and each should stay "within its own gate without invading the quotas and profits of the guilds." Each worker should "study to make his own work faster and more accurate, in order to be employed in preference to his peers." According to the lawgivers of 1777, the socioeconomic and, especially, the moral order were based on principles that could not be gainsaid: each person was to fulfil his own economic function without invading the territory of others. It was one thing to manufacture products, and another to sell them. By merging the two, the Jews upset the original concept that had inspired the entire history of the Republic.

By placing strict limitations on the activities open to the Jews, the new charter created changes in the relations between the Jews and their University, offering advantages to the leading merchants and freeing them from all obligations. These merchants were protected, *a priori*, from any attempt on the part of the University to burden them with taxes or duties. None of them, for example, could be obliged to "show the tax-collectors the assets and turnover of his business." No company could be taxed over a certain amount, and the end result was that even the ghetto tended to reproduce the traditional Venetian model of oligarchy.

The new charter of 1777 was therefore the occasion for a clash not only among competing groups, but also between two different mentalities, neither of which was probably in step with the times.

The new restrictions caused no great outcry in the ghetto; only a few Jews decided to leave. In 1766 there were 422 Jewish families in Venice, in 1780 there were 408, and in 1785, 410. Not a significant exodus, as confirmed by additional data testifying to the continuity of the Jewish presence on the Venetian mainland: in Verona there were

GL' ILLUSTRISS. ED ECCELLENTISS. SIGNORI

CATTAVERI

INFRASCRITTI

Ffinchè restino intieramente eseguite, nè in verun modo trasgredite le Pubbliche Prescrizioni espresse nelli sotto registrati Capitoli della Ricondotta degli Ebrei approvati dalla Sovrana autorità dell'Eccellentissimo Senato con suo Decreto 27. Settembre decorso, nè vi sia alcuno, che sotto qualsivoglia pretesto ardisca di fingere inscienza, o ignoranza di quanto restò nelli medesimi prescritto, e comandato.

Hanno perciò loro Eccellenze terminato, e terminando ordinato, sempre però a senso, ed in relazione delle prescrizioni dal prefato rispettabile Decreto stabilite, che li Capitoli 77. 83. 84. e 92. della Ricondotta medesima siano sotto la presente stampati, diffusi, e pubblicati a chiara intelligenza di ognuno, non che spediti in più esemplari a' N. N. H. H. Pubblici Rappresentanti della Terra Ferma, e da Mar, ove esistono Ebrei per la loro inalterabile esecuzione, cominando in caso d'inobbedienza, a qualsivoglia Trasgressore le pene tutte nelli medesimi espresse, al quale effetto sarà dal loro Eccellentissimo Magistrato tenuto sempre aperto Processo d'Inquisizione, col Rito dell'Eccellentissimo Senato contro gl'Inobbedienti, e Trasgressori, e saranno ricevute Denoncie Secrete, col premio al Denonziante da essi Capitoli stabilito, ed in tutto, e per tutto come nelli medesimi, alli quali &c. mandantes &c.

SEGUONO LI CAPITOLI

77. Che dagli Ebrei non possa tenersi in Casa alcun Uomo, o Donna Cristiana, nè come Servitor, nè sotto qualunque altro nome, impiego, o pretesto, niuno eccettuato, in pena all'Ebreo di Duc. 100. da esser applicati, come sopra, e di star in Galera con ferri ai Piedi, ed al Cristiano di essere castigato criminalmente, ed anche Banito da questa Città, ma possano servirsi di giorno di soli Uomini Cristiani, e non Femmine, per accendere unicamente il lume, e fuoco nelli soli giorni Festivi, ed anche per le occorrente di Traffico, che non ammettessero dilazione, il che pure dovrà osservarsi nella Terra Ferma.

83. Che non possa, nè debba alcun' Ebreo di che stato, sesso, o condizione si voglia, tanto in nome proprio, tanto sotto altro nome, per poco, o per molto tempo, posseder, acquistar, tener in affitto, Pegno, Feudo, o Livello, o sotto qualunque altro Titolo, e modo, niuno eccettuato, nemmeno a pretesto di Pieggiaria, o Cessione, Case, Terreni, Beni stabili, Possessioni, Livelli, ed altro, posti, e situati, tanto in questa Città, che in cadaun luoco dello Stato, a riserva delle Case destinate per loro Abitazione entro li Ghetti. Fuori de' medesimi Ghetti resta solo permesso ritener in affitto Magazzini, Volte, e Luochi ad uso di Mercanzia, e mai di Abitazione, come pure sia proibita l'Abitazione medesima in qualunque Villa dello Stato, senza permesso di Decreto del Senato, e ciò in pena di Duc. 500. da esser applicati un terzo al Denziante, il quale sarà tenuto secreto, e il rimanente diviso con le forme solite del Magistrato al Cattaver, do-

vendo anche dal Magistrato suddetto esser proceduto per via d'Inquisizione nel proposito contro li Trasgressori.

84. Che Ebrei non possano far Senserie nè in Ghetto, nè fuori, di cose, che appartenessero alla Senseria stessa, nè far dar Dinari a tempo, nè a Livello, in pena di Ducati 25. per caduna volta da esser applicati, come sopra.

92. Sopra il proibito Negozio di Biade in Terra Ferma di qualunque genere egli siasi, sarà così dal Magistrato al Cattaver, come da quello alle Biade tenuto Processo col Rito del Senato per scoprirne le delinquenze, e punir li Rei con tutte quelle pene afflittive, e pecuniarie, che riputassero di Giustizia, e di esempio a freno di ulteriori contraffazioni.

Data dal Magistrato Eccellentissimo al Cattaver li 5. Decembre 1777.

(MATTIO DANDOLO Cattaver.

(LAZZERO ANTONIO FERRO 1.° Cattaver.

Francesco Marinoni Nod.

ADDÌ 9. DECEMBRE 1777.

Pubblicati sopra le Scale di S. Marco, e di Rialto.

STAMPATI PER LI FIGLIUOLI DEL QU. Z. ANTONIO PINELLI STAMPATORI DUCALI.

A proclamation issued by the Cattaveri stressing scrupulous compliance with clauses 77–92 of the 1777 charter.

177 Jewish families in 1766, 172 in 1780, and 165 in 1785; in Padua there were 107 families in 1766, 111 in 1780, and 104 in 1785.

Tron himself had told an ambassador to Venice that in his opinion the severity of the new charter would not drive the Jews away; neither the Treves nor the Bonfil families, the most powerful in the ghetto, would leave Venice. His prediction was confirmed by events.

Approval of the charter did not attenuate the economic and political conflicts within the Venetian oligarchy, and the Avogadori de Comun suspended the charter in February 1778, in order to give the Maggior Consiglio a new opportunity to evaluate the situation. Tron was successful in obstructing this maneuver, but the "Jewish issue," as he called it, was not yet settled.

The new charter of 1777 had overlooked one delicate matter: the right of the Jews to own ships flying the Venetian flag. Despite the opposition of the Senate, the number of ships owned by Jews increased steadily during the eighteenth century. In September of 1779, in the wake of the latest repressive policies, the Sages of the Orders proposed revoking all Jewish licenses. The resulting discord created a deadlock in which the initiative could be neither approved nor rejected. After several consultations, the Five Sages of Commerce expressed an opinion dissenting from that of the Sages of the Orders. They reminded the Senate that the Jews, under the new charter, were not considered true citizens, but merchants in the Venetian marketplace, under public protection. The patricians, however, were increasingly divided on the question of the Jewish shipowners. On September 19, 1779, Tron wrote to Francesco Donà: "Marcello [Gabriel] can think of no other resource than granting licenses to the Jews."

The conference of the Five Sages of Commerce with the envoys returned from Constantinople was convened in May 1779, despite the opposition of Tron and his faction. Its purpose was to re-examine the situation and propose possible changes in the clauses of the revised charter of 1777 (which had caused considerable hardship on the mainland with the closing and liquidation of all the factories operated by Jews, in compliance with the public decrees). Issues vital to the Republic were discussed, including the naval industry, free maritime trade, and the privileges of citizens. After a heated debate, the new assembly issued some sensational rulings representing a true reversal of the restrictive provisions of the 1777 charter. The Venetian Jews were granted permission not only to participate in commerce, but to own and build merchant ships: "Having demonstrated that permission has been granted them to navigate and mix in the Levant trade, ancient and jealous seat of Venetian Commerce, it is appropriate to expound the point regarding the time they were admitted as partners [holders of a certain number of shares in a ship] and consequently enabled to obtain the Royal License. The first season of Jewish licenses appears to have been in 1689, sought by Aron Oxid who, having purchased a three-masted Portuguese merchantman, entreated, as a subject of this Most Serene Dominion, to be allowed to travel under the flag of San Marco and enjoy the prerogatives that the ships of this region generally have. From this time until the year 1777, an uninterrupted series of licenses affords further proof of the public willingness to accord the companies of Jewish traders permission to sail their vessels under the Venetian standard."

In June 1786, the Senate, after hearing the Sage Treasurer and giving due consideration to the University leaders' request for a new charter, keeping in mind the decree of March 22, 1760, convened a conference to be attended by the Inquisitors over the Jews, the Adjunct Deputies for the Provision of Money, the Cattaveri, the Sage Treasurers, the Five Sages of Commerce, and the Inquisitors over the Guilds. The Quarantia al Criminal would deal with the clauses concerning the banks, while the Cattaveri would be responsible for enforcing their decisions.

The surviving fragment of the minutes of this assembly is animated by the spirit of the Enlightenment. The patrician Nicolò Erizzo expressed the new trend, stating, "If the Jewish issue were to be governed according to real principles, we would not be holding this conference." He also said that in his opinion the Jews were like all other men, and that he was not bothered by any difference of religion. The words of this nobleman were spoken in a newly auspicious moment; many long-standing prohibitions fell and the Jews were allowed to act as purveyors to the State and hold State contracts. The patrician Gabriel Marcello stated: "It is well known to all that there have always been Jews in the resolutions and in the contracts . . . to all public benefit and without any private inconvenience." He was personally convinced, he added, that some recent laws had been more harmful than beneficial and in fact had never been obeyed.

Once more, the age-old question arose concerning the sale of grain on the mainland. To those seeking to maintain the anti-Jewish protectionism, Erizzo answered: "Those who have grain will sell it to greater advantage the more competitors there are. If the commodity abounds, it is well that it be sold; if there is a shortage or monopoly, we will open the granary of the Jew rather than that of the Christian." And further: "The old grain system has changed; once it was forbidden to send it out of the State; now we reward those who do." The conference sanctioned these free-trade policies and decided that the Jews should be allowed to buy grain on the mainland, but only for export.

In June 1788, the conference, which had been planned as early as 1786, resolved on a new charter. Sixty-three clauses concerned the banks and related questions, and thirty-three clauses dealt with issues related to the Jewish presence in Venice. The charter was to be valid for ten years, and like its many predecessors, it contained the usual threatening sentence: "the temporary approved charter." The Senate approved the latest clauses on June 5, 1788.

The last chapter in the relationship between the Serenissima and the University of the Jews unfolded in 1797; very soon both would disappear. That year the Republic was tottering under the impact of Napoleon's armies, and the Jews of the ghetto offered silver and cash to help the exhausted Republic one last time. On April 6 the Venetian Senate, in one of its last acts, issued a decree of thanks: "To the many demonstrations of attachment and loyalty toward our Republic manifested at all times by the Jewish class living in this city, and to the important free gifts and loans, is now added the spontaneous offer of silver in the sum of 6,214 ounces belonging to the Schools of this ghetto and not serving the immediate purposes of their religion, at the conditions set forth in the Decree of last March 18 . . . This new show of concern for the public name will be well deserving of manifest public favor, and in accepting it this Council instructs the Treasurer of the above Cabinet to deliver a copy of the present resolution to the Leaders of this University of the Jews, expressing to them at the same time the gratitude aroused in the mind of the Senate by such marked show of loyalty, and said Treasurer of the Cabinet will make all provisions necessary for receiving this silver, through due recognizance to each of these Schools, the Senate being certain of drawing ever increasing demonstrations of attachment from that class."

Revolution broke out in Venice on May 12. A new season was beginning, for Venice and for her Jews.

CHAPTER TWENTY-TWO

Freedom in Contrada Dell' Unione

The demolition of the ghetto gates — The report of Pier Gian Maria Ferrari, battalion leader — The article in the Gazzetta Veneta Urbana *— Speeches by Citizen Vivante and Citizen Grego — The 1797 census*

"In order that there be no visual appearance of a separation between them and the other Citizens of this City, let the gates be expeditiously removed which in the past closed off the Ghetto area." With these words, the exact opposite of those pronounced by Zaccaria Dolfin back in 1516, the age of the ghetto came to an end. The document was an order from the Provisional Municipality of Venice to the Committee on Public Health. A few days later, on 19 Messidor (July 7) 1797, the old gates were demolished.

Venice was living a brief, tumultuous period, never to be repeated. Pressed by the French armies, firmly believing in the supremacy of General Bonaparte, and undermined from inside by revolutionary sympathizers, the city had surrendered. On May 12, 1797, the government abdicated and approved the French occupation. On May 17 a Provisional Municipality was created. This government wielded no real power and was merely a tool in the hands of the occupying forces.

The Most Serene Republic was gone forever. The hard times that followed were well described by the historian Samuele Romanin: "Times of extreme humiliation under the illusion of independence, times of ruin for public and private fortunes, which the people attempted to hide with artificial exhilaration . . . times when everything was subject to innovation and the governors, deluded or deceiving, vied in high-sounding declamations, making government into a theatrical show."

Early in June, the Provisional Municipality received an appeal "from the Five Citizens, members of the University of the Jews who provisionally held the title of Leaders" and decided that they should stay at their posts, "continuing throughout June with the usual methods, and making the usual loans in the three ghetto Pawnshops, followed by the usual auctions through the agency of ministers, this Municipality meanwhile reserving the faculty to provide as hastily as possible for those further measures that may combine the justly envisaged objectives of Equality with the objectives of the public."

The Committee on Public Health then proposed to call all the Jewish citizens to a meeting in the ghetto, with a view both to ensuring the continued administration of the banks and endowing the Jews with new civil rights. It appealed to the Provisional Municipality: "Firstly, in conformity with the forms of Democracy, it feels that the above Leaders of the University of the Jews should no longer retain this title, but be called 'Deputies of the Jewish Citizens,' and secondly, in order that there be no visual appearance of a separation between them and the other Citizens of this City, let the gates be expeditiously removed which in the past closed off the Ghetto area."

The Jewish citizens were convened in the Spanish School on 21 Messidor (July 9), in Year One of the Italian Liberation, and the minutes of the meeting have been preserved. The final paragraph reads:

"The Citizen President delivered an eloquent speech, reading to the Nation the Rights and Obligations of Man and recommending love, Concord, and Brotherhood, and charity to all the indigent. He moved that tomorrow, when all signs of the abhorred segregation fall with the Ghetto gates, be solemnized by a charitable donation of 200 Ducats in cash, to be divided principally among the poor people not of his nation, in the neighboring parishes of San Geremia and San Marcuola; this meritorious Motion was greeted with enthusiasm, and the abundant voluntary offerings resulted in the collection of 314 Ducats in cash, which will all be shared out. Citizens Almeda, Morpurgo and Mortera were elected collectors, and the money will be sent tomorrow to the Parish Priests of the respective districts. The assembly was adjourned with the most clamorous cries of 'Long Live Brotherhood, Democracy, and the Italian Nation.' "

Barely twenty years earlier, the articles of the revised charter of 1777 had read: "The Jews of Venice and the State, or any other Jew, may never claim or enjoy any Right of citizenship, and because they cannot at any time or place enjoy any Privilege reserved exclusively for Venetian citizens, they must never at any time or place be considered as such."

The rabbis of the Venetian ghetto at that time were Jacob Emanuel Cracovia, who was born in Venice in 1746 and died there in 1820, probably a disciple of Simone Calimani, and Abramo Jona, a native of

Spalato, who arrived in Venice in 1784 to fill the post of Calimani, left vacant by his death that year. Known as a scholar and Kabbalist, Jona did not allow himself to be seduced by the impetuous surge of freedom, nor by the new Napoleonic policies culminating in the convocation of the great Synedrium in Paris in the early nineteenth century.

Many legends grew up around Jona. One especially colorful story is told by Rabbi Ottolenghi, a student of that historical period. "A few days before the fall of the Venetian Republic and the constitution of the Democratic Government, a group of Slavonians wanted to break into the Ghetto, and there was great excitement among the Jews when the Rabbi, or so runs the popular tale, having written three special Mezuzoth (probably the usual Kamioth with Kabbalistic signs and words), reportedly affixed them to the three Ghetto Gates where they were thought to have the power to repel the feared attackers. Another Kamiah, written by rabbi Jona, was jealously safeguarded by an old Venetian family, and its present owner, in compliance with his father's last wishes, walled it up in his house, so that I have not been able to examine it. But returning to the legend of the Slavonian attackers of the ghetto, it has a historic basis. In fact, Romanin tells us in his valuable book that on the evening of May 5, 1797, Friday, 13 Iyar 5557, a troop of Slavonians did surround the ghetto, not spontaneously but on the order of Morosini, who was in charge of internally guarding the city, and apparently only for reasons of security. But the people who are in the dark—nor can they know everything especially at certain times—in this case, too, began to imagine things; soon their imaginings became fear, and perhaps disproportionate, but they were also soon tranquillized by the timely intervention of the venerable rabbi with his soothing words, accompanied by that religious act of affixing the Mezuzoth, calling for the aid of Heaven to those very agitated souls." So calm returned to the ghetto.

The Municipality, a provisional government organ which included three Jews, Mosè Luzzatto, Isaac Grego, and Vita Vivante, sent an order to Citizen Ferrari, battalion leader of the National Guard: "The Provisional Municipality, by its Decree of 19 Messidor (July 7) has decreed that that the Ghetto Gates must be taken down in order to eliminate that mark of segregation between the Jewish Citizens and the other Citizens, where none must exist. You therefore, using such means as you may find necessary, will see to the execution of said operation, observing those precautions required to avoid any problems."

We have two first-hand documents describing that day, so exhilarating for the ghetto and its people. One is a report by Pier Gian Maria de Ferrari, leader of the Third Battalion, Second Bucchia Brigade, who relates:

"Early on the morning of the 22nd I went to fetch the three Deputies of the Hebrew Nation, Citizens Daniel Levi Polacco, Vidal d'Angeli, and Moisè di David Sullam, with whom I devised all possible measures to make the ordained demolition of the Ghetto Gates, which was to take place that day, both decorous and peaceful . . . At 5 in the afternoon the Officers of my Battalion no. 3, Second Bucchia Brigade, set out from the ordinary Square where they habitually drill, and accompanied by Band and beating Drums proceeded with me to the Ghetto Gate that faces the Fondamenta di San Gerolamo, which was lined with French and Italian troops, as were the other three Gates of Cannaregio, Caleselle and Aggui. A fair number of French Sentinels was already ranged in the New Ghetto square, and my Battalion of Officers took up its post in the middle of that Square, accompanied by many Officers of other Battalions of the National Guard, and by numerous Members of the Patriotic Society, in addition to a large crowd of People of both sexes, streaming out of every door. The three Citizen Deputies of the Hebrew Nation presented themselves, and the Order of your Committee was immediately read aloud to them by my Adjutant Major Goldoni . . . Having heard your Order the Jewish Deputies consigned all the Keys of the 4 above-mentioned Gates of the Ghetto, giving them into my hands, whence they were passed to the Workmen, including many Dockyard hands, who were ready for the demolition of these gates. Inexpressible were the satisfaction and the happiness of all the attending Populace, who with happy cries of 'Freedom' never tired of dragging those Keys on the ground, blessing the hour and the moment of Regeneration. The echo of these bright 'Viva's was almost a single sound with the pulling down of the four gates, one by one, under the direction of Adjutant Goldoni who distinguished himself with the zeal of a patriot . . . As soon as the gates were brought to earth, People of both Sexes without distinction wove joyful democratic Dances in the midst of the Square that remained covered by the National Guard, and it is to be remarked that the Rabbis danced too, dressed in Mosaic garb, which roused the Jewish Citizens to still greater fervor.

"The two Parish Priests of S. Geremia and S. Marcuola were also present, applauded by their Parishioners who thus acknowledged the removal of the prejudices of strict segregation not reconcilable with the sacred ideals of a pure Democracy.

"Later there were several popular addresses worthy of mention . . . Meanwhile the Ghetto Gates were borne in triumph by the crowd of People that had rushed up to the Gates to snatch them from the Citizens and the ordained Workmen, and were broken into pieces in the New Ghetto Square before the National Guard, where in the sight of all, and with exultant cries of joy, they were consigned to the flames, which rapidly consumed them. Then it was moved by Citizens Goldoni and Momolo Grego, suggested by their patriotic sentiment, that a Liberty Tree would be appropriate in that Square, and no sooner did the idea catch on, than all impatiently responded by searching for the object. The National Guard went off and, entering a nearby Garden, in a moment cut down a Tree which was carried in triumph with Patriotic Hymns to the middle of the aforesaid Square, where it was set up, and a virtuous Citizeness sacrificed the adornment of her National Cap from her Head to crown the Liberty Tree. The Patriotic Dances were repeated, with democratic disposition.

"The day finally ended with the sudden brilliant Illumination of the Spanish School, where the worthy Citizen Massa, President of the Patriotic Society, kept his promise by addressing the great Crowd with a speech worthy of his talents . . .

"This is the most detailed and exact description I can provide, oh Citizens . . . and the only thing wanting on your part would be to give a new name to the Ghetto and thus destroy this unhappy stigma, for the name still carries a reminder of the former segregation, and I would propose replacing it with the Name of Contrada della Riunione.* Greetings, and Fraternity. Venice, 24 Messidor Year One of the Italian Liberty.

Pier Gian Maria de Ferrari
Leader of the Third Battalion
Second Bucchia Brigade."

"Festivities in the ghetto on its emancipation from the political slavery in which it was held by the Aristocracy," read the headline on the city page of the *Gazzetta Veneta Urbana* of 24 Messidor (July 12), 1797.

The Civil Guard entered the ghetto, "forming a military circle that made a fine appearance with its dress uniforms and the gleam of its unsheathed weapons." The festive crowd included French soldiers, Jews, and Christians. Music filled the air and people were dancing. The ghetto gates were carried to the midst of the square, hacked into pieces, and burned. The reporter wrote that it was a fine sight "to watch the hatchet bravely swing to splinter a base barbaric prejudice. Citizen Vivante jumped up on a wall and harangued the crowd. The music, the sound of the hatchet blows, the confusion and the excitement of the crowd made it impossible to hear his heartfelt words." The report in the *Gazzetta* ends by describing a great meeting that evening in the Spanish School and a party at Vivante's house. The Venetian Society for Public Education decided, by acclamation, to print Vivante's speech.

"Brothers,

"That happy day has finally come, in which prejudice and superstition have been vanquished, and the injuries and offenses avenged which we have so unfairly suffered. The light of philosophy has shone from the blessed shores of France to this country, where an arid Aristocracy made our bonds and our ignominious chains heavier . . . The

---

*Reunion District

immense distance separating us from the other nations has been entirely removed, and here too, those formidable Gates have been overturned that held our Nation captive, strengthened by thousands of iron bars invented by the most heinous despotism. Yes, my brothers, those same men that formerly looked with indifference at our humiliation and oppression, now give us the means to rise again, to become enlightened and to improve; they invite us to love them and consider them no longer in the repugnant role of persecutors."

Isaac Grego, one of the protagonists of the day, delivered his address in Venetian dialect.

"Citizens!

"Democracy is built on virtue and Justice, and from these spring liberty and equality, but these two sacred words must be well understood, in order not to confuse liberty with license and equality with abuse, as is easily done . . . Freedom of action for all Mankind, for each citizen to do anything that brings no harm to others . . . Equality makes all Citizens peers . . . The Aristocracy needed the segregation of the citizens, to divide the Strength and interests of the people . . . These are the reasons that have led your Provisional Municipality to order the demolition of the Gates of this enclosure, with their tyrannical thunder, that kept Citizens separate from Citizens; Religion has nothing to do with Civil rights, for all men enjoy equal rights and each can worship the Supreme Being with the ceremonies he prefers . . . Likewise observe the Jews, for there are certainly honest Men among them, and these deserve your love; if you know of any bad ones, report them to the Authorities and let them be corrected according to their crimes, and I myself will make it my duty to participate, before all others, in their punishment. I know the goodness of this Venetian people too well to doubt the love you bear your regenerate Brothers. We have only to remember the fatal day of May 12 to understand the gentleness of this People albeit incited and driven to excess by those who had an interest in disorder; the publication of a single Proclamation sufficed to calm them and make them voluntarily give up most of the Property taken, and the greatest proof of your goodness is that despite Tyranny you have not lost your virtue."

Massa, the president of the Patriotic Society, also spoke that day in the Spanish School. He pointed out the sad conditions in which Jews still lived in other Italian cities, and said: "I will not speak to you of foreign lands. I know that beyond the mountains the Vatican influence has been less great; I will stop at our own Italy. The Jews have been banished from Naples. The Jews are derided. In Rome they are insulted and scorned with impunity. Cruel caprice! A Turk is respected and a Jew despised! Even the mark of ignominy is added. The Jews are marked in Rome like Beasts at the Market. But this has all finally given way before the development of reason, the progress of the Human spirit . . .

Thanks then be given to the immortal Bonaparte who has broken the bonds of Italian servitude. Thanks to the unvanquished Italian Army, which has blazed our path to freedom. Thanks to the most meritorious Minister Lalleman and to the most virtuous Citizen Villetard, two Pillars of the Venetian revolution. Thanks to the fervent Municipalists, who have destroyed the sign of that most unjust division, by having those infamous Gates, Trophies of ignorance, torn down."

The next day, it was decided to rename the ghetto Contrada dell'Unione.

In the words of Samuele Romanin: "One sign of progress was the recognition of the Jews as the equals of other citizens. Not only did three of them sit among ex-noblemen and churchmen in the municipal government, but on July 11 the ghetto gates were torn down, and that name, a reminder of barbarous times, was abolished and replaced by that of Contrada dell'Unione."

In the summer of 1797, the democratic Municipality, after its initial burst of enthusiasm, was obliged to provide for the needs of the city and the occupying French army, and decreed new taxes. Merchants and tradesmen, both Venetian and foreign, were obliged to pay a total of 867,000 ducats. About a quarter of this sum, or 223,100 ducats, was underwritten by the Jews. The Jewish companies Vivante and Treves and Bonfil paid more than anyone else in the city. Only one other foreigner, named Racek, paid a comparable sum: 50,000 ducats. The Greek Angelo Papadopoli paid 4,400 ducats. The distribution of the obligation to pay the special tax suggests a condition of wealth in strong contrast to the view offered by a critical analysis of the city registers, ordered on June 28, 1797, by the Committee on Public Health of the Provisional Municipality. The analysis of the ghetto population was conducted that summer by Saul Levi Mortera, the scribe of the University, and delivered to the Committee by the Jewish Deputies on October 5, just a few days before the end of the libertarian experiment.

The copy of the register (preserved in the Venetian State Archives, under *Atti della Municipalità Provvisoria*) reveals a true cross-section of the ghetto, with residents and transients totaling 820 men and 806 women. For each family group it indicates the address, relationships among people living in the same household, and economic condition. Levi Mortera broke the population down into eleven categories. His classification is somewhat abstract and not perfectly appropriate to each social group being studied:

A) Owners of land and real estate, none (not surprising, considering the Venetian laws).
B) Wealthy property owners, Isaac Todesco.
C) Wealthy shopkeepers, 98.
D) Moderately well-off artisan shopkeepers, 121.

E) Daily workers, 165.
F) Artists without employment and income, 10.
G) Nonartists without employment and income, 127.
H) Clergymen with property, 0.
L) Clergymen without property, 1.
M) Second-hand clothing brokers, 133.
N) Unknown foreign alms-seekers, 20.

Even in its incompleteness and approximation, Levi Mortera's table gives a fairly detailed picture of the situation at the time the ghetto was abolished. Isacco and Giuseppe Treves, well-known bankers and shipowners, employed twelve servants. Leon Vita, Jacob Vita, and Lazzaro Vivante, wealthy merchants, boasted seventeen employees. Other wealthy men were Marco and Gabriele Malta, Isacco Morpurgo, Beniamino Errera, Abramo Motte, and Salomone Curiel. Just over thirty families, totaling two hundred people, seem to be well off—not many, in a population of 1,620. In category D (moderately well-off artisan shopkeepers) Levi Mortera includes agents of businesses and pawnshops, food merchants, one bookseller, one furniture and one notions merchant, a surgeon, and a "seller of letters," but primarily second-hand clothing dealers. The category of daily workers comprises not so much manual laborers as salaried personnel employed by the various Jewish institutions, including *chazanim, shammashim,* and schoolmasters. Among the nonartists without employment are 127 individuals grouped together in a somewhat singular fashion, as more than one student has noted: doctors, teachers, shopkeepers, a custodian of wells, a farmer, one Giuseppe Sullam, petition-writer, and some alms-seekers. The clergyman with no property is Rabbi Abramo Jona of Spalato. Despite the number of synagogues in Venice, he is the only rabbi recorded here.

Gino Luzzatto, a famous student of the Venetian economy, noting certain inconsistencies between the data in the register and those relating to the distribution of the tax burden ordered by the Provisional Municipality, wrote: "The fact that this figure is so much lower (less than half) than that indicated in the contemporary tax distribution may be explained in various ways. In part, that is, the lower number is due to the fact that only the heads of households are listed in the census, whereas taxation extended to several members of a family. But primarily, the discrepancy is attributable to the fact that foreign merchants and shipowners were also obliged to pay the special tax. Not being members of the Community, they were not counted in the Census."

About 213 household heads were associated with business on a large or small scale, and to these we should probably add 141 private business agents. Artisans were few: 8 tailors, 3 printers, 3 painters, one mender of chairs, and 1 engraver. There were also 15 schoolmasters, 21 employees of religious institutions, 5 doctors, 3 surgeons, 1 midwife, 5 porters, 2 almshouse superintendants, and 3 mailmen. There were many servants (84, counting cooks), 19 people living from hand to mouth, 29 beggars, and only 1 farmer, named Aron Vita Latis.

That was the social makeup of the ghetto at the end of the eighteenth century. A third of the population enjoyed a fair degree of financial comfort, but the rest were little better than indigent.

Meanwhile the political situation in Venice was changing rapidly. Napoleon had ceded the city to Austria. The dream, begun on May 12, 1797, first with the arrival of the French and then with the destruction of the ghetto gates, was abruptly shattered. On October 17 of that year, under the Treaty of Campoformio, the Austrian troops entered Venice. On January 18, 1798, the ghetto took back its original name, abandoning the ephemeral title of Contrada dell'Unione. Almost immediately the Jews lost their civil equality and were again subjected to restrictions by the Austrian government. But the ghetto gates never rose again to close off the Jewish quarter.

CHAPTER TWENTY-THREE

Between Austria and Italy: Venice and the Jews in the Nineteenth Century

The Jews and the Republic under Manin — The Castillero-Ravenna case — Jewish integration into Venetian life — The unification of Venice and Italy

With the end of the Most Serene Republic and the fall of the old ghetto gates came the end of the University of the Jews. The history of the ghetto was over, but that of the Jews continued to evolve. Now they were simple Venetian citizens, even though it would still be a while before they enjoyed full civil rights. The old pawnshops were closed and the capital derived from their liquidation donated to the State as the Jews' contribution to the foundation of a *monte di pietà* in Venice.

When the Austrian troops entered Venice, total equality for the Jews proved to be a brief daydream. Until the return of the French in 1806, they would be once again subjected to restrictions. The year 1798 witnessed the foundation of the General Brotherhood of Religion and Charity, which would coordinate the activities of the Jewish institutions.

Nevertheless, the Venetian Jews enjoyed a fair amount of freedom. They were no longer subjected to heavy taxation or obliged to live in the ghetto. Many choices were open to them which would have been unthinkable a few years earlier: they could buy real estate, practice the professions, serve in the military, enter the public schools and civil service, and be admitted to such illustrious cultural institutions as the Venetian Atheneum, the Venetian Institute, and the Academy of Fine Arts. Certain anachronistic restrictions remained: they could not be pharmacists (even in the last years of the Most Serene Republic, there had been Jewish pharmacists) and they were excluded from the municipal organs of government. The United Sections of the General Jewish Brotherhood (the Small Council of the new Jewish institution) tried several times during the early nineteenth century to overcome this obstacle to complete emancipation. Early in 1848 two well-known Jewish figures of the day, Cesare della Vida and Isacco Pesaro Maurogonato, asked Daniele Manin,* whose political authority was unassailable, to assert his prestige with the Central Congregation of Venetia in favor of the Jews. Manin kept his word, and on January 8, in an address to the Central Congregation, proposed that the "unjust and odious distinctions of religion be eliminated and all the Jews, therefore, emancipated and allowed to partake of all political and civil rights on a par with every citizen." Niccolò Tommaseo,** who had arrived in Venice by chance, was also present at the meeting between della Vida, Maurogonato, and Manin. Tommaseo promised to champion the Jewish cause and thought it would be useful to send the government a petition signed by a number of Christians. He also promised that he himself, known as a staunch Catholic, would back the operation in writing. But Manin and Tommaseo were arrested as conspirators a few days later, and the Austrians' suspicions were further aroused when they found notes and writings in favor of total Jewish emancipation among the papers of both men. Moreover, Manin himself had Jewish ancestors. This is documented by the registry of the Priorate of Venetian Catechumens, which in April 1759 recorded the baptism of Samuel Medina, age twenty-four, and Allegra Moravia, age twenty—Manin's grandparents.

In the few days between his interview with Manin and his arrest by the Austrians, Tommaseo wrote a work entitled *Diritto degli ebrei alla Civile Uguaglianza*,† an impassioned discourse charged with strong moral and religious sentiment.

Even if complete emancipation was late in coming, it must be recognized that by this time many Jews were perfectly assimilated and enjoyed high esteem among the Venetian intelligentsia. The historian Samuele Romanin was one such figure, as were the noted doctors Giacinto Namias and Michelangelo Asson, the poetess Eugenia Pavia Gentilomo, the attorney Leone Fortis, Baron Treves de' Bonfili, Rabbi Abramo Lattes, and the land-reclaimer Girolamo Latis.

---

*Daniele Manin (1804–57), Venetian lawyer and patriot, president of the Venetian Republic formed in 1848, and leader of the city's defense until August 1849
**Niccolò Tommaseo (1802–74), a patriot and man of letters, and member of the Venetian provisional government in 1848–49, is known today chiefly as a writer and lexicographer. His dictionaries of synonyms and of the Italian language are still considered fundamental reference works.
†*The Right of the Jews to Civil Equality*

Meanwhile, all through Italy, popular unrest became overt disorder: riots broke out and barricades were erected in Naples on February 11, in Turin on March 4, in Florence on March 17, and in Rome on March 18. The contagion spread from Paris to Vienna. In Venice, Manin and Tommaseo were liberated by a popular uprising on March 17, 1848, and carried in triumph to St. Mark's Square. Barely five days later the Austrian troops vacated the city and the *Gazzetta di Venezia* appeared with a special supplement: the Austrian civil and military government had fallen.

It was replaced by a provisional Republic of Venice, with Manin as president. Among the seven men who contributed to its formation was a Jew, Leone Pincherle, appointed minister of agriculture and trade. One of the government's first acts, on March 29, was to proclaim the civil equality of all Venetian citizens. The Jews were now totally emancipated.

Since the University of the Jews no longer existed, all political action was a matter of individual choice. Yet, animated by a keen desire for independence and strong feelings of Italian patriotism, Jewish participation in the revolt had been massive. After centuries, the Venetian Jews were now discovering the appeal of politics and patriotism. On April 5 their most illustrious representative, Rabbi Lattes, urged them to enroll in the civil guard and made clear his personal religious position regarding the Sabbath and holidays.

"To my coreligionist brothers

"There is surely no need to urge you to hasten voluntarily to join the Civil Guard, which has served our dear Country so well, since you have already come in such great numbers to unite under its honored standard . . .

"What may be necessary for some is to know whether and to what extent the exercise of military duty may be obstructed by the obligation to keep our Sabbath and holy days; to tranquilize your consciences, therefore, and dissipate all doubts, I broadly declare that not only is there no opposition on the part of our Religion to fulfilling military functions on such days, according to each person's responsibilities and the orders received, but that on the contrary we eminently serve Religion by placing our best efforts at the service of our Country."

Total mobilization followed. In May, Rabbi Lattes organized an evening of amateur theatricals at the home of Citizen Girolamo Levi and donated the proceeds to Guard Headquarters.

One marginal but significant episode shows how greatly the climate had truly changed for the Jews. Jacopo Cardinal Monico, the patriarch of Venice, had asked the Central Prefecture for Public Order to repeal certain Austrian laws that made it more difficult for bishops to baptize Jews. According to this law, the prerequisites for conversion were four months in the House of Catechumens, notification of police head-quarters, and a meeting with the neophyte's family and rabbi. The patriarch requested the abolition of these rules in the interest of greater religious freedom. Tommaseo, probably in the name of his own Christianity, answered the cardinal in a letter dated April 16, 1848: "It is important to the defense of religious freedom, which cannot but contribute to the propagation of the truth and the dignity of the Catholic clergy, that the Baptism of Catechumens be free of all suspicion of violence or deception. Therefore, until a new law is passed on this important matter, abolishing the detailed Austrian precautions of 1817, this and the Italian law of 1803 should be retained in their entirety, enforcing them with flexibility and appealing in doubtful cases to the Government which, in agreement with the ecclesiastical Authorities, will always opt for the most liberal interpretation."

The first permanent assembly, instituted on June 3, 1848, and running from July 3, 1848, to February 1849, numbered among its members Isacco Pesaro Maurogonato as minister of finance, Jacopo Treves de Bonfili as postal minister, and Rabbi Samuele Salomon Olper. The second assembly also included Rabbi Abramo Lattes, the son of Jacob Levi, Angelo Abramo Errera, and Leone Pincherle. Abramo's sons Alessandro and Gabriele Levi were also politically active.

It was a time of great hardship for Venice. To find adequate funds, the Victualling Commission floated a loan of one and a half million lire. Angelo Levi, the son of Jacob Levi and Regina Greco, contributed with one hundred thousand lire; Cesare della Vida, the son of Samuele della Vida and Regina Pincherle, contributed so much money to the revolution that he severely eroded his own personal fortune. The Errera and Treves families also contributed considerable sums to the defense of Venetian freedom. Many young Jews enthusiastically enrolled in the Bandiera and Moro Artillery Regiments.

The National Assembly voted in favor of annexation to Piedmont on July 3, 1848. Manin dissented. But the military defeat of Charles Albert at Custoza altered the balance of forces drastically, and on August 11 Venice and Austria faced each other alone. The royal commissioners resigned on August 31. In this desperate situation, Manin was proclaimed dictator. At that time many subscriptions were raised to benefit the city, and many Jews contributed, as individual citizens. Several subscriptions were raised by women.

Relations between Manin's revolutionary government and the Venetian Jews were very cordial. This is further evinced by the fact that the president of the Jurisconsultants' Council consulted with rabbis Olper and Lattes, Pesaro Maurogonato, Treves, Fortis, and Namias for advice on the form and formula of oaths to be sworn by Jews, elaborated as follows in March 1849:

1) The Judiciary Committee will proceed to the first admonition of the Jew to be sworn, in accordance with the laws in effect for Christians and with no need for the intervention of a rabbi.
2) The formula of the oath for Jews will be identical, that is invoking the deity with the words: So help me God.
3) The Jew will pronounce it with covered head, placing his hands on the Torah.

Charles Albert's defeat at Novara in February 1849 shattered all illusions, but it could not weaken the desperate will to fight. The Revolutionary Assembly, in a decree dated April 2, 1849, refused the Austrian general's demand for surrender. Venice would resist at all costs.

Manin had obtained unlimited powers, but by the end of April the city was surrounded on all sides. The Austrian marshal Radetsky offered an honorable surrender, but Venice was determined to fight to the last. On May 1, young Isaac Finzi fell, and Tommaseo commemorated him as "one of the first to die a worthy death for Venice."

Fighting at Marghera, among others, was Alessandro Levi. He had devised an unusual way of communicating with his mother, Enrichetta, who lived in a palazzo in the Venetian parish of San Felice: they sent a dog back and forth between Venice and Marghera, carrying messages in its collar. Late in May, Marghera fell. Venice was isolated on her lagoon. Enrichetta Levi received no more messages from her son, for the dog had been intercepted and killed. Worried by the news from the nearby front, Alessandro's mother made the rounds of the hospitals and found her son with his head and face completely covered by bandages. She recognized him by his *arba canfot*, the little *tallit* she had sewn under his clothes.

In July, the first Austrian bombs fell on the city. One fell into the kitchen of the building at San Felice, and Enrichetta Levi moved with her children to a safer home: the Levi palazzo, headquarters of the bank of Jacob Levi & Sons, located near San Marco, at the Angelo Bridge. The Spanish synagogue was hit also. On the steps of the *Aron hakodesh* a Hebrew epigraph has been carved, which in English reads: "Here fell a bomb / plunging down with a crash / it did no damage / bursting in, but with discretion." Rabbi Abramo Lattes dedicated a special commemorative prayer to the event, to be read every year on the last Friday evening of Av in memory of the bomb that, according to some witnesses, fell on August 17, 1849. From that time on, the day was called "Bomb Friday." The *Gazzetta* reported: "The rain of fire shows no signs of abating, in fact it increases every day . . . hunger, disease, one half of the city pouring onto the other, are a sight posterity will not believe. In former, so-called barbarian times, such great suffering would have moved the Powers to implore a truce, out of pity. Today they barely show sympathy, a cold, sterile sentiment."

On August 13, a few days before the surrender, Manin spoke in the square. He never finished his address, for he was taken ill while speaking. Venice capitulated on August 23. French and English ships took on board many refugees to whom Austria had promised a safe departure. Manin went to Paris, in exile, on August 27. Leone Pincherle fled first to Turin and later to Paris. Samuele Olper went to Florence, then to Leghorn and finally to Casale. Pesaro Maurogonato chose Corfu, while the Levi cousins, Alessandro and Giacomo, fled to Turin. Some returned to a liberated Venice, but others died in exile.

The Austrians did not soon forget the Jews' collaboration with the Republic of Manin and Tommaseo, and kept the Jewish community under strict supervision. An Austrian guard was even posted to watch over the synagogue services. Those Jews who remained did so at their own risk and not without inconvenience: Angelo and Jacob Levi, for example, were fined three thousand florins for speaking out too freely. Jacob was later elected city councilman, but the Austrian government refused to accept him, on the grounds that he was too liberal. Cesare della Vida and Abramo Errera also had problems: della Vida, especially, had contributed so generously to the Republic that his private finances suffered. Errera, however, became increasingly involved with the Jewish community, acting as its president for thirty years. Manin died in exile, in 1867.

The epic was over, and dull routine set in. Austria was not overly repressive; in fact, she lost no opportunity to cultivate the minorities, and on more than one occasion attempted to insinuate that anti-Semitic, anti-Austrian, and revolutionary sympathies were three aspects of one and the same political view.

A seemingly insignificant episode caused a great furor throughout Venetia, in the cities and countryside alike. In the summer of 1855, a peasant woman named Giuditta Castillero accused Caliman Ravenna, a Jewish shopkeeper from Badia Polesine, of having kidnapped her and sucked her blood to use in his religious rituals. In Venice, and in every city and hamlet of Venetia, especially in the Po delta, as reported by the chief of police at viceregal headquarters, "the rumour, spread with all its variants, aroused indignation against the Jews, especially among the lower classes." At first there were a number of anti-Semitic reactions, and anonymous letters were sent to the Jews of Venice and their rabbi. One such letter read: "Death to the Jews! Burn the ghettos! Your nation will be extinguished by dagger-blows! Go wandering over the earth, fleeing the wrath of the Catholics. The misdeed you were about to commit in the Polesine* cries out for vengeance to all humankind,

*the region of the Po delta

to God himself: if we cannot avenge ourselves, there is a God to take up the defense of the Christian people He protects. Death to the Jew! Catholic spirits are enraged by the reported kidnappings of female children in the Polesine . . . perpetrated by those Jews, and in the fear that it may happen here too, they are about to organize a massacre of these Jews." The chief of police sent a copy of the letter to the viceregal headquarters on July 7, 1855, and the police did not sit idle. They conducted investigations to discover the author of the anonymous letters and establish the truth of the matter "which must contribute to silencing the rumors," for they were convinced there was a collateral campaign afoot, to "stir up ill will against the Jews."

Anti-Austrian sentiments found every possible outlet for expression, including attacks on a minority that constituted a convenient scapegoat, and the rumors were fed by popular imagination. The Austrian authorities, while defending the Jews from the virulent rumors, did not fail to turn the affair to political account, accusing of subversion those who had instigated the slander and thus disturbed the social order.

Rabbi Lattes, who had fought with passion for Manin's Venice, wrote a long article on the subject in the *Gazzetta Uffiziale* of July 9, 1855, in effect asking the authorities to intervene in favor of the Jews, who had become the target of anti-Semitic prejudice and a campaign more virulent than in the past. And while in the former ghetto any anti-Jewish measure affected a solid, cohesive group, such measures were now directed against individuals and families who, no longer forced to live under the old rules, were fast becoming assimilated into Italian society. Emancipation and civil equality had encouraged many of the wealthier families to leave the ghetto, leading gradually to the rise of a Jewish professional class that for the first time, with the enjoyment of full civil rights, was prominent in city life.

The Venetian Jews, estimated at around 2,500 in 1821, numbered 2,023 in 1857 (out of a population of 114, 164), according to the Austrian census, and 2,415 in 1869, according to the Italian census. 64 percent of these Jews lived in the ghetto or the adjacent parishes, and 23 percent lived in the parish of San Marco. The wealthy Jews, members of the middle and upper bourgeoisie, moved to the heart of the city, while the poorer families stayed in the ghetto. On the eve of the First World War, the Jewish community numbered approximately 3,000.

At the end of the nineteenth century, the Jews were no longer a compact group; they were Venetian citizens, entirely integrated into the life of the city. Several Jewish figures are remembered for their accomplishments. Luigi Luzzatti, the first Jewish government leader in Italy, in the early twentieth century, founded the Istituto commerciale superiore,* the present Ca' Foscari; Moisè Raffaele Levi founded

---

*Higher Institute of Business

the Sailors' Hospice; Michael Treves was responsible for important public works such as the renovation of the aqueduct and the gas company.

Many reports, however, agree that any integration between Jews and Christians had taken place only among the middle and upper classes. The lower strata of the ghetto had reacted with jealousy and less tolerance, and their weaker condition also may have made them less resistant to anti-Semitic propaganda.

As long as Austria held control over Venice and the Venetian provinces, the authorities were concerned primarily with keeping the peace. They were eager to reduce social tensions of any kind and to suppress all temptation to subversion. And, perhaps mindful of the anti-Austrian ardor of so many Venetian Jewish patriots, they attempted to preserve the status quo through a policy of moderation.

The Giuditta Castillero–Caliman Ravenna affair, mentioned earlier, and the Austrian response to it were emblematic of a situation of unrest that reached far beyond the specific episode. Castillero's trial, held in the provincial court of Rovigo, ran from September to November 1856 and caused a great sensation. The charges against her were slander through false insinuation, restriction of personal freedom, and drawing of blood. Caliman Ravenna was detained in prison for sixteen days, but it soon became clear that the accusation against him was false. Castillero herself withdrew the charge, turning it first against an unknown man, and then against an unknown carter who, she stated, had induced her to accuse Ravenna. The court's ruling: The peasant Giuditta Castillero, daughter of Lorenzo, age twenty-three, unmarried, a native of Baruchella and a resident of Nasi, was found guilty of the crimes of slander and theft and sentenced to six years in prison with additional punishments.

Relations between Jews and Christians in the small matters that made up their daily existence were full of contradictions. The priest of San Marcuola, one of the parishes closest to the ghetto, wrote in the 1850s, "The intermingling of Jewish families does great moral harm in a Christian parish." He emphasized the danger of friendships between Jews and Christians and his concern that the hunger of the poor and the exchange of small favors could encourage lapses in Christian morals. Confessors were warned not to grant the sacraments to Christian women who lived with Jews, nursed Jewish babies, or lived according to Jewish law. One reason for the priests' concern over integration was the increase in the number of illegitimate relationships, considered a symptom of moral decadence. In the most central parishes of San Marco, Santo Stefano, and Santa Maria Formosa, such things occurred frequently. The alarm and concern grew and spread in 1855 as a result of the Caliman Ravenna trial, and were not dissipated by Castillero's heavy sentence.

This confusion within the clergy was expressed, on the one hand, by defensive behavior, and on the other by the intensification of propaganda aimed at converting Jews and non-Christians in general. The House of Catechumens, three centuries after its founding, was always a threatening presence, although the provisional rules for the conversion of Jews afforded protection against abuse. From 1850 to 1866, as Gabriella Cecchetto notes, the baptismal registry at the House of Catechumens records thirty-five Jews, fifteen males and twenty females, aged seventeen to fifty-four, all unmarried with the exception of a man of fifty-four and a woman of fifty-two, the mother of five neophytes. Half were Venetian and the others came from many different places: Hungary, Prague, Galicia, and Vienna, but also Verona, Rovigo, Modena, and Ancona. Most of them were very poor. According to the house director, "The experience of three centuries has shown, as do the archives and testaments, that the people who come are almost all of poor condition, without assistance, and some even have recourse to that asylum in the hope of making their fortune."

The Jewish community took a keen interest in each individual case of conversion, and resisted each conversion tenaciously by both legal and psychological means. On the one hand, the Jews asked that the guarantees provided by the Ruling of 1803 and confirmed in the sovereign Resolution of 1817 (which required involvement of the rabbi and relatives and a four-month waiting period) be enforced; on the other, the Church tried to reduce the guarantees in order to convert the neophytes as quickly as possible.

In 1859, meanwhile, a new war between Austria and Piedmont stirred political passions in Venice. Several Venetian Jews joined Giuseppe Garibaldi and his Thousand in 1860, including Giuseppe Ancona, Enrico Uziel, Davide Cesare Uziel, and Alessandro Levi.

Levi, assigned by Garibaldi to a daring mission in Naples, was the hero of a perilous adventure: the little boat that was to carry him to shore was sunk by the Bourbon soldiers. Levi was rescued by fishermen, and as soon as he had recovered his strength he attempted to enter Naples dressed as a fisherman. He was arrested, summarily tried for espionage, and sentenced to death. Only the sudden arrival of Garibaldi saved his life.

In the Levi palazzo, meanwhile, his mother Enrichetta Levi was sewing tricolor cockades which she hid in a bedroom drawer. The Royal Imperial Police, despite their frequent searches, never found a thing.

1866 was a crucial year. We can relive its harsh international climate through an exchange of letters between Vita Arbib, a Jew originally from Tripoli but Venetian by adoption, and his employee Simone Vivante, a Venetian Jew who worked for the Bonlini and Arbib glass bead factory.

Though a Turkish subject, Arbib carried a Sardinian passport. He had gone to Tripoli to meet his uncle, and the sudden outbreak of war prevented him from returning to Venice. The Austrians were defeated at Sadowa on July 3. On the 11th, Simone Vivante wrote to his employer: "Political affairs are so confused that it is impossible to imagine the outcome. Everyone thought it was all over, but today the City issued an order to stock supplies for 4 months rather than 3, as stated in the first order."

On July 18, he wrote: "Until otherwise ordered, the Lloyd steamers will continue their journeys between here and Trieste, but all communications by land are cut off, and since yesterday travel to Mestre is forbidden even by boat. Here we are totally in the dark. All the factories have been closed since Saturday."

His words forecast the approaching storm. Vivante, in charge of Arbib's business in his absence, wrote again on July 25, "I do not think it prudent to delay the closing of this deal." He reported, in fact, that the land block had begun and a sea block seemed imminent, inevitably putting a stop to trade.

The armistice between Italy and Austria was signed on August 11. On September 26, Giacomo Sarfatti, Arbib's friend and employee, wrote: "In short let us hope everything will return to a satisfactory state, all the more so if the accursed cholera that threatens us and visits us daily with a few new cases disappears entirely. Here, meanwhile, special festivities are being organized for the Italian troops and the king, in which I am certain you, too, will want to take part." Vivante's mood, a few days later, was more pessimistic: "We have ever more reason to fear, seeing that instead of waning [the cholera] is increasing daily."

Early in October, the Austrians began to leave. They were gone by October 19, the last day of the Hapsburg government in Venice. The Italian troops entered three days later. Simone Vivante reports in his letters that the price of rice was disproportionately high, owing to the demand caused and sustained by the need to feed the soldiers, and that despite the tumultuous events, the Lloyd steamers continued to ply between Venice and Trieste.

Vita Arbib arrived in Venice just in time to attend the festivities organized for the arrival of King Victor Emmanuel II on November 7. Bianca Nunes Vais Arbib, the granddaughter of Vita Arbib and the Levi family (the ones who hid Italian cockades in the drawer at San Felice), colorfully described the events many decades later: "Victor Emmanuel II arrived in Venice on November 7 amid applause and acclaim, and endless festivities. Among these was a great reception in Palazzo Levi at San Marco (where the bank of Jacob Levi & Sons had its headquarters) given by Angelo Levi, who had been a deputy to the Venetian assembly, and his wife Giovanna Kaula. Giuseppina, their daughter who had married her cousin Cesare, the son of Abramo, was there too, and so was Enrichetta Levi, who eventually succeeded her father-in-law as director of the bank. Angelo's son Giacomo Levi was certainly there with his wife Nina Mondolfo, and all the other members of the Levi family. The flag, riddled with holes from Austrian bullets, waved from the balcony. It waved for many years thereafter on patriotic holidays, commemorating to the Levi descendants the heroic events of the past. I saw it myself as a child, when I went to my grandparents' house."

That was probably the moment of greatest patriotic elation for many Jewish families. But whereas this document has survived to describe the emotions of the Levi family, the experiences of other Jewish families have been forgotten, both because (it cannot hurt to repeat) there was no longer a community organism that made unified, if controversial, decisions for everyone, and because it is difficult to draw a cogent historical picture of a group now deeply integrated into Venetian society.

Evening was falling, too, on the protagonists of 1848. Abramo Lattes died in 1875, Samuele Olper in 1877 in Turin, and Leone Pincherle in Paris, in 1882. Cesare della Vida, who returned to Venice from exile, served as both city councilman and board member of the Cassa di Risparmio bank and the Chamber of Commerce, and later replaced his father as an executive of the Assicurazioni Generali insurance company, along with Isacco Pesaro Maurogonato. He died in 1876, leaving his mother, Regina, née Pincherle, and his sister, Adele, who founded the first Froebelian kindergarten in Venice, married a Levi, and had two daughters. The elder daughter married Enrico Castelnuovo, a fairly well-known writer of the period, and the younger married Luigi Luzzatti, a professor of constitutional law and successively a member of the Italian parliament, minister of the Treasury, minister of the Interior, and finally prime minister.

Now if up to 1797 our history was primarily that of groups and families that converged to form the German, Levantine, and Western Nations, emancipation and integration inverted the picture. From then on, individual family names emerge with their particular histories and destinies, while the Jewish community remains in the background.

Only once again, for a brief period, would the destiny of the group dominate that of the individual: during the coming dark age of Fascism, racial laws, and deportations.

CHAPTER TWENTY·FOUR

Can a Jew Be a Minister of the Realm?

*The telegram to the king — A violent press campaign — Senator
Musio's letters — Rabbi Mortara — Isacco Pesaro Maurogonato
declines the ministry*

F rancesco Pasqualigo, the deputy to Parliament from Lonigo,
generally considered "a liberal of sincere and diligent faith,"
had been practicing law in Venice for thirty years and had been a
staunch defender of the Republic in 1848 and 1849. In the summer of
1873 there was no doubt in his mind: he would send a wire directly
to the king. The Lanza government had recently fallen and the ensuing
crisis had lasted only fifteen days, until July 10 when a new government
was formed under Minghetti. But in that interval Pasqualigo had heard
an extremely disquieting rumor: Isacco Pesaro Maurogonato was being
considered for minister of finance. Something had to be done.

The deputy for Lonigo brazenly sent off his wire. Though much
talked about, the text, probably buried in the royal archives, has never
been found. Its substance, however, was certain: it would be inexpe-
dient to appoint a Jew minister of finance.

Pasqualigo's objection went unnoticed at first, overlooked by a dis-
tracted press. But soon a violent press campaign was unleashed, which
persisted for several months and which provides us with an ideological
and cultural picture, however incomplete, of the problem of Jewish
integration in Italy at that time. Curiously enough, both Pasqualigo
and Maurogonato were Venetians. Pasqualigo was not known as a rabid
anti-Semite; on the contrary, he was a liberal who had spoken in favor

of emancipation from feudal laws in the provinces of Venetia, voted against the Law of Guarantees, and even had a reputation as an anticleric. Maurogonato was an economist. He had been the administrator and later the director of the Assicurazioni Generali insurance company, finance minister in the Venetian Republic under Manin, deputy for Mirano in the Kingdom of Italy, president of the Parliamentary Budget Committee, and twice vice-president of the Chamber of Deputies.

It was *La Stampa,* a Venetian political daily, that lit the fuse on July 15, 1873, with the publication of an editorial entitled "A Venetian deputy." Among other things, it said, "The intolerance which may sometimes find justification in the blindness of an ignorant proletariat, the pawn of those who would make it a tool for domination and power, is incompatible with the sentiments that should inspire a representative of the Nation." *La Stampa* accused Pasqualigo of intolerant madness, of impropriety for having attempted to force the hand of the Crown, and of revealing his ignorance about the criteria governing a constitutional monarch's selection of his cabinet. The unsigned editorial commented sarcastically on the "humor of the strange missive, from which emanated a perfume of Inquisition which no doubt gently titillated the nostrils of all the reactionaries of Italy." The voters of Lonigo would certainly keep that in mind!

The official organ of the liberal left, *Il Diritto di Roma,* appeared on August 31 with an editorial that filled three columns: "The news is old, but certain regrets and certain statements make it sound new. For a while it seemed that Hon. Maurogonato would be called to govern Italian finance . . . At the time, when those rumors were circulating, someone sent a wire to Victor Emmanuel, begging him not to set his royal seal to the appointment of a Jewish minister. It was believed to be a joke. . . But the story was confirmed; it turned out to be serious, and it became known that the author of the telegram was not a priest but a deputy; Pasqualigo, in truth, was a man of little note who did not hesitate to state his firm conviction that Jews should not be called to govern the body public in a Catholic state. The statement was not even worth fighting, although it came from one of the five hundred lawgivers. It had been thought that his constituents, the citizens of Lonigo in Venetia, would disavow their intolerant deputy. But they did not. On the contrary, Hon. Pasqualigo was given a great banquet in Venice, and now, if we can believe certain letters and certain newspapers, the voters of Lonigo are preparing an address in his honor. So the matter has now become serious. What in one man might be judged madness or caprice, when upheld by many becomes a serious opinion that liberals must combat, unless they intend to step aside and concede defeat . . . The question is this: what is the connection between the government of a State and the religion of the governed? The Jews, it has been said before, cannot govern the State because it is not theirs; because they have a vaster, ideal fatherland, and because their class interests are too great and prevalent."

Pasqualigo, who had remained silent up to that point, countered with a long letter published in *Il Diritto* on September 8, and again in the Vicenza paper *Giornale della Provincia*. He claimed that his opposition stemmed not from religious intolerance, but from purely political considerations, and wrote: "My opinion as a politician is that the government of a people demands one sole indivisible patriotic sentiment . . . and I therefore think that the ministerial functions should be entrusted only to men who are *purely* Italian. My opinion is that the Jews, dispersed among other peoples since before the age of Christianity, have always constituted, and still do constitute a politico-religious association unto themselves; and that the interests of their own nation prevail, in their consideration, over those of the particular nation of which they may happen to be citizens; and that the alleged complete identification of their interests with those of the Italian Nation (perhaps due to the short time since their emancipation) has not yet come about and, according to some, may never come about. My opinion is, therefore, that a Jew should not be made a minister of the Kingdom of Italy. How can a man serve two masters? Nor is there any tinge of religious prejudice, hatred or intolerance in this, for I have never felt any." The deputy from Lonigo recalled that a colleague of his, a Jewish deputy, had had his children baptized to make them more Italian, and exclaimed: "There is a man who, although he be a Jew, I would not hesitate to take into the King's Cabinet. But is this not an exception?"

The next day, September 9, *La Stampa* replied with a two-column editorial entitled "Hon. Pasqualigo has spoken": "He does not want to recognize the Jews as citizens of any country in the world, or better, [although they may be] citizens before taxes, the draft, the provincial militia, etc., etc., he believes they lose this character when offered the portfolio of any ministry. And all this because the representative of the constituency of Lonigo is convinced that the Israelites—he says Jews, in homage to history—are neither Italian, nor French, nor German, but above all Jews and disposed to sacrifice all to the triumph of their religious nationality." Once more the telegram was criticized not only for its content, but for being in poor form, and its author was reproached for having sent it to the king, especially in the delicate circumstance of a government crisis.

By now the affair was public knowledge, and continued to provoke reactions. Around the end of September, a long letter signed D.G. was published in the *Giornale della Provincia di Venezia*. It was entitled, "A Christian reply to the Jewish letter of Hon. Pasqualigo, Deputy for Lonigo." The reader D.G. pointed out that many freethinkers and

Christians put their own interests before those of their country, and that no one would dream of barring them *en masse* from public office; he then discussed the problem of Jewish integration and concluded: "We can hardly wonder that the Jews are still very far from embracing Christianity, as the current events attest, when we see that the Christians themselves are none too attached to the faith of their fathers."

Senator Giuseppe Musio, former Sardinian secretary of state and chief justice of the Court of Appeals, known for his political and moral virtues, made his opinion known in a long series of letters printed in the Roman paper *Il Paese* and reprinted by several other papers in October of 1873. Could a Jew be minister? Senator Musio answered broadly: "If I understand it correctly, the question is: Does a Jew, having become an Italian citizen and therefore placed, like every other citizen, under obligation of allegiance, authority, protection, burdens and benefits of our Statute, like every other citizen have the ability and the right . . . unlimited and indistinct, to fill any civilian or military post of the State, or must he, for the sole reason of belonging to the Jewish religion, be considered a new species of *capite minutus* and proclaimed capable of certain inferior positions and incapable of the highest functions of the State and of sitting in the King's Cabinet?" Musio maintained that equality of rights must go with equality of obligations, and observed that Pasqualigo's idea of granting full social and political equality to the Jews only when, by assimilation, they had ceased to be Jews was inherently flawed.

The polemic, emblematic of the difficulties faced by the Italian Jews, only a few generations removed from the ghettos, attracted the attention of other illustrious figures, including Rabbi Marco Mortara of Mantua and, in a marginal way, Isacco Pesaro Maurogonato himself, whose possible appointment as minister of finance had triggered the famous telegram.

Mortara wrote personally to Pasqualigo in October 1873, and a month later had several articles printed in *Il Diritto* entitled, "On the nationality and the messianic aspirations of the Jews." Mortara accepted a debate with his adversary on the problem, real or presumptive, of double nationality. In his opinion the Jews had been a nation in ancient times, but now, after centuries, they no longer nurtured such aspirations. Certainly, Judaism was something more than a religion, but the special bond that united the Jews could not be called national according to the modern criteria that identified a nation in terms of territory, language, traditions, and civil constitution. Mortara reminded his readers that the Jews had assimilated the culture of their host nations, with regard to both food and language (as in the case of Yiddish and Ladino). The Jewish messianism that Pasqualigo considered a sign of transitory allegiance was, in Mortara's view, a religious aspiration to the victory of a monotheistic ideal. Faithful to the teachings of Moses Mendelssohn, one of the chief exponents of the German Enlightenment, Mortara proudly considered Judaism the religion best attuned to modern times and held that a Jew could feel completely Italian without in any way renouncing his Judaism. Judaic doctrine, in sum, was well suited to a complete civil education and total integration into an Italy striving for political emancipation of a liberal stamp.

At just about the same time, the Florentine daily *La Nazione* published an editorial entitled "On whether a Jew may be minister in Italy": "Today *Diritto* prints a long article by Signor Marco Mortara of Mantua, on the issue raised by Hon. Pasqualigo. For us, to tell the truth, the question has never seemed to exist, nor has it had any reason to exist. In any case it would be resolved and closed by Article 24 of the Statute, which reads: 'All subjects of the realm, whatever their title or degree, are equal before the law. All equally enjoy the same civil and political rights and are eligible for civil and military office, saving those exceptions provided by law.'" The paper then quoted *L'Unità Cattolica* and reprinted the conclusion of a long article that had appeared in that paper. "The Jews of Rome presented a chalice to Pius IX, a masterpiece that had been preserved for two centuries in the Ghetto. Balleydier, in his work *Rome and Pius IX*, relates that on July 13, 1846, the chalice was presented at the Quirinal by a Jewish delegation, and that the Holy Father welcomed the Jews with the most paternal affection. 'I accept,' he said, 'I accept your gift with great pleasure, and I thank you. How many scudi is it worth?' 'It weighs five hundred Roman scudi,' said the head of the delegation. Pius IX . . . took from his desk the first sheet of paper he saw and wrote on it: 'Good for 1,000 scudi. Pius P.P. IX,' and turning to the Jews, said: 'Accept this small sum, and divide it among the indigent Jewish families of Rome.' That is the story, and now let us talk. Ministers are the doctors of the State. If the Popes sometimes chose their doctors among the Jews, why should the Kingdom of Italy not choose her ministers among the Jews? If a Jew can be a deputy and make laws, why can he not be a minister and have them enforced? If Jews can serve as journalists, representing public opinion and constituting the fourth Estate of the realm, why can they not constitute the second, that is the executive Estate? Away with such reservations! Jews can be Ministers, and indeed we would like them to be."

The arguments of *L'Unità Cattolica* were actually not all favorable to the Italian Jews, but the latter, so little accustomed to hearing praise from Catholics, appreciated their substance and made much of certain statements in the articles, whose true purpose was to attack the Italian liberals, including Pasqualigo.

The affair was naturally easily exploitable as a political weapon. The *Veneto Cattolico*, an intransigent clerical periodical, joined the attack against Pasqualigo on the basis of his past, as well his present, politics. But neither *Veneto Cattolico* nor *L'Unità Cattolica* espoused a consistent pro-Semitic line.

It is interesting to note that the two sides in this controversy were never compact, nor did they reflect two clearly opposed political positions. There were anti-Semitic fringes in both the liberal and the clerical camps, just as there were currents in favor of a tolerant and pro-Semitic line on both sides. As far as the content of the polemic was concerned, those who felt that a Jew should not be appointed minister often mixed considerations of political expediency with emotional reactions and religious prejudice. Those who saw nothing scandalous in the possibility of Pesaro Maurogonato's appointment were divided according to two principal lines of reasoning: the constitutional one, summarized in *La Nazione*, which held all citizens equal before the law, and that of Rabbi Mortara of Mantua, who, with no intention of renouncing his Judaism, tried to make it acceptable by stressing the assimilation of the Jews and their patriotism and by denying the existence of Jewish nationalism. This position, derived from the theories of Mendelssohn, had gained support in Italy throughout the nineteenth century and strongly characterized Italian Judaism up to the early decades of the twentieth century, when double nationality became the subject of debate within the Jewish community between supporters and detractors of the rising Zionist movement. The question of Jewish identity was raised again in 1938, with the promulgation of the racial laws.

Isacco Pesaro Maurogonato's reaction was one of great measure and moderation. When Prime Minister Minghetti offered him the Ministry of Finance in 1873, he declined. He had already done so once before, when the post was offered him in 1869, on the pretext of family problems. But in December 1873 he told the king his true reasons. "I would certainly have never disobeyed Your Majesty's orders had I not felt in my conscience that, in the public interest and in that of the Crown, it was not appropriate that a man who does not profess the Catholic religion be called upon to enforce the laws regarding the religious Corporations in Rome. The wise direction taken and always so beneficially followed by Your Majesty's government has induced me to avoid anything that might, rightly or wrongly, be construed as a new exacerbation of provisions already too severe in themselves."

For reasons which, though more noble, were also influenced by considerations of political expediency, Pesaro Maurogonato himself felt it would be harmful for a Jew to become minister at that particular time, when he would have had to enforce the anticlerical measures about to be enacted.

The polemic that arose from one short telegram, while certainly a marginal episode, clarifies an important point: though the composite Jewish community had by now become integrated and scattered throughout the body of Italian citizens, it was still considered a separate entity. The question of whether or not a Jew could be a minister of the realm involved the group as a whole.

CHAPTER TWENTY-FIVE

The Twentieth Century:
A History Yet to Be Written

The ghetto at the turn of the century — The Nazi-Fascist
persecution

"In the quarter of Venice of which I speak, one hears nothing but poor everyday sounds, the days go by tediously almost as though they were one single day, and the songs one hears are a crescendo of laments that do not rise, but weigh heavily like smoke undulating over the streets. As soon as dusk falls, a timid, ragged populace wanders through those streets, innumerable children meet in the squares and in the cold, narrow doorways; they play with fragments of glass and chips of multicolored enamel, the same with which the masters composed the solemn mosaics of St. Mark's. Rarely does an aristocrat set foot in the ghetto."

Thus did the poet Rainer Maria Rilke, who visited Venice in the early twentieth century, describe his impressions of the ghetto in *Geschichte vom lieben Gott,** a collection of short stories.

Around the same period, the English writer Israel Zangwill used the hauntingly suggestive atmosphere of the ghetto as the setting for some of his best stories. One of these, "Had Gadya," portrays the crisis of a young Jew who returns to Venice to celebrate the Passover Seder with his family and ends by committing suicide in the Grand Canal. The story focuses on the identity crisis of the young man, who no longer finds any meaning in the traditions to which his father remains so

---

Stories of the Good God

strongly attached. Before dying, the youth asks himself why his brothers ever left the "serene slavery of the ghetto," why they sought emancipation, why his family left the home of his childhood for the palazzo overlooking the Grand Canal. The ghetto is security, a welcoming maternal embrace; the outside world is a hostile, unfamiliar environment. The ghetto is a means of preserving identity; emancipation is the loss of this identity.

Behind the literary fiction lies a real problem. The history of the ghetto in the past two centuries has also been that of the slow but inevitable loss of the Venetian Jew's cultural and psychological identity.

At the end of the last century, the ghetto still retained some of its old animation. A travel reportage dated July 1887, signed F.S., and published in the Jewish paper *Il Vessillo israelitico* with the title "Una scorsa nel Veneto"* contains a lively portrait of the Venetian Jewish community in the late nineteenth century. "The Jewish community of Venice is without doubt one of the most important in Italy, especially for the huge charitable donations distributed with great generosity, under the guidance of the spiritual leader who can thus, in all liberty and with no need to ask the opinion of others, alleviate much misery as he thinks best . . . in the public hospital, we were assured, there is a special ward run at the expense of the city for the Jews, who can thus eat according to our laws and freely observe the practices of our religion . . . In the Jewish Community of Venice there are so many institutions, thanks to the generous bequests and donations of the leading families, among whom we should mention the Treves, that there is assistance for every need. There is the House of Industry that provides work to indigent Jews and prepares the young people to enter the arts and trades. There is the Hanau Charitable Establishment that funds and subsidizes education; there is the Treves Foundation that alleviates the poverty of the aged; there are boys' and girls' schools, and an excellent Froebelian kindergarten; dowries are provided for marriageable young ladies . . . and yet there is no dearth of poor Jews in Venice . . . And all the millions of the millionaires Hirsch and Rothschild, and a hundred other benefactors, would not suffice to eliminate the poverty of certain people . . . in Venice, in Italy, and in the world."

In the late nineteenth and early twentieth century, the Spanish and Levantine Schools were restored. In 1925, during the construction of a new target-shooting range at the Lido, some very old Hebrew gravestones were uncovered, leading to the restoration of the tombs in the old Jewish cemetery. The engineer Guido Sullam contributed to this endeavor and designed the entrance to the new cemetery.

---

*"A Short Journey through Venetia"

Naturally the Venetian Jews took part in all facets of Italian government and made their contribution to Italy in World War I. A plaque on the facade of the Spanish School commemorates the fallen.

By this time many families lived outside the ghetto, which, however, was still the center of community life. There were a school and a kindergarten and a very active club called Cuore e Concordia, and the House of Industry was remodeled into a rest home for the elderly. There was, and there still is today, a matzoth bakery. The whole ghetto came to life on the holidays, especially Purim, when the open space in front of the Levantine temple (today the site of a municipal nursery school) became a bazaar with games, rides, and sweet-stalls.

The racial laws promulgated by Mussolini's Fascist regime in 1938, and the Nazi-Fascist persecution from 1943 to 1945, fell like a thunderbolt from a clear sky on these Jews, increasingly integrated and assimilated into the fabric of Italian society. Those years have remained etched in the memories of the many who suffered, including the few survivors of the German concentration camps. The memory of these tragic events has been kept alive by the many oral accounts of eyewitnesses, yet there are very few written documents able to provide us with insights into those dark days. A complete collection of whatever documents may exist is needed, to be handed down to future generations so that these events may be remembered in the future.

In short, the history of the Venetian Jews in the twentieth century and in the crucial years from 1943 to 1945 has yet to be written. But to conclude our story, here is a brief account of the Jewish settlement in Venice up to the present.

The racial laws of 1938 affected the entire Jewish community of Italy, then numbering about 40,000. The Venetian Jews, a population of about 1,200, integrated into the peaceable city, were the object of discrimination as a group, despite the fact that they had become thoroughly assimilated with the Catholics through frequent intermarriage, by then a common practice. Discrimination took many different forms: Jews were fired from civil service jobs and expelled from professional associations, so that many lost their means of livelihood and found themselves suddenly relegated to the margins of society. Such overt discrimination was compounded by small everyday humiliations: signs on the doors of certain public facilities read "Dogs and Jews prohibited," and in the summer Jews were barred from the Lido beach. Violent and arbitrary as were the racial laws, however, they had not yet brought physical annihilation, destruction, and death.

On July 25, 1943, the Fascist government fell, and with the arrival of the German troops in Italy on September 8, 1943, the situation took an abrupt turn for the worse. On September 16 of that year, Giuseppe Jona, the president of the Jewish community of Venice, committed suicide. His was a terrible gesture, the premonition of a future with no ray of hope. In October and November the situation deteriorated steadily. In Rome on October 16, and in Florence a few days later, the Nazis made their infamous sweeping roundups of Jews, who were then sent to the death camps in Germany. A few sporadic arrests were made in Venice, but the worst was yet to come.

The Buffarini Guidi decree of November 30, ordering the confinement of the Italian Jews in special camps, was made known to the press on December 1. The Italian police did not take immediate action, and the Jews had three or four days to escape. In Venice, too, a general alarm had gone out on December 2, as attested by a message from the Superintendant of Education to the chief of the Province of Venice: "Following the news of the Jewish provisions, published yesterday afternoon, the Jewish elementary school, operating by ministerial order, was totally deserted yesterday. The school's two teachers . . . left the school after having removed their personal belongings in the early part of the morning. I feel it my duty to advise Your Excellency of the above."

Slowly, during those months, the awareness of danger grew. Some Jewish families fled early to far-off lands, to South America or the United States, driven by the progressive worsening of the situation and their realization of increasing, imminent danger. On the other hand, some who could have gone chose to remain, either for family or other personal reasons, or even out of optimism. The Jews in Venice were not a homogeneous group. On the contrary, they were highly differentiated. Many families also had ties and relationships with Catholics, which strengthened their resistance to flight or an underground existence and encouraged the feeling that, all things considered, they were better off staying: the storm would pass. The refugees who had passed through Venice in the early forties were no longer coming; in any case, their tales had failed to reawaken an ancient, ancestral fear in the face of a more powerful feeling of disbelief. There was another factor, too, that contributed to keeping many Jews in Venice, although it now seems ironic, and that was their scrupulous compliance with Italian law and their desire, to the very last and even in the face of undeniable factual evidence, to avoid going underground and being hunted for the sole crime of being Jews.

On the night of December 5, the Fascist guard of the Republic of Salò and the police organized a huge roundup in Venice, Chioggia, and Trieste, on the islands of the lagoon and on the Lido. Over a hundred people were arrested, including children aged three to fourteen. A news article, based on eyewitness reports, said that "all those torn from their homes and those captured in the Rest Home were first taken to the Marco Foscarini school, which became an improvised prison with no beds." According to the police reports of December 31, 1943, they were all transported to Fossoli. A telephoned report from the Venetian police on January 18, 1944, to the directors of the Concentration Camp for Jews at Carpi reads:

"Re: Jews

"On today's date officers of this command accompanied here those Jewish minors found on December 31, 1943 in conditions such as to make them untransportable.

"1 LM child of Beniamino, age 4

"2 LL child of Beniamino, age 6

"3 TS child of Eugenio, age 4

"4 NN child of Eugenio, age 3

"The above children will find their parents in this concentration camp. Signed: the Commissioner."

The camp at Fossoli fell into German hands in mid-February, 1944. Until the first trainloads of people left for Germany, life in the camp still fell short of tragedy. It had been possible to send letters and care packages, and families had not been divided. A Venetian Jewish child of thirteen wrote from Fossoli on February 1, 1944, to a Christian friend in Venice: "Dear Mario, I haven't written you since the day they separated us in Venice, and I know you'll forgive me, because of the confusion here for the first few days after we arrived in camp. But we're better organized now, and I've found this free moment to write. We're in good company in our room, with my parents, Aunt Ida, cousin Bruno, and aunt Pina. During the day we live in a corridor, well heated by two huge stoves that send heat to the room, so it's not too bad, we sing and play, and even have some fun . . . Yours T.A."

But on February 21, on the eve of their departure for Germany, two sisters interned at Fossoli sent a short message in a different tone: "We're leaving. Pray God to protect us. Say good-bye to everyone. It is useless to send money or food. Now as never before we think of those who are distant. Our future is a question mark, and we hope for good health."

Throughout 1944, while war raged on all fronts, Venice was the scene of a manhunt, with continuous persecutions and deportations.

In the summer of 1944 a group of SS soldiers, returning from Treblinka, was especially active in hunting out and deporting Jews, on the orders of Franz Stangl. In their first roundup the SS deported about ninety people, including twenty-two inmates of the rest home, twenty-nine hospital patients, and the community's chief rabbi, Adolfo Ottolenghi, who was old and nearly blind. Early in October, the SS took some mental patients from the psychiatric hospitals on the islands of San Servolo and San Clemente. All these sick people, along with others now taken from the rest homes who had been judged untransportable at the time of the first roundup, were concentrated in the guardroom of the San Giovanni e Paolo hospital and deported on October 11. Some were eliminated at the extermination camp of Risiera di San Sabba at Trieste and others were sent to Auschwitz.

Despite their awareness of approaching defeat and the effect of the partisan resistance movement, felt especially strongly during the final months, the SS and its Italian collaborators continued hunting down Jews in Venetia, arresting them and deporting them to Germany.

Between September 8, 1943, and the final, longed-for liberation from Nazi Fascism on April 25, 1945, two hundred Venetian Jews had been killed. Entire families had been annihilated.

One by one, the survivors returned to Venice from the German camps. There were barely four or five, and while some talked about their terrible experiences, others preferred silence. Venetian Jews who had sought refuge in foreign lands returned. Others emerged from their hiding places in Venetian attics, or came back from the countryside or mountains of Venetia where they had been hidden, some by mere acquaintances, others by the parish priests of tiny villages. The alleys of Venice, freed from the Nazi-Fascist nightmare, breathed the exhilarating air of Liberation at the end of the long tunnel of war. Once again, life prevailed.

Conclusion

The story is not yet over. Today there are roughly six hundred Jews in Venice, totally integrated into the city's life. Today the splendors and miseries of the past are but memories, and many Venetian Jews are unfamiliar with the ghetto's tumultuous history.

The ghetto, the home of Leone da Modena, Simone Luzzatto, Sara Coppio Sullam, and Giulio Morosini, is no longer the focal point of Venetian Jewish life. The old stones, the synagogues where for long decades celebrated rabbis and scholars debated and argued over the most arcane meanings of Bible, Talmud, and Zòhar, are mute witnesses now.

Only a few years ago the attention of Venetians was once again called to the ghetto, when the broad wall adjacent to the rest home became the site of a monument in memory of the holocaust victims: seven bronze panels by the sculptor Arbit Blatas.

The cultural life of the Jewish community has revived. Annual seminars organized in Venice attract a large and attentive public.

The Jewish culture of past and present arouses keen interest today. For while the condition of the Jew in history has always been precarious, that of all mankind has now become so, in the shadow of nuclear weapons. In this sense contemporary man has become Jewish, despite himself.

But this is the thread of another story, which would lead us far afield.

If there is something to be learned from the effort to know our individual and cultural microcosm, it is tolerance and justice for all men and all peoples.

The history of the Jews of Venice is a long road traveled by a few thousand people toward a goal of tolerance and emancipation.

Shylock is gone forever.

Glossary of Hebrew Terms

by Raffaele Grassini

NOTE: Words and titles have been transliterated in the intent to reproduce the original Hebrew pronunciation as closely as possible.

a) All accents, except where otherwise indicated, fall on the last syllable of the word.
b) CH and KH correspond to the Hebrew *chet* and *khaf* and have a guttural sound.
c) TZ or Z correspond to the Hebrew *tzadi*, and are pronounced like "ts" in English.
d) T and TH, corresponding respectively to the Hebrew *tet* and *tav*, are both pronounced "t".

The spelling of Hebrew words and names in quotations or period documents has generally been left unaltered, although it may not always correspond to the traditional pronunciation.

In other cases proper names, given the variations due to Italian forms and pronunciation, and words that have entered into common English usage (such as "kosher") have been spelled as dictated by usage, maintaining the Hebrew form whenever possible.

Aggadah   The collection of rabbinical literature in narrative form, representing the most free and imaginative interpretation of the Holy Scriptures (see also Midrash).

Arba Kanfot   Literally "the four corners." A ritual mantle; each corner has a fringe (tzitzit) knotted according to a traditional system. Unlike the Tallit (see Tallit), it is worn underneath the clothing.

Arelim   Literally "uncircumcised." The term was sometimes used to indicate non-Jews.

Aron   The Holy Ark of the Synagogue, containing the Torah scrolls.

Barukh Habba   "Welcome." The words are chanted during circumcision ceremonies.

Bimah   The pulpit, from which the celebrant reads the prayers.

Cabbalah   See Kabbalah.

Casher   Literally "right" or "proper." The term generally indicates food prepared according to the Jewish dietary laws.

Casherut   The body of Jewish dietary laws.

Chanukkah   Literally "inauguration." A holiday during which a nine-armed lamp is lighted to commemorate the Maccabean resistance against the Syrians, who wanted to Hellenize the Jews.

Chassidim   (Sing. Chassid) Literally "the pious." The followers of certain mystical Jewish sects that originated around 1700 in Poland under the leadership of Rabbi Israel Ba'al Shem Tov.

Chaver   Literally "companion." A title indicating a high level of rabbinical training, despite the youth of the student.

Chazan The cantor of the synagogue.

Chazakah The right of occupancy or usufruct in certain properties.

Chatzer Literally "enclosure" or "courtyard." The popular name for the ghetto area.

Chèrem Excommunication from the Jewish community.

Dikduk Grammar.

Gabbaim The synagogue wardens or chiefs.

Gazakà See Chazakah.

Gemilut Chassadim Charitable actions toward the needy or the deceased.

Goyim Literally "peoples." Commonly used to indicate non-Jews.

Haftarah A passage from the Prophets read in synagogue on the Sabbath and holidays.

Haggadah The story of the Jews in Egypt. It is read on the first two evenings of Passover, while eating matzoth and bitter herbs.

Hassi Betulod A charitable organization that provided dowries for needy brides.

Haver See Chaver

Hoshana Rabba The seventh day of Sukkoth.

Kabbalah Jewish mysticism based on the Zòhar.

Kabbalat Shabbath Liturgical readings sung in the synagogue to honor the arrival of the Sabbath.

Kaddish The prayer for the dead.

Kahal Gadol Literally "large assembly." The Great Council of the Jewish community.

Kamiot Amulets against sickness and the evil eye.

Ketubot (Sing. Ketubah). Marriage contracts, specifying the duties of the couple and what each partner is to receive in case of divorce.

Kiddush Sanctification of the Sabbath and holidays with a ceremonial cup of wine.

Kohelet A book of Ecclesiastes.

Kosher See Casher.

Lashon Ha-Kodesh Literally "the holy tongue." Hebrew, the language of the Holy Scriptures.

Ma'amad The decision-making body of the Jewish community.

Maggid An angel who appears in a dream to prophesy the future; also, a preacher.

Mas Community tax.

Metatron The name of a prophesying angel, according to the Kabbalistic doctrine.

Mezuzah (Plur. Mezuzoth). A case containing a parchment inscribed with biblical passages, affixed to the doorpost of Jewish homes.

Midrash Literally "search." A manner of interpreting Holy Scripture, based on inquiry and discussion, and expressed in figurative terms. The word is sometimes used as a diminutive for Beth ha-Midrash, indicating the Talmudic school.

Mincha The afternoon prayer.

Minhagim (Sing. Minhag). The Jewish customs and observances.

Mishnah Literally "study." The Law handed down orally, as an addition to the Torah (Written Law). To preserve it, Rabbi Yehuda Ha-Nassi set it down in writing in the second century.

Mitzvoth (Sing. Mitzvah). The biblical commandments. According to rabbinical calculations, there are 613 mitzvoth—365 negative (prohibitions) and 248 affirmative (obligations).

Mohel The circumciser.

Parnas (Plur. Parnassim). A leader of the community and the synagogue.

Pidyon Sevuim The charitable fund for the ransoming of captives.

Pilpul Subtle Talmudic reasoning.

Pinkes Register.

Pirke Avoth A treatise of the Mishnah, containing moral teachings and wisdom of the Fathers.

Purim Holiday commemorating the miraculous salvation of the Jews in Persia at the time of Esther and Ahasuerus.

Shammash The beadle in the synagogue.

Shavuoth The festival of Pentecost, commemorating the revelation of the Ten Commandments.

Shema Yisroel "Hear, O Israel." The Jewish declaration of faith, recited daily. It consists of three biblical passages containing certain fundamental principles of Judaism, such as the unity of God.

Shèmen La-Maor Organization that collected funds for the oil used to illuminate the synagogue.

Shochet The butcher who kills animals according to Jewish law.

Shofar The ram's horn played on certain solemn occasions, calling the people to meditation and penitence.

Simchat Torah Literally "joy of the Torah." The holiday celebrating the completion of the Pentateuch readings, at the end of the Feast of Tabernacles. The Torah scrolls are carried around the synagogue, with joyous songs and dances.

Sukkoth The Feast of Tabernacles, lasting seven days, during which booths are built outdoors, with only greenery for their roofs. People sit in these booths to eat and converse, commemorating the life of the Jews in the desert after their exodus from Egypt.

Tallit The shawl worn by the Jew during worship. (See Arba Kanfot.)

Talmud Literally "study." The great collection of rabbinical interpretations and debates on the oral tradition (Mishnah). There are two editions: the Jerusalem Talmud (fourth century), the older and shorter of the two, and the Babylonian Talmud (sixth century), of considerably greater length and importance.

Talmud Torah Literally "Study of the Torah." The school where Torah, Talmud, and Jewish tradition are studied. The term is also used to indicate the Jewish Community (*Universitas Judeorum*).

Targum Literally "translation." The Aramaic version of the Bible.

Tefillah The Hebrew liturgy.

Tisha B'av A day of fasting to commemorate the destruction of the Temple in Jerusalem on the ninth day of the Hebrew month of Av in 586 B.C., and again in A.D. 70.

Torah Literally "teaching." The Pentateuch, written by Moses and read aloud in the synagogue. In a broader sense, the term connotes all the divine teachings contained in the Bible and Talmud.

Tzedakah Literally "justice." Charity to the needy, considered an act of justice.

Va'ad Katan   "Minor Council." The small council of the Jewish community.

Yeshiva   School of talmudic and rabbinical studies.

Yom Kippur   The Day of Atonement for sin, spent in fasting, prayer, and penitence.

Zòhar   The basic text of the Kabbalah, and a Biblical commentary.

Bibliography of Reference Works

Abbreviations used in the bibliography
A.J.S. = *Association for Jewish Studies Review*
J.Q.R. = *Jewish Quarterly Review*
R.E.J. = *Revue des Etudes Juives*
R.M.I. = *Rassegna Mensile di Israel*

1. AA.VV. *Gli Ebrei in Toscana dal Medioevo al Risorgimento*. Florence, 1980.
2. ———. *Gli Ebrei nell'Alto Medioevo*. 2 vols., Spoleto, 1980.
3. ———.*La stampa degli incunaboli nel Veneto*, in *L'editoria veneziana da Spira ad Aldo Manuzio*. Vicenza, 1984.
4. ———. *Storia della cultura veneta*. 6 vols. Vicenza, 1976–1983.
5. ———. "Venedig. Geschichte und Gestalt seines Ghettos." In *Emuna*, no. 10, 1975.
6. AMADOR DE LOS RIOS J. *Etudes historiques, politiques et littéraires sur les Juifs d'Espagne*. Translated by J.G. Magnabal. Paris, 1861.
7. AMINTA FRA' FILIPPO. *L'Ebraismo senza replica e sconfitto colle stesse sue armi*. Rome, 1823.
8. AMRAM W.D. *The Makers of Hebrew Books in Italy*. Philadelphia, 1909.
9. ANCONA C.E. "Attacchi contro il Talmud di Fra' Sisto da Siena e la risposta, finora inedita, di Leon da Modena, rabbino in Venezia." *Bollettino dell'Istituto di Storia della Società e dello Stato Veneziano*, nos. 5–6, 1963–64.
10. ———. "L'inventario dei beni appartenenti a Leon da Modena." *Bollettino dell'Istituto di Storia della Società e dello Stato Veneziano*, no. 4, 1962.

11. ANGELINI W. *Gli Ebrei di Ferrara nel Settecento*. Urbino, 1973.
12. ANTONIAZZI VILLA A. "Per la storia degli ebrei nel dominio sforzesco: un episodio di antisemitismo nel 1488." *R.M.I.*, nos. 11–12, 1980.
13. ARTOM E. "Gli Ebrei del Settecento" *R.M.I.*, no. 1, 1950.
14. ASHTOR E. "*Ebrei cittadini di Venezia?*" *Studi Veneziani*, vols. XVII–XVIII, 1975–76.
15. ———. "Gli inizi della comunità ebraica a Venezia." *R.M.I.*, nos. 11–12, 1978.
16. ———. "L'apogée du commerce vénitien au Levant. Un nouvel essai d'explication." In *Venezia centro di mediazione tra Oriente e Occidente*, vol. I, Florence, 1977.
17. ———. *Storia economica e sociale del vicino Oriente nel Medioevo*. Turin, 1982.
18. ———. "The Jews in the Mediterranean Trade in the Fifteenth Century." In *Wirtschaftskräfte und Wirtschaftswege, I: Mittelmeer und Kontinent*. Nuremberg, 1978.
19. Documents of the Conference on "The Jews in Venice," Venice, June 1983.
20. AVISAR S. *Tremila anni di letteratura ebraica*. 2 vols. Rome, 1980.
21. BACCELLI A. *Brevi note intorno al carattere del "Jus di gazagà" in Roma*. Excerpt from *La Legge*, vol. I, 1892.
22. BACHI R. "L'attività economica degli Ebrei in Italia alla fine del secolo XIX," in *Studi in onore di Gino Luzzatto*. Milan, 1950.
23. BAILLY A. *La Serenissima Repubblica di Venezia*. Varese, 1968.
24. BALLETTI A. *Gli Ebrei e gli Estensi*. Reggio Emilia, 1930.
25. BARBIERI G. *Il Beato Bernardino da Feltre nella storia sociale del Rinascimento*. Milan, 1962.
26. BARDUZZI C. *Bibliografia ebraica e giudaica in lingua italiana*. Rome, 1938.
27. BEDARIDA G. *Ebrei d'Italia*. Livorno, 1950.
28. ———. "Gli Ebrei e il Risorgimento italiano." *R.M.I.*, nos. 7–8, 1961.
29. BEDARRIDE J. *Les Juifs en France en Italie et en Espagne*. Paris, 1859.
30. BELOCH G. "La popolazione di Venezia nei secoli XVI e XVII," *Nuovo Archivio Veneto*, 1902.
31. BELTRAME D. *Storia della popolazione di Venezia dalla fine del secolo XVI alla caduta della Repubblica*. Padua, 1954.
32. BENZONI G. "Una controversia tra Roma e Venezia all'inizio del '600: la conferma del Patriarca," *Bollettino dell'Istituto di Storia della Società e dello Stato Veneziano*, no. 3, 1961, pp. 121–38.
33. BIALIK H.N. " 'Il giovane padovano': M.H. Luzzatto." *R.M.I.*, no. 1, 1948.
34. BLAU L. *Leo Modenas Briefe und Schriftstücke*. Budapest, 1906.
35. BLOCH J. *Venetian Printers of Hebrew Books*. New York, 1932.
36. BLUMENKRANZ B. "Les Juifs dans le commerce maritime de Venise, 1592–1609," *Revue des études juives*, vol. II, 1961.
37. BOCCATO C. "Il caso di un neonato esposto nel Ghetto di Venezia alla fine del '600," in *R.M.I.*, no. 3, 1978.
38. ———. "La disciplina delle sensarie nel Ghetto di Venezia," *Giornale economico*, Nov.–Dec. 1974.

39. ———. " 'L'amor possente, favola pastorale di Benedetto Luzzatto hebreo da Venetia' composta durante la peste nel 1630." *R.M.I.*, nos. 1–2, 1971.

40. ———. *L'antico cimitero ebraico di San Nicolò di Lido a Venezia.* Venice, 1980.

41. ———. "Lettere di Ansaldo Cebà, genovese, a Sara Copio Sullam, poetessa del Ghetto di Venezia," *R.M.I.*, no. 4, 1974.

42. ———. "Licenze per altane concesse ad ebrei del Ghetto di Venezia (sec. XVI–XVII–XVIII)," *R.M.I.*, nos. 3–4, 1980.

43. ———. "Nuove testimonianze su Sara Copio Sullam." *R.M.I.*, nos. 9–10, 1980.

44. ———. "Ordinanza contro il lusso e sul 'suonatore del sabato' nel Ghetto di Venezia nel secolo XVII." *R.M.I.*, nos. 6–7, 1979.

45. ———. "Processi ad Ebrei nell'archivio degli Ufficiali al Cattaver a Venezia." *R.M.I.*, no. 3, 1975.

46. ———. "Testamenti di israeliti nel fondo del notaio veneziano Pietro Bracchi seniore (sec. XVII)." *R.M.I.*, nos. 5–6, 1976.

47. ———. "Testimonianze ebraiche sulla peste del 1630 a Venezia." *R.M.I.*, nos. 9–10, 1975.

48. ———. "Un altro documento inedito su Sara Copio Sullam: il 'Codice di Giulia Soliga.' " *R.M.I.*, nos. 7–8, 1974.

49. ———. "Un processo contro Ebrei di Verona alla fine del Cinquecento," *R.M.I.*, no. 9, 1974.

50. Bokser B.Z. *Il Giudaismo: profilo di una fede.* Bologna, 1969.

51. Bosisio A. "La nazione ebraica tra Venezia e Mestre." *Quaderno di studi e notizie*, Center of Historical Studies, Mestre, Dec. 1964–Jan. 1965.

52. Braudel F. *Civiltà e imperi del Mediterraneo nell'età di Filippo II.* 2 vols. Turin, 1976, II ed.

53. Bouwsma W.J. *Venezia e la difesa della libertà repubblicana.* Bologna, 1977.

54. Brown H.F. *The Venetian Printing Press, 1469–1800.* Amsterdam, 1969.

55. Calimani R. *Introduzione al Dialogo sull'ebraismo di S. Calimani.* Venice, 1984.

56. Calimani S. *Esame o sia catechismo ad un giovane israelita.* Verona, 1821. (reprint *Dialogo sull'ebraismo*, Venice 1984)

57. Camerini D. *Storia del Popolo Ebreo.* Vol. I. Turin, 1921.

58. Canepa A.M. "Emancipazione, integrazione e antisemitismo liberale: il caso Pasqualigo." *Comunità*, no. 174, June, 1975.

59. ———. "L'atteggiamento degli ebrei italiani davanti alla loro seconda emancipazione: premesse e analisi." *R.M.I.*, no. 9, 1977.

60. ———. "L'immagine dell'ebreo nel folclore e nella letteratura del post-Risorgimento." *R.M.I.*, nos. 5–6, 1978.

61. *Capitoli della Ricondotta degli Ebrei di Venezia e dello Stato Veneto*, 1777.

62. Caracciolo Aricò A. (a cura di). *Marin Sanudo il giovane, De origine, situ et magistratibus urbis Venetae, ovvero la città di Venezia (1493–1530).* Milan, 1980.

63. Carletto G. *Il Ghetto veneziano nel Settecento.* Assisi/Rome, 1981.

64. Carpi D. "Alcune notizie sugli Ebrei a Vicenza (secoli XIV–XVIII)." *Archivio Veneto* LXVIII, 1961.

65. Carpi D. (a cura di). *Bibliotheca italo-ebraica (bibliografia per la storia degli Ebrei in Italia 1964–1973)*. Rome, 1982.
66. Carpi R. "Le premesse giuridiche e l'ordinamento amministrativo della Comunità israelitica di Padova nel secolo XIX." *R.M.I., Scritti in memoria di Federico Luzzatto*, Venice–Rome, 1962.
67. Cassuto D. *Ricerche sulle cinque sinagoghe (scuole) di Venezia*. Jerusalem, undated.
68. ————. "The Scuola Grande Tedesca in the Venice Ghetto." *Journal of Jewish Art*, 1977.
69. Cassuto U. "Alcune note ebraiche di contabilità del secolo XVI." *Rivista Israelitica*, VIII, 1912.
70. ————. "Chi era David Reubeni?" *R.M.I.*, no. 2, 1969.
71. ————. *Gli Ebrei a Firenze nell'età del Rinascimento*. Florence, 1918.
72. ————. "Leon da Modena e l'opera sua." *R.M.I.*, nos. 3–4, 1933.
73. Castelbolognesi G. "Il centenario del Collegio Rabbinico di Padova." *R.M.I.*, nos. 5–6, 1930.
74. Cattaneo C. *Interdizioni israelitiche*, reprint. Turin, 1962.
75. Cecchetti B. *La Repubblica di Venezia e la Corte di Roma nei rapporti della religione*. 2 vols. Venice, 1874.
76. Cecchetto G. "Gli Ebrei a Venezia durante la III dominazione austriaca." *Ateneo Veneto* 13 (1975) no. 2.
77. *Cenni storici e amministrativi delle Comunità israelitiche italiane*. Rome 1914.
78. Cessi R. *La condizione degli ebrei banchieri in Padova nei secoli XIV e XV*. Padua, 1908.
79. Cessi R. *Storia della Repubblica di Venezia*. Florence, 1981.
80. Chabod F. *La politica di Paolo Sarpi*. Venice–Rome, 1968. (reprint)
81. Chiuppani G. *Gli Ebrei a Bassano*. Bologna, 1977. (reprint)
82. Cicogna E.A. "Notizie intorno a Sara Copia Sulam." *Memorie del R. Istituto Veneto di Lettere, Scienze, e Arti*. Venice, 1865.
83. Ciriacono S. *Olio ed Ebrei nella Repubblica veneta del Settecento*. Venice, 1975.
84. Ciscato A. *Gli Ebrei in Padova (1300–1800)*. Padua, 1901.
85. Cohen I. *Israel in Italien*. Berlin, 1909.
86. Cohen M.R. "Leone da Modena's Riti: a seventeenth-century plea for social toleration of Jews." *Jewish Social Studies*, no. 34, 1972.
87. Colbi P. "La vita e l'opera di don Izhac Abrabanel statista, pensatore, esegeta." *R.M.I.*, no. 6, 1932.
88. Colorni V. "Autonomie ebraiche in Italia nel Medioevo e nel Rinascimento." *R.M.I.*, no. 7, 1966.
89. ————. *Gli ebrei nel sistema del diritto comune fino alla prima emancipazione*. Milan, 1956.
90. ————. *Judaica minora*. Milan, 1983.
91. Coppin P. *Sommario storico dei costumi del popolo d'Israello*. Padua, 1820.
92. Coryat T. *Coryat's Crudities* (reprint of the 1611 edition). 2 vols. Glasgow, 1905.
93. Cozzi G. "Paolo Sarpi tra il cattolico Philippe Canaye de Fresnes e il

calvinista Isaac Casaubon." *Bollettino dell'Istituto di Storia della Società e dello Stato Veneziano*, I, 1959.

94. ———. *Paolo Sarpi tra Venezia e l'Europa*. Turin, 1969.

95. ———. *Repubblica di Venezia e Stati italiani*. Turin, 1982.

96. DA MOSTO R., Private collection: letters, documents, newspaper articles on the Pasqualigo case.

97. D'AZEGLIO M. *Sull'emancipazione degli israeliti*. Florence, 1848.

98. DEL BIANCO COTROZZI M. *La comunità ebraica di Gradisca d'Isonzo*. Udine, 1983.

99. *Della influenza del Ghetto nello Stato*. Venice, 1782.

100. DELLA PERGOLA S. *Anatomia dell'ebraismo italiano*. Assisi–Rome, 1976.

101. ———. "The Geography of Italian Jews: Country wide Patterns." In *Studi sull'ebraismo italiano*. Rome, 1974.

102. DELLA TORRE L. "La cultura presso gli Ebrei in Italia nel secolo decimottavo." *Il Corriere Israelitico*, no. 9, January 1866.

103. DE POMIS D. *De medico hebreo. Enarratio apologetica*. Venetiis 1588.

104. DE POMIS D. *Discorso intorno a' l'humana miseria e sopr'al modo di fuggirla*. Venetia, 1572.

105. DE ROSSI G.B. *Dizionario storico degli autori ebrei e delle loro opere*. Parma, 1802. (facsimile reprint, Sala Bolognese 1978)

106. DIENA S. *La repubblica di Venezia*. Venice, 1898.

107. DI PORTO B. "Niccolò Tommaseo e gli ebrei: una meditata simpatia." *R.M.I.*, no. 11, 1969.

108. *Discorso sopra gli accidenti del parto mostruoso nato di una Hebrea in Venetia nell'anno 1575.*

109. DISEGNI D. "Gli Ebrei in Verona." *Il Corriere Israelitico*, no. 9, 1911.

110. DI SEGNI R. "Nota sul secondo soggiorno veneziano di David Reubeni." *R.M.I.*, nos. 6–7, 1979.

111. DOLCETTI G. *Le bische e il gioco d'azzardo a Venezia, 1172–1807*. Venice, 1903.

112. DOUGLAS M. *Purity and danger: an analysis of the concepts of pollution and taboo*. London, 1978.

113. *Ebrei e sinagoghe* (guidebook). Venice, 1973.

114. *Emuna*, special issue. AA.VV., *Venedig. Geschichte und Gestalt seines Ghettos*, 1975.

115. ERDELYI N. "Incontro con Shylock." *R.M.I.*, no. 4, 1950.

116. ERRERA A. *Daniele Manin e Venezia*. Florence, 1875.

117. FERORELLI N. *Gli Ebrei nell'Italia meridionale dall'età romana al secolo XVIII*. Turin, 1915.

118. FICHMANN J. "La poesia di M.H. Luzzatto." *R.M.I.*, no. 1, 1948.

119. FINLAY R. *La vita politica nella Venezia del Rinascimento*. Milan, 1982.

120. ———. "The foundation of the Ghetto: Venice, the Jews and the war of the League of Cambrai." *Proceedings of the American Philosophical Society*, no. 126, 1982.

121. FOÀ S. *Gli Ebrei del Risorgimento italiano*. Assisi–Rome, 1978.

122. FORTIS U. "Riferimenti agli ebrei in un inedito del Settecento veneziano." *R.M.I.*, no. 5, 1972.

123. FORTIS U. (editor). *Venezia ebraica*. Rome, 1982.

124. FORTIS U. - POLACCO B. "Quarant'anni fa (tre tempi in giudeo-veneziano)." excerpt from *R.M.I.*, nos. 11–12, 1972.
125. FORTIS U. - ZOLLI P. *La parlata giudeo-veneziana.* Assisi–Rome, 1979.
126. FOSCARINI M. *Necessità della storia e Della perfezione della Repubblica veneziana* (edited by L. Riscaldone). Milan, 1983.
127. FRANCO M. *Essai sur l'histoire des Israélites de l'Empire Ottoman depuis les origines jusqu'à nos jours.* Paris, 1897.
128. FRIZZI B. *Difesa contro gli attacchi fatti alla Nazione Ebrea.* Bologna, 1977. (facsimile of the 1784 Pavia edition)
129. ———. *Elogio dei rabbini Simone Calimani e Giacobbe Saraval.* Trieste, 1791.
130. FUBINI G. *La condizione giuridica dell'ebraismo italiano dal periodo napoleonico alla Repubblica.* Florence, 1974.
131. FULIN R. *Breve sommario di Storia Veneta - Breve storia di Venezia.* Venice, 1972.
132. GABRIELI G. *Italia Judaica.* Rome, 1924.
133. GALLICCIOLLI G.B. *Storie e memorie venete profane ed ecclesiastiche,* 8 vols. Venice, 1795.
134. GAON S. "Abravanel and the Renaissance." In *Studi sull'ebraismo italiano.* Rome, 1974.
135. GEIGER A. *Leon da Modena Rabbiner zu Venedig (1571–1648).* Breslau, 1856.
136. GEORGELIN J. *Venise au siècle des lumières.* Paris, 1978.
137. GINSBORG P. *Daniele Manin e la rivoluzione veneziana del 1848–49.* Milan, 1978.
138. GRENDLER P. *L'Inquisizione romana e l'editoria a Venezia (1540–1605).* Rome, 1983.
139. GRENDLER P. "The destruction of Hebrew books in Venice, 1568." *Proceedings of the American Academy for the Jewish Research,* no. 45, 1978.
140. GROSS B. "L'idea messianica nel pensiero di Isaac Abrabanel." *R.M.I.,* no. 9, 1969.
141. GRUNEBAUM-BALLIN P. *Joseph Naci duc de Naxos.* Paris, 1968.
142. HARRIS A.C. "La demografia del ghetto in Italia (1516–1797 circa)." *R.M.I.,* nos. 1–5, 1967.
143. IOLY ZORATTINI P.C. *Battesimi di fanciulli ebrei a Venezia nel Settecento.* Udine, 1984.
144. IOLY ZORATTINI P.C. "Fervore di educazione ebraica nelle Comunità venete del '700." *R.M.I.,* no. 10, 1968.
145. IOLY ZORATTINI P.C. (editor). *Gli ebrei a Gorizia e a Trieste tra "Ancien Régime" ed emancipazione.* Udine, 1984.
146. IOLY ZORATTINI P.C. "Gli ebrei a Venezia, Padova e Verona." In *Storia della cultura veneta,* vol. 3. Vicenza, 1980.
147. ———. "Gli Ebrei del Veneto dal secondo Cinquecento a tutto il Seicento." In *Storia della cultura veneta, il Seicento.* Vicenza, 1984.
148. ———. "Gli insediamenti ebraici nel Friuli Veneto e la Ricondota del 1777." *Archivio Veneto,* CXXI, 1983.
149. ———. "Il 'Mif'Aloth Elohim' di Isaac Abravanel e il Sant'Offizio di Venezia." *Italia: studi e ricerche sulla cultura e sulla letteratura degli ebrei d'Italia,* I, 1976.

150. ———. "Il testamento di Caliman Belgrado." Excerpt from *East and Maghreb*, VI, 1985.

151. ———. *Leandro Tisanio un giudaizzante sanvitese del Seicento*. Florence, 1984.

152. ———. "L'Università degli Ebrei di S. Vito al Tagliamento e il suo antico cimitero." Excerpt from *Studi forogiuliesi* in honor of C.G. Nor.

153. ———. "Note e documenti per la storia dei marrani e giudaizzanti nel Veneto del Seicento." In *Michael: on the history of the Jews of the Diaspora*. Ed. S. Simonsohn, I. Tel-Aviv, 1972.

154. ———. "Note sul S. Uffizio e gli ebrei a Venezia nel Cinquecento." *Rivista di Storia della Chiesa in Italia*, year 33, 1979.

155. ———. "Processi contro ebrei e giudaizzanti nell'Archivio del S. Uffizio di Aquileia e Concordia." *Memorie storiche forogiuliesi*, no. 58, 1978.

156. Ioly Zorattini P.C. (editor). *Processi del S. Uffizio di Venezia contro Ebrei e Giudaizzanti (1548–1560), and (1561–1570)*. 2 vols., Florence, 1980–82.

157. Ioly Zorattini P.C. (editor). *Processi del S. Uffizio di Venezia contro ebrei e giudaizzanti (1570–1572)*. Florence, 1984.

158. Ioly Zorattini P.C. "Un giudaizzante cividalese del Cinquecento: Gioambattista Cividin." *Studi geografici*, I. Pisa, 1977.

159. Ive A. "Banques Juives et Monts-de-Piété en Istrie: les Capitoli des Juifs de Picane." *Revue des Etudes Juives*, II. 1881.

160. Jacoby D. *Les Juifs à Venise du XIV au milieu du XVI siècle, in Venezia centro di mediazione tra oriente e occidente (secoli XV–XVI): aspetti e problemi*. 2 vols. Florence, 1977.

161. ———. "Venice, the Inquisition and the Jewish Communities of Crete in the early 14th century." *Studi Veneziani*, XII. 1970.

162. Kaufmann D. "A contribution to the history of the Venetian Jews." *J.Q.R.*, no. 2, 1890, reprinted 1966.

163. ———. "Die Vertreibung der Marranen aus Venedig in Jahre 1550." *J.Q.R.*, no. 13, 1901, reprinted 1966.

164. Klausner J. "Don Jehuda Abravanel e la sua Filosofia dell'Amore." *R.M.I.*, nos. 11–12, 1932; no. 6, 1931–32; nos. 11–12 and no. 7, 1932–33.

165. Kobler F. (editor). *Letters of Jews through the ages*. New York, 1952.

166. Lane F.C. *I mercanti di Venezia*. Turin, 1982.

167. ———. *Le navi di Venezia*, Turin, 1983.

168. ———. *Storia di Venezia*. Turin, 1978.

169. ———. "The funded debt of the Venetian Republic, 1262–1482." In *Venice and history: the collected papers of Fredric C. Lane*. Baltimore, 1966.

170. Laras G. "Diego Lorenzo Picciotto: un delatore di Marrani nella Livorno del Seicento." In *Scritti in memoria di U. Nahon*. Jerusalem, 1978.

171. Lattes D. "Cabbalah e Hassidismo." *R.M.I.*, vol. 1, no. 2, 1925.

172. ———. "Mosè Chaim Luzzatto (Ramchal), autore del Trattato morale 'Mesillath Jesharim.' " *R.M.I.*, *Scritti in memoria di Federico Luzzatto*, 1962.

173. Lattes M. "Documents et notices sur l'histoire politique et littéraire de Juifs en Italie." *R.E.J.*, V, 1882.

174. ———. "Gli Ebrei di Norimberga e la Repubblica di Venezia." *Archivio Veneto*, Vols. IV, II, 1872.

175. ——. *La libertà delle banche a Venezia, dal secolo XIII al XVII.* 1869 (reprinted Sala Bolognese 1977).
176. ——. "Notizie e documenti di letteratura e storia giudaica." In *Antologia israelitica*, 1879.
177. LAZAR H. "Raffigurazioni di Gerusalemme." *Ketubbòth italiane*, nos. 11–12, 1980.
178. LEVI A. "Il ghetto ebraico nella sua univoca natura." *R.M.I.*, no. 3, 1973.
179. LEVI C.A. *Dante a Torcello.* Treviso, 1906.
180. LEVI E. "Lo 'Jus Kazagà' in Piemonte." *R.M.I.*, nos. 3–4, 1977.
181. LEVI L. "Tradizioni liturgiche, musicali e dialettali a Corfù." *R.M.I.*, no. 1, 1961.
182. LEVI DELLA VIDA G. "Quattro lettere di Samuele Romanin." In *Miscellanea in onore di Roberto Cessi*, III vol. Rome, 1958.
183. LOGAN O. *Venezia: cultura e società (1470–1790).* Rome, 1980.
184. LOMBARDO A. (editor). "Nicola de Boateriis notaio in Famagosta e Venezia (1355–1365)." in *Fonti per la storia di Venezia*, sec. III, Venice, 1973.
185. LONARDO P.M. *Gli Ebrei a Pisa sino alla fine del secolo XV.* Bologna, 1982.
186. LOWRY M. *Il mondo di Aldo Manuzio.* Rome, 1984.
187. LUZZATTO F. *Cronache storiche della università degli ebrei di San Daniele del Friuli: cenni sulla storia degli ebrei del Friuli.* Rome, 1964.
188. ——. *La comunità ebraica di Conegliano Veneto ed i suoi monumenti.* Rome, 1957.
189. LUZZATTO G. "Armatori ebrei a Venezia negli ultimi 250 anni della Repubblica." *R.M.I.*, *Scritti in memoria di Federico Luzzatto*, nos. 3–4, 1962.
190. ——. "Brevi cenni introduttivi ad una guida dei templi veneziani." *R.M.I.*, no. 5, 1964.
191. ——. *Storia Economica d'Italia—Il Medioevo.* Florence, 1963.
192. ——. "Sulla condizione economica degli ebrei veneziani nel secolo XVIII." *R.M.I.*, *Scritti in onore di Riccardo Bachi*, 1950.
193. ——. "Tasso d'interesse e usura a Venezia nei secoli XIII–XV." In *Miscellanea in onore di Roberto Cessi*, I. Rome, 1958.
194. ——. "Un'anagrafe degli Ebrei di Venezia del Settembre 1797." In *Scritti in memoria di Sally Maier*. Jerusalem, 1956.
195. LUZZATTO L. "Giuda Chaiug primo grammatico." *Il Vessillo Israelitico*, no. 11, 1896.
196. ——. "Norme suntuarie riguardanti gli Ebrei - 27 Febbraio 1697." (translated from the Hebrew) in *Archivio Veneto*, a. XVII, 1887.
197. ——. "Un ambasciatore ebreo nel 1574." *Il Vessillo Israelitico*, no. 7, 1893.
198. LUZZATTO S.D. "Essenza-socialità del Giudaismo. Della letteratura ebraica in Italia." Excerpt from *Giudaismo illustrato*. Padua, 1908.
199. ——. "Lettera a Samuele Romanin." *L'educatore israelitico*, no. 21, 1873.
200. LUZZATTO S. *Discorso circa il stato de gl'Hebrei et in particolar dimoranti nell'inclita città di Venetia* (facsimile of the 1638 Venetian edition). Bologna, 1976.

201. ———. *Discorso circa il stato de gl'Hebrei et in particolar dimoranti nell'inclita città di Venetia.* Ed. G. Colleoni. Venetia, 1638.
202. Maestro R. *Le attività commerciali svolte in Venezia dagli Ebrei Levantini e Ponentini dal 1550 al 1700.* Graduate thesis, Gino Luzzatto adviser, 1935.
203. Maranini G. *La costituzione di Venezia.* 2 vols. Florence, 1974. (reprint)
204. Maravall J.A. *Potere, onore, elites nella Spagna del secolo d'oro.* Bologna, 1984.
205. Margulies S.H. "La famiglia Abravanel in Italia." *Rivista Israelitica,* nos. 3–4, 1906.
206. Maternini Zotta M.F. *L'ente comunitario ebraico; la legislazione negli ultimi due secoli.* Varese, 1983.
207. Mayda G. *Ebrei sotto Salò.* Milan, 1978.
208. Mc Neill W. *Venezia il cardine d'Europa (1081–1797).* Rome, 1979.
209. Medici P. *Riti e costumi degli ebrei.* Venezia, 1746.
210. Medin A. - Tolomei G. *Per la storia aneddottica dell'Università di Padova.* Padua, 1911.
211. Melamed A. "The myth of Venice in Italian Renaissance Jewish thought." *Italia Judaica,* Rome, 1983.
212. *Memoria che può servire alla storia politica degli ultimi otto anni della Repubblica di Venezia.* London, 1798.
213. Meneghin V. *Bernardino da Feltre e i Monti di Pietà.* Vicenza, 1974.
214. Mihaly E. "Isaac Abravanel on the principles of faith." *Hebrew Union College,* XXVI, 1955.
215. Milano A. "Bibliografia degli studi sulla storia degli Ebrei d'Italia." *R.M.I.* no. 11, 1966.
216. ———. "Considerazioni sulla lotta dei Monti di Pietà contro il prestito ebraico." In *Scritti in memoria di Sally Mayer: saggi sull'ebraismo italiano.* Jerusalem, 1956.
217. ———. "Gl'inviati di Terrasanta in Italia: un singolare testamento riguardante Safed." *R.M.I.,* nos. 7–8, 1952.
218. ———. "I 'banchi dei poveri' a Venezia." *R.M.I.,* no. 6, 1951.
219. ———. *Il ghetto di Roma: illustrazioni storiche.* Rome, 1964.
220. ———. "I primordi del prestito ebraico in Italia." *R.M.I.,* nos. 5–10, 1953.
221. ———. "L'Editto sopra gli Ebrei di Pio VI e le mene ricattatorie di un letterato." *R.M.I.* no. 2, 1953.
222. ———. "L'Editto sugli Ebrei di Papa Pio VI." *R.M.I.,* no. 3, 1953.
223. ———. *Storia degli ebrei italiani nel Levante.* Florence, 1949.
224. ———. *Storia degli Ebrei in Italia.* Turin, 1963.
225. ———. "Un sottile tormento nella vita del Ghetto di Roma: la predica coattiva." *R.M.I.,* no. 12, 1952.
226. Miozzi E. *Venezia nei secoli,* 4 vols. Venice, 1957.
227. Mocatta F.D. *Gli Ebrei della Spagna e del Portogallo e l'Inquisizione.* Naples, 1887.
228. Modena (da) L. "Historia de' Riti Hebraici." *R.M.I.,* nos. 7–12, 1932.
229. ———. *Historia de' Riti Hebraici.* Reprint of the 1678 Venetian edition. Bologna, 1979.
230. Modona L. *Sara Copio Sullam, sonetti editi ed inediti.* Bologna, 1887.

231. MOLMENTI P.G. *Curiosità di storia veneziana*. Bologna, 1919.
232. ———. *La storia di Venezia nella vita privata dalle origini alla caduta della Repubblica*, II. Bergamo, 1925.
233. MOROSINI G. *Via della fede mostrata a' gli ebrei*. Rome, 1683.
234. MORPURGO E. "Inchiesta sui Monumenti e Documenti del Veneto interessanti la storia religiosa, civile e letteraria degli Ebrei." *Il Corriere Israelitico*, March 1911.
235. ———. *L'Università degli Ebrei in Padova nel XVI secolo*. Padua, 1909.
236. ———. "Monografie storiche sugli Ebrei del Veneto I Gli Ebrei a Treviso, II Gli Ebrei a Conegliano—Gli Ebrei a Ceneda." *Il Corriere Israelitico*, no.8 (1909), nos. 9, 10, 11 (1910).
237. ———. *Notizie delle famiglie ebree esistite a Padova nel XVI secolo*. Udine, 1909.
238. MORPURGO FANO L. *Diario. Ricordi di prigionia*. Venice, 1966.
239. MORTARA M. *Indice alfabetico dei rabbini e scrittori israeliti di cose giudaiche in Italia*. Padua, 1886.
240. MUELLER R.C. "Charitable institutions, the Jewish Community, and Venetian Society. A discussion on the recent volume by Brian Pullan." *Studi veneziani*, XIV, 1972.
241. ———. "Le prêteurs juifs de Venise au Moyen Age." *Annales: Economies, Sociétés, Civilisations*, 30, 1975.
242. MUIR E. *Il rituale civico a Venezia nel Rinascimento*. Rome, 1984.
243. MUSATTI E. *Storia di Venezia*. 2 vols., Venice, 1968–1969. (reprint).
244. MUSSO G. *Per la storia degli ebrei in Genova nella seconda metà del Cinquecento*.
245. ———. "Le vicende genovesi di R. Josef Hakoen." In *Scritti in memoria di Leone Capri*. Jerusalem, 1967.
246. MUTINELLI F. *Del commercio dei Veneziani*. Venice, 1835. (facsimile reprint, Venice 1984).
247. NAHON U. "Il lunario di Venezia." *R.M.I.*, no. 8, 1966.
248. NELSON B. *Usura e Cristianesimo*. Florence, 1967.
249. NETANYAHU B. *Don Isaac Abravanel, statesman and philosopher*. Philadelphia, 1968. (second edition).
250. ———. *Don Isaac Abravanel*. Philadelphia, 1972.
251. NISSIM D. "Gli Ebrei a Piove di Sacco e la prima tipografia ebraica." *R.M.I.*, Scritti in memoria di Paolo Nissim. 1972.
252. ———. "Modernità di vedute in un nostro illuminista: Benedetto Frizzi e le sue opere." *R.M.I.*, no. 5, 1968.
253. NISSIM P. "Le tappe del soggiorno in Italia di Elia Levita." *R.M.I.*, no. 8, 1966.
254. ———. "Sulla data della laurea rabbinica conseguita da Moshe Chajim Luzzatto." *R.M.I.*, no. 12, 1954.
255. NORSA A. "Carlo Cattaneo e le Interdizioni israelitiche." Excerpt from *R.M.I.*, no. 12, 1969.
256. NORWICH J.J. *Storia di Venezia*. 2 vols., Milan, 1982.
257. NUNES VAIS ARBIB B. "La comunità israelitica di Venezia durante il Risorgimento." *R.M.I.*, nos. 5–8, 1961.
258. *Opera pia Moisè Vita Jacur in Venezia*. Venice, 1885.

259. *Opere pie amministrate dalla congregazione di carità. Fondazione Grazia Consiglio Ricchetti.* Venice, 1903.
260. OSIER J.P. *D'Uriel da Costa à Spinoza.* Paris, 1983.
261. OSIMO M. *Narrazione della strage compiuta nel 1547 contro gli ebrei d'Asolo.* Casale Monferrato, 1875.
262. OTTOLENGHI A. "Abraham Lattes nei suoi rapporti colla Repubblica di Daniele Manin." Excerpt from *R.M.I.,* no. 1, 1930.
263. ———. "Il Governo democratico di Venezia e l'abolizione del Ghetto." Excerpt from *R.M.I.,* no. 2, 1930.
264. ———. *Il tempio.* Venice, 1929.
265. ———. *L'azione di Tommaseo a Venezia.* Venice, 1933.
266. ———. "Leon da Modena e la vita ebraica del ghetto di Venezia." *R.M.I.,* no. 12, 1971.
267. ———. "Origine, vicende dell'Historia de Riti Hebraici di Leon da Moena." *R.M.I.,* nos. 7–8, 1932.
268. ———. "Spigolature storiche di vita ebraica veneziana." *R.M.I.,* nos. 5–6, 1931.
269. OTTOLENGHI A. - PACIFICI R. "L'antico cimitero ebraico di S. Nicolò di Lido." Excerpt from *Rivista di Venezia,* May 1929.
270. PACI R. *La "scala" di Spalato e il commercio veneziano nei Balcani fra Cinque e Seicento.* Venice, 1971.
271. PACIFICI R. "Il regolamenti della Scuola italiana a Venezia nel secolo XVII." *R.M.I.,* nos. 11–12, 1930.
272. ———. *Le iscrizioni dell'antico cimitero ebraico a Venezia.* Alexandria (Egypt), 1936.
273. PADOA P. "Daniele Manin e gli Israeliti di Venezia nel 1848–49." *Il Vessillo Israelitico,* no. 52, 1904.
274. ———. "Gli Israeliti di Venezia e il Risorgimento italiano." Excerpt from *Il Vessillo Israelitico,* July-August 1911.
275. ———. *Scuole religioso-morali maschili israelitiche in Venezia.* Padua, 1901.
276. PARDO E. *Brevi cenni sulla "Associazione israelitica di previdenza Cuore e Concordia" di Venezia.* Rome, 1962.
277. ———. *Luci e ombre.* Venice, 1965.
278. PARENTE F. "Il confronto ideologico tra l'Ebraismo e la Chiesa in Italia." In *Italia Judaica.* Rome, 1983.
279. PASCHINI P. *Venezia e l'Inquisizione Romana da Giulio III a Pio IV.* Padua, 1959.
280. PAVONCELLO N. *Antiche famiglie ebraiche italiane.* Rome, 1982.
281. ———. *Gli ebrei in Verona dalle origine al sec. XX.* Verona, 1960.
282. ———. *La letteratura ebraica in Italia.* Rome, 1963.
283. *Per l'Università degl'Ebrei di Venezia* (Collection of Decrees), Misc. A 2672, Marciana Library Venice.
284. PEROCCO G. - SALVADORI A. *Civiltà di Venezia.* 3 vols. Venice, undated.
285. *Pia Fondazione Enrichetta Consolo-Treves dei Bonfili in Venezia.* Venice, 1887.
286. *Pia Opera Marco Reiner in Venezia.* Venice, 1888.
287. PIATTELLI A. " 'Ester': l'unico dramma di Leon da Modena giunto fino a noi." *R.M.I.,* no. 3, 1968.

288. ———. *Un'antica usanza per il Capodanno*. Rome, 1979.

289. ———. "Un arazzo veneziano del XVII secolo." In *Scritti in memoria di Attilio Milano*. 1970.

290. ———. "Una severa disposizione in un tempio veneziano del '600." *R.M.I.*, no. 1, 1969.

291. ———. "Un inno per Simchat Torà di Rabbi Elia Aharon Lattes." *Annuario di Studi Ebraici*, 1977–79.

292. PINETTI A. "Una supplica alla Serenissima contro gli Ebrei." *Nuovo Archivio Veneto*, XIX, 1900.

293. *Pio Stabilimento Hanau in Venezia*. Venice, 1887.

294. POLIAKOV L. *I banchieri ebrei e la Santa Sede dal XIII al XVII secolo*. Rome, 1974.

295. ———. *Storia dell'antisemitismo*. 3 vols. Florence, 1974–76.

296. ———. "Un tentativo di Venezia per attirare gli ebrei di Livorno." *R.M.I.*, no. 7, 1957.

297. PRETO P. *Peste e società a Venezia, 1576*. Vicenza, 1978.

298. ———. *Venezia e i Turchi*. Florence, 1975.

299. *Processo Giuditta Castilliero*, suppl. to no. 641 dell' "Eco dei tribunali," sec. I, 1856.

300. *Progetto di Statuto organico della Fraterna Generale di Culto e Beneficenza degli Israeliti in Venezia*. Venice, 1910.

301. PULLAN B. *La politica sociale della repubblica di Venezia 1500–1620*, vol. I (*Le scuole grandi, l'assistenza e le leggi sui poveri*), vol. II (*Gli ebrei veneziani e i Monti di Pietà*). Rome, 1982.

302. ———. "Poverty, charity and the reason of state: some Venetian examples." *Bollettino dell'Istituto di Storia della Società e dello Stato Veneziano*, II, 1960.

303. ———. *The Jews of Europe and the Inquisition of Venice (1550–1670)*. Oxford, 1983.

304. RABELLO A.M. "Gli Ebrei a Ceneda e a Vittorio Veneto." *R.M.I.*, *Scritti in memoria di A. Milano*. 1970.

305. *Raccolta di decreti, processi, verbali e discorsi concernenti li cittadini ebrei di Venezia dopo la loro felice rigenerazione*, Venice, 1797.

306. RADZIK S.G. *Portobuffolè*. Florence, 1984.

307. RAVÀ V. "Ebrei in Venezia." *L'educatore israelitico*, XIX, 1871; XX, 1872.

308. RAVENNA A. "La scuola rabbinica di Padova e il Risorgimento italiano." *R.M.I.*, no. 7, 1957.

309. RAVID B. " 'A Republic Separate from an Other Government'; Jewish Autonomy in Venice in the Seventeenth Century, in Thought and Action." In *Essays in memory of Simon Rawidowicz*. Haifa, 1983.

310. ———. "Contra Judaeos in Seventeenth-Century Italy: two Responses to the Discorso of Simon Luzzatto by Melchiore Palontrotti and Giulio Morosini." *AJS review*, vols. 7–8, 1982–83.

311. ———. *Economics and toleration in seventeenth-century Venice: the background and context of the Discorso of Simone Luzzatto*. Jerusalem, 1978.

312. ———. " 'How profitable the Nation of the Jewes are': the Humble Addresses of Menasseh ben Israel and the Discorso of Simone Luzzatto." In

Essays in Jewish Intellectual History in Honor of Alexander Altmann. Durham N.E., 1982.

313. ———. "Money, love and power politics in sixteenth century Venice: the perpetual banishment and subsequent pardon of Joseph Nasi." *Italia Judaica*, Rome, 1983.

314. ———. "The establishment of the Ghetto Vecchio of Venice, 1541." *Proceedings of the Sixth World Congress of the Jewish Studies*, II, Jerusalem, 1975, pp. 153–67.

315. ———. "The first charter of the Jewish merchants of Venice, 1589." *Association for Jewish Studies Review*, I, 1976. 187–222.

316. ———. "The Jewish mercantile settlement of twelfth and thirteenth century Venice: reality or conjecture?" *A.J.S.*, vol. 2, 1977.

317. ———. "The legal status of merchants of Venice." Thesis, Harvard University, 1973.

318. ———. "The prohibition against Jewish printing and publishing in Venice and the difficulties of Leone da Modena." *Studies in medieval Jewish history and literature*, Cambridge 1979, pp. 135–153.

319. ———. "The socioeconomic background and the expulsion and the readmission of the Venetian Jews, 1571–1573." In *Essays in modern Jewish History: a tribute to Ben Halpern*. Rutherford-Madison-Teaneck, 1982.

320. *Regolamento dei riuniti sovvegni spagnuolo e tedeschi in Venezia.* Venice, 1873.

321. *Regolamento interno d'amministrazione della fraterna misericordia e pietà degli Israeliti in Venezia.* Venice, 1888.

322. *Regolamento per la fraterna generale di culto e beneficenza di Venezia.* Venice, 1828.

323. *Regolamento per l'istruzione religiosa e morale degli Israeliti in Venezia.* Venice, 1827.

324. *Regolamento speciale d'amministrazione della casa israelitica d'industria e ricovero in Venezia.* Venice, 1890.

325. *Regolamento speciale di amministrazione della sezione beneficenza della fraterna generale di culto e beneficenza degli Israeliti in Venezia.* Venice, 1888.

326. REVAH I.S. "Chi sono i Marrani." *R.M.I.*, nos. 1–2 and 3–4, 1959.

327. ———. "Les Marranes." *R.E.J.*, I, 1959.

328. RILKE R.M. *Le storie del buon Dio.* Milan, 1978.

329. RIVKIN E. *Leon da Modena and the Kol Sakhal.* Cincinnati, 1952.

330. RODRIGUEZ F. "Shylock, l'ebreo di Shakespeare." *Communità*, no. 178, 1977.

331. ROMANIN S. *Storia documentata di Venezia.* 10 vols. Venice, 1912–1921. (reprint).

332. ROMANIN JACUR S. "Le Sinagoghe Spagnole." *R.M.I.*, no. 1, 1958.

333. ROMANO G. *Bibliografia italo ebraica* (1848–1977). Florence, 1979.

334. ———. "Di una filastrocca pasquale in italiano e delle sue lontane origini." *R.M.I.*, nos. 2–3, 1974.

335. ROTH C. *A History of the Marranos.* Philadelphia, 1932.

336. ———. *Gli ebrei di Venezia*, Rome 1933.

337. ———. "I Marrani a Venezia." *R.M.I.*, nos. 5–6, 1933.

338. ———. "I Marrani in Italia. Nuovi documenti." *R.M.I.*, no. 9, 1934.
339. ———. "Immanuel Aboab's proselization of the Marranos." *J.Q.R.* n.s., XXXII, 1932–33.
340. ———. "Joseph Nassì, duca di Nasso e i Savoia." *R.M.I.*, no. 8, 1968.
341. ———. "L'Accademia musicale del ghetto veneziano." *R.M.I.*, no. 4, 1928.
342. ———. "La ricondotta degli ebrei ponentini, Venezia 1647." In *Studi in onore di Gino Luzzatto*, II. Milan, 1950.
343. ———. *Leon de Modène, ses Riti Ebraici et le Saint Office à Venise*. Paris, 1929.
344. ———. "Leone da Modena e gli ebraisti cristiani del suo tempo." *R.M.I.*, no. 10, 1937.
345. ———. "Les Marranes a Vénise." *REJ*, LXXXIX, 1930.
346. ———. "Lettere della Compagnia del riscatto degli schiavi in Venezia." *R.M.I.*, no. 1, 1949.
347. ———. "Nel Ghetto italiano." *R.M.I.*, nos. 3–4, 1926.
348. ———. *Storia del popolo ebraico*. Milan, 1962.
349. ———. *The house of Nasi: Dona Gracia*. Philadelphia, 1947.
350. ———. *The house of Nasi: the Duke of Naxos*. Philadelphia, 1948.
351. ———. *The last Florentine Republic 1527–30*. London, 1925.
352. ———. "Un'elegia giudeo-italiana sui martiri d'Ancona." In *Scritti in onore di Riccardo Bachi*. 1950.
353. SACCO P. *Il Beato Bernardino da Feltre*. Feltre, 1940.
354. SAMAJA N., "La situazione degli Ebrei nel periodo del Risorgimento." *R.M.I.*, nos. 7–8, 1957.
355. ———. "Le incerte vicende di un manoscritto di Leon da Modena." *R.M.I.*, no. 7, 1955.
356. ———. "Le vicende di un libro: 'Storia dei riti ebraici' di Leon da Modena." *R.M.I.*, no. 3, 1955.
357. SANDRI M.G. - ALAZRAKI P. *Arte e vita ebraica a Venezia (1516–1797)*. Florence, 1971.
358. SANSOVINO F. *Venetia città nobilissima e singolare*. Venice, 1663. (facsimile reprint in 2 vols., Venice, 1968).
359. SANUTO M. *I Diarii*. Edited by R. Fulin et. al. 58 vols. Venice, 1879–1903.
360. SARPI P. *La Repubblica di Venezia, la Casa d'Austria e gli Uscocchi*. Bari, 1965.
361. SCHAERF S. *I cognomi degli ebrei d'Italia*. Florence, 1925.
362. SCHIAVI L.A. "Gli Ebrei in Venezia e nelle sue colonie." In *Nuova Antologia*, 3rd series, XLVIII, 1893.
363. SCHIRMANN H. "Una invettiva 'Contro i vizi dei contemporanei' di Simon Calimani, poeta ebreo italiano del XVIII secolo." In *Scritti in memoria di Umberto Nahon*. Jerusalem, 1978.
364. SCHOLEM G. *Sabbatai Sevi, The Mystical Messiah*. Princeton, 1975.
365. SCHWAB M. *Storia degli ebrei dall'edificazione del secondo tempio fino ai giorni nostri*, Venice, 1870.
366. SCHWARZ S. "I Marrani del Portogallo." *R.M.I.*, n. 2, 1925.
367. SCHWARZFUCHS S. "I Responsi di Rabbì Meir da Padova come fonte storica." In *Scritti in memoria di Leone Carpi*. Jerusalem, 1967.
368. SERENI P. "Della comunità ebraica a Venezia durante il fascismo." In *La resistenza nel Veneziano*. Venice, 1985.

369. ———. "Gli anni della persecuzione razziale a Venezia: appunti per una storia." In *Venezia ebraica*. Rome, 1982.

370. SERMONETA J. "Sull'origine della parola 'ghetto.' " In *Studi sull'ebraismo italiano*. Rome, 1974.

371. SERVI F. *Gli Israeliti d'Europa nella civiltà*. Turin, 1872.

372. SHAZAR Z. "Il 'fatto di R. Josef della Reina' nella tradizione sabbatista." *R.M.I.*, no. 4, 1973.

373. ———. "L'attesa messianica per l'anno 5500–1740 nel pensiero di R.Y. Chayim Kohen Cantarini." *R.M.I.*, no. 9, 1971.

374. SHULVASS M.A. *The Jews in the World of the Renaissance*. Chicago, 1973

375. SIMONSOHN S. "Lo stato attuale della ricerca storica sugli Ebrei in Italia." In *Italia Judaica*. Rome, 1983.

376. SIPORIN S.C. *Continuity and innovation in the Jewish festivals in Venice, Italy*. Ph.D. 1982, Indiana University.

377. SOAVE M. "Mosè del Castellazzo, distinto pittore." *Il Corriere Israelitico*, nos. 9–10, 1882.

378. ———. "Sara Coppio Sullam." *Il Corriere Israelitico*, 1863–65 and 1877.

379. ———. "Vita di Giudà Ariè Modena." *Il Corriere Israelitico*, 1862–1864.

380. *Statuto della Società Israelitica di previdenza Cuore e Concordia Venezia*. Venice, 1906.

381. *Statuto di riuniti sovvegni, spagnuolo e tedeschi in Venezia*. Venice, 1906.

382. STEINHAUS F. *Ebraismo sefardita*. Bologna, 1969.

383. SUMMO G. *Gli Ebrei in Puglia dall'XI al XVI secolo*. Bari, 1939.

384. TABACCO G. *Andrea Tron e la crisi dell'aristocrazia senatoria a Venezia*, II ed. Udine, 1980.

385. TAGLIACOZZO A. "Lo jus Gazagà nell'ordinamento giuridico italiano." In *Scritti in onore di Umberto Nahon*. Jerusalem, 1978.

386. TAMANI G. *Catalogo dei manoscritti ebraici della Biblioteca Marciana di Venezia*. Florence?

387. ———. "Manoscritti autografi di S.D. Luzzatto." *R.M.I.*, nos. 3–4, 1977.

388. ———. *Alcune delle più clamorose condanne capitali eseguite in Venezia sotto la Repubblica*. Venice, 1966.

389. ———. *Curiosità veneziane, ovvero Origini delle denominazioni stradali*, new edition edited by L. Moretti. Venice, 1888.

390. ———. *Curiosità veneziane*. Venice, 1983 (facsimile reprint)

391. TEBEKA E. "Gli ebrei europei nell'Ottocento: l'ora della scelta," *R.M.I.*, no. 11, 1968.

392. TEMANZA T. *Antica pianta dell'inclita città di Venezia delineata circa la metà del XII secolo*. Bologna, 1977. (reprint of the 1781 edition)

393. TENENTI A. *Naufrages, Corsaires et Assurances maritimes à Venise, (1592–1609)*. Paris, 1959.

394. *Terminatione et ordini de . . . Signori Essecutori contro la Biastemmia —1619, adì 23 marzo in materia delle estorsioni et violenze usate a banchieri del gheto*.

395. *Tesori d'arte ebraica a Venezia*. Venice, undated.

396. TESSADRI E. *L'arpa di David: storia di Simone e del processo di Trento contro gli ebrei accusati di omicidio rituale, 1475–1476*. Milan, 1974.

397. *Testo unico di Statuto della fraterna generale di culto e beneficenza degli Israeliti in Venezia.* Venice, 1887.

398. Teza E. "Intorno alla voce ghetto: dubbi da togliere e da risvegliare." *Atti dell'Istituto Veneto,* vol. VI, 1903–1904.

399. Tivaroni C. *Mazzini e Parenzo nella cospirazione veneta (1865)* excerpt from *Nuova Antologia,* July 1898.

400. Toaff A. "Nuova luce sui Marrani di Ancona (1556)." In *Studi sull'ebraismo italiano.* Rome, 1974.

401. Toaff E. "La vera fonte del Mercante di Venezia di Shakespeare." *R.M.I.,* no. 4, 1956.

402. Todeschini G. "Teorie economiche degli Ebrei alla fine del Medioevo. Storia di una presenza consapevole." *Quaderni storici,* 52, no. 1, 1983.

403. Tommaseo N. "Diritto degli Israeliti alla civile uguaglianza." *R.M.I.,* nos. 5–6, 1975.

404. Tranchini E. *Gli Ebrei a Vittorio Veneto dal XV al XX secolo.* Vittorio Veneto, 1979.

405. Turcato G. - Zanon dal Bo A. *1943–1945: Venezia nella Resistenza. Testimonianze.* Venice, 1975–76.

406. Vanzan Marchini N.E. "Il dramma dei convertiti nella follia di una ex-ebrea." *R.M.I.,* nos. 1–2, 1980.

407. ———. "Medici ebrei e assistenza cristiana nella Venezia del '500." *R.M.I.,* nos. 4–5, 1979.

408. Vecchi A. *Correnti religiose nel sei-settecento veneto.* Venice-Rome, 1962.

409. Venturi F. *Settecento riformatore.* Turin, 1976.

410. Viola A.A. *Compilazione delle leggi in materia d'officij e banchi del Ghetto.* Venice, 1786.

411. Vivante R. *Discorso . . . tenuto il dì 22 Messidor anno I della Libertà Italiana, in cui per decreto della Provvisoria Municipalità di Venezia furono levate e bruciate le porte del Ghetto.* Venice, 1797.

412. Volli G. *Breve storia degli ebrei d'Italia.* Milan, 1961.

413. ———. "Il Beato Lorenzino da Marostica presunta vittima d'un omicidio rituale." *R.M.I.,* no. 9, 1968.

414. ———. "I Processi tridentini e il culto del beato Simone da Trento." Excerpt from *Il Ponte,* no. 11, 1963.

415. Volpi E. *Storie intime di Venezia Repubblica.* Venice, 1893. (facsimile reprint 1984).

416. Von Ranke L. *Venezia nel Cinquecento.* Rome, 1974.

417. Weinberg J., *The collection of Hebrew printed books in the Antoniana library of Padua.* Excerpt from *Il Santo,* September–December 1974.

418. Wirth L. *Il ghetto.* Milan, 1968.

419. Yahuda A.S. "Napoleone e uno Stato Ebraico." *R.M.I.,* no. 5, 1950.

420. Yerushalmi Y.H. *From Spanish Court to Italian Ghetto - Isaac Cardoso - A study in Seventeenth-Century Marranism and Jewish Apologetics.* University of Washington Press, 1981. (reprint).

421. Zacuto M. *L'inferno preparato, poema ebraico.* Turin, 1819.

422. Zago F. (edited by), Consiglio dei Dieci, deliberazioni miste. Registri I —II (1310–1325), *Fonti per la storia di Venezia,* sec. I, Venice 1962.

423. Zanelli A. "Di alcune controversie tra la Repubblica di Venezia e il

Sant'Officio nei primi anni del Pontificato di Urbano VIII (1624–1626)."
Archivio Veneto, no. 6, 1929.

424. ZANGWILL I. *Il meglio*. Milan, 1955.

425. ZORDAN G. *Le persone nella storia del diritto veneziano prestatutario*. Padua, 1973.

426. ZORZI A. *La Repubblica del Leone*. Milan, 1979.

427. ZORZI E. *Osterie veneziane*. Venice, 1967.

428. ZUCCAGNI-ORLANDINI A. "Notizie concernenti la storia degli Ebrei in Portogallo." *R.M.I.*, no. 2, 1950.

Index

Aaron, 74–76
Abenacar, Abram, 225
Aboab, Samuel, 213–214, 215–216, 217
Abrabanel, Isaac, 42–43, 86, 87, 145, 179, 180
Abrabanel, Josef, 43
Abramo (physician), 9
Accademia degli Impediti, 144
Adriatic, 44, 106, 107, 113, 114, 202, 222
Alexander III, 17
Alexander VII, 191
Alfarin, Baruch, 225
Alfarin, Mosè, 208
Ancona, 46, 48–49, 56, 121
Ancona, Clemente, 171
Aprosio, Angelico, 175, 177
Aquinas, St. Thomas, 17, 59
Arbib, Bianca Nunes Vais, 266
Arbib, Vita, 265–266
Archivolti, Samuele, 143, 153
Arezzo, Baruch d', 213, 216, 217
Argoli, Giovanni, 170

Asher, Rabbenu, 152
Ashkenazim, 141, 144, 145. *See also* German Jews
Ashtor, E., 4, 12
Askenazi, Salomon, 103, 104–105
Asser, 74–76
Asson, Michelangelo, 258
Auctions, Rialto, 119
Augustine, St., 17
Austria, 106
   armistice, 266
   and Venice, 256–259, 261–263
Avogadori de Comun, 29

Badges, yellow, 9, 10, 11, 12, 13
Banco, Anselmo del. *See* Meshullam, Asher
Banco, Emanuael Levi Dal, 208
Banks, 6, 16, 29, 127–128. *See also* Moneylending; *Monti di pieta*
Baptism, forced, 42, 124–125
Barbarano (preacher), 25
Barbarigo, Daniele, 95
Barbarigo, Marco, 25

Barbaro, Marcantonio, 98, 103, 104
Barozzi, Pietro, 26
Barsiza, Vincenzo, 240
Baruch, Jacob di Samuel, 208
Baseve, David, 145
Bassan, Isaia, 231, 233, 234
Battista, Zuan, 66, 67, 68, 69, 71–72
Bechinat ha-kabbalah, 166
Belgrado, Calonimos, 144, 154
Bellagno, Giust'Antonio, 127
Beloch, 148, 149
Beltrame, D., 149
Bembo, Nicolò, 229
Bembo (patrician), 204
Benetelli (censor), 228
Benincasa, Sabbatai, 156
Berardelli (painter), 176, 177
Bernardino da Feltre, 23, 24–25, 26, 34
Bernardino da Siena, 21, 23
Bertinoro, Ovadia da, 142
Bessarione, Cardinal, 13
Bezochrenu et Zion, 144
Bialik, Chaim, 234
Bignamin, Haim Hai di, 225
Bolani, Nicolò, 220, 221
Bomberg, Daniel, 81–82
Boniface VIII, 59
Boniface IX, 9
Bonifacio, Baldassare, 175
Book publishing (Hebrew), 80–86, 228
Bookburning, 47, 83–84, 85
Boswell, William, 163
Bracchi (notary), 147
Bragadin, Alvise, 82–83, 84, 85
Bragadin, Francesco, 35
Bragadin, Marcantonio, 99
Bragadin, Nicolò, 111
Bragadino (podestà), 26
Braudel, Fernand, 42, 99
Brokers, 119
Brustolon, Andrea, 134
Buffarini Guidi decree, 278

Calimani, Simone, 235–236
Calonimos, Calò, 40
Canal, Giovanni da, 6

Candia, 205
Cantarini, Isaac Chaim Cohen, 231
Canton School (synagogue), 134
Capsali, Elia, 12
Caravaglio, Isach Hai di Moisè Baruch, 225
Cardoso, Isaac, 187, 211
Castelfranco, Jacob Chaim, 232
Castellazzo, Mosè da, 143
Castelnuovo, Enrico, 267
Castillero, Giuditta, 262, 264
Castro, Paolo di, 17
Catalano, Abraam, 151
Cattaveri, 33, 119, 121, 126, 204, 217–218, 220, 224, 228, 230, 243
Cavalli, 84, 85
Cebà, Ansaldo, 173, 174–175
Cecchetto, Gabriella, 265
Cemetery, Jewish, 9
Censorship, 84–86, 228
Census (of Jewish population), 2, 148–149, 244–245, 254–256, 263
Chabiglio, Joshua, 150
Charities, 139, 165
Charles V, 54
Charters (for Jews residing in Venice), 6, 7–8, 10, 18–19, 20, 22, 30–31, 36, 37, 49–51, 113, 115, 126, 202, 205, 208, 229–230, 239, 242–247
Chesterfield, Lord, 222
Christians, relationships with, 10, 120, 121, 142–143, 223, 224–225, 264
Church, conflict with Venice, 117, 121, 122–123
Cicogna, Emanuele Antonio, 173, 175
Circumcision, 192–193
Citizenship (granted to Jews), 12, 125, 242
Clement IX, 191
Clement X, 191
Clothing, second-hand, selling, 27
Codice di Giulia Soliga, 176–178
Codice Diplomatico Veneziano, 5
Coen, Benjamin, 232

Coen, Moisè, 208
Colon, Joseph, 16
Colorni, V., 4
Condulmer, Antonio, 35
Conegliano, Israel, 181
Conegliano, Salomon, 208
Contarini, Francesco, 58
Contarini, Nicolò, 125
Contento, 148
Conversion, 60, 259–260, 265
Converts. See Marranos
Corfu, 127, 240
Cornaro, Caterina, Queen, 96
Corner, Alvise, 11
Corner, Andrea Giulio, 241
Corner, Gieronimo, 150
Corner, Giovanni, 6
Corner, Marco, 6
Correr, Nicolò, 110
Coryat, Thomas, 149
Costa, Licentiato, 72–74, 93
Costa, Uriel da, 167, 168
Council of Rheims, 16
Council of Rome, 16
Council of Ten, 5, 36, 37–38, 43,
    57–58
Cozzi, Gaetano, 123, 124, 125, 146,
    147
Cracovia, Jacob Emanuel, 249–250
Cremonese, Giovanni Giuseppe
    Gregorio, 86, 88
Cristiani, Paolo, 5, 15
Curfew, 204
Curiel, Salomone, 255
Cyprus, 95–96
    and Turks, 51, 97–100, 103

Dattolis, Giuseppe de, 87
Dattolis, Joseph de, 40, 119
Dattolis, Mosè de, 119
Dattolis, Simone de, 119
Della Scala, Antonio, 8
Dietary laws, 196–197
Dina, Shelomoh, 232
Diritto di Roma, II, 269
Discorso circa il stato de gl'Hebrei,
    181, 187
Dolfin, Zaccaria, 32, 129, 248

Domenico da Gargnano, 26
Donà, Antonio, 125
Donà, Leonardo, 117, 118, 121, 122
Donà, Nicolò, 125

Eletti, Marco Antonio degli, 76–79
Elijah, Gaon of Vilna, 234
Emancipation, 257–259
Emigration of Jews, opposition to,
    224
Emmanuel Philibert of Savoy, 56, 96
Emo, Piero, 243
Emo, Zuan Alvise, 240, 241
Enriquez, Augustiro, 70–72, 93
Ercole II d'Este, 46
Erizzo, Francesco, 181
Erizzo, Nicolò, 246
Errera, Angelo Abramo, 260, 262
Errera, Beniamino, 255
Esame ad un giovane israelita, 236
Este, Cardinal Alvise d', 153
Ethnic diversity, 141, 164–165
Executors against Blasphemy, 57–58,
    117, 121, 223
Expulsion decree, 8, 11, 13, 28, 47–
    48, 100–101

Facchinetti, 98
Fano, Azaria da, 140–141
Fano, Diana. See Modena, Diana da
Fano, Menahem Azaria da, 142
Fascism, 277
Felice da Prato, 81
Ferdinand of Spain, 30
Ferrari, Pier Gian Maria, 250
Ferro, Marco, 163
Finzi, Rabbi, 153
Fires
    arsenal, 98
    ghetto, 240
Five Sages of Commerce, 109–110,
    111, 112, 126, 201, 202, 203–
    204, 205, 225, 226, 245
Fondaco dei Turchi, 38
Forti, Jacob Israel, 232
Fortis, Leone, 258
Foscarini, Sebastiano, 241, 243
Fossoli, camp of, 279

Franciscan Friars Minor, 21–22, 26, 27, 34
Francisco of Aragon, 91
Francoso, Giuseppe, 62–63
Frederick II, 9
Free trade, 108, 127, 240–241, 246
Freschi Olivi, Elena de, 66–70, 71
Fricele, 101
Frizzi, ben Zion, 187

Gabirol, Ibn, 82
Gaffarel, Jacques, 163, 170
Gallicciolli, G. B., 2, 3, 4, 8, 9
Gama, Vasco da, 42
Gambling, 159–160
Gara, Giovanni di, 85, 86
Garibaldi, Giuseppe, 265
Gaztelu, Dominique de, 92
Geiger, Abraham, 170
General Brotherhood of Religion and Charity, 257
Gentili, Amselmo, 224
Gentili family, 224
Gentilomo, Eugenia Pavia, 258
German Jews, 10, 11, 39, 45, 47, 57, 112, 119, 121
German School (synagogue), 133–134
Ghetto
  edict establishing, 1, 32–33
  etymology, 129–132
  gate removed, 248–251
  New ghetto, 32, 45–47, 129, 130, 132–133, 135
  Newest ghetto, 133, 135, 202
  Old ghetto, 45–47, 130, 133, 135
Giovanni da Feltre, 24
Giovanni de l'Anzolina, 34
Giovanni, i, 117, 121
Giuda, Nachman, 204
Giudecca, origin of name, 2–3
Giustinian, Alvise, 156
Giustinian, Giuffredo, 99–100
Giustiniani, Marco Antonio, 82–83, 84
Goldoni, Adjutant Major, 251
Gomez, Odoardo, 70–72, 93
Gomez, Simon, 124
Gordon, Jequtiel, 232–233

Greco, Regina, 260
Greeks (in Venice), 39
Grego, Isaac, 250, 253
Grego, Momolo, 251
Gregory X, 17
Gregory XIII, 24, 118, 120
Griffio, Giovanni, 84, 85
Grimani, Alvise, 100–101, 105
Grimani, Antonio, 35
Gritti, 204
Grossi, Carlo, 144

Ha-Cohen, David, 132
Ha-Cohen, Joseph, 83, 103, 141
Hagiz, Moshe, 233
Harrington, James, 187
Harris, A. C., 148
Hat, yellow, 11, 29, 30, 31, 37
Hebrew, 141, 165
Henry II, 54, 95
Heresy, 59–60
Historia de' Riti Hebraici, 15, 163–164, 166, 191
Holidays (Jewish), 193–196
Holy League, 99, 103
House of Catechumens, 48, 60, 260, 265
Hunderbach, Bishop, 24
Hunna, Reb, 14

Iberian Jews, 42, 44–45, 109, 210–211. See also Levantines; Marranos; Spanish Jews
Infant, abandoned, 217–221
Inquisition, 49, 57–61, 62–81, 123, 124, 163, 164
  Portugal, 54
  Spain, 41–42
Inquisitors over the University of the Jews, 226, 227, 228, 229, 230
Interdict, 122–123
Interest rates, 5, 6–7, 16, 19–21, 30, 47, 102, 118. See also Moneylending
Isaia ben Chayim, 12
Isaia da Trani, 4
Israel, Menasseh ben, 149, 187
Israel, Moisè, 127
Isserles, Israel, 214

Isserles, Moses, 83, 85
Italian School (synagogue), 134, 138–139

Jacob ben Elia, 15
Jacob ben Elia "da Venezia," 5
Jacob the Jew, 5
Jacoby, David, 12
James I, 163
Jewelry, Jews forbidden to sell, 204
Jona, Abramo, 255
Jona, Giuseppe, 277
Julius II, 30
Julius III, 47, 83

Kabbalah (doctrine), 140–141, 232
Kahal Gadol, 135–136
Karo, Joseph, 85, 232
Katzellenbogen, Meir, 82–83
Katzellenbogen, Samuel Judah, 140, 233
Keter, 4
Kol Sakhal, 166, 167, 168, 169, 170

Labia, Francesco, 229
Lalleman, Minister, 254
Landau, Jacob, 15
Lateran Council, 16
Latis, Girolamo, 258
Lattes, Abramo, 258, 259, 260, 261, 263, 267
Lazaro, Master, 32
League of Cambrai, 27, 30
Leo I, 16
Leo X, 81
Leone da Modena. See Modena, Leone da
Lepanto, battle of, 96, 99–100
Levantine School (synagogue), 134, 276
Levantines, 10, 11, 44–45, 46–47, 49, 51, 98, 109, 111–112, 113, 120, 121, 126–127, 203, 204, 207
Levi, Alessandro, 260, 261, 262, 265
Levi, Angelo, 260, 262, 266
Levi, Corona, 220–221
Levi, Diana. See Modena, Diana da
Levi, Enrichetta, 261, 265

Levi, Gabriele, 260
Levi, Giacobbe, 156
Levi, Giacomo, 262
Levi, Isaach, 145
Levi, Isacco, 156, 159, 161
Levi, Jacob, 262
Levi, Moisè Raffaele, 263
Levita, Isaac ben Jacob de, 214, 215
Levitas, Elias, 45, 82
Libowitz, 170
Libro Grande, 145–147, 160
Lippomano (family), 4
Loans. See Moneylending
Longhena, Baldassare, 134
Loredan (patrician), 149
Loredan, Alvise, 109
Loredan, Giacomo, 37
Loredan, Pietro, 98
Lorenzino of Marostica, 25
Luna, Beatrice de, 90–94
Luna, Brianda de, 90–93
Lunel, Emanuel, 208
Luria, Isaac, 232
Luxury, ordinance against, 146, 208–209
Luzzatti, Luigi, 263, 267
Luzzatto, Gino, 255
Luzzatto, Mosè, 250
Luzzatto, Mosè Chaim, 231–235
Luzzatto, Simone, 4, 107, 114, 141, 142, 179–188, 190, 191, 199, 200

Maggior Consiglio, 2, 5, 13
Maimonides, 82
Malta, Gabriele, 255
Malta, Marco, 255
Manin, Daniele, 258, 259, 260, 261, 262
Mantino, Jacob, 40
Marcello, Gabriel, 241, 245, 246
Marcello, Lorenzo Alessandro, 241
Marcuzzo, 101
Marini, Isaac, 232
Marranos, 42, 47–49, 52–57, 60, 107, 113–114, 120–124, 126, 141–142, 166–167. See also Levantines
Martin, Pope, 26

Massa, 253
Maurogonato, Isacco Pesaro, 258, 260, 262, 267, 268–273
Mavrogonato, David, 11
Maximilian, Emperor, 30, 33
Medici, Paolo Sebastiano, 200
Medici, Sisto, 18
Medigo, Joseph del, 181
Meir da Mestre, 217
Mendelssohn, Moses, 271–272
Mendes, David Franco, 236
Mendes, Diego, 90–91
Mendes, Francisco, 90
Mendes da Silva, Roderigo, 211
Meshullam, Asher, 31–32, 34, 36, 203–204
Meshullam, Chaim, 34
Meshullam, Jacob, 34
Mesillath Yesharim, 234
Messiah, false, 212–217
Mestre, 6, 9, 28, 29, 30
Micanzio, Fulgenzio, 146
Micas, Joao. *See* Nasi, Joseph
Miches, Giovanni. *See* Nasi, Joseph
Military service (allowed), 259
Minghetti, Prime Minister, 273
Minister, Jew appointed (debate), 268–274
Minotto, Leonardo, 46
Mocenigo, Alvise, 220, 221
Mocenigo, Alvise (doge), 98–99, 100
Mocenigo, Pier, 25
Mocenigo, Tommaso, 35
Modena, Diana da, 155, 156, 159, 161, 172
Modena, Isacco da (grandson), 155, 159, 161
Modena, Isacco da (son), 155, 159, 161
Modena, Leone da, 15–16, 141, 142, 143, 145, 152–172, 175, 178, 180, 190, 191, 196, 197, 198, 233
Modena, Marco da, 154, 155
Modena, Marino da, 155, 156
Molin, Daniele da, 114
Molin, Francesco, 98
Molmenti, Pompeo, 12, 29
Moneylending, 5–9, 10, 13, 14–24,

26, 51, 118, 200. *See also Monti di pieta*; Pawnshops
Monico, Jacopo, 259
Monti de pieta, 13, 22, 23–24, 26, 35–36, 51, 101–102, 118, 229
Morin, Marco, 130
Moro, Cristoforo, 13
Moro, Gabriele, 36–37
Morosini, Giulio, 143, 147, 181, 189–200
Morosini, Zuane, 146
Morpurgo, Isacco, 255
Mortara, Marco, 271–272, 273
Mortera, Saul Levi, 254–255
Motte, Abramo, 255
Mueller, Reinhold, 6
Muia, Jacob Levi, 228
Muratori, Ludovico, 2
Murder, ritual, 24–25
Music (and synagogues), 143–144
Musio, Giuseppe, 271

Nahmanides, Moses, 82
Namias, Giacinto, 258
Namias, Samuele. *See* Morosini, Giulio
Napoleon, 248, 254, 256
Nasi, Joseph, 49, 85, 90–92, 94–96, 97–100, 104, 105
Nathan of Gaza, 212, 216–217
Navarro, Davide, 127
Naxos, Duke of. *See* Nasi, Joseph
Nazione, La, 272
Nazis, 278–280
Nevo, Alessandro de, 17
Noghera, Vincenzo, 170

Oliviero, Francisco, 63–65
Olper, Samuele Salomon, 260, 262, 267
Oral Law, 167–169
Ottolenghi, Adolfo, 250, 279
Overcrowding (ghetto), 108, 135, 149–150, 204
Oxid, Aron, 246

Pacifici, Riccardo, 138
Pakuda, Ibn, 82

Paluzzi, Numidio, 175–176, 177
Pancieri, Salomon, 220
Papal States, 118. *See also* Church, conflict with Venice
Parenzo, Meir, 82, 84
Paruta, Paolo, 121
Pasqualigo, Francesco, 268–273
Paul III, 24–25, 47, 58
Paul IV, 48, 49, 87, 93
Paul V, 118, 122, 123
Pavoni, Giuseppe, 174
Pawnshops, 5, 8, 15, 18, 19, 20, 22–24, 26–27, 29, 35–36, 47, 51, 102, 118, 137, 207, 223, 225, 227, 229–230, 238, 241
Penso, Joseph, 202
Pescaruol, Samson, 101
Philip II, 105
Physicians, 8–9, 10, 39–40, 87, 139
Piattelli, Abramo, 139
Piero da Cà Pesaro, 35
Pincas Calvo, Josef, 225
Pincherle, Leone, 259, 260, 262, 267
Pius II, 13
Pius IV, 84, 87, 131
Pius V, 51, 86, 99
Pius VI, 242
Pius IX, 25, 272
Plague, 150–151, 160–161, 201
Plantavit de la Panse, Jean, 170
Poliakov, Leon, 15, 21, 102
Pomis, David de, 40, 86, 87–88, 179, 180
Portugal, 44, 54
Primo, Samuel, 215
Priuli, Girolamo, 31
Priuli, Lorenzo, 120
Prostitutes, 38
Protectionism, 108, 202, 240–241, 246
Pullan, Brian, 60, 119, 136
Purim, 142, 196, 213, 277

Quarantia, 6
Querini, Andrea, 240

Rabbis, 137, 145
Racial law of 1938, 277

Radetsky, 261
Ragusa, 56, 110, 114
Rashi de Troyes, 14
Ravenna, Caliman, 262, 264
Ravid, B., 2, 46, 113, 130, 148, 186
Real estate, possession of forbidden, 9, 10
Reggio, Isacco, 166, 167, 170
Rental rights (of Jews), 135
Rieti, Ercole Zaccaria, 220
Rilke, Rainer Maria, 275
Rivkin, E., 170
Rocca, Mosè della, 153
Rodriguez, Daniele, 107–115
Romanin, Samuele, 12, 99, 248, 254, 258
Romano, Shlomò, 83
Rossi, Azaria de, 140
Rossi, Salomone de, 143
Roth, C., 149

Sabbath, 199
Sagredo, Agostin, 240
Salomone (physician), 8
Salomone da Camposampero, 34
Sansovino, Francesco, 2, 130
Sanudo, Alvise, 115, 126
Sanudo, Marin, 18, 31, 32, 34, 35, 143
Saraval, Giacobbe, 214, 216, 235
Sarpi, Paolo, 122, 123, 124, 140
Scherzi di Purim, 15, 19
Schools, 236–237
  Jews forbidden to run, 10
Second-hand shops, 27, 119
Sedecia ben Abramo ha Rofe, 4
Sefer Torah, 193
Selden, John, 163, 170
Selim II, 95
Senate, Venetian, 5, 36, 57–58, 117, 123, 140, 227, 238–239, 241, 242–243
Senese, Sisto, 157
Sephardic Jews. *See* Iberian Jews; Marranos; Spanish Jews
Serati, Serafin, 228
Serenissima Signoria, 124
Sermoneta, Joseph Baruch, 131–132

Sexual relations (Jews with Christians), 10
Sforno, Salomone, 153, 155
Sforza, Francesco, 17
Ships, right to own, 245–246
Shofar, 147
Siamese twins, birth of, 88
Simchat Torah, 193–194, 195–196
Simone, 24
Simonsohn, S., 116
Sixtus V, 24, 118
Soares, Isach Mugnon, 208
Soave, Moisè, 156, 161, 162, 170, 175, 178
Sokolli, Mehemed, 99, 104
Soliga, Giulia, 176, 177
Sonino, Yehoshua, 55
Soranzo, Pietro, 150
Soranzo, Senator, 103–104
Spain, 41–42, 44, 106
Spalato, port, 108–114, 127, 201
Spanish Jews, 10, 11, 26, 107, 111–112, 113–114. *See also* Marranos
Spanish School (synagogue), 134, 210, 276
Spinalunga, 2, 3, 130
Spinoza, Baruch, 167, 168
Stampa La, 269, 270
Stangl, Franz, 279
Stringa, Giovanni, 130
Students, university, 139–140
Suleiman the Magnificent, 49, 94
Sullam, Giacobbe, 173
Sullam, Guido, 276
Sullam, Sara Coppio, 142, 173–178
Synagogues, 133–135, 138–139, 193

Talmud, 59, 81, 82–84, 157–158
Talmud Torah Brotherhood, 154, 157, 236–237
Tam, Rabbenu, 15
Tassini, Giuseppe, 130
Tax collectors, 137
Taxes (paid by Jews), 2, 7, 11, 27, 30, 32, 36, 37–38, 47, 120, 136–137, 186, 203, 205–208, 223–224, 225–226, 254, 255
Temanza, Tommaso, 3, 129, 130

Tentori, Cristoforo, 4
Teza, Emilio, 129
Theater, 143
Thiene, Alvise, 25
Three Sages on Heresy, 58–59, 84
Tiepolo, Nicola, 58
Todesco, Isaac, 254
Tofteh Aruch, 211–212
Toland, John, 180, 187
Tommaseo, Niccolò, 258, 259, 260, 261, 262
Torah, 144, 167–168, 169
Torquemada, Tommaso de, 41
Torre, Lelio della, 231, 235
Trade, free, 108, 127, 240–241, 246
Trades (in ghetto), 139, 239
Treaty of Noyon, 34
Trento, Giacomo, 25
Treves, Giuseppe, 255
Treves, Isaac di Mandolin, 227
Treves, Isacco, 255
Treves, Israel, 232
Treves, Jacob Mosè, 214, 216
Treves, Johannes, 82
Treves, Michael, 264
Treves, de' Bonfili, Jacopo, 258, 260
Treves Foundation, 276
Trevisan, Zaccaria, 37
Tron, Francesco, 240, 241, 242, 244, 245
Turks, 106–107, 111, 112, 114
  and Cyprus, 51, 97–100, 103
  Marranos, 49
  in Venice, 38
  and Venice, 205, 206, 210, 222

Ulimidus, 5
Unita Cattolica, L', 272–273
University of Padua, 87, 139–140
University of the Jews, 57, 112, 116
Usque, Salomon, 143
Usury. *See* Interest rates; Moneylending
Uziel, Aron di David, 225

Va'ad Katan, 135–136, 137, 187
Valensi, Josef, 214
Valenzin, David di Salomon, 225
Valiero, Agostino, 100, 104

Valmarana, Prospero, 240
Vanzi, Pietro, 2
Varallo, Cardinal, 47, 82
Varisco, Giovanni, 87
Veltuyck, Gérard, 82
Veneto Cattolico, 272–273
Venier, Antonio, 58
Venier, Marc'Antonio, 229
Venier, Nicolò, 12
Venier, Sebastiano, 146
Via della fede, 189, 191
Victor Emmanuel II, 266, 269
Vida, Cesare della, 258, 260, 262, 267
Vigevano, Isacco, 162
Vislingio, Giovanni, 170
Vita, Jacob, 255
Vita, Leon, 255
Vital of Safed, Chaim, 232
Vivante, Lazzaro, 255
Vivante, Simone, 265–266
Vivante, Vita, 250
Volli, Gemma, 25

Way of Faith, 189
Weddings (Jewish), 165–166
Western Jews. *See* Marranos; Spanish Jews

Wills, 147–148
Wine, Kosher, 197–198
Wolf, S. A., 132
Wotton, Henry, 163

Yaffe, Mordechai, 233
Yellow badges, 9, 10, 11, 12, 13
Yellow hat, 11, 29, 30, 31, 37
Yiddish, 141

Zacuto, Mosè, 211–212, 214, 216, 217
Zane, Gerolamo, 97
Zanetti family, 84–85
Zangwill, Israel, 275
Zante island, 204
Zarfati, Joseph Moro, 83
Zevi, Sabbatai, 212–213, 215–216, 233
Zòhar, 140
Zohr, Ibn, 5
Zorzi, Alvise, 101
Zorzi, Emo, 32
Zulian, Antonio, 241
Zulian Maria di Arezzo, 32
Zustinian, Sebastian, 240

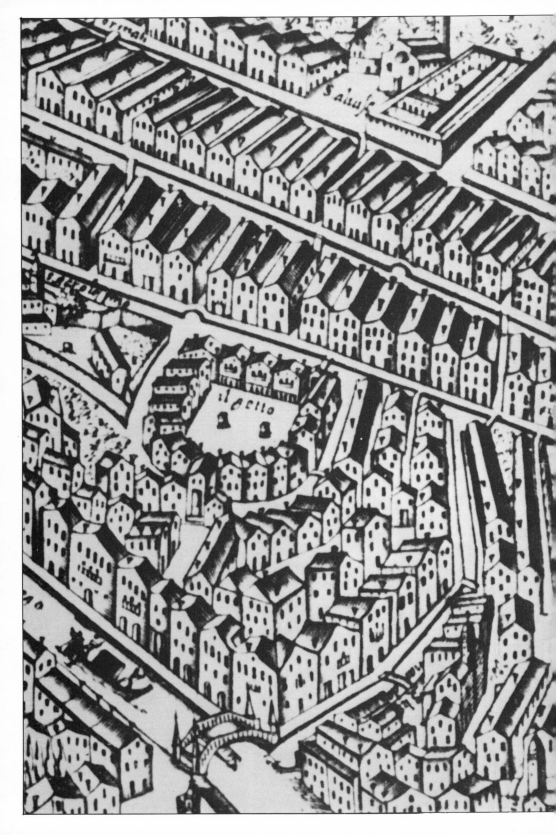